In memory of the photographers Depara from the Democratic Republic of Congo (ex Zaïre), Mohamed Amin from Tanzania, Felix Diallo from Mali and Philip L Ravenhill (National Museum of African Art, Smithsonian Institution Washington DC), who passed away during the publication of this book.

Thanks to Dr Berhanu Abebe, Bruno Airaud, Gilbert Albany, Ricardo Aleixo, Salim Amin, Emanoel Araújo, Francis Articlaut, Roger Barnard, Azra Chaudhry, Philippe David, Daniel Fra, Denis Gérard, Louis Girard, Aïda Gomes Da Silva, Henrike Grohs, Agnès de Gouvion Saint-Cyr, Bertrand Hosti, Françoise Huguier, Marie Human (Bailey's African History Archives), André Jolly, Abdoulaye Konaté, Orla La-Wayne Garriques, Bernard Leveneur, Romain Louvet, André Magnin, Yves Marguerat, Marylin Martin, Odile Meyer, Jean-Luc Monterosso, Erika Nimis, Maï Ollivier, Edimilson de Almeida Pereira, Catherine Philippot, Sabine Vogel, Mark Sealy ...

and the numerous people and photographers who worked with us on this book.

First French edition published in by Revue Noire in 1998. ISBN: 2-909571-30-0
First Portuguese edition published in by Revue Noire in 1998. ISBN: 2-909571-43-2
First English edition published by Revue Noire in 1999. ISBN: 2-909571-49-1

© Revue Noire 1998, 1999
8 rue Cels, 75014 Paris, France

with the participation of

Maison Européenne de la Photographie, Paris. Ministère français de la Culture et de la Communication. Ministère français des Affaires Étrangères. South African National Gallery, Cape Town. Pinacoteca, São Paulo.

Anthology of african Photography

of

Revue Noire

and Indian Ocean

Contents

P r e m

Doubt

One cannot consider something to be an unassailable truth unless it is written down in some form, somewhere. This principle points to the mission of this book. As a first general exploration of the photography of a continent – the African continent, excluding Mediterranean Africa but including the Indian Ocean – its sole aim is to achieve an initial gathering together of photographs. It in no way sets itself up to be encyclopaedic. There will probably have to be many other collections of photographic material, reflecting approaches and sentiments different from those which shaped this book, before it will one day be possible to publish a true history or encyclopaedia of African photography.

A Collage

The selection criteria for both photographers and photographs are historical, geographical and aesthetic. They are also, quite simply, pragmatic, making use of the little research that has already been conducted. The book comprises a collage of views, analyses and condensed research. Each item in this book makes an important contribution in terms of both knowledge and feeling. Our aim has been to reflect the scope of African photography with as broad a vision as possible.

A Refusal to define African photography

We do not attempt to define what African photography is, or to present it as homogeneous in any way. On the contrary, the intention is to include all the techniques and forms of artistic expression that have been represented on the continent, making no assumptions about an African style or specific African identity.

Humility towards the subject

While the scope of this book and the arguments contained in it may appear to give the opposite impression, the work is presented in a genuine spirit of humility: current knowledge is too fragmentary, recent and lightweight for any claims to an objective assessment of African photography as a whole. Research – which has hitherto been mostly conducted by non-Africans – conveys two main benefits. On the one hand, it casts light on the Western view of Africa, and disseminates knowledge about certain practices in and views of African photography; and on the other, it can support specific efforts in this field. These include the work of *Revue Noire* and the work of the prime movers behind the Bamako Biennale of African photography (first held in December 1994), Francoise Huguier and Bernard Descamps. However, sometimes « research » runs the danger of ignoring the facts. Since 1991 Revue Noire has published more than 300 photographs from Africa, as well as producing special issues on photography (*Revue Noire* no. 3, December 1991; no.15, December 1994; and no. 28, June 1998). It mounted the first exhibition of African photography – showcasing 90 photographers and 300 photographs - at the Centre Wallonie Bruxelles in Paris (October 1992), and later the exhibition, l'*Afrique par elle-même*, at the Maison Européenne de la Photographie in Paris (May to August 1998). It has also contributed informally to many other exhibitions, such as the 1996 Guggenheim exhibition in New York. The extent of these efforts perhaps explains a certain frustration one feels at seeing selections of photographs presented with total disregard for the reasons they were taken, so that they are distorted to the point of meaninglessness. The purpose of this book is also to stress that while there is still so much to bring to light, it is important not to set out to establish taboo areas of research, opportunistic markets and ultimately a form of plunder that could parallel the plunder of the ritual arts which has continued unabated for over a century.

HARDLY ANYTHIN

HARDLY ANYTHIN

NO HOUSE

NO OBJECT

BUT WOMEN

MEN

THOUSANDS

LOOKING AT THE LEN

PERHAPS ENCOMPASSE

THEY WANT TO CHARM, OR PERHAPS THEY AR

NOT AS IF WAVING AT THEI

BUT OFFERING A GREETING OF KINSHI

THEIR FAMIL

HAVING NO IMPACT BEYON

AN IMAGE OF THEMSELVES PROJECTE

PHOTOGRAPH

AS IT SEEM

BUT IT I

FOR THOSE WHO CA

THE POSITIONING OF HANDS AND BOD

– EXTRAORDINARY FOR OTHERS

QUITE SIMPL

i s e s

Revue Noire

IO SCENERY OR HARDLY ANY,

)R HARDLY ANY,

)R HARDLY ANY,

GIRLS,

3OYS, CHILDREN,

MILLIONS OF THEM

S IF IT HELD THE WORLD,

THEMSELVES IN IDEAL FORM.

SIMPLY GREETING THE VIEWER,

)WN REFLECTIONS IN A MIRROR,

VITH THE WORLD, WITH SOCIETY,

THEIR CULTURE,

VHAT THEY THINK THEY CAN OFFER:

NTO THE SOCIETY THAT GAVE THEM BIRTH.

N AFRICA IS NOT AS EXOTIC

ROM EUROPE OR AMERICA,

UST AS RICH

)IVINE EXPRESSIONS,

THE SETTING

3UT SO COMMONPLACE FOR THEMSELVES –

MEN AND WOMEN.

The duty to reveal, to research, to record the memory and preserve this photographic heritage must not become a treasure hunt: the work should ideally be done anonymously, without any ambition to make history. This applies whether the work is done by Africa alone, or with international involvement.

THE DANGERS OF GEOCENTRISM

Given how limited current knowledge of African photography is, it is all too easy for each new research project to fall into the trap of geocentrism, seeing its own little sphere of study as the centre of the universe, as the birthplace of a style, technique or some other characteristic. For example, a newspaper article in Mali reported that Seydou Keita had trained Mama Casset in Senegal, while a good 30 years of photographic experience separate the two, and the controlled, premeditated, constructed style of Mama Casset, expressing a strong personal identity as an artist, could in no way be seen as common practice among the thousands of other contemporary studio photographers. Much research and investigation is still needed to cover vast expanses of territory, and it is misleading to state that it all started in St Louis, Freetown, Lagos, Accra or Cotonou. However, the few facts that are certain show that photography followed the path of European colonization, beginning with the first trading posts. Harbour towns with large foreign populations introduced the first signs of urban culture to Africa, ushering in the widespread use of photography by 1945. After the Second World War, each area had its own direct links with Western countries – the main producers of images – mainly through more democratic access to the different processes and equipment, as well as the development of international press photography and the advent of the airport; previously, harbours and railway stations had been people's only way of escaping their geographically circumscribed domain.

A FEW CERTAINTIES

For these obvious reasons, photography started late in areas far from the coast and harbour towns. And the limelight afforded by the recent Bamako Biennale cannot guarantee Mali the status of being the alpha and omega of African photography. Far from it: even taking into account only the coastal areas, photography was practised here in Africa, without any shadow of doubt, as early as 1880 in Sierra Leone (50 years before Bamako) and in 1900 in Senegal (30 years before Bamako); and the full scope of its inventiveness and wealth has yet to be discovered. Countries in the south and along the Indian Ocean, on the main passage to India and the rest of Asia, followed developments in photography in both Europe and America almost simultaneously. The striking feature of photography, despite the relative technical difficulty in the early days, is that it immediately became a universal medium, adopted and adapted by anyone and everyone, rendered democratic in practice throughout the world, while following the pace of inventions and technical advances. (In this sense it could be compared to radio, at a much later date – but not to film or television, which require much greater financial and technical support and always attempt to assert themselves.) The fact that African photography developed simultaneously with photography elsewhere, is perhaps the most important thing to bear in mind.

Approaches

Approches

Shifting Africa

Elikia M'Bokolo

There is a general belief that today's map of Africa was drawn up by the European states at Bismarck's Berlin conference, which ran from 15 November 1884 to 26 February 1885. But this view fails to take into account the fact that the two World Wars disrupted the European spheres of influence. It also ignores the reality that preceded the creation of the African borders we know today, for the first colonial powers denied the existence of structures that were already in place before Europeans arrived on the African continent. We must not forget that Africa has always experienced population shifts which make today's divisions totally arbitrary – for example, the division of Africa into different linguistic areas, notably English-speaking and French-speaking zones.

Elikia M'Bokolo is a Congolese historian and a professor at the Institut des Hautes Etudes en Sciences Sociales in Paris.

Artificial frontiers, arbitrary division of territories, conflicts among the colonial powers of Europe over the control of Africa: such is the post-colonial heritage of the African continent today. The celebrated expression « spheres of influence » was officially used for the first time at the Berlin Conference in 1885. The objective reality conveyed by the expression had long existed, and is still operative today. Yet to a great extent Europe's division of Africa into colonial territories, which commenced at the dawn of the modern era and reached its apex at the end of the 19th century, was predicated upon the specifically non-African interpretation of the movements and internal dynamics of the continent's indigenous population.

We therefore need to question this European vision and its underlying assumptions, grounded as they are in the commonly accepted belief that Africa lacked its own internal system of dynamics governing the appropriation and settlement of territory, and the organization of its societies.

I. FRONTIERS, REGIONS AND TERRITORIAL DISTRIBUTION IN PRE-COLONIAL AFRICA

False ideas are often extremely tenacious. One such erroneous idea which would certainly be better forgotten is the enduring belief that prior to its colonization by Europe, « traditional » Africa was composed of a series of ethnic groups permanently established on their respective territories, controlling, for better or worse, their own little piece of an immense continent.

« ETHNIC » TERRITORIES?

This interpretation is supremely European. Traces of it appear in certain late 19th and early 20th century photographs which conveniently categorize Africans within a series of simplistic typologies based on supposedly objective « racial » characteristics which alleged men of science could measure and describe, or « tribal » and « ethnic » characteristics, « revealed » in « distinctive signs « such as « costumes », ritually-inflicted scars or tattoos.

Although the segmentation of the African continent and its inhabitants into categories based on physical or cultural criteria produced many admirable photographs, it was also unfortunately far from representing their objective reality. Even worse, it established and perpetuated a totally erroneous idea which on occasion was deliberately or unconsciously employed by Africans themselves in their analysis and conception of the history and social organization of their own continent.

INTERNAL DYNAMICS AND
TERRITORIAL ORGANIZATION

No matter how far one goes back in time, the African continent has always seen perpetual movement, whether of individuals and populations, social and political structures or ideas and value-systems.

As ancient as the continent itself, movement and transformation in all their manifestations existed up to and throughout the colonial period, and have continued into the present era. The 19th century, generally considered as the apex of European expropriation, provides both an excellent example of this phenomenon and the possibility of interpreting it within a perspective of purely African dynamics. From this perspective, and despite the full inhibitory force of the colonial presence, we can see that 19th century Africa continued to experience the migratory flux of many of its inhabitants, particularly in most of the southern and much of the eastern and central regions of the continent.

One of these migratory fluxes, known as *mfecane* or *difacane* (« the tumultuous movement of peoples ») was produced by the Zulu revolution and its leader Chaka. The emergence of Zulu ideology and its transformation of the Zulu nation into a powerful and militant movement principally dedicated to war and conquest resulted in the displacement of local populations. Their mass-migration to new territories in present-day Mozambique, Zimbabwe, Malawi and Tanzania began in 1820 and continued through the 1800s (see below).

Another migration, essentially motivated by economic factors, saw Chokwe hunters move from central Angola to resettle the north and east of their former lands on territories situated in present-day Zambia and the Democratic Republic of Congo.

There was also the lesser-known and progressive descent of the Fang population to the south of Cameroon, Equatorial Guinea and much of Gabon. Many other similar examples could be cited, for they were a general phenomenon of 19th century Africa and touched nearly every region of the continent.

The main objective of Europeans during this period was the physical occupation of territory rather than the overt control of its inhabitants.

Incapable of understanding the true nature of these population movements, Europeans adopted the comforting idea that the regions that they occupied were abandoned or under-exploited by their « primitive » inhabitants and therefore could be rightfully claimed as their own property. A prominent example of this is the Zulu mfecane (a controversial issue in South African history circles), which was used by the supporters of apartheid to justify the allocation of land in South Africa.

A multitude of states which in their own fashion divided up the continent's space, existed in Africa prior to, during and after the European conquest. Schematically speaking, they can be localized within four main regions and can be characterized by the presence of durable and coherent social and political structures (city-states, kingdoms, empires, etc.) of diverse origins and historical destinies. In time, each of these regions acquired a quasi-mythical aura which exercised an irresistible attraction for explorers, adventurers and pioneer photographers, all of whom were questing after the « discovery » of what at the time was considered to be a « mysterious continent ».

The first of the four regions was the greater Sudan. In the middle ages, this ancestral territory of fabled kingdoms was known to Arab geographers as Bilad al-Sudan: « the land of the blacks ». Encompassing present-day Senegal and Chad, its northern limits extended from the Sahara to the tropical forests and savannahs of the south. In the *Livre des Itinéraires et des Royaumes*, a manuscript dating from 1068, the Arab geographer El-Bekri identified no less than ten different states which were established in the region; over the ensuing centuries, Ghana, Mali and the Gao Empire would successively fire Arab and European imaginations. The Gao Empire encompassed an immense territory whose limits, expressed in contemporary terms, extended from Senegal in the west to Niger in the east and from Téghazza in the Sahara to the region of present-day Ouagadougou. The tensions inherent in its specific social and political organization, as well as the expansionist policies of neighbouring countries to the north, and particularly Morocco, resulted in the Empire's disintegration in 1591. Under the impetus of Islam or anchored in the worship of local deities, other states emerged thereafter: Kanem-Bornou in Chad, the Caliphate of Sokoto in Nigeria and the Mossi kingdom in the territory of present-day Burkina-Faso.

Further south, beyond the great forests and savannahs which stretched from the Congo and Angola to Malawi and Mozambique, one saw the creation of impressive political structures, of which some – such as the Kingdom of the Kongo and the « Monomotapa » Empire – were well-known in both the Islamic world and Renaissance Europe. There were also lesser states that were noteworthy for their dynamism: the Lunda Empire, at the height of its power during the 18th and 19th centuries, occupied a territory corresponding to the present-day Angola, the Democratic Republic of Congo and Zambia, and maintained ongoing commercial relations with traders established along the Atlantic coast and the Indian Ocean. Even in the 20th century, in spite of the colonial borders, the Lundas continued to offer a variety of material, political and symbolic tributes to their « Emperor » Mwata Yanvu, who had been reduced to the simple rank of « Supreme Chief » by the European colonial powers and their African successors.

The third region, in the form of a semicircle running from the Abyssinian Plateau to the Great Lakes, contained the « traditional » East African states. Among them, Ethiopia was a unique example of continuity within a long succession of states.

Axum, the oldest of these, dated from the beginning of the Christian era. The *Kebra Nagast* (« The Glory of Kings »), a book probably written in the 14th century, sets out the ideological vision of the Ethiopian kings of their own history, and establishes the tradition according to which the lineage of the Ethiopian royal family originated with Solomon and the Queen of Sheba, whose son Menelik was the first Negus (monarch) of Ethiopia. Thousands of years later, his distant descendant and namesake, Menelik II (1844-1913), established the country's current borders. To the south, in the region of the Great Lakes, Bunyoro, Buganda, Ankole, Rwanda and Burundi emerged in the 15th century. Recent tragic events have focused the attention of the world's news media on this region.

The fourth region comprised an area encompassing present-day Senegal and Ghana. With the exception of Benin (today part of Nigeria), few states emerged prior to the development of commercial exchanges between West Africa and Europe in the 16th century. The Ashanti kingdom (Ghana), Dahomey (the Republic of Benin) and Bamum (Cameroon) were characterized by the intersection of two factors: the external influence of the Europeans, which represented both a threat and an opportunity, and an internal dynamic which offered elements of a response to the European challenge.

Despite their diverse origins, the majority of these ancient African states survived for centuries: although some ultimately collapsed after the European conquest others, after accepting the necessary compromises, were able to maintain their specific national identities both within the colonial system and into the present period.

II. THE RESTRUCTURING OF THE AFRICAN CONTINENT

The influence of Europe began transforming Africa well before the colonial era, which in certain respects was simply the culmination of a process which had commenced centuries earlier. A little-known aspect of this long process was the role played by various Islamic populations – including the inhabitants of Shiraz in Iran and the Berbers of North Africa – who opened up the continent to the outside world before being progressively overtaken and finally eliminated by the Europeans.

EXTERNAL INFLUENCES

The first persistent external influence – one which continues to exercise an ever-widening impact was that of religion. Aside from the legendary « Nine Saints » credited with the Christianization of the Abyssinian Plateau in the 4th century, Islam – preached by Mahomed – took root on the continent. Ethiopia generously granted asylum to his early companions who had been driven from Mecca, and the theological conflicts which divided Muslims after Mohamed's death resulted in the resettlement of a number of the inhabitants of Shiraz in Zanzibar and along the east coast of Africa.

Islam long remained confined to the region before commencing its progression over the rest of the continent in the 1860s moving counter to the effects of colonization.

In the 8th century, Islam fanned out over West Africa and solidly established itself in the Maghreb. Militantly imposed by the Almoravides in the 11th century, the religion was more or less freely adopted over the following centuries.

Significantly, princes were among the first to convert to Islam and display the external signs of their new faith. Wholesale conversion of entire West African populations occurred only in the 18th and 19th centuries, following a series of religious wars in Senegal and northern Nigeria. Other conversions were more pacific, such as those of the « Mourides » in Senegal, which accelerated with the arrival of colonialism. From their external perspective, Europeans saw the continent of Africa – and especially its people – as being rich in « primitive » traditions and essentially pagan. At the same time, « African Islam » and its legendary shrines and holy places contributed to the fascination that the continent held for outsiders.

Both in the Sudan and east Africa, the frontiers of Islam delimited areas of commercial activity. Known since antiquity as « the land of gold », the *Bilad al-Sudan* developed an extensive international trade network around the 11th century. Caravans of slaves and gold bullion traversed the Sahara to the north, where they were exchanged for food products and other goods from the Maghreb and Europe, and particularly blocks of salt from mines in the Sahara. According to some historians, it was this same Sudanese gold that fuelled the commercial expansion of the Occident during the 14th and 15th centuries, prior to the discovery of the New World. In the Middle Ages, sumptuous and legendary cities emerged along the caravan routes: Djenné, Gao, Sokoto, Kano and Timbuktu. From the Arab point of view, they were integral elements of the « geography of the Muslim world » (André Miquel).

The fascination exercised over the European imagination by these distant cities began in the 15th century. Jealous of the Arab traders who had established a flourishing trade with Sudan, Italy was the first European power which attempted – and failed – to gain a foothold in the region. There was also an audacious plan by Portuguese navigators to eliminate the Arab intermediaries and access the coastal towns directly by ship. The interior of the region nevertheless remained as mysterious and inaccessible as ever; Timbuktu and other Sudanese cities continued for a long time to attract European explorers and adventurers. Accounts of their voyages, such as René Caillié's *Journal d'un voyage à Tombouctou et à Jenné dans l'Afrique Centrale (1824-1827)*, were followed by numerous other 19th-century publications written by geographers, amateur explorers and other individuals fascinated by the region's mystique.

THE ARAB AND EUROPEAN CONQUEST OF AFRICA

European ships' navigation around the coast of Africa led to the establishment , starting with the coastal cities of the Atlantic ocean, of a kind of shifting and expanding frontier behind which western influences steadily penetrated the continent. The fortresses that ran from St-Louis in Senegal to the Cape favoured the development of adjacent towns and the emergence of black or half-caste commercial agents who specialized in long-distance trade. Two principal types of structure developed: « commercial relays », in which goods passed from one community to another, with each controlling its own territory and receiving its share of profits on transactions, and « commercial networks », in which a group of individuals transported goods – or in the case of the slave-trade, accompanied their human merchandise – from a point of origin to a given destination.

The overall effect of this activity was considerable in the coastal cities, and gradually produced an effect of biological (through inter-marriage) and cultural hybridization. In some cases, steps were taken to counter this. In South Africa, a law prohibiting mixed marriages was passed in 1685, and was followed over subsequent centuries by an arsenal of discriminatory and racist legislation. The inland communities were also affected, and even traditional agriculture changed as communities adopted the cultivation of groundnuts and manioc, imported from the New World.

By virtue of its scope and rapidity, the wave of external influences that penetrated the eastern half of the continent from approximately 1820 to 1849 was perhaps more powerful than anywhere else in Africa.

The expansionist policies of the Kédive Mohammed Ali of Egypt (1805-1849) and his successors resulted in the creation of various commercial structures in neighbouring countries to the south. These were over-seen by agents and intermediaries such as the jallaba (merchants specializing in trade with the south), bahhara (« river-people », specializing in trade along the Nile) and the Khartomians, a heterogeneous group of Arab, European, Sudanese and Levantine traders drawn to the region by a common desire for financial gain. Their network of zaribas (warehouses and offices), daym and dem (fortified outposts) had a profound impact on the economic and political organization of the region.

By the 1880s, Egypt's sphere of influence extended to the regions situated within the borders of present-day Sudan, the Central African Republic, the Congo (Kinshasa), and in its ultimate ramifications, even to the Bugandas and the inhabitants of the neighbouring regions.

An important factor in the transformation of East Africa was the progressive rise to power of the Swahilis, descendants of Arab and Shirazi merchants who over the centuries had intermarried with Islamic Africans in Zanzibar and the city-states that dotted the coasts of Kenya and Tanzania.

The Swahilis were financed by Indian businessmen and were nominally the subjects of the Sultan of Oman. The latter, supremely aware of the rich opportunities offered by the region – and particularly the ivory and slave trade – transferred his capital from Oman to Zanzibar in 1840. Between 1850 and 1860, the commercial activity of the Swahilis gained momentum and gave rise to a commercial network that extended from Tabora in the centre of Tanzania to Ujiji on the shores of Lake Tanganyika. From there, the Swahilis rapidly established themselves on the opposite side of the Lake in the eastern portion of the Congo (Kinshasa) and created a series of strategic outposts in Kasongo, Nyangwe and Kisangani. They also established trade relations with the old Lake kingdoms in the north, and in the region of Katanga in the south. The Swahili presence prevented these countries from becoming nominal or effective possessions of Zanzibar. Europeans were obliged to negotiate their passage with Arabs and Swahilis before entering the territories: the logistical support of the expedition into « darkest Africa » by the explorer Stanley was organized by Swahili merchants and their porters, and even King Leopold II of Belgium adopted the structures created by the Swahilis – and Swahili agents like Tippo Tip – to govern the eastern provinces of his « Independent Congo State » (the present-day Democratic Republic of Congo).

The influence of Egypt and Zanzibar was an enormous obstacle for the Europeans. As a first step to eliminating this influence, they did everything in their power to discredit their « Arab » competitors. Although slavery had been abolished in Europe only in the early 19th century, Europe attempted to create an association in the public mind between Arabs and Islam on the one hand, and the slave trade on the other. To justify colonialism as a « humanitarian » and « civilizing » crusade, photography was used as a means of manipulating public opinion.

Shocking images of long lines of chained slaves carrying heavy ivory tusks appeared in newspapers, magazines, children's school books and religious publications.

III. THE COLONIAL PARTITION OF AFRICA AND ITS CONSEQUENCES

The origins of the colonial partition of Africa can be traced back to the « discoveries » of the early Portuguese navigators; the activities of the various intermediaries involved in the slave trade; and the exploratory expeditions of the 19th century. Once formally established, European colonialism would transform – with an influence lasting up to the present – the destinies of territories and their inhabitants, national borders, political and economic allegiances, and even certain behavioural characteristics.

GREAT BRITAIN, FRANCE AND OTHER COLONIAL POWERS

Once the Arab trade monopoly had been broken, the territorial division of the continent was primarily a European affair.

The United States of America, which had decided against having colonies, was busy establishing economic control over South America and the Far East; and being assured by the Europeans that American businesspeople, manufacturers and missionaries were free to operate as they pleased, had little time for Africa. Europe was another story: its most industrialized countries willingly filled the vacuum left by the Arabs, and in so doing, eliminated several of their own neighbours who logically could have been expected to receive their share of the African pie. Holland and Denmark, both of which had previously been highly active in the slave trade, closed, abandoned or sold their commercial holdings on the continent after the prohibition of slavery in the 19th century. After doing the same, Russia, whose orthodox religion was similar to that practised in Ethiopia, reinforced its diplomatic ties to the latter country.

The advantageous positions of France and Great Britain were not only due to their economic superiority, but also rested upon the strategic positions that they had already established. The British controlled much of West Africa (Gambia, Sierra Leone, the Gulf of Guinea, the Cape Coast and Mauritius); the French had long been a presence in Senegal and Reunion, and had more recently established commercial outposts in the Ivory Coast and Gabon. The veritable free-for-all began in 1873 within the context of a severe economic depression , and lasted until 1896. As the competition among the industrialized European countries became ferocious, they all – with the exception of Great Britain – erected solid trade barriers. As the economy stagnated, colonial expansion was perceived as a solution. As Jules Ferry so aptly stated, « colonial policy is the daughter of industrial policy ».

In addition to the major players, other European countries long established or newly arrived in Africa also vied for their share of the continent. Spain succeeded in retaining small portions of northern Morocco, the Sahara and the Gulf of Guinea (the present-day Equatorial Guinea).

Although Portugal had never become industrialized, it nevertheless had developed close economic ties with Great Britain, and with the latter country's support was able to impose its « historical » claim to Guinea, Angola and Mozambique. But Portugal's long-standing dream of controlling an immense territory extending « from Angola to the opposite coast » (i.e. Mozambique) was nevertheless quashed by Britain's determination to possess everything « from the Cape to Cairo ».

If Italy yearned for a portion of sub-Saharan Africa to compensate for the long-lost Roman Empire, other and newer players in the African arena were even more voracious. Germany, despite having achieved the status of a unified state only in 1871, was highly industrialized and possessed one of the strongest armies in Europe. Its ambitions to world power were well-served by Chancellor Bismarck, who adroitly organized the famous Berlin Conference (15 November 1884 – 26 February 1885), which established the rules which would long govern the distribution of territories to Europe's colonial powers.

In the context of the Weltpolitic of Emperor Wilhelm II, Germany's objective was the creation of a Mittelafrica extending from Cameroon to Tanganyika.

There was also Belgium, whose King Leopold II cultivated the « humanitarian » image of an enlightened sovereign with a passion for discovery and exploration, and an almost religious desire to alleviate the suffering of Africans by rescuing them from the evil designs of their « Arab » masters. This transparently hypocritical discourse (for at the same time Stanley and other agents were setting up new outposts in the name of the King of Belgium) pleased the great powers, who believed that they had nothing to fear from Belgium, and looked forward to taking possession of Leopold II's possessions in Central Africa at the opportune moment.

THE INTERMINABLE PROCESS OF PARTITION

Europe's division of the African continent was a long and ongoing process. Nothing could be further from the truth than the idea that portions of Africa were distributed like so many pieces of cake to the participants of the Berlin Conference. In reality, the ambassadors of the colonial powers defined a certain number of criteria governing the recognition of each country's colonial possessions by the European community. After having condemned slavery and affirmed the principles of free trade in the territories bordering the Congo and Niger Rivers, the Congress issued a final « declaration of the basic conditions governing the occupation of new territories on the African continent ». Among its various articles, the declaration stated that « The Powers signing the present document recognize their obligation to exercise a level of authority capable of assuring the respect of acquired rights and the freedom of trade and passage as stipulated in the territories occupied by them on the African continent ». If there was a winner at this conference, it was an individual: Leopold II of Belgium, whose personal ownership of the « Independent Congo State » (today the Democratic Republic of Congo) was recognized by all the participants.

The Congo became a Belgian colony only in 1908. In the interim, the distribution of territories among the European powers, which had steadily accelerated after the Berlin Conference, proceeded in two distinct ways. In the first, representatives of a given country rushed to Africa, where they extorted treaties from local chiefs. From 1880 to 1890, for example, France obtained 226 such treaties; Great Britain's Royal Company of the Niger did even better, with a score of 389 between 1884 and 1892. According to the second method diplomats in Europe negotiated the limits of spheres of influence as precisely as if they were national borders, and when necessary, exchanged territories to consolidate their presence and control over them. Thus, after the second « Moroccan Crisis » in 1911, Germany recognized France's « rights » to the country after receiving a portion of the French Congo in exchange.

The exact frontiers of the various territories thus acquired were later ratified by representatives of the colonial governments concerned.

The partition of Africa had largely been completed by 1914. The historical rivalry between France and Great Britain was reflected in the equally generous portions of the continent which they accorded themselves. Portugal, which had long been a presence, also obtained a sizable share, as did Germany and Belgium.

As the dust of the continent settled after the years of struggle for its ownership, only Ethiopia and Liberia emerged relatively intact. Since 1822, the latter country had been populated by runaway and freed slaves from North America. Despite having proclaimed itself an independent state in 1847, Liberia's situation was somewhat unusual: on one hand, the country was entirely controlled by the United States and in a certain sense, was what could be termed an unofficial colony; on the other, its black American immigrants had instituted a system that was colonial in all but name, exploiting the original inhabitants. Ethiopia had managed to preserve its independence and national sovereignty despite Italy's repeated attempts to invade and colonize it. In 1896, the Italian expeditionary army was defeated by Menelik II at Adoua. Although Mussolini ultimately succeeded in invading the country in 1935-36 and proclaimed King Victor Emmanuel III as its new Emperor, his victory was short-lived: in 1941, the joint efforts of the Negus Haile Selassie and Great Britain effectively rid the country of its Fascist occupants.

Three observations can be made concerning the contemporary effects – and problems – resulting from Africa's colonial heritage.

First of all, the rivalry among the European powers was continuous, and was reflected in the redistribution of their African possessions following the First and Second World Wars. According to the terms of the Treaty of Versailles (1919), Germany was held responsible for World War I. In reprisal, it was divested of its African colonies in favour of Great Britain (which received the present-day Namibia, Tanzania and a portion of the Cameroon and Togo), France (likewise, a portion of the Cameroon and Togo) and Belgium (Rwanda and Burundi). In 1950, as a result of its participation in the Second World War, Italy was forced to relinquish Somalia, which was then placed under the supervision of the United Nations.

Decolonization resulted in other changes, many of which still continue today. Despite the progressive emancipation of the African continent, its relationship with Europe has remained fundamentally unchanged. Hundreds of years of exploitation have created a lasting economic dependence and placed Africa within an Occidental sphere of influence. In the decades following the Second World War, the internationalization of business activity created a series of new economic contexts which considerably reduced the 19th century pattern of European spheres of influence.

The former colonial powers were progressively eclipsed by the Soviet Union (whose repeated attempts to affirm its presence in Africa ended with the collapse of Communism) and above all, the United States. By both covert and overt operations, the Americans succeeded in evicting a number of European countries – and in particular, Great Britain and Belgium – from their zones of influence, while at the same time interfering with the activities of France, the only former colonial power which developed an « African policy » for its former possessions.

This economic and strategic conflict has often been reduced to mere linguistic rivalry between French- and English-speaking Africa. In reality, the problem is much more complex. On one hand, the colonial heritage left more languages than just French and English on the African soil: there was also Spanish and above all, Portuguese. On the other, linguistic barriers were not as inflexible as one might think. Portuguese-speaking Mozambique was admitted as a member of the English-speaking British Commonwealth, while Equatorial Guinea (Spanish) and Guinea Bissau, Cape Verde and Angola (Portuguese) participated in Franco-African summit conferences and operated in French trade zones. Last, and this is perhaps one of the most important considerations for the continent's future, the ongoing existence of powerful African influences should never be underestimated.

If one examines Africa from a linguistic perspective, it is clear that colonial geography fails to correspond to the inherent realities of the continent itself. This is not only because the majority of Africans in any given region do not speak (or have barely mastered) the foreign languages imported by the colonial occupants, but also because African languages themselves have undergone profound transformations. Some have disappeared, only to re-emerge later within other languages; still others, such as Swahili in East and Central Africa, Lingala in Central Africa, and Hausa and Dioula in West Africa, have consistently gained popularity.

Other examples of transformations such as these can be found on all levels of economic, political and cultural life in Africa. From start to finish, colonization encountered a resistance. This was particularly acute in the border regions, where inhabitants attempted to defy, abolish or simply ignore the often arbitrary divisions which were among the most tangible manifestations of the colonial presence. The independence movement was accompanied by the emergence of a pan-African consciousness, itself a reaction against the effects of the colonial heritage. Despite the difficulties encountered by the Organization for African Unity (OAU) in the realization of this ideal, the « Renaissance » currently underway in post-apartheid South Africa indicates a possibility which is perhaps the most promising of present-day Africa.

Elikia M'Bokolo

Photographer ZACCHARIA KABA ©
Kan Kan, Conakry, Guinea ca. 1962.

ZACCHARIA KABA

b. Kan Kan, Guinea ca. 1910 - lives in Kan kan

He is the oldest living portraitist in his country, living in the North of Guinea.

Africa of gods, Africa of people

Agnès de Gouvion Saint-Cyr

Agnès de Gouvion Saint-Cyr is in charge of photography for the Délégation aux Arts Plastiques du Ministère Français de la Culture et de la Francophonie.

Recent projects on the photographers of black Africa have emphasized the strange paradox in which photography evolves: we master its major scientific principles, we are constantly breaking new ground in photographic technology, but we have a very imperfect grasp of its customs and history.

This « humble servant of the arts », as Baudelaire described it, emerged as a tool that was capable of pushing the limits of the world further than ever before. Although photography appeared on the scene before the Anglo-Boer War and Livingstone's first journeys of exploration, it did not develop rapidly in black Africa, which could have become a field of photographic experimentation.

Photography was still a complicated process, especially in such an unfavourable environment, so the first major explorers preferred to draw sketches, while the first missionaries tended to turn to the written narrative.

Photography first emerged in the 1870s, when the colonial powers laid the foundations for new administration. Ethnologists, geologists, geographers, soldiers and merchants all needed images to understand, describe or organize the colonized countries. They were not interested in individuals, but concentrated on social groups, their physical environment or their customs. The photographs taken with this aim in mind, mostly by the above individuals themselves, had a primarily utilitarian function and are still hard to date with any precision: in the final decades of the 19th century there was little change in clothing or architecture; this, with the exception of the buildings in the major cities, was fragile and often ephemeral, and therefore not a reliable way of recording the passage of time.

1 & 4. Claude Roy, *Arts Sauvages*, Published by Delpire.
2. Michel Leiris, *Afrique Noire*, Univers des Formes, Gallimard
3. Jacques Lipchitz.

ANTOINE FREITAS

Democratic Republic of Congo
b. Angola 1919 – d. Kinshasa, Democratic Republic of Congo 1990

Antoine Freitas was taught photography by a white priest in Angola. He moved to Kinshasa in 1932 and became a travelling photographer in 1935 when he started working all over the Congo. This extraordinary photograph shows him working with his «box» in the midst of a crowd of children and villagers in the Kasaï, ready to take a photograph of three young women posing in front of a classical painted canvas backdrop. At the time, travelling photographers had to deal with the apprehension of villagers who were faced with their own image for the first time. Two of Freitas' children became photographers. The elder son, Georges, was a photographer for several years before working in a bank. Oscar, well-known for his sports photos, was a photo-reporter for a news weekly until the 1970s and a freelance for various newspapers, photographing social topics from the 1960s to the present day.

front of card :
A de Freitas, First snapshot photographer in Bena Mulumba (Kaïsa)

back ot card :
to Mr. Manuel Barros Mecaca
B.M.S. nurse
in Songololo (S. Salvador)

Luluabourg, 27-1 1939

« My dear Barros,
You must think I have forgotten you. On the contrary, but I have been travelling a great deal. I could have sent this note before the New Year, but I keep moving from village to village. In this photo I am with the Kasaï natives. I have always been called « Muene Mumpongo » (witch doctor) in this village. They wanted to kill me with magic but I managed to escape their clutches by giving them ground rice. I am the first person to do snapshot photography in the Congo and am always ready to give advice and a helping hand. As you can see, I am looked on with admiration.
My compliments to my wife. Tell her that her old husband hasn't lost the fire of his youth yet. He braves rain and hunger, carries heavy loads and paddles a dugout like a spritely 18 year-old. My compliments to Roque.
Your dear friend, »
Antoine Freitas

At the turn of the century photographs became easier to make and reproduce and photography became more diversified. With images to illustrate books or postcards, souvenir photographs by amateur colonial photographers, and positives given to future missionaries, the representation of black Africa became more complex and more precise. Yet it was still an interpretation made by white men for white men.

In fact, with the exception of the work of a few studios that were generally set up by former soldiers who had learned photography in the colonial armies, photography was not the medium generally chosen to describe or represent the continent, its inhabitants and their culture.

Claude Roy rightly remarked that « black sculptors carve out images »[1] that are inspired by magic and religion because «according to ancestral beliefs, all things are linked to these forces with which good relations are vitally important »[2].

By extracting the lifeblood of the trees used to sculpt statues or fetishes, or by pouring wax into the layer of clay that encases the body of an insect, African artists used nature to represent their daily world and plead with the gods: they had no need to use photography to do so.

In fact, at the beginning of this century, these masks and fetish objects were subverted from their purpose for ancestral worship by explorers who wanted to reveal them to the western world.

Apollinaire described himself in this way in *Zone*:

> « *You walk to Auteuil you want to walk home*
> *To sleep among the fetishes of Oceania*
> *and Guinea*
> *They are Christs of a different form, a different creed*
> *They are the inferior Christs of obscure expectancy.* »

Tristan Tzara, Blaise Cendrars, Jean Cocteau, Vlaminck, Picasso and Juan Gris examined these « images » from Africa and praised their authors for « their true understanding of proportion, their feeling for drawing, their keen sense of reality ... »[3].

On 25 October 1923 the Théâtre des Champs Elysées presented the première of the *Creation of the World*, a ballet inspired by African art with a narrative by Blaise Cendrars, music by Darius Milhaud and sets by Fernand Léger.

The enthusiasm for African art became widespread and photography now accompanied and enhanced this discovery of Black Africa and its art forms.

In July 1925, André Gide set off on his *Journey to the Congo*, which he wrote up a few years later. It was illustrated by the first photographs taken by a young photographer, Marc Allégret.

A few years later the surrealist journal *Le Minotaure* published excerpts from *l'Afrique Fantôme*, an account of a long journey made by Michel Leiris and the ethnographer Marcel Griaule. The work was described as an « allusion to the answers to Africa's taste for the supernatural ».

These two years of travel and discovery were marked by the collection of objects, extensive documentation and, above all, a corpus of photographs exceptional for the understanding of the African peoples.

Shortly after publication, the Museum of Modern Art presented the *African Negro Art* exhibition in New York in 1935. Alfred Boer, the museum director, was so convinced of the importance of this event that he called on Walter Evans to document all the works presented. It took him two months and resulted in several thousand negatives.

Many artists drew their inspiration from African art at the time, including Man Ray with his famous photograph *Black and White*.

Meanwhile, the first studios were opening in Africa in the early 1930s, owing to the necessity to conduct population censuses: the authorities needed to photograph every individual to fix his or her identity in the context of the frequent migrations from the countryside to the cities or from one country to another. The most notable photographers in this field, Seydou Keita in Bamako and Mama Casset in Dakar, became exemplary exponents, developing a model that others could follow by making notes on different types of dress, cloth and jewellery.

Photography was very interested in people: major ritual events (circumcisions, initiatory celebrations) or major personal events (weddings, births) fell under the scrutiny of Malik Sidibé and Cornelius Augustt; Samuel Fosso went as far as representing himself as the hero of his innermost dreams.

Photographs covered the walls of homes far and wide, particularly as clan and family units began to disintegrate.

At the dawn of independence, when official press agencies like the Amap in Mali or Congo Presse started to develop, photography became a tool used to display political commitment. From the 1950s on, South African photographers like Peter Magubane, Bob Gosani, Billy Monk or Roger Balen denounced apartheid. Some of them were regularly published in the magazine Drum, which proved to have a large readership and widespread influence.

While this form of political struggle condemning the massacre of entire populations still continues in our time, contemporary photographers like Santu Mofokeng and Andrew Tshabangu use photography to denounce everyday poverty and misery.

And while poets may think that « art, along with love and knowledge, is the only real solution that can tear man away from the nightmare of time, from the minor colonized hell we call life, »[4] other photographers, like Pierrot Men in Madagascar or Cathy Pinnock in South Africa, have more aesthetic preoccupations in their research.

Having praised the Africa of gods, photography is today intent on understanding the Africa of human beings.

Agnès de Gouvion Saint-Cyr

The writer, the griot and the photographer

Simon Njami

Simon Njami was born in 1962 to Cameroonian parents, but has been living in Paris since 1976. He is co-founder and editor-in-chief for *Revue Noire*.

The young woman took a photograph and returned to the young man she had just photographed. She lay down beside him and closed her eyes.

- You are part of my life. I have your image. I have stolen your soul.

Photography, like literature, no doubt, is not an affair of the soul. The young woman here, in a state of obvious confusion, conflated the emotional abduction she was aware of committing - her desire to possess - with the act of taking a photograph. Her goal was presumably to record the moment on film as an enduring reminder of what she and the young man had experienced together. It was not him she wanted to capture on film; it was certainly not his soul. Instead, it was her own desire: her craving for eternity. She put photography and memory side by side, as if they were the same thing. She was telling herself a story. Now photography is more than just a matter of memory - although for this particular woman, photography, and specifically this photograph, will be the sole instrument of memory. The experience she and the young man shared, no matter what it was, became nothing more than an interpretation filtered through her own memory; it became mixed into the jumble of elements that give an image life. Memory will then be the paintbrush with which she endlessly repaints an image which is, a priori, devoid of meaning: memory is a painting, a blank canvas onto which she transfers her own soul.

Photography is not writing. Its task is to restore to us the reality of a moment: that is, one version of reality. And it is into the space opened up by these myriad interpretations that narrative, which may become writing, surges. Photography then becomes the medium, the setting, the point of departure for a story. For stories that are not rigidly linked to the reality presented as a referent. For such reality, no matter what its aspiration, could never disclose any truth other than the truth of the point in time already past.

This may explain why a photograph has never struck me as being essential. Quite the contrary. Lost in a moment in time, I devote all my energy to the present, the fleeting moment which I need to live to the full. I cannot recall my finger being ready to press the shutter. I have never wanted to take over any pictures I might produce. Pictures have their own life which should not be confused with ours. Any forced appropriation is suspect, disturbing. For the photograph depicts only a fraction of a moment. It is not the moment. Photography can lure us into the trap of believing in the intrinsic value of the document, seeing it as a function of reality or as a symbol of a truth which, inevitably, will be conferred upon it. Photographers whose vocation is to record the fleeting moment believe they are at an advantage over us with their knowledge and free use of their eyes, while they themselves are merely a plaything in the hands of time. They have the advantage of being able to choose.

And the choice is imposed on us. What difference does it make if, here or there, we think we can recognize a place, a light or a colour? There will always be a discrepancy between the still image, still for eternity, and life which goes on. The picture of the young man which the young woman wanted to capture, is no longer the man. It is obsolete. Gone. Void. The void left behind can be filled by feelings, comments or narrative bringing a second or third life to the image: a life beyond the moment which suddenly takes on a new dimension.

A photograph can be made to say whatever we want, simply because, as for any other instrument devised by human hands, it does not have its own life, or any reality other than the reality endowed on it at a given point in time. It lives solely through the eyes of another, when it becomes art, casting off the trappings of reality it so often wears. But that is another story. Here we are referring to these pictures of ourselves which photography shows us; to pictures of others, of people we love and think we know but no longer recognize: a poor copy, as it were, a usurped identity. For identity is only worthwhile when asserted. The young woman gave the young man an identity on her own terms, which was not necessarily the identity he may have imagined - as if taking the picture was not enough for her. She had to take possession of it; as if the original, neutral snap-shot could only be of value once it was named, possessed and permanent.

Indeed, while time and the moment expressing feeling need no intermediary, no concrete delineation to exist, photography is non-existent without its paraphernalia. It is not feeling, but technique. It is not being, it is artefact. It is *Another Country*. The country we can only dream of, where the sole purpose is in fact to remain in a dream state. This is the domain which, above all, transcends the frame of a photograph, because it depicts the essence. My fascination for Baldwin's novel will go on, because of the beauty and myriad meanings of the title; because of the narrow relationship between the title and the content. « Another country » has no form of physical legitimacy. It is an illusion which we all carry within ourselves. Our sexuality, our career, our friends, our family, all comprise the many different countries which make us the individuals we are. We cannot be considered without taking these into account; without these we are nothing, merely a mass of flesh and bone devoid of life. Photography shows its limits to us in its incapacity to record this other country on film.

And in this space left vacant, the writer may find a position somewhere between fixed reality and the shifting world of feelings. We need to project our minds, to extend ourselves in time; in a word, to feel our being; to have proof of our material essence, of our existence, quite simply. And while photography can record appearances, only writing, poetry, can offer a means for grasping the fleeting and the fragile - the immaterial - in the irresistible urge to control all the miscellaneous data that make and unmake our existence, to record them in black-and-white, lest we ever forget; as when marking a record on a blank film. Perhaps this is the only reason for writing: to assert our existence, to establish a world for ourselves to our own scale where everything would be possible and known.

To establish something which would remain; a record; proof for disputes in the future; a plea held in reserve and revised on a daily basis, in case ... Refusal. Refusal of old age, which dooms us forever to be strangers unto ourselves, refusal of death, of disappearing without having experienced the sincerity and inanity of things. Write so as not to die. Stop time and impose our own individual pace on it. Render time continuous, spread out, with neither beginning nor end, like a story starting over and over again. Fill in gaping holes, chasms. Silence this anguish of not knowing. The anguish of never being able to know, the anguish that cannot be identified, the anguish of not existing. A vain quest, a utopia. A refusal to decline into madness. Nothing is invented. Memory wavers. Understanding falters. For here is all the beauty of all true writing. It lies in approximation, amnesia, cautious smokescreens thrown up like a modest veil over our ambitions for our lives. It is in the very insignificance of things which remain that we manage to draw a little strength. A confrontation between the real image and the dream image. Writing for reinventing and contesting the image, as on a blank page, a photograph on an eternally blank film. Inventing our own history. A novel. A work of fiction. There is no such literary thing as bluff. From the outset, literature acknowledges the artificial nature of the referential world, unlike photography which, while sometimes arguing the opposite, becomes only too often a substitute for reality. The young woman, to be sure of stealing the soul of the young man, of stealing the part of his soul which was of interest to her, should have written it down; invented it; as a character is invented, as a perfect match to the specifications of our desires. She expected photography to perform a miracle it was incapable of performing.

The only miracle of such pictures of beings made of flesh and blood, whether close or distant, is in the reality we confer on them ourselves. In many ways, family photographs are perfect examples of this trap of subjectivity. Most of the time they show perfect strangers: we are told they were uncles, aunts, cousins, grandparents, great-grandparents, sometimes even ourselves, in other words a whole procession of characters we have not always been personally acquainted with and who mean nothing to our memory. But these strangers provide us with a mooring in history and an ambiguous sense of belonging to a clan. These images which, with time, have developed into emblems, figures of heraldry, are simply the image that our family wanted to preserve of its own history. They are invariably devoid of expression, posed, in accordance with an immutable technique and aesthetic. Such a pretence of belonging, based on images which have become historic documents and part of our heritage, blinds us, creating obligations we cannot always fulfil. Surely the ancestral legend is an essential component of our perception of ourselves, and the main purpose of such photographic portraits is to confront us with ourselves? Is there another way of seeing ourselves, of taking root in another land or geographical area, outside our own history written down as one of the chapters of a saga dating back to time immemorial, and which will obviously outlive us? The images interfere with each other, combining and cancelling one another out. Where is the reality to which one refers? It no longer exists: faces are both familiar and unfamiliar, indeed deriving their familiarity from the fact that, at last, they are anchored somewhere.

JOSÉ ONDOA

Cameroon
b. Yaoundé, Cameroon 1938
- lives in Yaoundé

After having travelled and worked in different fields, José Ondoa decided to devote himself to photography and studied at the École Louis Lumière in Paris from 1964 to 1966. Back in Yaoundé, Cameroon, he became a freelance photographer, then opened a studio. His studio closed in 1989, because of financial problems due to the emergence of colour photography. Pascale Marthine Tayou discovered his work and completed his archives.

1. Griot: a member of a class of travelling poets, musicians and folk-historians in North and West Africa.

Photographer JOSÉ ONDOA ©
Cameroon, ca.1985.

The images of these people, reinterpreted ad infinitum, no longer belong to them. They are the basis for a legend beyond our grasp. They constitute the material from which the griot[1] will write, will tell his story. They are the proof which, despite their obvious lack of material existence, will nourish the legend suddenly transformed into timeless truth. And the word of the griot, historian and artist, holds us in its clasp, hypnotizing us, strengthening our clan-based moorings which we might, quite legitimately, have doubted. These moorings, once again, are entirely dependent on subjectivity and our need to see articulate images in every snapshot whose subject touches us. Hence the oft-stated argument that an image only exists when invested with something else. Apparently contradictory at a first glance, this view is really nothing more than the tale of a tale, confirming, if indeed it were necessary, the disembodied nature of photography. Familiarity is strange, disturbing. But what does a certain shot of a house really show? Or of a deserted street? This stretch of wall? A house. A deserted street. A stretch of wall. The rest, if it exists, exists entirely in our minds.

No doubt this is the way photography is seen by the writer, as the realm of the ambiguous, the abyss, the optical illusion. While the griot can rely on a portrait to legitimize his truth, a writer devotes all his energy to contesting the same truth; seeing beyond the obvious inference; seeking time before and time after, which alone can validate the moment recorded on the film. The writer is bound to contest the archetype of these shapes, objects, faces, which, nevertheless, endure and withstand time; there, in their stubborn immobility, reminding us of our lies, overstatements, liberties taken with what we shall continue to call, for want of a better term, reality. The contrast between blank paper and printed paper. But the strength of the writer emerges entirely from this contrast, in the capacity to circumvent the most irrefutable evidence, in the intuition and ability of the constant pursuit of another country.

« It was snowing outside, and our mother was telling us how she had met our father. How they fell in love. How they had loved us. How they loved us. She told the story and it was hard to link these words to any form of reality; the contrast was too striking; long hot nights spent outside talking and fooling around. Outside the wind wailed through the branches of the bare trees. She talked about her childhood, so that we too could feel some of it. And in a haphazard way, we understood her efforts; and loved her for it even more. The tales about our father, of his life before, with us, sounded bitter in her mouth. There was the time, for example, when he turned up in slippers at university, in front of his students. How many times had she told us the story? We had even been there ourselves. As if she were afraid that with time the images might fade and in the end we would only be left with the memory of a memory? Images always fade. »

The image, the photograph I have kept of this scene shows us all around the table, smiling at the camera. My elder sister is missing: no doubt because she had been asked to take the photograph. An ordinary photograph. Of no interest for anyone other than me. Because I was there. I am both the player and the spectator. And the spectacle reflected back to me has nothing to do with the picture being shown. As if the disappearance of the people in the photograph would take all the meaning away. Would make it just one of any number of photographs. A friend of mine told me one day that memory only works with ruins or remains. The remnants of feelings, the ruins of physical areas, the vestiges around which we reconstructed reality. We rebuild it to our scale. Life would then be nothing but a pile of charred ruins. What photograph would be capable of restoring the meaning of these ruins? Literature, as I see it, has no other function.

Perhaps it starts where photography stops.

Simon Njami

UNKNOWN photographers ©
Democratic Republic of Congo
Album of the Henri-Désiré Faye Assani family from Kinshasa.

The Icon and the Totem

Jean-Loup Pivin

Words and Photographs

Why, when writing and photography come together, does one feel that the exercise is a waste of time, that it will be in vain? There are many texts written on photography that are both enriching and relevant, while avoiding any claim to be definitive. Yet theoretical considerations of photography are distinguished by their lack of impact on either the taking of pictures or the myriad interpretations made by billions of eyes around the world.

At the time when photography was exploding onto the scene, modern European painting was being born out of theory and thought: for more than a century and a half not a single new art form or new art movement has come into existence without a preliminary declaration of theory, always drawn up by the artists themselves, the archetypal examples being Kandinsky, Duchamp and Breton.

In the field of photography, no major theory of aesthetics, no matter how vast, has ever had the slightest impact on the concept or production of the photograph. Handbooks emphasize techniques, making recommendations about how to frame a shot; since the subject is highly technical, the discussion inevitably becomes academic. Today's cameras with automatic diaphragm settings and autofocus still attach great importance to the centre of the viewfinder, so that the focus is determined by technical needs. The history of photography has mainly been influenced by technical advances, with new practices and new aesthetics being linked to the increasing potential afforded by the camera and by developing techniques. Theoretical writings on aesthetic issues involved in depicting reality in photographs are virtually non-existent, and the few texts there are have had no impact on the taking of pictures.

Photography is a technique that uses machines. The use of these machines is functional or commercial; it is not artistic. From the very outset, a vast number of photographs was taken outside the scope of art and art-related issues, so that photography was able to set up and develop in total autonomy.

With time, photography will have its own critics, criticism and history, far removed from art criticism and history. Less than 20 years ago we often heard art historians and critics confessing to knowing nothing about photography, which was why they refused to exhibit photographs in museums or galleries. This isolation from the artistic mainstream, which confined photography for many long years to the ranks of inferior art forms, left it free to explore reality without suffering from any complexes, allowing it to become a form of expression so common and widely practised that it can now claim to be a truly popular art form free of all the trappings of « High Art ».

Photography is now on an equal footing with painting or sculpture as an art form in its own right; it has no outside references, no influence other than its own. A photograph can only be compared to another type of photograph. What the photograph evokes or tells us is autonomous.

Interpretations must always be made with caution and will inevitably remain an exercise external to the object. If text must be written to accompany a photograph, the only forms of writing which are equal to the task are poetry and metaphor – writing in images. All we can therefore do is to sort a series of photographs, collecting, combining or discarding them in different orders, attempting to incorporate or fathom the different worlds of forms created by photography: the setting, the pose, the expression of the subject photographed (particularly for portraits); the light, the movement, the framing; the inspiration, the expression, the environment. The written text will review and describe contextual references: the date and place, the biography of the photographer and of the subject (whether human or inanimate). It will be impossible to stop the written text from conveying a moral message, a statement, even while we remain aware of its relativity.

Sometimes writing and photography are closely interrelated, as with books and posters (for example, posters for advertising, information, or political purposes). The famous slogan of the French weekly magazine *Paris Match* - « the weight of words, the impact of photos » - acknowledges the inevitable manipulation of photographs by words. The words offer an instant interpretation of the visuals, stirring both the individual and the collective subconscious, so as to endow the photograph with one specific, easily decipherable meaning. It is the slogan that uses the picture. Written comment and the caption or « legend » (a quaint choice of terminology for the few words accompanying a photograph, and a term which highlights the ambiguity of written comment) guide and steer the eye across the image.

REALISTIC ABSTRACTION OF THE REAL

Photography is abstract by nature. As primary evidence of this we can put forward the two-dimensional paper on which it is printed, the decontextualization of the reality it shows, and the suspended image of the real situation, which has no life outside the moment when the shot was taken. The aspect of the photograph that is obvious to us then obliges us to reconstruct a true or fictitious story to explain the picture, without any real knowledge - despite all the allegedly « scientific » precautions we may observe, despite all the contrivances (literary or otherwise) which may surround it. Such is the case for photographs that do not sink into oblivion. The second piece of evidence in support of photography's abstract nature is the permanent doubt that exists as to the validity of the photograph as objective proof, as absolute truth, as a material rendition of reality. And so meaning is reversed, so that the photograph's most « realistic » aspect may be less reliable than its most « abstract » aspect. This reversal of meaning may apply in either of two different approaches to photography: one artistic, whereby photography becomes an artistic process and an artistic object; the other behavioural and philosophical, whereby photography becomes an icon, a symbol that may be used for different purposes. Such an icon may be used as a symbol of an affiliation (family or social) on the one hand, or the image of an attraction or repulsion on the other.

THE PAPER TOTEM

It is possible that photography in Africa could be less a realistic representation of reality than an example of the iconic vision. By renouncing documentary value or personal, private value, the photographic image itself may become not a depiction of reality, but a social and spiritual counterpart of the subject photographed. Hence the choice of the photographer in terms of personal qualities as a mediator, as an interpreter of social values and an intercessor, going beyond the role of the clever technician to become the producer of icons. This may be an explanation for the reluctance certain communities feel at the prospect of being photographed, not wishing to have their souls stolen away. African photographers are not exempt from this suspicion: the Congolese-Angolan photographer, Antoine Freitas, described this in notes made during a visit to a village in Kasai country in 1939. Similar observations were reported by Youssouf Tata Cissé in his recent book on Seydou Keita (in 1995).

We are not trying to quantify the level of subjectivity in a picture, which would involve acknowledging the obvious – namely, that each viewer interprets as his or her heart and mind see fit. Instead we are speaking of the values carried by a photograph. These are never what the photograph is; instead, they are what it signifies, at the point where the photograph carries its own inner meaning (independent of any intended by the photographer) not simply for an individual, but on a universal scale; thus enhancing the intrinsic value of a visual image in the perception of reality, without recourse to writing and words. Yet this does not imply that universal values are conveyed by photographic images, because it is clear that the cultural essence of each civilization will develop meanings and significances of its own, which may be contradictory. This fork is not a fork, it is a fork only for the person who knows what a fork is and who wants it to be a fork: we can see this again and again, especially in surrealist and conceptual paintings.

The icon not only expresses the being: it also prevents it from becoming anything other than its portrayal. If photography were a mirror of reality it could merge the being and its photographed counterpart, as the being is indeed realistic, although the counterpart is abstract and does not content itself with being a mere portrayal: it is part of a much greater reality. Can this be why people being photographed are so willing to be shown in costume, or even disguise, right up to the 1980s? « I am my portrayal. » « My portrait is myself. » In the same way, a totemic portrayal, the emblem of the person, embodies broader values and is far more than just a realistic depiction of the subject. The resemblance between the photograph and the subject, or the totemic portrayal and the subject, is not intended to be absolute, even if it actually is. Instead, it is the attitude, the gestures and the costume which proclaim the inner identity, the being in society and the values expressing it. The use of traditional costumes and ritual poses by the man or woman for whom the photograph is being taken illustrates this clearly. And the use of modern costume or disguise is not intended to have a different purpose: on the contrary, it is the revival of the traditional social values of the ancestors displayed in new attire.

Such a photograph parallels the poster of a singer or footballer on the bedroom wall of any young person anywhere in the world: both express values and confer an identity, even « protection », on the person associated with them. The sports star and singer are not gods, but totems in which gods are embodied.

This is similar to young people's tendency to adopt nicknames borrowed from current stars – rap stars especially - for their music groups, or even fashion houses, such as Yves Saint Laurent or Versace, with whom young people from the United States or Zaire identify in competing groups. The image of the other person becomes a fragment of oneself; similarly, one's own image is also a fragment of oneself: and thus we have the icon and the totem. The above phenomenon is also a means of anchoring one's individuality in a communal value, shared by as many people as possible.

We are far removed from what had originally seemed to be a self-evident truth: we are now at a point where photography is not a neutral object observed as if it were a fixed reality at a given point in history, but has a different value, no doubt deep down inside each and every one of us at the most fundamental level. Photography is not the proof that something has existed (a meeting, birth, political event, accident or war); it stands as testimony of what such reality depicts. Once again, photography has become an icon.

COMMUNAL VALUES OR THE RELEVANCE OF A PARENTHESIS IN THE FLOW OF TEXT

In Africa, the extended family of fathers and mothers, plus aunts and various spouses, underscores the broad concept of community which can include the even wider dimension of the cultural family, name, caste and civilization. And this is indeed the key issue when a photograph is taken: it is taken in relation to the imagined or real social context of the subject; the photograph defines the role the subject has there or intends to have there.

Something crucial has disappeared in Europe along with the loss of the concept of the social individual – that is, of the individual who does not exist outside society. In the past, it was not the mother and father who procreated, but society that produced the children. This is how things were all over the world, including Europe, until the 18th century, but this concept completely disappeared in the West in the latter part of the 20th century, and is fading - although without disappearing entirely - in the rest of the world, including Africa. The European family, reduced to the procreating couple, is no longer the first link in society, but merely a barrier behind which the child not yet born withdraws. The victory that was won for the respect and freedom of the individual has been transformed into rampant individualism. Relationship with others has been reduced to a sharing of commodities on the international market, and these commodities have in turn become moral values: as the shoe manufacturer, Nike, says, « Just do it! » Consumer goods have become the promised land of individual fulfilment that can be found through images manufactured for the territory they can occupy in the subconscious of each individual: again they are images which portray not reality, but a value carried by reality.

Societies in a state of weightlessness regarding the communal values by which each individual lives, no longer bind individuals on the basis of common rules, other than rules of material values; they can no longer break down the loneliness they have produced. And yet this does not mean that we must return to a state where the individual is negated and confined to a social mould offering nothing more than communal contentment: the price paid for individual liberty over the past century has been too great for us to find ourselves at such a dead end.

The nuclear family as the sole bond in society has led to such a narrowness in Europe that the only prospect is to extend outwards again in a new movement of sociability; the communal destiny will have be to redesigned so that we can once again share common values and act together, not only in a local context but also at the level of our small planet, Earth. This is probably the angle we need for understanding the contemporary upheavals in modern cities around the world, each of which has become the world (as the song says, « We are the world! »); and this includes the cities of Africa today.

The « moral » contained in this view is not an essential prerequisite for understanding the statement which a photograph attempts to convey, or its scope as an icon expressing communal values, as shown so clearly by photography in Africa. It does, however, cast light on the issue involved. It also casts light on the objective view of photography in Africa and probably on an entire area of photography generally. An icon is not merely for the use of the individual, as a source of reassurance, but primarily for use by others, or in fact, for the society which produced that individual. Could a photograph from independent Africa of the 1950s to the 1970s – or indeed the future - be seen as anything other than an expression of communal values overlaid with the external manifestations of modern style? During this period, photography was a special form of expression, as was music, providing abundant proof to the individual, to his or her family and to the colonizing power, that attitudes were ready for the modern age: this meant honouring everything in the way of autonomy, liberation and respect for the individual, but always in the context of shared community values. Clearly this interpretation also applies outside Africa and can be seen in a more structured and conscious way in all propaganda photography, where people are represented as groups rather than as individuals.

THE PHOTOGRAPHER

In such a context - which could transform the African subject into the actor playing his own role, staking his claim in society - the photographer is not the brilliant artist living as a recluse, but the mediator, the stage director, the iconographer. He is not making art, he is on the sidelines of the artistic, he is the manufacturer of a paper icon, producing a two-dimensional material rendition duplicating the other being. His expertise lies in the attention he pays to what the actor wants to convey of his own image, and in his help with the staging of the scene. This aspect of staging is more obvious in regions with « animistic » traditions. Such careful composition of the scene and deliberate attention to the posture of the subject can be seen in the ritual postures of speech and prayer seen from the Ivory Coast to the Congo, but these features are less obvious in Muslim countries, although they are just as strong. One finds evidence of this if one examines photographs of a number of men crouched praying on their mats, in the same studio where ten minutes earlier a couple had been embracing and where, ten minutes later, a young girl would appear in a new dress or two boys would announce their friendship to the world. In Ghana, Kenya and Ethiopia the relationship is even stronger because icons, which in the past were painted and placed on coffins, were quickly replaced by photographs. These photographs were often touched up using colour and the fine airbrushing of features. They literally played the role of icons, not because the photographic depiction was more realistic, but because it provided a better likeness of the deceased person and his or her values: it was a twin. There had been a meeting between the photograph and the person photographed.

THE AUTONOMY OF AFRICAN PHOTOGRAPHY

The best way to illustrate what was different about the way photographs were taken in Africa is the persistent gulf, whether conscious or unconscious, one sees between the aesthetics of European teaching and apprenticeship and the aesthetics found in practice in Africa. One of the important aspects of African photography in its early days was that despite the colonial photographic model, it developed an autonomous form quite unrelated to colonial subjects and styles. The first African photographers, mostly apprenticed to European photographers (who had settled in the country or were there as expatriate civil servants), had their own parallel and privately run businesses, taking photographs which displayed not the slightest stylistic connection to those of their tutors. The distinguishing feature was the practice - almost standard among African photographers - of capturing their fellow countrypeople on film, attired in their finest robes, in carefully arranged poses, with expressions suggesting that they were « conversing » with the photographer and the camera lens. In these photographs, Africans were showing themselves to themselves. By contrast, shots taken by European photographers, even those who had been based locally for many years, have a tangible quality of awkwardness and distance; it feels as if they have been taken « from the outside ». European photographers also favoured a particular choice of dress for their sitters, at least in the early years, preferring costumes that created an impression of strangeness or wildness. Such anthropomorphic, ethnological, tourist or exotic photographs served to endorse one single viewpoint: that which was designed to show that the other person was indeed other, different, unknown. Otherwise, why photograph the person? Such an argument obviously served to bolster the legitimacy of the foreign presence as a civilizing influence over these noble or ignoble savages. Photographs taken by Africans were clearly seen as representing a neutral technique rather than an artistic approach. Within the European tradition, the apprentice painter in an art school – or even the ordinary observer of those Western paintings that were in circulation - learnt not only the technique, but also what it conveyed regarding assumptions about portraying reality. The same applied to the person teaching or the source of the reference pictures, as the paintings and drawings were mainly bought by Europeans. The autonomy of African photographers was therefore absolute from the outset; they operated within a free zone because they were not targeting the external white market.

The same relationship between producer and consumer of art may apply to all portrait photographers around the world, including European ones. But while the quest of European and American photographers has been to understand the individual personality, enhancing its individuality and uniqueness, in Africa it was quite the opposite; here it was a case of ritualizing the personality and endowing it with its social potential. This explains the number and variety of the props and disguises which are present in these photographs: their purpose is not to reveal an image of a desired future, but to *be* the future. Thus the photograph is not a wish or ambition, but a proving ground that makes you become what you are, both socially and within yourself. The visible proof of social success, such as a telephone or motor-scooter, may belong not to the person in the photograph, but to friends or the photographer. Yet this must not be seen as deceit: the telephone is an attribute showing that the person is prepared to be identified in such a way.

This point leads us to consider the practice of art as a collective exercise, emancipated from the burdens of art for art's sake and the artist as brilliant genius, where instead the artist is a member of the community who plays a leading role in producing forms.

TOWARDS A THEORY OF ANONYMITY

In Africa we are dealing with a different practice of image-making, no doubt coming out of thousands of years when everyone in the community could create images of reality. We are all artists, as Joseph Beuys said - which is another way of saying that no-one is, in the context of the modern definition of art and in view of the great pressure of social values that has been exerted on image-makers over the last two centuries in Europe and over the past few decades in the rest of the world.

Music and dance can still be enjoyed either individually or in a group, without each and every participant having to be a dancer with the New York City Ballet or a musician with the Berlin Philharmonic, to be watched with religious devotion. The reason lies in popular music and dance, which we all enjoy, whether we sing in the bathroom or play a musical instrument for pleasure, whether we dance in night-clubs or in groups at parties. In the visual arts, what has clearly disappeared is an unselfconscious community involvement in portraying reality through (for example) painting or drawing. At the moment photography offers the only possibility of this. For many years formal photography was disdained, but now there are billions of faithful followers although, fortunately, only a few see themselves as artists and some want to be photographers without really knowing what is involved.

When 20 000 photographers in the Ivory Coast register with the professional union, what is their understanding of photographic practice, and what awareness do they really have of it? It is probably less a claim to art and more an opportunity for earning a living with the licence to take photographs; and, even more importantly, it could be an entrée to social status in the context of modern society. In addition to this so-called professional practice, there is private photography which, over recent decades, has been carried to every corner of the earth by the democratic spread of technology.

Can photography be seen as the return to a communal form of visual expression in a world where the tendency is for spectators to be passive? Does this mean we can see it as part of the traditional practice of making images that our common ancestors passed down to us? More specifically, can we link it to prehistoric rock paintings, where it seems that the most accomplished hands worked side by side with the most inept, all being totally anonymous? Could we dare see a practice such as rock painting, which was built around a ritual as a spiritual exercise achieved through a communal artistic act, as being similar - even in flippant argument - to the practice of photography? This may very well be the case, if we allow for an intuitive inclusion of three objective components: communal practice, artistic experience and anonymous initiatives. However, one distinction must be made: photography aims exorcise reality, while prehistoric rock art aimed to transcend it.

Even if drawing a link between photography and rock paintings in prehistoric times is simply a leap of intuition, it may help to provide an understanding of the meaning of things unspoken, of the form in art in general and in photography in particular. Such practices are not to be seen as spiritual in the limited religious sense.

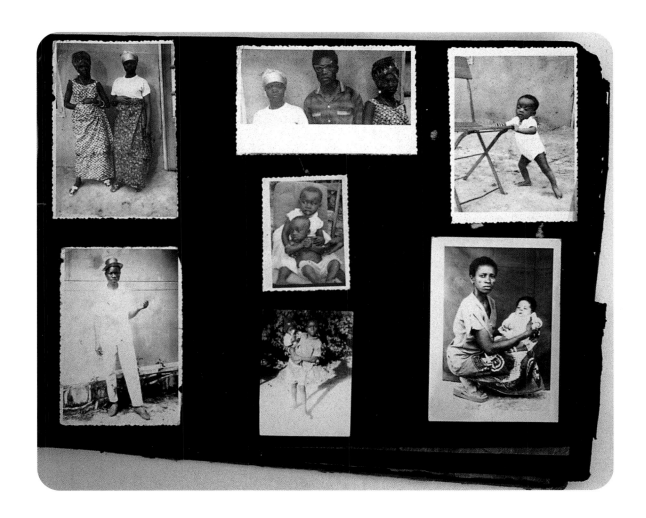

Any art form is a carrier of spirituality. Without attempting to develop an argument about art and the nature of producing different forms, it is essential to at least contemplate the anonymous aspect of photographic work for which Africa offers a live illustration on a grand scale.

ART AND THE HERO

The disappearance of communal values in Europe has coincided with a fading of the charisma surrounding the hero who fights for his country, defending the widow and the orphan (i.e. community values). There has been a parallel shift towards a glorification of the individual, standing alone, confronting his or her destiny, whether as athlete or researcher, entrepreneur or explorer. The European artist is one of these individualists, and artists themselves have gradually been shaped by this image of themselves as both rebellious and misunderstood, both medium and mediator of the irrational: the only ones able to challenge society, society's jesters, much like the jester in the royal courts of long ago, but also the purest spiritual protector (being unstained by any religion: they are not priests), in a lay world guided by reason and science. Such a vision of the artist is spreading to every civilization around the world, with varying effects. Europe, the United States and various other countries around the world had a number of photographers at the turn of the century who endeavoured to impose artistic values on their work and thus share in the glorious aura of the artist who signs (often with great ostentation) each print - mostly with a view to increasing the market value of the work rather than out of pure egoism. However, photographers did not manage to achieve for their craft the status of an art in its own right, even if some recognition was given to a certain relationship between photography and artistic feeling and thought - although only ever on the same level as the applied arts. Rare indeed were the leaders of artistic movements at the time who allowed a photographer into their ranks, or even into their circle of friends, observers or promoters. Yet Man Ray is not an isolated case and over recent years a number of contemporary works have been uncovered featuring the abstraction of the reality photographed.

The legend of the suffering artist has only recently found its way into the world of photography. Very few photographers die lonely and misunderstood. Some even forget that they were photographers and ask of their « art » no other form of recognition than the pleasure they experience in practising it. In Africa, those who claim to be artist-photographers are from the younger generation, earning more on the non-African market than the local market and following paths already opened up in affluent countries.

Over the last 30 years photography has become a more common means of expression for artists producing works that are recognized as art for museums. Yet the camera is still seen as that funny machine with the button we press without knowing why; its sole purpose seems to be the fascination of seeing one's own image seen through the eyes of another. It is nevertheless difficult to understand why photography, being « multiple » (i.e. infinitely reproducible) by nature, has been forced to remain within the confines of the single, original object: a photograph is made unique by the viewer's perceptions and the accidents of history, where this may never have been the intention of the photographer. While attempts have been made, if only over recent years, to bring photography onto the art market, with numbered prints, vintage photographs and the application of famous signatures with a view to financial speculation, it is still clear that photography is an art of a multiple nature that can be reproduced ad infinitum without any concern for the restrictions governing a market based on one-off objects.

The value of the multiple object that can be shared by everyone coincides with the basic communal value. In this way, photography has built a community around the world, in a series of radically different contexts, depending on the geographical areas and civilizations concerned.

From the outset the photographer is working with multiples that infinitely reproduce what can be shared as an image. His or her subject is reality and the reproduction of the subject is reality: the photographer is only a medium brandishing a gadget, really no more than a simple technician in a communal enterprise. For the public, the art of the photographer is always secondary to the reality effect produced. The subject is the superstar, not the photographer, unlike the painter, who creates seemingly out of nothing. Yet the photographer is equally an artist, with the mind of an artist, which is expressed in his or her photographic vision. The process may not be arduous - a mere fraction of a second to take the picture, instead of hours wielding a brush, pencil or chisel - yet it is quite autonomous in the choices made and the intuitive qualities behind the work. Yet this craft is at the reach of millions of fingers and eyes which, every second, press the shutter release or see a picture.

And this is no doubt the point where the shift occurs between practising one of the « fine arts » and the art of photography. On the one hand, the revered artist-turned-iconoclast sets up cliques and gradually moves away from the general public to orient his or her message solely towards a cultivated audience of specialists, speculators, paying patrons-of-the-arts and critics (museum curators get added to the list later). On the other hand, photography has invaded the shared public visual imagination. The subject is no longer god or the hero, but me and my relatives, the countryside where we were on holiday or, in the case of pictures taken by others, the countryside we dream of visiting, special moments in the community, new superstars with whom we all identify, advertising and reporting.

AFRICA BY AFRICA

For all these different reasons, which can be seen in the context of concerns of a more universal nature, rather than being strictly African, we are not presenting the photography of Black Africa in order to introduce it into a general history of photography - which will inevitably happen, with all the attendant confusion and simplistic misinterpretations. Our ambition is rather to have these pictures play a part in an African view of Africa, both for the continent itself and for the world at large. Hence our reservations when African photography was finally noticed in the early 1990s and was shown to the world through the work of only one or two photographers - a situation that persisted for years in some cases. The quality of the work of Malian photographers Seydou Keita and Malick Sidibé is unquestioned, even though they have both produced work which is of unquestionable quality, but this situation arose simply because the combination of the market and international archives could not absorb any more and did not have the courage to go out and discover anything else.

Quite clearly, the sum total of the photographers and photographs being presented in this anthology aims to display to the world not only a continent and its talent, but also an entire dimension of photography so superbly epitomized by Africa in the relationship with form, art and the artist. This book embraces both levels, as a tool for knowledge and a tool for stimulating thought.

Jean-Loup Pivin

UNKNOWN photographers ©
Democratic Republic of Congo
Album of the Henri-Désiré Faye Assani family from Kinshasa.

Beginnings

Le premier âge

Studio photography in Freetown

Vera Viditz-Ward

In the first half of the 19th century, two African territories, Liberia and Sierra Leone, were favoured by emancipated and runaway slaves from the United States. In Sierra Leone, these former slaves, who called themselves Creoles, started photography in the second half of the 19th century, turning the territory into a land of plenty for all kinds of photography, from portrait work to city and country landscapes. Despite complex internal problems, photography is still very much alive in Sierra Leone today.

In recent years there has been considerable interest in the early use of photography by non-Western peoples. Frequently, these early photographs show how non-Western peoples created new forms of artistic expression by adapting European technology and visual idioms for their own purposes. The photographs represent a rich synthesis of European and indigenous imagery. The long history of contact between Sierra Leoneans and Europeans made Freetown a logical starting point for photographic research in West Africa. The information presented here is based on 20 years of researching photographs on the part of Sierra Leonean photographers. These photographs represent what is probably the oldest continuing tradition in West Africa of black African photographers producing photographs for an African audience.

In 1839 the daguerreotype was presented to the world as a gift from the government of France. This early form of photography involved complicated procedures and cumbersome equipment and each mirror-like image was unique and non-reproducible. Described as a victory for both science and art, the daguerreotype endured for several decades and revolutionized image-making both practically and conceptually. The appearance of photography in the mid-19th century was opportune, to say the least. The public in Europe and America desired to see the « exotic » and « mysterious » peoples and countries who were the subjects of military campaigns and innumerable romantic paintings and novels.

Vera Viditz-Ward is an associate professor of Photography at Bloomsburg University in Pennsylvania, USA. She is a photographer and a photography historian. She has lived and worked in Sierra Leone for the last 20 years, has published numerous articles and given lectures on the development of black photography in Sierra Leone, from the 19th century to the present day.

< UNKNOWN photographer © ca.1870
Visiting card.
Courtesy of Viditz-Ward

Beginnings

Also, the 19th-century concepts of realism, materialism and scientific method created an intellectual need for « objective » or realistically correct imagery. Daguerreotypists immediately exploited the new medium's ability to reproduce reality; the more adventurous of them set off to document foreign lands visited by few Europeans.

Late in 1839 French daguerreotypists were travelling to North Africa, the Middle East and South America to photograph indigenous peoples, geographic formations and historical ruins and architecture. The British and some Americans were soon to follow to India and Australia. It was through these early photographers that the medium was introduced on the African continent. Since the most practical and direct route to India and Australia was round the Cape of Good Hope, the daguerreotype process was introduced to South Africa as early as 1840[1]. Ships travelling to Cape Town always stopped at various ports of call along the West African coast and photography was certainly introduced to coastal West Africa before 1845 through contact with these ships and the daguerreotypists travelling on them.

By the mid-19th century, Freetown was already a bustling city with an active commercial, administrative and social life, and was a major West African port of call. Its history dates from 1787 when the Black Poor, a small group of destitute former slaves from London, established a self-governing colony with the help of a British benevolent society. Over a period of more than 50 years the British settled three other groups of liberated Africans: escaped American slaves who had fought for Britain during the American Revolution; Jamaicans who had waged guerrilla attacks on European plantations from mountain strongholds; and thousands of slaves released from ships by the British Navy after Parliament prohibited the transatlantic slave trade in 1806. At mid-century Freetown was the hub of the British Crown Colony of Sierra Leone, which encompassed the fast-growing urban area and surrounding peninsula. The various groups of liberated slaves and other ethnic groups in Freetown were welding themselves into a new ethnic group called Creoles. In their private lives the Creoles continued with many of their African social and religious customs, but in public, with the active encouragement of missionaries and colonial administrators, they emulated European customs. Victorian Creoles took pride in their churches and public buildings. Missionaries had built several secondary schools and a teacher-training institution, which was to become the first university college in West Africa. Business was active between enterprising Creole merchants and traders arriving from other African and European countries. Social events included lectures, concerts, plays, horse races, charity balls and Victorian high teas. Several local newspapers kept the public informed of international events, news of which arrived regularly by ship since Creoles travelled often to Britain and Europe. The information which did not reach the city through other channels was sure to arrive with a returning Freetonian. Creoles of this period proudly called their thriving city, « The Athens of West Africa ».[2]

In such a sophisticated environment it is not surprising that photography took root quite early. The first professional Freetown photographers were probably itinerant merchants who travelled between the main ports of the West African coast. Although circumstantial evidence suggests the existence of African daguerreotypes in Freetown by the mid-1840s, the earliest documentary evidence, so far, dates to 1857. A newspaper advertisement in the *New Era* that year announced the arrival in Freetown of a daguerreotypist named A Washington, who had worked in the United States and Liberia[3]. While daguerreotypes from northern and southern Africa have survived, since those areas are located in climates with average humidity, none by Washington or any other photographer from this period have yet been discovered in Freetown. Freetown's location in a tropical environment, which receives over 500 mm of rainfall each year, would be extremely destructive to the fragile, many-layered daguerreotype.

By the 1850s, numerous technical innovations made photography considerably easier and more portable while the photographs became more durable. Even with these innovations, the 19th-century photographer required a formidable array of equipment and chemicals to make a photograph. Cameras were large and cumbersome in order to accommodate the standard glass negative sizes of 8 x l0 inches or 16 x 20 inches. The glass negatives used by photographers had to be coated with collodion and sensitized with silver nitrate immediately before exposure. Chemicals, bottles, trays and glass plates were necessary for sensitization and printing on albumen paper. Since the process required total processing while still wet, a darkroom or light-resistant tent was essential during the entire procedure.

During this time there were African and some European portrait photographers who ran studios or travelled as itinerant photographers along the West African coastal towns.

The Europeans making photographs in British West Africa usually came out in capacities other than that of photographer. Backed by such institutions as the Royal Geographical Society, maritime expeditions, or the Colonial Office, these soldiers, administrators, scholars and adventurers produced photographic documents of the people and places they were sent to observe and control. The Europeans brought up-to-date technology and the latest photographic styles, and they usually left behind equipment, supplies and technical knowledge with their African assistants and colleagues.

Africans had established permanent photography studios in Freetown by at least the late 1860s. In that decade newspaper advertisements appeared for local studios which made photographic portraits and frequently sold photographic chemicals and supplies ordered from Liverpool. News articles from the *British Journal of Photography* were occasionally reprinted in the Freetown papers, and Freetonians appear to have been fairly interested in the variety of photographic methods in use at this time. Indeed, the text of one 1881 advertisement presents an astounding variety of locally available photographic processes:

Pictures of the best quality will be produced by the company in the following processes, viz; The Gelatine Instantaneous Process, The Platinum Type Process, The Improved Daguerreotype Process, The Woodbury Type Process, The Albert Type Process, The Imperishable Carbon Process, The Art Silver Printing Process etc ...[4]

This advertisement was placed by Shadrack Albert St John, one of the many Creole studio photographers working in Freetown in the late 1880s. E Albert Lewis, J Nutwoode Hamilton, Nicholas May, Tom Johnson and Dionysius Leomy also advertised their studios during this period. Each of these photographers offered work in the contemporary European formats of carte-de-visite (3 x 5 inches) or cabinet (5 x 7 inches) and hand-tinted photographs. Another service most studios offered was the sale of landscape photographs, urban scenes of Freetown, and photographs of typical scenes from the countryside. The Creoles responded to this new art with an enthusiasm equal to that of their European contemporaries. They collected photographs of family, friends, 19th-century celebrities, public buildings, social events and local scenery. These pictures were purchased by Freetonians and expatriates to be preserved in their personal photograph albums. Whether in London or Freetown, the family album was an essential part of the respectable Victorian parlour.

∧ Photographer JP DECKER © ca.1870
The Port of Freetown.
Courtesy of S. L. Museum.

JP DECKER

Sierra Leone

Photographed the British headquarters in Sierra Leone, Gambia, Ghana and Nigeria for the Colonial Office in London.

1. Bensusan. 1966. 9.
2. Fyfe 1962. 459.
3. *New Era* (Freetown),
29 June 1857.
4. *Watchman* (Freetown),
25 October 1881.

Very little biographical information exists about these early photographers. The newspaper advertisement of Shadrack Albert St John states that he learned photography in London and also took photographs in Gambia. Nicholas May was the brother of a prominent Creole headmaster, and E Albert Lewis worked as both a trader and a professional photographer. The only extant photographs from this group were made by Dionysius Leomy, who worked in Freetown from the 1880s until the early l900s. There are several examples of his work in various archives in London as well as in three albums at the Sierra Leone National Museum. Leomy's photographs are easily identifiable by his name, printed diagonally in the lower right-hand corner of each albumen print. His most interesting photographs are of Freetown street scenes which capture the vitality of market women and hawkers as they talk to each other and sell their wares. He also specialized in « bird's-eye-view » photographs of Freetown streets. This style of photograph would have been considered innovative and was popular with those who collected photographs for their albums or as a souvenir of Freetown.

Another photographer of this period was JP Decker. Decker ran his own photography studio and worked for the colonial government in the capacity of photographer. He was commissioned locally on a directive from the Colonial Office in London to document British colonial headquarters in Freetown, Bathurst (Banjul in Gambia), the Cape Coast, the Gold Coast (Ghana) and Nigeria. These images are primarily of government buildings and military quarters. J P Decker's skill and technical control over his equipment and materials is consistently apparent in his architectural photographs, and his artistic ability is reflected in his sensitive compositions and unusual vantage points.

One of the most important early innovations in photography was the development of the gelatine dry-plate negative in the late 1870s. Gelatine was substituted for collodion on the glass negative. The gelatine significantly reduced exposure times and negative plates could now be purchased presensitized and stored in light-tight boxes until needed. Cameras were becoming smaller and more portable.

Beginnings

After the invention of the snapshot camera in 1889 there were many African and European amateur photographers in West Africa, taking pictures as a hobby. These innovations made the itinerant photographer's life considerably easier. Photographers continued to travel through Freetown on their way to or from such places as Gambia, Liberia and the Gold Coast. They usually appeared in Freetown around December and again in May or June, before the rainy season made travel more difficult. Their stay would last a few weeks; besides making portraits, itinerants frequently sold photographs of other countries they visited in West Africa, along with supplies and equipment for local photographers. In May 1893 the following advertisement appeared on the front page of the *Sierra Leone Times*:

> WS Johnston, photographer, begs to inform the public that he is prepared during his visiting tour to Sierra Leone, which will only extend to a few weeks, to receive sitters at his residence in Howe Street and to solicit their kind patronage. Specimens can be seen during business hours from 7 to 11 am and 1 to 5 pm. Pictures of all sizes taken, negatives kept. Copies may be had always. Landscapes, views of the Gold Coast, Lagos, Sierra Leone and Native Types are always on hand. Charges Moderate.[5]

A second advertisement appeared in July 1893 in which Johnston thanked his patrons and announced the intention of making his stay permanent. Freetown photographers must have enjoyed an active business if an itinerant was able to settle permanently after only two months of work. While biographical data on Johnston is sparse, he was most likely an itinerant Creole photographer who was finally able to establish a permanent business at home. Whatever the situation, the success of his Freetown studio is evidenced by the fact that he was ultimately able to turn the business over to his sons. Johnston's photographs can be found in archives in London as well as in private collections in Freetown. Dating from the 1880s to about 1910, they cover a vast array of subjects, ranging from baby pictures, to group portraits, to the 1910 visit of the Duke and Duchess of Connaught. All his photographs show consistently high quality in terms of artistic composition and technical execution.

The work of one photographer appears frequently in archival collections, colonial publications and historical texts from the period just prior to World War I. The photographer, Alphonso Lisk-Carew, was born in Freetown in 1887 and, at the age of 18, opened his first photographic studio. As was the custom, Lisk-Carew probably learned photography while serving as an apprentice in another Freetown studio. The Lisk-Carew photography studio was a great success and it thrived until his death in 1969. An early albumen print shows his large two-storey building with framed photographs displayed on the open doors and a large sign indicating his name and business. His photographic output was extensive and diverse. Studio portraits of Creoles and expatriates are found alongside images of native life and landscapes. Creole to the

core, he displays a special enthusiasm for photographing his home town. One finds among his oeuvre photograph after photograph of urban panoramas, the harbour, markets, factories, bicycle tracks and many other urban scenes and social events.

Lisk-Carew was the official photographer when the Duke and Duchess of Connaught visited in 1910. His success in recording this event was such that afterwards each photograph he produced carried the stamp, « Patronized by HRH the Duke of Connaught ». Alphonso Lisk-Carew's active business benefited from the support of his large, extended Creole family. Around 1914 the stamp on his photographs was altered to read, « Lisk-Carew Brothers », recognizing the involvement of his younger brother Arthur in the operation of the photography studio. Alphonso Lisk-Carew became famous in Sierra Leone for his photography and his reputation has lived on to the present day. In 1970, a memorial retrospective exhibition of his work mounted in Freetown gave homage to his talent and work, which was described as « striking and original. »[6]

Alphonso Lisk-Carew's career served as the nexus between the Freetown photographers of the 19th and 20th centuries. Two World Wars, the changing relationship between Sierra Leone and her colonial rulers, and national independence in 1961, all helped draw attention to Sierra Leone's African cultural heritage. Africans migrated from the Sierra Leonean countryside and other West African countries to live and work in the capital city. The culture of Freetown was no longer dominated by the Creoles. Although photography studios proliferated in the capital city, their owners were no longer exclusively Creole, but were often immigrants from Nigeria who wanted to replicate the success of photography studios in the rapidly growing capital of Lagos. These photography studios were no longer exclusively family-run businesses: studios, complete with equipment, props and inventory, frequently changed owners.

Changes in attitude and self-perception enabled Freetown photographers to begin developing a distinctive photographic tradition with both European and African influences. Although the materials and equipment used by local photographers continued to be of European manufacture, the aesthetics of the photographic image began to be dictated by local African styles. Studio backdrops were no longer painted to imitate European parlours or street scenes, but were now local artists' paintings of Freetown, of village scenes or of mosques. Locally made and dyed cloth and woven mats became popular backgrounds for studio photographs. The concept of what made a good photograph was no longer based on formal European poses, but instead on local styles such as double exposure and split imaging. Indeed, even today, as Sierra Leone struggles to survive almost a decade of internal fighting and extreme economic hardship, the photographic studio trade is still functioning and local photographers are still devising new styles to please their patrons and challenge their competition.

Vera Viditz-Ward

Bibliography

Bensusan, AD. 1966. *Silver Images: History of Photography in Africa*, p.9. Cape Town: Howard Timmins.

Fyfe, Christopher. 1962. *A History of Sierra Leone*. London: Oxford University Press.

Porter, A. 1963. *Creoledom: A Study of the Development of Freetown Society*. London: Oxford University Press.

Spitzer, Leo. 1974. *The Creoles of Sierra Leone: Responses to Colonialism, 1870-1950*. Madison: University of Wisconsin Press.

Sprague, Steven. 1978. *Yoruba Photography: how Yoruba see themselves* .African Arts, XII, 1 (November): 52-9.

Viditz-Ward, Vera. 1985. *Alphonso Lisk-Carew, Creole Photographer*. African Arts, XIX, I (November): 46-51.

1987. *Photography in Sierra Leone, 1850-1918 in Africa*, Vol.51, No.4,p. 510-518. Manchester University Press.

1991-92. *Notes Toward a History of Photography in Sierra Leone*. Exposure, Volume 28, Number 3 (Winter): 14-21.

DIONYSIUS LEOMY

Sierra Leone

A Black American exiled in England to escape from slavery, he left with many others for Sierra Leone. Between 1880 and 1900 he worked in Freetown.

Photographer WS JOHNSTON © ca.1870
The Baker family.
Private collection, Courtesy of Viditz-Ward.

5. *Sierra Leone Times* (Freetown), 6 May 1893.
6. University of Sierra Leone, *Exhibition of Sierra Leoneana, 1895-1970*, Section 26.

ALPHONSO LISK-CAREW

Sierra Leone
b. Freetown, 1887 – d. 1969

A Creole, he opened his studio at the age of 18. He was one of the most prosperous photographers in the country, doing portraits, panoramic landscapes and lively views of the city.

< Photographer WS JOHNSTON © ca.1870
The botanical gardens, Freetown.

UNKNOWN photographer ©
Portrait, visiting card.

Photographer ALPHONSO LISK-CAREW ©
A group of friends.

> Photographer DIONYSIEUS LEOMY ©
The market.

Photographer ALPHONSO LISK-CAREW ©
Main street in Freetown.
Courtesy of Viditz-Ward.

Photographer-publishers in Togo

Philippe David

In 1927, the Togo Professional Photographers' Association already had at least ten members. These photographers distinguished themselves in the publication of postcards, an aspect of photography that was highly instructive for future research.

1. Buchner, Max. 1914. *Aurora Colonialis, 1884-85*. Munich.

2. Initially in the British colonies, and in particular, Sierra Leone.

3. The Protestant missionaries of Basle (Switzerland) and Bremen (Germany), as well as the Catholic missionary organizations of the Netherlands, have preserved 150 years of archival material, including period photographs. They arrived in the southeast part of present-day Ghana in 1840 and progressively occupied the south and central area of Togo during the German colonial period. The northern part of the country remained inaccessible until 1911.

4. Philippe David. 1988. *Mémoires et Confidences de Deux Pionniers de la Photographie au Togo à la Fin du Siècle Dernier*. Études Togolaises, no. 35, Lomé.

< Photographer ALEX A ACOLATSE © Lomé, Togo. ca.1930.

No one knows who he was or why he happened to be there. The only certainty is that an anonymous African photographer was present when Gustav Nachtigal disembarked on the beach at Baguida on 5 July 1884.[1] As a special emissary of Bismarck, Nachtigal would - almost by accident - sign a charter which ultimately resulted in the creation of the country known today as Togo. Well before Nachtigal's arrival, photographers were already active on the West Coast of Africa.[2] Over the past 20 years, research into the history of African photography has revealed Togo's particularly rich heritage in this domain.

The origins, as well as many of the specific characteristics of photography as it was practised on the territory corresponding to present-day southern Ghana and Togo are essentially ascribable to the influence of 19th-century Catholic and Protestant missionaries.[3] Their names, trials and tribulations are known: from 1885 to 1890, several of these early missionary-photographers, such as the Pastor Ernst Bürgi, kept journals in which they related their experiences.[4]

In time, the missionaries passed on their techniques and equipment to African nationals who were their friends or assistants. Heinrich Klose, an administrator of the German colonial government and pioneer photographer who lived in the Bassar territory of northern Togo in 1897, described how he taught Meppo, his ten-year-old assistant, how to develop film in a tent serving as a portable darkroom.[5]

Philippe David was born in 1932. After graduating from l'École Nationale de la France d'Outremer, he was appointed as a government magistrate in Niger (1960-64), Senegal (1966-78) and Togo 1986-92). He also had an administrative position with UNICEF from 1978 to 1985. The author of a number of historical, sociological and juridical studies (notably of the Ivory Coast and Benin, published in the *Meridians* collection by Editions Karthala), Philippe David is the president of the *Images et Mémoires* Association of Paris. Under the aegis of the association, a team composed of a historian and geographer, the directors of the archives of the National Library of Togo and three Togolese photographers, are currently documenting photographic activity in Africa from its inception to the present.

Beginnings

It is probable that Lutterodt, a half-caste who lived in the Gold Coast at Cape Coast or at Accra in the final years of the 19th century, trained a number of young African photographers in the region between Accra and Lagos. In any event, the doyen of Togo's photographers, Alex Acolatse (1880-1975), claimed Lutterodt as his mentor and source of inspiration.[6] Acolatse had encountered him at the turn of the century and was already established as a professional photographer prior to the First World War when Togo was still a German colony. A deacon of the local Evangelical church and a member of a Masonic Lodge, Acolatse came from an influential and highly respected African family which became particularly prominent during the successive British and French colonial periods. He also presided over Togo's Association of Professional Photographers which, as a group portrait dating from 1927 attests, numbered at least 13 members drawn from the capital's total population of 10 000 inhabitants.

Acolatse's professional career is all the more interesting insofar as it encompassed the entire western extremity of the Gold Coast and Nigeria with its English- and French-speaking inhabitants. Versatile and ambitious, Acolatse created a series of 80 picture postcards captioned in French or English from 1920 to 1930. He was far from being the first to have this idea: at the turn of the century, three other Togolese photographers of Afro-Brazilian origin, FF Olympio and the Aguiar Brothers[7], had done the same. There were, in fact, approximately 40 other creators of photographic postcards in the territory during the German colonial period prior to the First World War. Before the popularization of photography, illustrated postcards had been available in the region since the opening of the territory's first post office in Klein Popo (the present-day Anecho) in 1888. By 1900, several photographers were established in Lomé: apart from Olympio and the Aguiars, three others were inscribed in Lomé's municipal tax register: Mamatta, Djallemann and an apprentice photographer named Benjamin Acolatse. It is not clear whether the latter was related to Alex, for no information exists as to his origins and career.

Following his retirement in 1956, Acolatse's studio passed into the hands of a member of his family. He lived well on into his nineties, and by the time of his death in 1975, he had become the inspiration for two new generations of Togolese photographers, many of whom he had personally trained. The majority opened their own studios; a few others created their own line of illustrated postcards or worked for the newly-independent government's news and information services (Radio Togo, Togopress, Editogo, the Ministry of Tourism, etc.).

In addition to Alex Acolatse, other postcard photographers active in Togo during the French colonial period after the First World War included CM Santo, Gustave Darboux (of Dahomey) and Monor-Lawson (probably of Togolese origin, but an inhabitant of Douala in Cameroon). After the Second World War, and until the arrival of large-format (10 x 15 cm) colour postcards in the early 1960s, the photographer John Badohu continued the tradition.[8] Interviewed in 1988, Badohu, who was born in 1926, had known Kokouvi and Oklou, members of the preceding generation, as well as his contemporaries, Ametozion and Fumey, in the early 1950s. He also related how he had been trained by Barrigah (rather than Acolatse) in Kpalimé in the mid-1940s, and described his sojourn in Bordeaux in 1948, and the types of clientele and prices that were common in the 1950s.

At least 150 different examples of work by these photographers have survived: 80 by Acolatse, 15 by Aguiar, 10 by Olympio, 30 by Santo, 5 by Darboux and 15 by Badohu. Approximately 1 000 more photographic views of Togo in postcard format were produced by other African photographers in the 1970s. More recently, Amousou (« Eka ») became interested in photographic postcards when he was still a student in Toulouse. By the late 1980s, he had created a superb line of 10 x 15 cm cards and posters of Togo.

Today, the Togolese Photographers' Association represents the majority of the country's professional photographers. Only two or three of Togo's biggest studios can be considered profitable operations; foreign competition has also emerged in the form of photographers and publishers established both in Togo and France, and the near-monopoly for film development by Korean- or Lebanese-owned studios equipped with the latest processing systems.

In 1988, a mixed group of Togolese and French researchers, historians and technicians began an overall inventory of the country's photographic history, beginning with its origins over a century ago.[9] Within the context of this project, an inventory of photographic postcards (from 1890 to 1960) has recently been completed.

At present, it is to be hoped that one of the members of the new and talented generation of Togolese photographers will devote himself to documenting the rich possibilities offered by spontaneous street scenes and the details of daily life in the capital and the rest of the country, a theme which remains to be explored both in Togo and the majority of other African countries.

Philippe David

Photographer ALEX A ACOLATSE © Lomé, Togo. ca.1930. >

5. Philippe David, 1992. *Le Togo Sous Drapeau Allemand, Selon Heinrich Klose*. Editions Haho, Lomé, Karthala and Paris.

6. Phillipe David. 1993. *Alex A Acolatse: Hommage à l'un des Premiers Photographes Togolais*. Editions Haho/the Goethe Institute, Lomé. An exhibition of Acolatse's work was organized in Lomé in June, 1992.

7. The Aguiars, who arrived in Lomé from Lagos at the turn of the present century, were in fact three brothers: two twins (Cosme and Damiano) and a third and younger brother (Jacinto). By 1906, they had established themselves as retailers of construction materials and tools for the African and European community and, in 1907, had Germanized their family name. With the exception of an advertisement for a series of photographic postcards bearing their name, little evidence of their activities in the domain of photography has survived the passage of time.

8. Maguerat and Péléï. 1993 *Si Lomé M'était Contée, Vol. II, No. 4*. Benin University Press.

9. Archives Nationales du Togo. 1996. *Lomé, un Siècle d'Images, Vol. I and II*. Benin University Press.

ALEX AGBAGLO ACOLATSE

Togo
b. Kedzi, Togo 1880 - d. Lomé, Togo 1975

In 1914 he opened his studio in Lomé. One of the earliest African photographers, he began by taking outdoor photographs of groups of people, the city's monuments, and important political events between 1920 and 1940. He stopped taking photographs in 1953.

Photographer ALEX A ACOLATSE ©
Lomé, Togo. ca.1930.

The pioneers of St Louis

Frédérique Chapuis

The story of the oldest photographer in Senegal, Meïssa Gaye, is much like the history of St Louis, the first European-African city in Africa, where the first daguerreotype studio was set up as early as 1860. St Louis was full of shop-keepers, administrators, soldiers, adventurers yearning for excitement - and photographers. In 1958, St Louis handed over the role of economic and political capital to Dakar, where the strong personalities of photographers Mama Casset and Mix Gueye were very much in the foreground.

The portrait on page 50 is pasted on a rectangle of heavy cardboard backing - a technique used at the beginning of this century. The young man is dressed in a richly-appointed tchawali, the traditional ceremonial costume of collarless tunic, flowing white trousers and matching white cummerbund surmounted by an ample boubou made of carefully-assembled bands of woven cloth. He also wears a silver necklace from which hangs a protective talisman. He is holding the hand of an aristocratic young girl adorned in traditional jewellery. The design of her boubou, whose black-and-white checkerboard motif echoes the background against which they are posing, is a transposition of Arabian geometrical figures used in ceremonies of magic. As they face the camera, both the young man and his companion communicate a sense of dignity and quiet elegance. Boubacar Dieng, the young man in the photograph, was born in 1905. It is difficult to determine his precise age at the moment that the portrait was taken. The girl whose hand he holds, according to the photographer's grandson, was descended from the Queen of Walo. The photograph is from an album belonging to the family of Meïssa Gaye, the oldest known photographer of Senegal and perhaps all of West Africa. Little remains of his work: the majority of his archives disappeared under the floodwaters of the Senegal River after his death in 1982. Today, all that remains is the album, itself a precious link to the past, recalling the memory of a man whose name is still cited from St Louis to Dakar when the subject of conversation turns to photography.

Frédérique Chapuis is a journalist and photo-editor for the weekly magazine *Télérama*.

< UNKNOWN photographer © ca.1920
Young girl in her bedroom.
Saint-Louis, Senegal.
Adama Sylla collection.

One afternoon, Meïssa Gaye's grandson initiated me into the history of the family - in which Gaye, with his richly complex personality, remains the central figure. One by one, the grandson spread out the photographs which had been preserved in the precious album; the commentaries which accompanied them were pure examples of an oral tradition. Ignoring chronological logic, we began a voyage across a hundred years of Senegalese history, and with it, the history of African photography.

In one portrait), Meïssa appears to be about 20 years old and is wearing a distinctive red felt toque known as the chéchia. Although the photograph has faded with time, his adolescent features already express the self-assurance and inner determination possessed by strong-willed individuals. Gaye was born in 1892 in the Guinean town of Coyah, where his parents, originally from St Louis, had joined Sambacor Diop, an uncle on his mother's side, who ran a general store. Gaye's family would later move back to St Louis, where they would open their own shop. As an only child, Gaye received an excellent education: initially from his uncle, Sélé Gaye, the director of a school for Islamic stu-

dies, and afterwards at the Catholic missionary school from which he graduated. After working as an apprentice carpenter, he left for the Congo at the age of 18, where he worked in shipyards and on bridge construction.

Prior to the abolition of slavery in 1848, St Louis was principally a centre of trade and commerce. Fortunes were amassed from the exportation of gum arabic, leather hides, amber, peanuts, ivory and indigo. France's policy of territorial expansion and the arrival of Faidherbe as the new colonial governor of Senegal from 1854 to 1865 resulted in a significant upsurge of activity within the interior of the country. To ensure peace and defend the frontiers, which he was attempting to extend to the distant city of Timbuktu, Faidherbe gathered a group of African and European adventurers and explorers, military men and civilians.

St Louis was a legendary city: constructed on an island situated between the mouth of the Senegal River and the ocean, it was sheltered by the Langue de Barbarie, an immense sandbar inhabited by Lebou fishermen in their village of Guet N'dar. In addition to supplying the early population of St Louis

with fresh fish, the Lebou transported passengers, crew and cargo over the sandbar to the ships anchored off the coast. On the opposite bank of the river from St Louis, the agricultural village of Sor was also home to the ferrymen whose pirogue canoes were the only connection between the island and the continent. (The construction of the Faidherbe Bridge was only completed in 1865.) Exceptional for its geographic location, St Louis's destiny was equally unusual. Traders from Bordeaux constructed long, one-storeyed brick warehouses with terraced roofs. The *tapats* (palisades of brushwood, planks and corrugated iron), were torn down. Native architecture no longer corresponded with the colonial idea of «civilization» and was replaced by an ever-increasing number of colonial-style brick houses whose facades were adorned with wrought-iron balconies, verandas and slatted shutters for filtering the hot afternoon sun. The interiors were comfortable, gracious and often superbly appointed: symbols of civilization and modernity were important in the colonies. Above all, the city's character was determined by its grid system of paved streets, dotted with sidewalks and shaded by palm trees.

∧ Photographer MEÏSSA GAYE © ca.1918
Self-portrait, aged 20.
Saint-Louis, Senegal.
Selé Gaye Collection.

< Photograph attributed to
MEÏSSA GAYE © ca. 1910
*Boubacar Dieng and Astou M'Bodj,
granddaughter of the Queen of
Waalo.*
Saint-Louis, Senegal.
Selé Gaye collection.

Newly-constructed administrative buildings flanked the enlarged and embellished Governor's Palace, with its large square protected on both sides by identical military barracks. In the centre of the square, facing the ocean like a homage to distant France, was a bandstand - a perfect replica of those found in the public gardens of Paris - whose music accompanied the promenade of elegantly-dressed citizens in their carriages along the esplanade. Such was the image of Senegal's capital city at the dawn of the 20th century.

West Africa itself was dotted with construction sites during this period: roads were being built, canals dug, railway lines established and new bridges constructed. Rich and varied, colonial life offered opportunities for everyone: the «civilizing» mission of the army and the church, trade and commerce for the business-minded, and the lure of exotic new horizons for adventurers of all sorts ... Photography was an ideal means of giving a certain tangible reality to the objectives and ideals of the colonial undertaking: army engineers equipped with rifles and cameras were sent into the interior on surveying expeditions, while missionaries documented the benefits that Christianity had brought to the newly-converted natives.

On 20 January 1857, the French *Ministre de la Marine et des Colonies* sent a dispatch to the Governor of Senegal concerning the first official photographic mission to the country: a naval infantry captain named Dérème was arriving with the equipment necessary for creating a photographic map of St Louis. The camera arrived damaged after *The Podor*, the ship which was transporting it, capsized. A second attempt to ship a camera to St Louis in 1862 was successful. St Louis boasted more than 700 shops, among which was the first daguerreotype studio, created by Washington de Monrovée in 1860, followed by that of Decampe in 1861. The photographer Bonnevide also opened a studio, before relocating to Dakar in 1885. Other early photographers established in St Louis included Hautefeuille, Hostalier (Bonnevide's former assistant), Tacher - who published picture-postcards - and Etienne Lagrange, who opened a studio in 1908 and trained a number of African photographers.

Everything was a potential subject of interest, and everything interesting was photographed. In the shipyards of the Congo, Meïssa Gaye made friends with a European who possessed a glass-plate camera. His friend taught him how to take and develop photographs, and gave him the camera when he left the Congo. Photography was not yet a profession: it was more of a hobby, and at best a new means of expression offering the possibility of limited financial returns.

As in Europe, it was practised as a sideline by shopkeepers. Many of its early adepts were either artists or experimenters hailing from a variety of horizons, including chemists, opticians and mechanics.

In 1912, Meïssa travelled to French Guinea where, after passing an examination, he became a customs agent. He also continued taking photographs. He left the customs service for a position in the office of the Governor of Conakry. In 1923 he returned to Dakar and worked in the branch office of the Governor of St Louis. In the meantime, photography had become his second profession. When not working at the Governor's office, he would strap his bulky wood-framed camera with its home-made magnesium flash-gun on to his bicycle. Traversing the administrative and residential quarter of the Plateau with its quiet gardens, lush vegetation, colonial villas with their shaded verandas, and neat government buildings, he would head for the working-class neighbourhoods and commercial arteries near the port. There, he set up his camera and practised the art of *jooni-jooni*. Roughly translated within the context of photography, the expression means « instant portraits ».

Meïssa Gaye, a cultivated man passionately interested in art and music, thus became an itinerant photographer, taking photographss of his fellow citizens during his off-duty hours from his job at the Governor's office. A portrait of Gaye, selected from the album by his grandson, reveals a man of imposing stature and youthful features, elegantly dressed in a dark suit and white shirt with an unhappy-looking baby sitting in his lap. It is impossible to tell from what epoch in his life the portrait dates.

At the end of the First World War, Dakar was still a sleepy and somewhat dull provincial town, overshadowed by the more cosmopolitan St Louis. The lives of the French colonial inhabitants were lived within a series of closed circles and precisely delimited neighborhoods. The colonies, which had long been perceived as distant, dangerous and unfit for normal human existence, began to benefit from an influx of new administrators and their families from France. With their arrival, a new and more positive image emerged: that of a way of life characterized by ease, comfort and the special elegance of a new and emerging society of unlimited opportunities. This concept was promoted by a number of specialized magazines, such as *Le Monde Colonial Illustré*, *Le Journal de Voyage* and *Le Tour du Monde*. The often fascinating and seductive images which illustrated their articles played a large part in modifying the public's perception of life in the colonies.

During the same period that Meïssa Gaye was plying his trade as an itinerant photographer, permanent studios were opening up in the principal cities of Senegal. One of the first, established by Bonnevide in 1885, was frequented by the French colonial population. As in the Parisian studios, clients were photographed in settings which faithfully reproduced upper middle class interiors, complete with heavy velvet curtains, elegant tables and vases with freshly-cut flowers.

Beginnings

The images communicated prosperity and success; here, as in France, the photographic portrait was a symbol of an entire social class. Among the most popular studio photographers of Dakar in the 1920s were Tennequin, Oscar Lataque (among whose apprentices in 1920 was a 12-year-old boy from St Louis who would later become one of Dakar's best-known photographers, Mama Casset) and Edmond Fortier, who later became a pioneer news photographer. Many of the studios also sold picture postcards: the public demand for them was so great that at one point, more than 5 000 different images were available. The photographss of monuments, landscapes and the bush circulated within France and often around the world, nourishing a stereotyped vision of Africa that was tinged by an underlying racism. But whatever their drawbacks, they were the only images of Africa available to the general public for many years.

If photography had become a second source of income for Gaye, it was also a personal passion. After mastering the techniques of photography and development, he became an accomplished retouching artist. As one of his sons, who had worked as his assistant, said, « My father was a magician ». Gaye's enthusiasm for his craft increased to the point where in 1929 he requested a prolonged leave of absence from the colonial administration and for the next three years worked as a portrait photographer in the town of Kaolack. Kaolack is situated on the banks of the Saloum River in the heart of Senegal's fertile groundnut country. It experienced an economic boom in the 1860s, when gum arabic production declined in favour of groundnut cultivation. After 1910, the groundnut harvest in and around Kaolack attracted thousands of migrant workers from the north and even from neighbouring countries. All year long, boats made the journey up the river to Sangomar and thence to Kaolack for their cargoes of groundnuts. The town was a charming community with well-planned streets bordered by low houses. On market-days, throngs of inhabitants arrived from the neighbouring villages: it was the perfect place for an itinerant photographer. Gaye worked there for three years before returning to a civil service position with the local government of Ziguinchor in Casamance.

At that time, Gaye's camera was an enormous (125 x 70 cm) wood-framed box which he had constructed himself; its large format images were particularly well suited to portrait photography. Today, opposite the Leona Pharmacy in Kaolack, an old man named Mamadou Diop offers portrait sittings to passersby. His camera, an enormous handmade affair, pierced by a tiny hole covered by a rubber plug, is of the same type used by Gaye some 70 years ago. Primitive yet efficient, the camera uses individual sheets of film rather than rolls. The negative is then re-exposed to create a print. The development process, which is manual, takes place inside the camera, which has its own self-contained miniature darkroom complete with the appropriate chemical baths. Sitting in the chair reserved for the purpose, Diop's clients, for the most part countryfolk and youngsters, pose for their « instant portrait ». Long ago, a Lebanese shopkeeper taught Diop the technique. When asked about his own age, he becomes evasive: « I must be over 75, because when God took Cheikh Ahmadou Bamba back to Him back in 1927, I was already planting groundnuts in my father's garden. »

In Dakar in the early 1930s, a young man named Amadou « Mix » Gueye worked as an assistant at the Tennequin photographic studio on Avenue Roume. An excellent cyclist and swimmer, Mix was given his nickname by his mother, in memory of her favourite perfume, Mixte. As the assistant to a French photographer, Mix early on became a familiar presence in the homes and clubs of Dakar's colonial administrators and military personnel. In time, he became an indispensable element of the city's social life: no event of any importance was complete without Mix and his camera to photograph it. His role as the colony's semi-official photographer led him to open his own studio in the Medina quarter.

∧
UNKNOWN photographer © ca.1930
Saint-Louis, Senegal.
Adama Sylla collection.

Beginnings

In the years that followed, he was the director of photography for the Federation of Mali and subsequently the director of photographic services at the Ministry of Information of Senegal. Mix thrived in his new career at the Ministry, and even today is still considered the doyen of Africa's press photographers. Cultivated and non-conformist, Mix is a sociable man whose openness to others has made him friends at every level of Senegalese society. His sense of humour and equanimity have helped him to endure and even overcome the humiliations imposed upon Africans by the colonial occupants: the story of the time he jumped fully clothed into the swimming pool of an exclusive Dakar club (off-limits to blacks « for reasons of hygiene ») has since become a legend in Senegal. During the early years of his country's independence, Mix took thousands of photographs of Senghor, all of which have either been dispersed or destroyed. Today, only a few of his studio photographs have survived the ravages of time.

Meïssa Gaye returned to St Louis from Ziguinchor in 1939. His passion for photography and his career in the colonial administration finally coincided when he was appointed as the official photographer for the city's justice department. At the same time, he pursued his freelance activities. Elegant in his impeccably-tailored suit, white shirt and inevitable hat, Gaye was a familiar figure in the crowds that massed at important events. Using a Rolleiflex camera, he photographed military parades, visiting dignitaries and political meetings (years before its independence, Senegal already had seven political parties and eleven newspapers).

He also continued his activities as a portrait photographer. In St Louis, a city known for its legendary signares (from the Portuguese, *senhora*, designating a particularly attractive young woman), elegance and a pronounced taste for self-representation were part of daily life. People adored having their photographs taken: in the street, as in one of Gaye's portraits of a radiant young woman proudly wrapped in her boubou and flanked by two timid children, or at home, as in the image of a middle-class couple posing on their veranda, while a third person - it is impossible to say whether he is a servant or a member of the family - stands behind them in the background. Still other haunting images from the past: three friends in European dress, lounging on a street corner; a modest couple posing in their garden with an obvious lack of self-assurance.

People also liked to pose in more intimate settings, as in the photograph of two lovers, his hand lightly resting on her arm as they pose on the edge of a bed covered by a richly-embroidered spread. It is not clear whether the scene takes place in their bedroom or the sitting-room, which often contained a bed which served as a sofa. Gaye's prolific activity during this period - in addition to his administrative duties - was motivated less by a desire for financial gain than by his profound love for photography. His grandson described with feeling Gaye's habit of analysing the play of light and shadow on his features, as if trying to determine the best angle for photographing his portrait.

In the years between the two World Wars, portrait photography was enormously popular. Many of these portraits can still be seen in family albums or on the walls of peoples' homes, such as the charming image of a seated woman in a matching dress and jacket, hands folded in her lap. Her hair is arranged in a characteristic St Louis style and partially covered by a silk taffeta handkerchief that frames her upper forehead with its series of fine braids to which small gold coins have been attached. Taken in the subjects' homes, portraits such as these are more natural, unposed and intimate than studio photographs. As such, they are an even richer source of information about peoples' lives and lifestyles in the often culturally and occasionally racially-mixed micro-society that developed on the fringes of the dominant French colonial model.

St Louis and its women: among them, the linguères (members of the elite classes) and the gourmettes (women converted to Christianity and often taken as mistresses by the English and, later, the French). These were women whose love and devotion enabled the successive waves of soldiers, adventurers, traders, shopkeepers and civil servants to survive the rigours of life in a country whose language and customs were totally foreign to them. Even the august Governor Faidherbe had his liaison: a Sarakolé woman, who gave birth to his half-caste son, Louis-Léon. These women, who were neither totally of one culture nor of the other, possessed a talent for business and love that foreshadowed the role they would play in the creation of a new hybrid society that combined elements of both. Accompanied by their servants and traditional musicians, regally dressed and adorned from head to toe with filigree jewellery handcrafted by Arab artisans, they frequented afternoon gatherings where the company was selected by age and social class, and where conversations were simply for pleasure - and occasionally for profit. Even today, the scent of their perfume lingers on the verandas and balconies where long ago, in the cool of the early evenings, they charmed their admirers with their grace and elegance.

St Louis was also the birthplace of Senegal's first political party. Its origin can be traced back to an association known as L'Aurore de St Louis, whose members shared a common interest in theatre, music and politics. Their activities gave rise to a more politically-oriented group called the *Jeunes Sénégalais*, whose president, Lamine Gueye, was elected mayor of St Louis in 1925.

∧
UNKNOWN photographer © ca.1920
Saint-Louis, Senegal.
Adama Sylla collection.

The few surviving portraits of the members of these associations testify to the vitality and diversity of the men and women who struggled for the liberation of their country. These mute and distant images are, for many citizens of St Louis, a reminder of individuals whose determination and courage contributed to the making of present-day Senegal. We must also acknowledge the social and political truth of these images, which were ignored or simply dismissed by the partisan and ethnocentric vision of colonialism.

In the two decades that followed the First World War, other African photographers began working in St Louis. In some cases, friendships with members of the colonial administration were decisive in launching new careers for, like jazz, photography had the power of forging common bonds and transcending cultural and social barriers, as in the example of Alioune Diouf. Diouf was born in 1910, but even today the memory of this venerable gentleman is perfectly intact as he remembers the past: his first position as a secretary in the colonial administration of Cotonou; the first time he saw a movie, which terminated in an altercation and his arrest; a new posting in the Niger, and the racism, humiliations and conflicts which were his daily lot. Then at Conakry, where he worked as a court clerk for Octave de Saint-André, the chief magistrate from 1937 to 1942, followed by his return to St Louis and a new posting in Mali, far from his home and family. With the exception of the period spent in Conakry, where he was befriended by Saint-André, whose gift of a camera and darkroom equipment launched his career as a photographer, Diouf's existence was punctuated by a long series of struggles and conflicts - generally with the colonial occupants of his own country. Upon his retirement after working for 36 years in various administrations, Diouf rounded out his meagre pension by working as itinerant photographer in the outlying villages of St Louis. Although never a personal passion, photography proved to be an ideal means of assuring his financial security. More importantly, it remains the indelible reminder of his friendship with Octave de Saint-André, whose rare humanity and encouragement were decisive factors in his life.

Doudou Diop, born in 1920, was another pioneer photographer of St Louis. In the cool interior of his house, he proudly displays an unusual relic from another age: the « Pagivolt », a photograph album whose pages turn automatically. As the electrical motor of the album gives off a soft, mechanical purr, the portraits of his family pass under our eyes as if on parade. Many of the images are indicative of the modest performances of his camera; others have been delicately retouched and hand-coloured. Today the guardian of a neighbourhood mosque, Diop nostalgically recalls his

long career as an accountant for the French colonial army, and the day in 1952 when he received a camera and enlarger as a gift. It was the beginning of his second career as a photographer, and led him to open the Studio Diop in the Sor quarter of St Louis. The studio was an enormous success: opening hours were in the evening, and by 7 pm, up to 50 people would be waiting in front of the door. On holidays, Diop would often have to work far into the night to satisfy the demand. But if the customer was the king, Diop remained the master: his conception of portrait photography was precise, and his clients had no say in the choice of their pose. After being photographed, the customer paid a modest sum and received a numbered receipt to exchange the next evening for the finished 13 x 18 cm portrait. Even if Diop's attachment to photography was motivated by financial considerations, it nevertheless gave him special status as an artist among his friends and neighbours in the Sor. Unfortunately, he was also influenced by a persistent rumour concerning the long-term «health hazard» of the chemicals used for the development of negatives, and every ten years, to avoid exposing his family to this supposed danger, he would dig a hole in his garden and burn his archives. Today, as we visit his former studio (he finally retired in 1987), only a few boxes of negatives remain, miraculous survivors of the disaster.

Another studio located in the same quarter of Sor is still in business. This afternoon, Doro Sy is waiting for a customer to pick up his identity photographs. The studio opens at 5 pm; before that, Sy is usually occupied in his garden. Like his father before him, Sy is a gardener; the family was the first to have water piped in to irrigate their vegetables. Born in 1930, Doro Sy is still a handsome man whose eyes twinkle with pleasure as he reminisces about the past. As a teenager, he spent one summer vacation with his uncle, an electrician in Dakar. One day, Sy accompanied him to the studio of Mama Casset, which had just opened in the Medina. Fascinated by what he saw, Sy felt himself irresistibly drawn to photography. A few years later, he returned in a military uniform to have his portrait taken. Sy takes a photograph out of his wallet, as if offering the tangible proof of his story; its corner bears the official seal of Mama Casset's African Studio.

In 1953, Sy went to Paris and trained as a photographer. The following year, after returning to St Louis, he opened the Doro Sor Photo Studio. The studio's legendary trademark is the palm tree backdrop painted by a Nigerian friend. All the rituals of portrait photography are respected here: one's hair is carefully arranged, a light veil of powder is applied to even out the complexion, and after a final stroke of the hairbrush, the client poses once (and once only) between the studio's two spotlights.

∧
UNKNOWN photographer © ca.1920
Saint-Louis, Senegal.
Adama Sylla collection.

Beginnings

Doro Sy also works outside the studio: he was the official photographer for the city's football association and often photographed crime scenes for the police. But above all, Sy owes his success to the charming painted palm tree in his studio: « That tree is known in every corner of Senegal, » he laughs, adding, « And probably beyond as well; everybody wanted to be photographed in front of the palm tree! »

Of all these pioneer photographers, Adama Sylla is the most recent. Born in 1934, he initially pursued a career with the Musée de la Mer in Gorée. Upon his return to St Louis in 1957, he accepted a position with the municipal museum. After learning photography at the city's Maison des Jeunes, he began working in the museum's laboratory, where he was in charge of the photo-reproduction of documents for the archives. In 1965, Sylla opened a modest studio in the Guet N'Dar district. The Lebou fishermen who inhabited this quarter, situated between the ocean and the river, were among the most prosperous of Senegal. On special holidays or after their return from a long fishing trip, they flocked to Sylla's studio for a photograph commemorating the event. On such occasions, Sylla remembers bringing, literally, bags full of money back home after closing his studio for the evening. For his own pleasure, he also photographed landscapes (a rare subject for African photographers), the ongoing transformation of his neighbourhood, and the ever-changing contours of the coastline and ocean. From the years spent working in museums, Sylla has preserved a passion for documents and archives. He is an avid collector of period photographs (an equally unusual activity here) and is highly conscious of Senegal's inexorable loss of a precious heritage. By way of explanation, Sylla notes that, « In France, you have huge brick and stone barns to store objects from your past. In Africa, even our fortresses are made of earth. »

During each of my meetings with these photographers, the name of Meïssa Gaye, the city's first studio photographer, was invoked like that of a revered ancestor. Like Mama Casset, he had transcended the mere techniques of his discipline and transformed it into an art. As in Europe, photography in Africa is generally seen in financial terms; Gaye was among the few to also use it as a means of personal expression, endowing it with an added dimension of modernity. Gaye left the colonial administration in 1945 and opened his Tropical Photo studio in the north of St Louis; along with the Caristan studio, it rapidly became the city's most popular place to have one's portrait taken. St Louis was Senegal's most fashionable city in the years following the Second World War: visitors came there on weekends to shop in its well-stocked boutiques and dance to the latest jazz music in its clubs. Despite the two successive changes of colonial government in 1908 and 1958, St Louis remained the vibrant capital of Senegal's intellectual and artistic community.

As Gaye's children grew older, he taught them all he had learned about photography during his long career, while on their respective graduation days, each of his 17 grandchildren received a camera from him. Some have continued in his footsteps, while others have chosen to pursue different professions. Gaye's passion for photography continued through the final years of his life. He would often work for hours, experimenting with techniques for transferring images onto cloth or glass, or absorbed in his hobby of painting miniature landscapes on empty Perrier bottles. In the evenings, he would entertain his children by playing the mandolin and accordion. A photograph taken in the 1950s shows him seated with two of his grandchildren on his lap. He had abandoned his elegant suits and white shirts for a comfortable boubou, and there is a half-amused, half-mocking smile on his face.

Frédérique Chapuis

Λ
UNKNOWN photographer © ca.1925
Saint-Louis, Senegal.
Adama Sylla collection.

THE SIGNARES

St Louis, in Senegal, is a special kind of place. No question, for the French civil servant or trader appointed to this tropical city, of bringing wife and children; instead, following the « custom of the country », he would form a union with an African woman whom everyone in town then regarded as his legitimate spouse. These spouses, known as signares, were initially black, but subsequent generations of Europeans living here were quick to show a preference for the light-skinned daughters of their predecessors. Thus it was that a veritable mixed-blood middle-class, a link between Wolof (a local Senegalese people) and European society, emerged in St Louis in the late 19th century. A group of 9 x 13 cm photographic plates show us one of these *signare* families. The white middle-aged husband with his top hat, gleaming moustache and neat suit seems straight out of provincial France. The young women, elegantly dressed in the European style, pose in a middle-class interior. On the wall, between the wardrobe where the linen and lace are kept and the mirror in which the presence of the photographer can be detected, the calendar indicates Friday 12 February 1915, the day when the family assembled for a ritual lunch. On the veranda the dignified grandmother, wearing the traditional bou-bou of indigo dimity, remains motionless before the camera. And meanwhile the children play in the shade of the patio.

∧
UNKNOWN photographer © ca.1920
< *The Signares of Saint-Louis.*
Senegal.
Adama Sylla collection.

Aminata Sow Fall
VAGUE MEMORY OF A CONFISCATED PHOTO

First, the setting: Saint-Louis de Senegal, a magical island set down in the north of the country beguiled by the roar of the ocean and the murmur of the river. You immediately feel something charmed in the air: no doubt it is muted clamour that fills the atmosphere, contrasting with the nonchalance of the soft silhouettes that glide slowly, softly down the streets, quays and pathways. But above all, it is the faces lit with a love of life, the laughter, the cries of the women selling fish, dressed up in their finery, the rumbling of horse and cart, the thundering of cars and the wailing of beggars on the streets and in open doorways, singing moving melodies with such fine voices and such talent that they manage to evoke everyone's generosity, including those who only have a coin or a little food to share.

This was about 50 years ago. As today - except for the decrepit buildings, the economic crisis, the stress of a generation worried about its future - elegant gestures, words, attire, gait and cuisine were cultivated as a cardinal virtue, just like any other moral principles, like honesty, a sense of honour, human respect, dignity and hospitality. It was a deadly sin to be sloppy or slovenly. Each person had to offer the community the most positive image of themselves possible, according to their means or situation. Anything that could tarnish this image was banned: walking too fast, for example, running down the streets like a lunatic. How many times was I called to order? « What do you have to be in such a hurry about? Walk slowly, it won't stop you getting where you're going! » And I would stand there sheepishly, not understanding because I wasn't aware of the speed they so reproached me for. I would try to slow down by counting my footsteps. The funniest thing is that you were never given any lessons: no one ever taught you how to walk, you were just reprimanded so that you would look at the other rushing children and teach yourself, adopt the general rhythm, take the road to responsibility and avoid the scorn heaped upon people in a hurry.

Small, slow steps: a way of celebrating the perfect correlation between indispensable peace of mind, dignity in dress and the poetry of the human body. You have to deserve the distinguished honour of being created in God's image.

It is easy to understand the importance of images in this context of meticulous grooming. The arrival of photography must have been seen as a gift from the gods, to conspire against the grotesque and often insulting caricatures produced by the colonists. We could finally all enjoy looking at ourselves in a snapshot of happiness, immortalized on a card. A photograph should only reflect the beautiful, admirable, dazzling side of our existence. That is why we were photographed for major ceremonies. The day before a wedding, the walls of bridal bedrooms were magnificently illustrated with a multitude of photographs borrowed for the occasion from all four corners of the island, and judiciously laid out by one of the masters of ceremony who dictated fashion in St Louis.

People were all dressed up in their Sunday best to have their photograph taken, probably a universal practice at the time. Small children were awe-inspired by the perfumes, clothes and buzz of activity that accompanied a sitting for one of the two most highly-rated photographers: Meïssa Gaye in the North district and Karistan in the South district, a few yards away from my home, on the banks of the great river.

I must have been thoroughly elated the day that Dioundiou, one of my cousins, accompanied me to Meïssa Gaye's studio. The memory has faded with time, but I imagine that, dressed in my white dress with the flounced skirt and puff sleeves, I must have avoided everyone's eye because I was overcome with a dreadful shyness as soon as I reached the door of our house, miraculously devoid of my capacity to pester my family, who would pretend to complain about it to hide the deep affection - I would say weakness - that made them put up with my wild and wilful behaviour.

Meïssa Gaye's studio was in fact a very dark sitting room in his home: a few armchairs, one straight-backed chair and a camera on a tripod. I can still see the photographer telling me to sit down and giving me a bunch of flowers to hold. I can hear Dioundiou saying «Smile, smile!» and the photographer asking me to look into the black hole in the camera. I hear a « click! » It's over.

Two or three days later, Dioundiou brought the photograph home, causing much laughter and mockery. « Look at your cheeks! ... Your eyes! ... Your expression ... It all shows how boisterous and unbearable you are! » I thought the bunch of artificial flowers was the most important element; it inspired a feeling of amazement that I couldn't explain but which was enough to obliterate the teasing of my nearest and dearest, especially as three of my cousins, Dioundiou, Aram and Khady, quickly shared the three photographss among themselves, promising they would remind me of my boisterous, unruly little face once I was all grown up.

Here I must explain a cultural trait: in St Louis, when an adult wanted to insult a naughty child without swearing, they would say: « Watch out or I'll tell you about your grandparents' *pakk* ». Which meant that they were threatening to recount your grandparents' childhood in the days when they hadn't reached puberty and still had the *pakk* hairstyle, i.e. tufts of hair in between the bald patches that had been shaved to reproduce the geometric shapes of each clan, family or ethnic group. Telling someone about their childhood means reminding them of their naughtiness, their naked bottom, the pee rolling down their leg, the snot and tears all over their face and all the other things that adults have to hide. That is why it was never a good idea to mention the childhood of your parents or elders.

Dioundiou, Aram and Khady had confiscated the photograph. It may be in the back of a cupboard or at the bottom of a pile of forgotten papers somewhere. Dioundiou has lost her copy; Aram threatened me with it right up to her death ten years ago, and Khady categorically refuses to let me have a look. « You'll rip it up! » « No I won't, please let me look!» She cannot believe that, if I were given the pleasure of seeing and smelling the precious photograph, my only reaction would be to say: « Isn't childhood wonderful! »

Aminata Sow Fall

< Photographer Meïssa Gaye °
Self-portrait with hat, ca.1940.
Saint-Louis, Senegal.

∧ Photographer MAMA CASSET °
Comptoir Photo of the AOF.
Dakar, Senegal ca. 1925.

Photographer Meïssa Gaye ° >
Meïssa Gaye with his
grandchildren, ca. 1956.
Saint-Louis, Senegal.

MEÏSSA GAYE

Sénégal
b. St-Louis, Senegal 1892 – d. 1982

An inventive personality who was the most famous photographer in Saint-Louis in the 1940s. He is considered to be the father of Senegalese photography.

Photographer Meïssa Ga
Women, cards 9x14
Saint-Louis, Senegal ca.19

∧
Photographer Meïssa Gaye ©
Women, cards 13x18 cm.
Saint-Louis, Senegal ca.1920.

The Black Photo Album

Santu Mofokeng

Some of the images in the photograph album compiled by photographer Santu Mofokeng date back to the late 19th century, revealing a little-known world. In a country caught in the grip of racism and attempts at Darwinian classification, these photographs depict black men and women who belonged to the working and middle classes that the South African authorities wanted to erase from the history books.

These are images that urban black working- and middle-class families had commissioned, requested or tacitly sanctioned. They have been left behind by dead relatives, where they sometimes hang on obscure parlour walls in the townships. In some families they are coveted as treasures, displacing totems in discursive narratives about identity, lineage and personality. And because, to some people, photographs contain the shadow of the subject, they are carefully guarded from the ill-will of witches and enemies. In other families they are being destroyed as rubbish during spring-cleans because of interruptions in the continuity of the history they represent or disaffection with the encapsulated meanings and the history of the images. Most often they lie hidden to rot through neglect in kists, cupboards, cardboard boxes and plastic bags.

If the images are not unique, the individuals in them are. Painterly in style, most of the photographs are evocative of the artifices of Victorian photography. Some of them may be fiction, a creation of the artist insofar as the setting, the props, the clothing or pose are concerned. Nonetheless there is no evidence of coercion. When we look at them we believe them, for they tell us a little about how these people imagined themselves. We see these images in the terms determined by the subjects themselves, for they have made them their own. They belong and circulate in the private domain. That is the position they occupied in the realm of the visual in the 19th century. It was never intended that they should be hung in galleries as works of art.

Extracts from *The Black Photo Album, Johannesburg (1890-1950)* by Santu Mofokeng.

Santu Mofokeng was born in 1956 in Johannesburg. A black photographer heavily committed to the fight against apartheid (see the account of his experience), he has been a researcher at the Institute for Advanced Social Research at the University of the Witwatersrand in Johannesburg since 1992. He has collected old family photographs from people living in the townships of Johannesburg.

< Photographer HF FINE STUDIO ©
26 West St. Johannesbourg, 1900.
Rozetta Dubula and friends.
Rozetta Dubula, born Duma was born in Thaba-Nchu 1901. Her granddaughter, who was named after her, knows little about her life.
Albumen print

UNKNOWN photographer ©
Boshoek, 1900.
Cleophas and Martha Moatshe.
Cleophas and his wife Martha were
from Boshoek where he was a mode-
rator in the breakaway Anglican chur-
ch. He died in 1923 from « drie dae »
(three-day) influenza. This information
is from Moatshe Mohlakeng,
Randfontein.
Albumen print.

Their significance lies outside the framed image. They were made in a period when the power of the South African state was being entrenched and policies towards people the government designated as «natives» were being articulated. It was an era mesmerized by the newly discovered social sciences, such as anthropology, which was informed by social Darwinism. It was a time which spawned all kinds of « experts » (so dearly loved by politicians), who could be conjured up to provide « expert knowledge » on any number of issues, including matters of race. Race thinking was given scientific authority in this period and was used to inform state policy on « the native question ».

Officially black people were frequently depicted in the same visual language as the flora and fauna - represented as if in their natural habitat - for the collector of natural history or, invariably, relegated to the lower orders of the species on occasions when depicted as belonging to the «great family of man». Designated « natives », a discrete group who were considered « in a sense citizens, but not altogether citizens » (Cecil John Rhodes), these people had images made of them which contributed to schemes of «authoritative» knowledge about the natives and served no small part in the subjection of those populations to authoritarian power.

Images informed by this prevailing ideology have been enshrined in the public museums, galleries, libraries and archives of South Africa. In contrast, the images in this book portray Africans in a very different manner.

Yet all too often these images run the risk of being dismissed or ignored as merely bourgeois. However, it should be pointed out that right from the turn of the century and even earlier there were black people who spurned, questioned or challenged the government's racist policies. Many of those integrationists were people who owned property or had acquired Christian mission education, and considered themselves to be « civilized ». These people, taking their model from colonial officials and settlers, especially the English, lived a life in manner and dress very similar to those of European immigrants. The images reproduced here reflect their sensibilities, aspirations and view of themselves.

The beauty of these photos makes me wonder if they are not some kind of trick or illusion. The veiled, time-worn image has taken on a silvery sheen that reflects like the dirty puddle of my memory. Images of people in a state of contemplation, self-dramatization - or maybe - at a moment of conflict - confrontation.

Photographer DEALE © >
Bloemfontein,
Orange River Colony, 1890.
Bishop Jacobus G. Xaba and his fami-
ly. Bishop Xaba was the presiding Elder
of the AME Church in Bloemfontein
1898-1904. The church participated
strongly in the events leading up to the
formation of the South African Native
National Congress in 1912. This pho-
tograph was found in a wooden box
labelled (in Afrikaans), « Aan M.V.
Jooste van die persooneel van Die
Vaderland ». In the box there were 68
images including one of « Their most
Gracious Majesties, Edward VII and
Queen Alexandra – In their robes of
State ». This box belongs to Moeketsi
Msomi whose grandfather, John Rees
Phakane, was a bishop
in the AME Church.
Albumen print.

A world between the real and the imaginary, made of insignificant experiences noted and pulled out of context. Moments reduced to simple apparitions, flashes of reflected light captured and stored in the film's memory. An obscure assemblage of lives called up, then forgotten.

This selection of photos was initially conceived as a metaphorical biography, although I now have doubts about this aspect of my approach. The tendency of the pictures towards the obscure, the weird and the allegorical directly reflects my personal choices. Like Ezekiel in the Bible, I embrace the apocalypse. I could blame my parents for my obsessive desire to explain and analyse everything, and to find the detached beauty of truth insignificant; yet the foundations of my character are hidden elsewhere and have to be looked for in my history between 1956 and today, during the time of apartheid. These photographs explore a part of my being which up until now I had neglected - my spirituality, I mean. There are several possible explanations for my repression of it: its ambivalence, the embarrassment it causes me, the fear of the political and the loss of direction it can give rise to.

This exploration is a personal attempt to come to terms with my own schizophrenic existence. The expression I've chosen as a title for this series - « Chasing Shadows » - may sound fanciful, but in African languages its meaning is the exact opposite. « Shadow » does not conjure up the same image or significance as the word *seriti* or *is'thunzi*. This word cannot easily be given a single meaning. In everyday use it can mean equally aura, presence, dignity, confidence, strength, spirit, essence, prestige or wellbeing. It can also express the experience of being loved or feared. A person's *seriti/is'thunzi* can be positive or negative and exert a powerful influence. Having a good or bad *seriti/is'thunzi* depends on the whims of enemies, witches, relatives dead or still living, friends and acquaintances, circumstances and time. Having one's own *seriti/is'thunzi* and defending it against the forces of evil, or attacking the *seriti/is'thunzi* of those perceived as enemies, preoccupies and torments many Africans. Even those not directly concerned are at least conscious of *seriti/is'thunzi*, although this consciousness is often denied, especially by the African elite living in contact with South African whites.

<

UNKNOWN photographer ©
Johannesburg, 1900.
Tokelo Nkole with friends.
Tokelo Nkole was a great follower of Marcus Garvey and he also worked with Alan Paton at the Diepkloof reformatory School before he died in 1940. This image belongs to the Ramela family of Orlando East. The information was supplied by Emma Mothibe.
Silver gelatine print.

UNKNOWN photographer © >
Johannesbourg, 1900.
Elizabeth and Jan van der Merwe.
Elizabeth and Jan were siblings born to a family of « inboekselings » in Lindley, Orange River Colony now called the Free State. Inboekselings loosely translated means forced juvenile apprenticeship in agriculture. Her family became prosperous livestock and grain farmers at the turn of the century.
This information was supplied by Emma Mothibe.

<

Photographer SCHOLTZ STUDIO ©
Lindley. Orange River Colony, 1900.
*Ouma Maria Letsipa and her daugh-
ter, Minkie Letsipa.*
*Maria was born to a family of
« inboekselings » in Lindley, Orange
River Colony now called the Free
State. « Inboekseling » loosely translated means forced juvenile apprenticeship in agriculture. Her family
became prosperous livestock and
grain farmers at the turn of the century. The image belong to Ramela
family of Orlando east. This information was supplied by Emma Mothibe.*
Albumen print.

Photographer >
ALIWAL NORTH LOCATION SCHOOL ©
P.G. Mdebuka.1900.
*At the back of this print is written
« A present from (and stamped P.G.
Mdebuka – Location School, Aliwal
North) to Jane Maloyi ». PG Mdebuka
was hymn composer and minister of
the methodist church. This photograph
was found in a wooden box labelled
(in Afrikaans), « Aan M.V. Jooste van
die persooneel van Die Vaderland ». In
the box there were 68 images inclu-
ding one of « Their most Gracious
Majesties, Edward VII and Queen
Alexandra – In their robes of State ».
This box belongs to Moeketsi Msomi
whose grandfather, John Rees
Phakane, was a bishop in the AME
Church.*
Albumen print.

I grew up on the threshing floor of the faith, a faith as much ritual as spiritual: a bizarre cocktail embracing pagan rites and Catholic beliefs. While aware of my reluctance to become entangled in this universe, I identify with it: and this does not seem to me out of the ordinary. Yet I always try to avoid the trap of its hypnotic embrace, which seems to deride my patiently cultivated indifference and self-confidence. I feel myself ambivalent about my ambivalence, embarrassed by my embarrassment.

This project took me into places in which the real and the unreal freely intermingle, and in which my knowledge of photographic technique was tested to the limit. While the pictures are a record of rituals, fetishes and places, I am not sure I have caught on film the essence of the feeling I thought I was showing. Perhaps I'm looking for something that refuses to be photographed. Perhaps I've only been chasing shadows.

Santu Mofokeng

Portrait photographers

Les portraitistes

It wasn't until the early 20th century that the first African photographers started working privately before setting up their own studios in the major cities and capitals of Africa. Many of them had been employed in the European studios scattered around the continent or had discovered photography after doing military service in the colonial armies. African photography developed mainly through portrait photography carried out in homes, then studios. It initially evolved in response to demand from the burgeoning African middle classes, before centralized administration turned it into a popular phenomenon in the 1950s and 1960s.

There may have been fear or defiance of photography and photographers, both European and African, in certain regions, particularly rural areas. But urban life was transforming traditional customs, producing a radical change in general behaviour and attitudes in Africa and the rest of the world. Photography was welcomed with the same enthusiasm as elsewhere: it was seen as a memory, a sign of modernity, a symbolic message, a proof of, or desire for, social standing. Costumes, accessories and attitudes were never present by chance; they contributed to the social image of the person or group being photographed.

African photography appropriated an existing technique without being subjected to its aesthetics. This is perhaps the sense in which one can say that there are several different types of African photography, not one single style.

Pascal Martin Saint Léon & Jean Loup Pivin

Photographer
MAMA CASSET © 1955
Dakar, Senegal.

Mama Casset

Senegal
*b. Saint-Louis, Senegal 1908
– d. Dakar, Senegal 1992*

Mama Casset learned photography at the age of 12 in Dakar, under the guidance of French photographer Oscar Lataque. After his studies, Tennequin hired him to work for the photographic desk of the organization, Afrique Occidentale Française (AOF). He soon joined the French Air Force, where he took numerous aerial photographs, opening his own private studio, African Photo, in the Dakar Medina at the end of the Second World War. Mama Casset was not content to be the fashionable studio photographer of the Dakar bourgeoisie, he also produced work that he himself described as artistic, using his second wife as both muse and principal model. Halfway between postcard and poster, his prints were used as models by numerous clip-frame painters. Mama Casset's highly personal aesthetic acquired a wide following: a few props, a highly structured composition, the frequent use of slants and diagonals, attention to bodily expression, attention to costumes and tight framing. When you look at a Mama Casset photo you breathe in heavy scents - tchourais - you feel suppressed laughter or profound sadness, strong and weak characters and lithe sensuality.
Mama Casset stopped working in 1980 when he went blind. His studio burned down a few years later, but his works have been saved from oblivion by the photographer Bouna Medoune Seye.

Photographer MAMA CASSET © 1955
Dakar, Senegal.

Photographer MAMA CASSET © 1955
Dakar, Senegal.

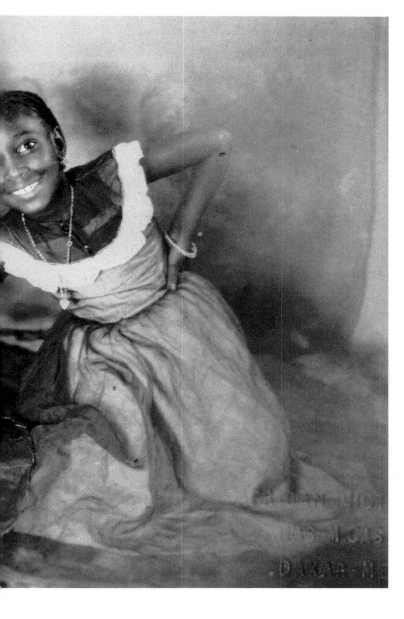

Joseph Moïse Agbojelou

Benin
b. Védo, Benin 1912 – lives in Porto-Novo

Joseph Moïse Agbojelou started taking pictures in France while he was part of the French army in 1935. In 1960 he opened a studio, France Photo, in memory of the man who showed him the tricks of the trade in Perpignan, France. Weddings, funerals, wakes, communions, political, cultural and religious ceremonies, various happenings and portraits: nearly 50 years of the life and history of Benin today slumber in boxes piled up on two tables on either side of his favourite armchair. He was the Kodak representative and president of the Dahomey professional photographer's association. Joseph Moïse Agbojelou finally gave up photography in 1994.

Photographer
JOSEPH MOÏSE AGBODJELOU © ca. 1950

Photographer
JOSEPH MOÏSE AGBODJELOU © ca. 1950

DANIEL ATTOUMO AMICHIA

Ivory Coast
b. Behine, Ghana) ca. 1908
– d. Grand Bassam, Ivory Coast 1994

Daniel Attoumo Amichia's older brother introduced him to photography in the 1920s. In 1948 he moved into the French neighbourhood of Grand-Bassam, where he stayed in close contact with the Ghanaian English-speaking community working at the local English trading post. He worked as an itinerant photographer, using natural light and producing mainly portraits of families or of different groups within Grand-Bassam society. Cancer forced him to give up photography and when he died in Grand-Bassam at the age of 86, his family threw all his photos and equipment into the sea. A very few prints have survived - thanks to Joseph Ernest Kouao, a collector and Amichia's former associate - together with a handful of photos preserved in family albums.

Photographer
DANIEL ATTOUMO AMICHIA © ca. 1950

Twilight of the studios

Jean-François Werner

After doing extremely well in the 1960s, studio photographers are now deep in a crisis from which they seem unlikely to emerge. The arrival of colour photography, Korean minilabs and itinerant photographers needing no particular skill to practise their profession, have placed studio-based photographers in a very difficult situation: unlike the itinerants, they were faced both with overheads and the « democratization » of the identity photo trade that had come to represent their sole source of income. The example of the Ivory Coast provides us here with a chronicle of a death foretold.

Jean-François Werner is an anthropologist who has made an extensive study of photography in West Africa.

An examination of photographic activity in West Africa reveals that the vast majority of professionals exercise their activity in what is called « family (domestic) photography ».[1] Owing to unfavourable economic conditions, the practice of amateur photography by the inhabitants of this region of Africa has yet to become widespread. The opposite phenomenon can be observed in industrialized Western countries, where after the Second World War the popularization of photography led to elimination of many neighbourhood photographic studios.

Despite the fact that the practice of amateur photography in Africa is still limited to a relatively affluent minority, studio photography has suffered from a deep structural crisis since the early 1980s. This transformation has either eliminated or threatens the survival of professional photographers such as Mama Casset, Seydou Keita or Cornelius Augustt, whose work is doubly marked by the mastery of their craft and their respective artistic sensibilities.

The following article will attempt to explain the factors that have led to the ruin of hundreds of West African studio photographers. The role played by the owners of the colour laboratories will be discussed, as will be that of the new generation of itinerant photographers who currently dominate the market. We will also examine the situation of the remaining traditional studio photographers as the 20th century draws to a close.

1. By which is meant images characterized by the nature of the referent - effectively, portraits.
This is an activity touching practically all social classes and geographical regions, easily accessible and destined for private rather than commercial use.

In the 1980s, the golden age of the studios, photographers were solidly established in their neighbourhoods and appreciated by the local population, for whom they played an important role by visually documenting the events of individual lives and the life of the community. These men (women did not engage in the profession) were generally non-nationals who had emigrated from neighbouring English-speaking countries (especially Ghana and Nigeria) to open studios in cities such as Niamey (Niger), Ouagadougou and Bobo-Dioulasso (Burkina-Faso), Abidjan, Bouaké and Korhogo (the Ivory Coast).

During this period, black-and-white studio photography was both immensely popular and governed by strictly-defined aesthetic norms. The demand came from all classes of the population, including the poorest members of the urban and rural proletariat. In addition to this activity, the need for identity photographs, which had always constituted an essential part of the business of the studios, increased sharply owing to new obligations regarding their use on identity cards, drivers' licences, school applications and a variety of other administrative documents.

At the same time, photographers increasingly began leaving their studios to document private events (marriages, baptisms and funeral ceremonies), and public events (the visits of politicians and sports competitions), and even began working for the police (car accidents, homicides, etc.). Their work was facilitated by the arrival of compact 24 x 36 mm flash cameras, which replaced the bulky studio box cameras and the need for artificial lighting.

In the early 1980s, colour photography made its appearance in the region. For studios which experienced a heightened demand for portraits using the new colour medium, the effects were initially positive. Given the higher prices charged for colour portraits, the available income of photographers increased sufficiently to permit the purchase of motor cars, which increased their professional mobility. The increased income also permitted the renovation of studios (the creation of new decor, the installation of a telephone and air-conditioning, etc.) and the acquisition of new cameras using the 24 x 36 cm colour negative film - a norm imposed by the new development laboratories whose automatic machines accepted only that format. The older cameras and studio equipment were thus progressively phased out.

The Ivory Coast, via France, played a decisive role in the introduction of colour photography in the region. In effect, colour film was initially marketed and distributed by a French firm, Direct-Film, whose laboratories were in France. Exposed film was thus collected from a network of local depots and sent to France for development. The completed prints were then sent back to the Ivory Coast by mail. A local laboratory eventually opened in Abidjan, and by copying the same system used by their French competitors, succeeded in gaining the monopoly for colour development until the arrival of the Japanese-made Noritsu minilabs.

The majority of the owners of the new automatic colour development systems were Asians (principally South Koreans). After initially dominating the market, they were joined by African businessmen and Lebanese investors. An analysis of respective market share in 1995 reveals that in the Ivory Coast (which has a population of approximately 12 million), fully half of the 85 laboratories in the country belonged to Asians and only a third to Ivory Coast nationals. The proliferation of these laboratories was naturally detrimental to the studios, except when their owners had enough capital to invest the several hundred thousand French francs necessary for the purchase of the same system.[2]

Ultimately, the introduction of colour film and laboratory processing has had disastrous consequences for the traditional activities of the studios, to the point where it now threatens their very existence. All of the purely technical operations that they had previously carried out (film development and prints) are today done by sophisticated minilabs capable of processing hundreds of rolls of film per hour. The role of the photographer, whether professional or amateur, has been reduced to that of simply taking pictures - an activity which in itself requires no special talent or competence.

The situation has favoured the massive influx of formerly jobless young men who today offer their services as portrait photographers throughout West Africa. Lacking the financial means to establish permanent studios, this new generation of itinerant photographers methodically canvasses the region's cities and rural villages in search of potential clients. Their mobility and low overheads permit them to charge prices significantly lower than those charged by the studios (which are obliged to pay rent, various taxes and telephone and electricity bills), giving them rapid dominance of the family photography market.

2 - Although the devaluation of the CFA franc (the franc of Francophone Africa) in January 1994 stimulated the local economy, it also made the purchase of imported products even more expensive.

Portrait photographers

For these young photographers, their professional training could be obtained in a number of ways: a long apprenticeship in a studio (perhaps several years); a short apprenticeship (three to twelve months) or simply hands-on experience. With the exception of a minority capable of developing film and prints, their professional competence is limited to posing their subjects and taking their pictures, skills which are much the same for all photographers, whether based in one location or itinerant.

The itinerant photographers invest little in their equipment;[3] conversely, the possession of a bicycle or a small motorbike is a valuable tool for rapidly covering a territory which, according to the size of the area in which they exercise their professional activity, can range from an entire city to simply a neighbourhood.[4] Day and night, with their distinctive camera bags slung across the shoulder, they canvass their territory and in particular its most-frequented places: markets and bus stations, churches, temples and mosques, restaurants, nightclubs, hotels and swimming pools, schools, military barracks, etc. In the larger cities, each photographer has his own speciality, such as bars and nightclubs or the exclusive contract for a particular school.

Photographing domestic events, although an intermittent activity, is particularly profitable, whether the photographs are directly commissioned by the organizers or the result of the uninvited presence of the photographer. Given the competition among photographers, it is not unusual for them to come to blows outside the local town hall where, on Saturday mornings, marriages are performed in succession. Traditional ceremonies, religious celebrations and funerals also constitute choice subjects for these photographers.

Since the public's taste has shifted from posed portraits to more spontaneous, natural and even « candid » photographs, the traditional studio photographers currently occupy a negligible portion of the market: their professional activity and economic survival are now principally based on identity photographs. Recently however, even this last bastion of their activity has been eroded by the encroachments of the ubiquitous itinerant photographers and the replacement of the traditional identity photograph by tamper-proof snapshots taken by official government photographers.

Although the itinerant photographers' access to the market for identity photographs has until now been limited by their lack of development equipment and ignorance of the necessary techniques, the situation is changing in their favour. This is less because of the acceptance by studio photographers - desperate for additional revenue - of the need to develop the films of itinerant photographers in their laboratories than because of the new possibility offered by West African minilabs of producing black-and-white prints from colour negative film. For the first time, the studio photographers have succeeded in acting as a group to persuade the laboratory owners to refuse this practice, which would have put many of them out of business. Faced by the progressive erosion of their traditional activities, studio photographers have attempted to use their professional association to protect one of their last remaining markets: student identity photographs.

At the beginning of each academic year, hundreds of thousands of students require such photographs for their registration files. In the Ivory Coast, local chapters of the Synaphoci [5] obtained the exclusive rights to student identity photographs from the school principals of their respective regions. At present, however, certain laboratories have succeeded in persuading the local authorities to open this extremely lucrative market to their own photographers.

Today, the laboratories have succeeded in laying down the law: on the one hand they pay their affiliated photographers less than the established standard rates and on the other, they have also created their own professional association which now competes with the Synaphoci. Their motivations are purely financial: a maximum of profit in a minimum of time. Given the fierce competition for clients, each camp makes an all-out effort to attract them. As one development laboratory owner put it, « In the Ivory Coast today, it's the laboratories who decide who is a professional or not. For example, if someone starts taking pictures for a living, even on a part-time basis, we accord him professional status as soon as he becomes a regular customer. » Accused by the studios of lowering professional standards, the laboratory owners defended their position with the assertion that technical progress and affordable, sophisticated cameras made it easier for more people to attain professional results, and that the distinction between professionals and amateurs was no longer valid. Furthermore, the laboratories argued, it was absurd to deprive newcomers of the opportunity to earn a living from photography by imposing technical competencies that were totally obsolete.

Under the guise of good intentions, these self-serving rationalizations were in reality an effective commercial strategy for gaining new clients. In addition, the laboratories offered services ranging from temporary office space with telephone and mail facilities, lounge areas with television, and discounts or gifts for repeat customers. No efforts were spared to attract new business and ensure the loyalty of customers who were quick to change to laboratories which offered even more. Speed of development was another important factor which attracted itinerant photographers to the laboratories, since their remuneration depends on their being able to distribute the finished photographs of marriages, baptisms, business meetings, religious ceremonies or other group events to the participants before they disperse.[6]

To satisfy the demand, the laboratories have opted for speed rather than quality. The development machines have been modified to run faster, the chemicals are changed less frequently and prints are made on cheaper paper. The results are often mediocre, a problem which is accentuated by the heat and humidity of the climate. All of these factors present a potential long-term threat to the photographic market itself: the quest for rapid profits may well backfire when people begin seeing the images on the photo-souvenirs they expected to last a lifetime fading to nothing in the space of a few years.

Behind the mask of the paternalistic behaviour of the laboratory owners lies a strategy of total market domination, as was revealed in their recent victory over the studio photographers of Bouaké in February 1996.

Photography Jean-François Werner ©

In collaboration with the Synaphoci, these photographers organized a boycott (which included pickets at the doors) of the Bouaké laboratories in an attempt to obtain lower prices for film processing. After pretending to negotiate, the laboratories not only maintained their prices, but also succeeded in putting a competing laboratory that was actually offering lower rates in a nearby city, out of business.

The studio photographers are the ultimate losers in this war which is not only economic and technical but also symbolic, for it is also centred around the laboratories' power to determine who is considered to be a professional photographer and who is not. Whatever the outcome, it is clear that the ongoing activity of studio photographers is doubly threatened: on one hand, the technical skills on which they have established their professional identity and commercial activity have gradually become obsolete; on the other, the demands of their customers have also changed, resulting in the progressive erosion of their traditional client-base. The most dynamic of the studio photographers have managed to adapt themselves to the new conditions, principally by becoming as commercially aggressive and mobile as their itinerant competitors. The older studio photographers, unable or unwilling to change their methods, have seen their business dwindle away. A number of the latter (originally emigrants from other countries, but often established for decades in their country of adoption) have found themselves in a particularly tragic situation: unable to make a living where they are, while at the same time unable to return to their countries of origin, with which they have broken all connection.

THE CURRENT STATE OF STUDIO PHOTOGRAPHY IN THE IVORY COAST

It was within the context of this crisis that I began investigating the activity of all photographers, whether studio or itinerant, in a secondary city of the Ivory Coast - Bouaké, population 500 000 - in 1994.

There were 85 studio photographers practising in Bouaké at that time. All were men and, on average, older than their itinerant colleagues. The question of nationality was another decisive factor separating the two groups. A full 80 per cent of the studio photographers were foreigners, while the same percentage of itinerant photographers were Ivory Coast nationals. The studio photographers were relatively well educated and, like the itinerants, many of them had previously practised other professions. For two-thirds of the studio photographers, their choice was motivated by a personal attachment to the profession rather than purely financial reasons. Many of them used terms such as «love» or «passion» to describe an activity which for them was both a source of pleasure and the means of earning a living. At least half of the studio photographers had learned their craft as assistants or apprentices to members of their own family already established in the profession.

3. In general, their equipment is relatively unsophisticated: a basic 24 x 36 mm camera with a standard 50 mm lens and a flash unit.

4. The phenomenon of itinerant photographers is not limited to cities. In the rural regions, young villagers practise this activity as an additional occupation between the planting and harvesting seasons.

5. Created in 1982 to defend the interests of professional photographers, the Synaphoci (Syndicat National des Photographes de la Côte d'Ivoire) accepted numerous members in the 1980s on the basis of criteria which were never clearly defined.

6. In the larger cities, some laboratories are open 24 hours a day on holidays such as Christmas, Tabaski, Easter or New Year's Eve.

The skills they acquired (in the absence of formal theoretical training) were principally of a practical nature: posing subjects, operating the camera and lighting systems, film development and print-making.

THE STUDIO

By definition, studio photography requires a fixed locale. Many of the studios were easily identifiable by names which recalled their function, such as the Studio du Nord; Studio Photo Plus; Studio Photo Central; Photo Studio Welcome; Studio Photo Cosmos N°1, etc. In general, photographers rent suitably-situated commercial space and divide it (using partitions or curtains) into three distinct areas: the waiting room for clients, the room where the photographs are actually taken, and the darkroom.

The waiting room also often serves as an office in which the commercial transactions between the photographer and the client are carried out. As such, it is usually equipped with a desk (or a counter) and one or more chairs. The walls are covered with samples of the photographer's work, typically colour portraits and black-and-white identity photographs, all of which were commissioned but never paid for by their clients.[7] In the studios which are still in business today, these photographs often reflect the efforts made by photographers to adapt to the latest styles and the public's demand for novelty. Still other images may adorn the walls: advertising posters from the suppliers of photographic products; calendars distributed by the laboratories, illustrated with scenes from Japan or Korea; postcards and official portraits of political leaders, religious dignitaries, sports stars, etc.

The actual studio (the room in which the photographs are taken) is always separated from the waiting room/office by a partition or curtain to preserve the sacrosanct privacy of the client and photographer. The studio lighting is totally artificial and generally consists of a series of ordinary light-bulbs or fluorescent tubes. The drawbacks of such lighting systems are that they tend to blind clients with their harsh glare and further increase the heat in the already airless room. The stifling heat in turn augments the client's lack of comfort and the haste of the photographer. The subject usually poses before a painted backdrop (urban scenes or rural landscapes) or a large colour poster representing an « exotic » landscape (snow-covered Alps, for example) whose purpose is to create an impression of being somewhere - or someone - else.[8]

The use of backgrounds is complemented by the possibility of being photographed in front of coloured curtains which can be changed during a single shooting session. Colours are chosen to provide the best contrast with the subject's clothing or skin-tone. The attention given to the latter factor is regarded by both parties as being of extreme importance. In general, photographers attempt to lighten rather than darken skin-tones, and the majority of the development laboratories have adjusted their machines to produce lighter hues. In addition to the backgrounds, the studios offer a variety of accessories (props), ranging from artificial flowers and plants to elegant wrought-iron balconies, a variety of seats (traditional stools and modern armchairs), end-tables with false telephones, etc.

These stereotyped elements appear with astonishing regularity in photographic studios across West Africa. Clients desirous of « dressing up » can also select appropriate clothing (such as sports jackets, dark suits, white shirts, ties and hats) kept by the photographer for that purpose. Studios are also equipped with dressing-alcoves complete with mirrors, combs, hairbrushes and talcum powder for absorbing perspiration.

TAKING THE PORTRAIT

Without exception, all the photographers interviewed possessed at least two cameras. The first (a medium-sized or 24 x 36 mm format) is permanently installed on a tripod, and serves for black-and-white identity photographs. The second (always a 24 x 36 mm camera equipped with a flash unit) is used for colour studio portraits as well as for exterior work (special events or commercial photography and portraits taken at the client's home).

Film is obtained on the informal market (also known as the « underground » or « black » market) at prices lower than those current in the shops. The film used is invariably 135-format in colour or black-and-white and 120-format exclusively in black-and-white. The informal market for photographic supplies came into existence in the late 1980s, following the bankruptcy of several Abidjan wholesalers (and in particular, the distributor of Kodak products).

The technical approach of studio photographers is essentially empirical. For example, although the majority of their Japanese-made 24 x 36 cameras come equipped with a light-meter as standard equipment, most studio photographers employ the same shutter speed and diaphragm opening, and adjust for light values manually.[9] For exterior shots, photographers use one of two habitual diaphragm-openings, depending on whether the subject is in the sunlight or shade.

THE DARKROOM

The portion of the studio reserved for developing and printing film is generally cramped (sometimes no larger than a closet), lit by an ordinary light-bulb (covered in red paint or black paper), without running water and usually cluttered and dust-filled. The lack of ventilation and the heat favour the decomposition of the development chemicals and print-paper. The enlarger (often an ancient model) is generally on a wooden table, but is only used for producing black-and-white identity photographs. The remaining accessories include plastic development pans and occasionally tongs, clips and a calibrated print-cutter.

Chemicals, developing baths, fixing solutions and print paper are obtained either on the informal market or from merchants, who enjoy a flourishing trade. In general, the photographers complain about the irregularity of supply, the poor quality of the products offered to them and the lack of variety. As for chemicals for fixing and developing, known as « medications »,[10] these are available only in powder form.

Once prepared, these products cannot be kept for more than a few months without deteriorating, which penalizes photographers for whom business is slow.

The straitened circumstances prevailing in their darkrooms have not prevented West African photographers from producing excellent photographs and at times, even veritable works of art. Their creativity and ability to improvise have triumphed over technical conditions which are far removed from those recommended by the instruction books. Film is manually developed, being passed in successive movements in and out of three different chemical baths. The temperatures of the chemical baths are never monitored; reserves of new chemicals and unexposed prints are regularly exposed to levels of humidity and heat which rapidly affect their quality.

THE PRESERVATION AND ARCHIVING OF NEGATIVES

Although the majority of the photographers interviewed were perfectly aware of their right to royalties in the event of the reproduction of their photographs, their economic situation has become so difficult that it is rare for them - particularly the older generation of studio photographers - to refuse a cash offer for the outright purchase of the original negatives. The physical preservation of their negatives leaves much to be desired. Even if certain photographers stock their negatives in pro-

tective cellophane envelopes and classify them in chronological order, the majority take no special precautions for their preservation. Some photographers even admitted that, after moving to a new studio or upon their retirement, they threw out hundreds of negatives which they considered to be valueless. When negatives are preserved, it is only because of the potential client demand for new prints: it is for this reason that when a studio is sold to a new owner, the previous photographer's negatives are included along with the furnishings and equipment as a package deal.

DAILY ECONOMIC SURVIVAL

The preceding description of photographic activity in West Africa would not be complete without calling attention to the economic and material difficulties experienced by many of its professionals. Although the majority of photographers who were interviewed described the current situation as critical, given the lack of relevant economic data (most photographers do not keep records of their business activity), it is impossible to evaluate this precisely.

What is clear, however, is the shabby state of the studios, the financial problems of the older generation of photographers (unpaid rent and electricity bills, etc.) and the necessity for some of them to sell part of their equipment, often to younger itinerant photographers.

For the majority of the studios, identity photos remain the principal and often only source of revenue, far ahead of colour portraits. Even this activity has become minimal (in general, only a few clients per day) and has resulted in the necessity for finding complementary sources of income. These secondary activities can range from the sales of non-photography-related products (gasoline, newspapers, charcoal, etc.) to hairdressing (a Nigerian speciality) and the rental of chairs and canopies for outdoor events and ceremonies.

It is within the context of this profound professional crisis that, since 1990, a wide variety of individuals (specialists of art and culture, representatives of foreign cultural agencies and non-governmental organisations, historians, collectors, art merchants, etc., the majority of whom are European) have discovered African photography. The effects of this belated recognition of what is regarded as a new chapter in the history of African art has benefited a handful of photographers. Conversely, at the present time, this new development has had little effect on the even more pressing need for the conservation of Africa's unique and precious cultural heritage.[11]

Jean-François Werner

7. In Senegal, photographers hang the portraits of clients who owe them money upside-down as a form of public humiliation.

8. In Ghana, the painted canvas backgrounds (often with a different scene appearing on either side) exhibit a wide variety of themes (urban scenes, well-furnished home interiors, luxurious villas with swimming pools, expensive automobiles, mosques, gardens, etc.). This phenomenon may explain why Ghanaian photographers have resisted the current crisis more successfully than their other West African colleagues. (See Tobias Wendl's observations on this subject.)

9. The practice can be ascribed to the difficulties of obtaining replacement batteries for these light-meters as well as their inaccuracy after being subjected to the usual operating conditions (heat, humidity and repeated mishandling).

10. Its probable origin was in the period when these products were sold in pharmacies - a practice which continued until fairly recently. On another level, it also evokes their utilization in processes which in the popular imagination are invested with a quasi-magical quality.

11. Although a project (under the auspices of the West African Museum Programme) for the preservation of the West African photographic heritage has recently been set up, it applies only to public collections and totally neglects the problem of the immense quantity of negatives and photographs existing in private archives.

CORNELIUS YAO AUGUSTT AZAGLO

Ivory Coast
b. Palimé, Togo 1924
– lives in Korhogo, Ivory Coast

Cornelius Yao Augustt Azaglo taught himself photography at the age of 18, but did not really become a photographer until the 1950s, after having practised various other professions. In 1955 he set up in Korhogo in the north of the Ivory Coast, not far from Ghana, where his family was living; there his Studio du Nord met with resounding success.

Equipped with his «box», he would set off regularly by bicycle along the Ivory Coast-Ghanaian border, and on village squares would take portraits of the local farmers under the harsh sun, against a simple painted backdrop fixed to a mud wall.

Photographer
CORNELIUS YAO AUGUSTT AZAGLO ©
October 1960.

Photographer
CORNELIUS YAO AUGUSTT AZAGLO ©

AMBROISE NGAIMOKO
STUDIO 3Z

Democratic Republic of Congo
b. Angola 1949 – lives in Kinshasa

Fleeing the war of independence in Angola, Ambroise Ngaimoko arrived in Kinshasa at the age of twelve with his mother and sisters. As the only male member of the family, he worked first as a mechanic, then as a projectionist in open-air cinemas. He took up photography thanks to his uncle, Marques Ndodal, owner of two studios, who gave him his first camera. In 1971 he set up his own 3Z Studio, in Kitambo, and continues to work there. The poses captured by his lens conjure up screenplays in which local dandies, often with artificially whitened skin, become the heroes of some great adventure.

Photographer
AMBROISE NGAIMOKO — STUDIO 3Z © ca. 1970
Kinshasa, Democratic Republic of Congo.

The golden age
of black-&-white in Mali

The first Malian photographers learned photography in the French army when African subjects were massively recruited to become the famous Senegalese fighters of the two World Wars. After 1945 they worked as assistants in studios owned mainly by European photographers, before setting up their own businesses after independence. Teachers were also very prevalent in the first generation of Malian photographers, which reached its peak in the 1960s. Colour photography rendered studios virtually obsolete, replacing them with on-the-spot flash photographs taken by photographers who learned their trade in the field.

IN THE BEGINNING

Mali, a land with an ancient culture, was discovered by Europe after the journey of René Caillé in 1827. It would become entirely colonized by France in 1898 with the fall of Samory, « the Black Bonaparte », after the siege of Sikasso. Photography was the medium favoured by many of those involved in colonial conquest. Apart from explorers, soldiers and missionaries, some attention must be given to the activity of civilians, civil servants and tradesmen. The idea of organizing photographic missions alongside military expeditions was fast adopted. The coastal towns of West Africa, such as St Louis in Senegal, which had been open to western influence from a much earlier date, were in contact with photography well before the inland regions, which remained relatively isolated until the 1880s. The first traces of commercial photography date back to the 1930s. Beforehand, photography only existed through the publishers of postcards from 1900 onwards: there were 15 of them in Mali and more than 50 in Dakar.

The role of the colonial army in the spread of photography was at its height during the two World Wars. Over 100 000 Sudanese were dispatched to fight for France. Some of the old Bamako photographers we met broadened their knowledge of photography owing to an enforced stay in Europe.

Text based on a dissertation for an MA in Contemporary History: « Being a photographer in Bamako, the evolution and realities of a profession born of modernity, 1935-1995 », written by Érika Nimis, African Research Centre of Paris University I, September 1996, published by Éditions Revue Noire in Bamako Photographers, Paris, March 1998.

< Photographer MOUNTAGA DEMBÉLÉ ©
Young girl, Bamako. ca. 1935.

Portrait photographers

Mountaga Dembélé, who was born in 1920, came back as a lieutenant of the Colonial Infantry in 1945.

Mamadou Cissé, born in 1930, was very young when he took his first lessons with the Allied Forces in Great Britain, taken in hand as he was by a British quartermaster by the name of « Mister Johnny ». He was then drafted into the Colonial Army and sent to Indochina (from 1954 to 1956) and Algeria (1957 to 1959). This is how he became a « regimental photographer ».

The first photography shop, Photo-Hall Soudanais, was opened in the Sudanese capital by Pierre Garnier in 1935. The shop rapidly became successful and from 1940, Pierre Garnier hired Sudanese employees: Tiékoura Samaké dealt with developing and printing; Nabi Doumbia started at the bookstore in the shop, as did Felix Diallo (from 1952 to 1955). Nabi Doumbia left the shop in 1942 to work for the Sûreté Nationale as a photographer.

Felix Diallo « started out in photography » in 1952. It was very hard for him to do his job: « Nobody knew what photography was in Kita in 1955, mothers did not want their children to be photographed », neither did old people wish to go before the camera.

IN THE DAYS OF BLACK-AND-WHITE

The 1930s saw the birth of the first generation of Sudanese photographers. All of them, with a few exceptions - such as Felix Diallo and Nabi Doumbia - were teachers, like Mountaga Dembélé and Samba Bâ, who are often referred to, although no trace of their work remains. By photographing on commission during his time off, Mountaga Dembélé, who was only an amateur, managed to earn as much as a professional. Many photographers, most of whom are also teachers, still follow the same path today, spreading photography beyond the major centres.

Photographers had to be extremely ingenious when it came to developing and printing their photos, whether in the bush or in town, where only the European areas had access to electricity. « When there wasn't any electricity we had to use Petromax lamps to take photos at night ». All the photographers of the time applied the principle of direct printing, using a 13 x 18 cm « frame-press ».

After the Second World War, photographic activity began to develop among eminent Bamako personalities, led by Seydou Keita. In order to get his customers ready for a studio portrait, the photographer would supply the accessories, clothing and furniture needed for any scenario: « I had three different European suits at the studio, with ties, shirts, clothes, hats ... the works. Plus the accessories: pens, plastic flowers, wireless, telephone at the customers' disposal ». A pedestal table and tablecloth were also among the accessories offered. Apart from the background, which was a simple cloth stretched over the earthen wall; these accessories recall the great feeling of ceremony that characterized European photography studios at the turn of the century.

INDEPENDENCE

For the small group of Bamako photographers, the independence of Mali in 1960 marked the end of various constraints and of being confined to the role of « subordinates ». Photographers could now get out and view the outside world, thanks to new techniques: medium and large formats, and flashes. As the young Republic of Mali celebrated its beginnings, the first years under Modibo Keita saw reportage photography flourish, and two new names distinguished themselves throughout Bamako: Abderramane Sakaly and Malick Sidibé.

Abderramane Sakaly, of Moroccan origin, was born in St Louis in 1926. He started out as a chauffeur, then sold « fabrics, beads and necklaces ». After arriving in Bamako, he opened his first studio in 1956. He started photography through the intermediary of two men: Claude Rollin, a young artist who had just arrived in Bamako, and Nabi Doumbia, who taught him developing and printing techniques. The Sakaly house used to buzz day and night; the entrance was always full of people. His archives, consisting of more than 400 000 negatives, are still methodically preserved. Sakaly remains in Bamako memory as *the* photographer in the city after independence. Along with his apprentices and colleagues, he photographed all the events of Bamako life: from advertisements to school portraits, as well as accidents, society gatherings and official portraits. Sakaly trained many people, including those who worked at Information, an official photographic service created following independence.

What with this boom in the profession, photographers from neighbouring coastal countries, especially the English-speaking countries (Ghana and Nigeria), arrived on the scene in the 1960s. There was a great demand for passport photos following independence and all the ensuing electoral processes. The street photographers worked close to the markets, both in towns and in the bush, with « box cameras » - handmade wooden chambers fitted with just a lens and no diaphragm stop or shutter speed control. In Bamako, the « koun don wola » (literally « those who put their head in the hole ») set up with the hairdressers next to the large mosque. Their working procedures have not changed since the early 1960s.

There are still many wary clients in the bush, where photography takes place mainly on market days. There is a fair every Monday in Badinko, a township close to Kita on the railway line: a makeshift studio has been set up there, far from prying eyes, mainly for « passports ». Youssouf B Touré, himself a teacher in Kita, started photography in 1980. He says that some villagers still don't know what photography is: «The people think it's something to do with medical treatment! They run away as soon as the light goes off!»

Certain Muslims, called « wahhabites », are also reluctant to be photographed. « The law of Mohamed condemns the reproduction of animate beings as being an impious infringement of God's rights. He alone can give life to the beings he created. » Mamadou Wellé Diallo, « Moussa Traoré's personal photographer » from 1978 to 1984, followed the imam of Mecca during his first visit to Mali in 1981: the latter managed to make him give up his career.

MOUNTAGA DEMBÉLÉ

Mali
b. Bamako, Mali 1919 – lives in Bamako.

Mountaga Dembélé was born in Bamako in 1919. He started photography in 1935 when he was a teacher. He was drafted into the colonial army and sent to Europe during the Second World War. He returned to Bamako in 1945, and went back to teaching in different parts of Mali, where he pursued his passion for photography by taking numerous 9 x 12 cm and 13 x 18 cm format photographs. He is now retired and lives in Médina Coura. Unfortunately, his archives have disappeared.

∧ Photographer MOUNTAGA DEMBÉLÉ ©
Family photograph, Bamako. ca. 1935.

THE COLOUR YEARS

In the West, colour photography started to take off in the 1960s. In Mali, as in most parts of French-speaking West Africa - perhaps with the exception of Senegal - it was not until the early 1980s that laboratories specializing in colour work began to appear. Demand for colour had, in fact, begun very early on and Mountaga Dembélé had started out tinting black-and-white photos using a brush, «wallpaper» and a little water. « I was turning out hand-made colour photos … on matt paper », he recalls. From 1975 onwards, studio photographers were making healthy profits out of colour; they were the sole inter-mediaries between clients ready to pay high prices for processing, and the laboratories in France or at Tiger Photo in Dakar. Demand was such that 1982 saw the opening of the first labo-ratory, Photo-Kola, in Bamako. « Kola » means « to wash » in Bambara, and in French-speaking Africa to wash a photo means to develop it. But their brand-new prosperity was already under threat from the devastating impact of the South Koreans on the local colour scene.

In the 1980s most studios were on the wane: they were still around, but business was slow and relied mostly on identity shots. The old hands opted for discreet early retirement, while the youngsters who had started up just before colour came along had enormous difficulty getting through the crisis period. The studio photographers brought up on black-and-white are universally hostile to colour. « Some time or other colour's going to lose in value, » declares Malick Sidibé, stressing that black-and-white retains its quality better and longer than colour - which is true in that colour chemistry is very delicate and requires a scrupulous attention that the Bamako laboratories, for reasons of profitability, rarely provide. But history marches on.

The recent upheavals have not improved the profession's already fragile standing. Even the photographer's professional skills are being challenged. Is being a photographer in Bamako today a real occupation? And where do you draw the line bet-ween professionalism and amateur status? So just what do they have in common, those dedicated photographers from the 1940s with all the practical and theoretical knowledge han-ded on to them by the colonialists - and the young itinerants of today, inexperienced and with no real interest in photography except as a source of income? Photography might be losing in quality, but it is gaining in quantity, with colour photographs now being part of everyday life in Mali.

FÉLIX DIALLO

Mali
b. Kita, Mali 1931 – d. Kita, 1997

Félix Diallo was born at the Catholic mission in Kita in 1931. When his father died he left school and became a tailor. In 1951 he moved to Bamako where he worked for photographer Pierre Garnier, printing enlargements. He returned to Kita in 1955 to become the town's first photographer. He died in Kita in 1997. Most of his archives have been destroyed but some were saved by Érika Nimis who presented his work in her thesis on Bamako photographers.

Photographer FÉLIX DIALLO ©
Group of friends, Kita, ca. 1957.
The old lion. ca. 1960.

Seydou Keita

Mali
b. Bamako, Mali 1923 – lives in Bamako

Born in Bamako in 1923, Seydou Keita has kept nearly all his photographs. A trained cabinet-maker, he started out in photography in 1949 and invested in a second-hand 13 x 18 cm chamber after a few attempts with the Kodak Brownie (6 x 9 cm format). He set his studio up in the courtyard of his home and photographed a significant part of Malian society until 1962, when he became a photographer for the criminal investigation department. He lives in Bamako.

Photographer SEYDOU KEÏTA ©
Courtesy of the Maison Européenne de la Photographie.
< *Bamako, 1956.*
∨ *Bamako, 1952.*
> *Bamako, 1952.*

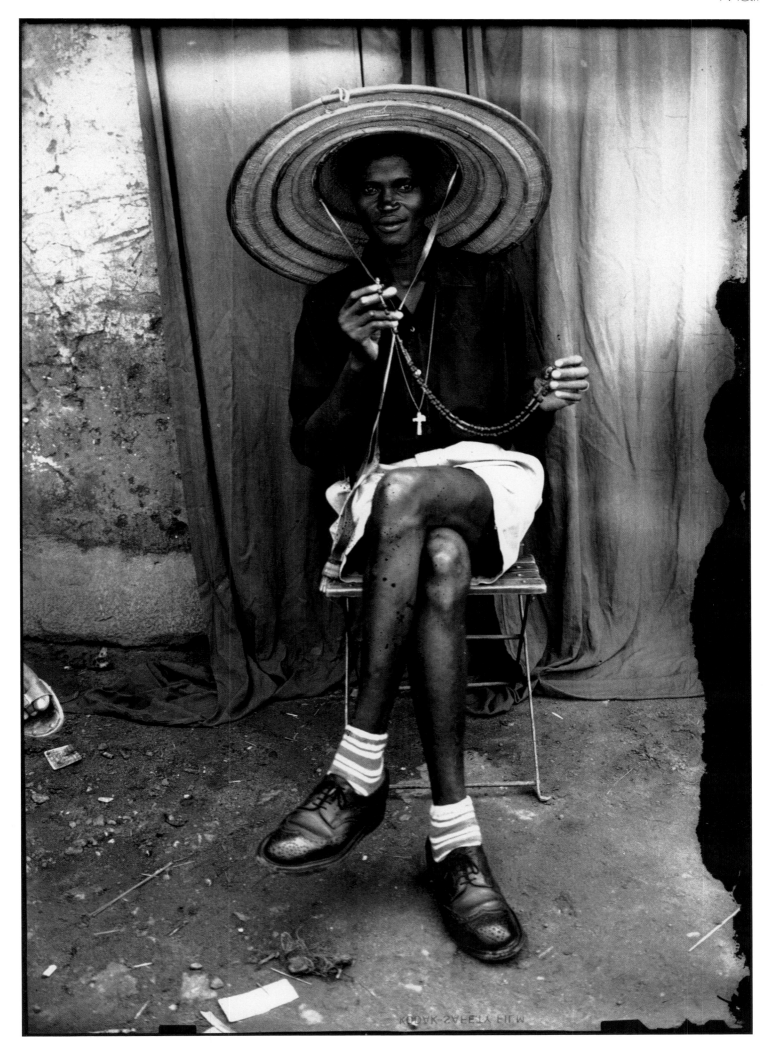

Photographer SEYDOU KEÏTA ©
Courtesy of the Maison Européenne
de la Photographie. ∧
Bamako, 1952. <
Bamako, 1949. >
Bamako, 1956. >

Photographer ABDERRAMANE SAKALY ©
Portraits, ca..1955-1965.

ABDERRAMANE SAKALY

Mali
b. Saint Louis, Senegal 1926 – d. Bamako, Mali 1988

Born in St Louis in Senegal where his Moroccan father worked as a shopkeeper, Sakaly trained with St Louis photographers, possibly Meïssa Gaye or Mix Gueye. He settled in Bamako in 1956 and opened a studio that was very fashionable in the 1960s and 1970s. Sakaly's images radiate a great sense of both poetry and friendliness. He also shot numerous reportage photographs during demonstrations and photographed the exhibits at the Mali Museum. He died in 1988. Since then, his children, Jamal, Naby and Wahal, have been trying to preserve his priceless heritage of thousands of 6 x 6 cm negatives.

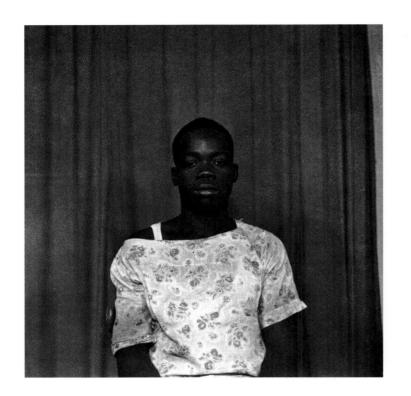

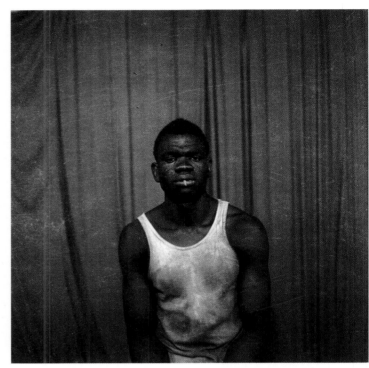

Photographer ABDERRAMANE SAKALY ©
Portraits, ca.1955-1965.

Court photographers

Richard Pankhurst & Denis Gérard

Ethiopia, an ancient country with a written history dating back almost two millennia, enjoys a unique position in African history. The Ethiopian monarchy, unlike most other polities on the continent, survived the European Scramble for Africa with its traditional political, social and other institutions largely intact. The coming of the camera to Ethiopia reflected the above politico-economic reality. Ethiopian rulers began their honeymoon with the camera by making use of foreign visiting photographers to take the pictures they desired. Later, in the 20th century, they employed the services of resident Armenians, in many cases of Ethiopian nationality. Several of the latter established studios in the Ethiopian capital, Addis Ababa.

The country, unlike most in Africa, therefore had a succession of independent rulers, who, quick to appreciate the value of photography, were among the first of their compatriots to be immortalized by the camera. Ethiopian monarchs and some of their principal chiefs were thus the subject of carefully staged photographs. Some of these reflected the European ideal of a posed portrait, with the dignitary seen beside a stone column or between two large vases. Other pictures, however, reflected Ethiopian ideas of royal etiquette, as well as symbols of power. These might be represented by a crown, ceremonial clothing, including a lion's hair headdress, firearms and, in at least one case, a small statue of the Lion of Judah. Ethiopian rulers and other potentates were generally seen in splendid royal dress, in posed portraits. In group scenes the persons depicted were almost invariably positioned to reflect what was considered the all-important hierarchy of state. Such works were reminiscent of, and probably influenced by, traditional Ethiopian paintings in which biblical and other kings, as well as holy personages and saints, were depicted with their followers and other dependants hierarchically arranged around them.

The history of Ethiopian photography also reflected the country's politico-economic condition as a technologically unsophisticated country, whose rulers were intent on modernization. Ethiopian monarchs, who were free of race- or colour-consciousness, had since medieval times made extensive use of foreigners: to import firearms and build palaces, to conduct foreign trade, and to serve as doctors and surgeons. The utilization of foreigners, until relatively recent times, seemed far easier than the training of their Ethiopian subjects in new and untried skills.

Professor Richard Pankhurst has been living in Ethiopia for 30 years and is the founder-director of the Institute of Ethiopian Studies at the University of Addis Ababa. He has devoted a substantial part of his life to the study of Ethiopian history and culture, about which he has written extensively.

Denis Gérard is a French agronomist working on rural development in the Afars region and has spent the last 24 years in Ethiopia. For him photography is a veritable passion - especially old photographs, which he sees as the purveyors of dreams.

Professor Pankhurst and Denis Gérard are joint authors of *Ethiopia Photographed: Historic Photographs of the Country and its People Taken Between 1867 and 1935* (Kegan Paul International, London and New York, 1996).

< Photographer PAUL MEJAT © 1890
*Menelik II, Emperor of Ethiopia
at his coronation.*
Courtesy of the Institute of Ethiopian
Studies (IES).
New print by Denis Gérard.

119

Prominent among the foreigners in Ethiopian government service since the early 16th century were Armenians, who were regarded as an integral part of Ethiopian Christian society. Adherents of a Monophysite Christian faith akin to that of the Ethiopians, they were often born in the country, spoke the local language, attended Ethiopian church services, married locally-born Ethiopians, and were buried in Ethiopian Christian graveyards. The status of Armenians in Ethiopian society, though taken for granted within the country itself, tended to be incomprehensible to outsiders. Matthew, an Armenian whom Empress Eleni, or Helen, of Ethiopia despatched in the early 16th century to appeal for urgently needed military assistance from the Portuguese, learnt this to his cost. On arriving in Portuguese India, and later in Portugal itself, he found himself rejected on the grounds that he was white and not black. For that reason he was regarded not as an envoy, but as an impostor. When the Portuguese, with many misgivings, eventually agreed to travel to Ethiopia with him, they were amazed, on reaching the Red Sea coast to see Ethiopians rushing into the sea to embrace him with love and affection!

The coming of the camera to Ethiopia reflected the above politico-economic reality. Ethiopian rulers began their honeymoon with the camera by making use of foreign visiting photographers to take the pictures they desired. Later, in the 20th century, they employed the services of resident Armenians, in many cases of Ethiopian nationality. Several of the latter established studios in the Ethiopian capital, Addis Ababa. Though the training of Ethiopians abroad was initiated by Emperor Menelik at the end of the 19th century, priority was given to studies other than photography, and we have a record of only one Ethiopian photographer prior to the Italian occupation of 1936-41, and he was merely an amateur.

The earliest photographic initiative in Ethiopia began outside Ethiopian control. The first known photographer to reach the country, in 1859, was Henry Aaron Stern, a British Protestant missionary of German-Jewish descent. He came to convert the Ethiopian Falashas, or Beta Esra'el, to Christianity. Keenly interested in photography, he took many shots of people and places, but was later arrested by the then ruling Ethiopian monarch, Emperor Tewodros, or Theodore, for reasons entirely unconnected with his camera. Stern's photographs are apparently no longer extant, but engravings based on them were later reproduced in his book, *Wanderings Among the Falashas* (London, 1862).

Photograph ∧
attributed to F GUILLAUME © 1906
Menelik II, Emperor of Ethiopia
and his retinue.
Courtesy of the Institute of
Ethiopian Studies (IES).
New print by Denis Gérard.

Photographer HAÏGAZ BOYADJIAN © >
Portrait of Haile Selassie,
last Emperor of Ethiopia.
Collection Dr Berhanu Abebe
New print by Denis Gérard

Photographer BOYADJIAN FAMILY ©
An Ethiopian noblewoman.
Denis Gérard collection.

The next important photographs of Ethiopia were taken by the British Royal Engineers. They were attached to a military expedition despatched by the British Government against Emperor Tewodros's mountain citadel of Maqdala, in 1867. This force was sent to punish the Ethiopian ruler, who was the country's first reforming Emperor of modern times, for his temerity in imprisoning several British officials, as well as a number of British and other European missionaries - including the aforementioned photographer, Stern. The Engineers, who were well supplied with photographic equipment of all kinds, took many shots of Maqdala, and of the route to it from the Red Sea port of Zulla. They also photographed a masenqo, or traditional fiddle, player, and reproduced a posthumous sketch of Tewodros, drawn by a British officer after the Emperor's defeat and dramatic suicide in April 1868. These pictures were later included in a large photographic album, a considerable number of copies of which were acquired by the British officers who had participated in the expedition.

Emperor Tewodros's orphaned son, Alemayehu, had meanwhile been taken to Britain by order of the British expedition commander, and was photographed in England by Julia Cameron, a well-known British woman photographer of the day.

The decades which followed witnessed the visit to Ethiopia of numerous other foreign photographers, who took a variety of shots of prominent personalities and important places and events. One of these photographers, an Italian, took the first photograph of an Ethiopian ruler: this was Emperor Yohannes IV (1872-1889), who was the second of Ethiopia's great 19th-century reforming monarchs. It was an impressive posed picture, in which the monarch was seen with his beloved son, Ras Araya Selassie.

Perhaps the next important photographer, and the first in Ethiopian government service, was a Swiss craftsman, Alfred Ilg, who, on graduating from the Zurich polytechnic, became an employee of King Menelik of Shawa in 1879. An enthusiastic photographer, he took numerous pictures with a large camera. He was also obliged, he relates, to teach his royal master the laws of optics. Menelik, the third of the country's notable 19th-century reforming rulers, was fascinated by innovations of all kinds. He is said to have been a willing pupil and a great lover of the camera. Ilg's photographs, largely unpublished, are still extant, in the possession of his family and in institutions in Switzerland. Several of them are to be seen in Willi Loepfe's study, *Alfred Ilg und die Äthiopische Eisenbahn* (Frauenfeld and Zurich, 1978).

<
UNKNOWN ITALIAN
photographer © ca. 1885
*Emperor Yohannes IV of Ethiopia
and his son Ras Araia Selassie.*
in *Chronique du Régne de
Ménélik II, Roi des rois
d'Ethiopie* by Guebre Selassie.
New print by Denis Gérard.

Other prominent personalities photographed in the 1880s included Abdullahi, the last local ruler of the independent Muslim city-state of Harar. This portrait was taken by the Austrian ethnographer Philipp Paulitschke, who reproduced it in his book, *Harar* (Leipzig, 1888). The chief later lost power to Menelik, and was replaced by the latter's cousin, Ras Mekonnen, who was soon afterwards photographed by an Italian engineer, Luigi Robecchi-Bricchetti. The Ras's picture is reproduced by the Italian in his book, *Nell'Harrar* (Milan, 1896).

Many other travellers with cameras made their appearance in Ethiopia in the last decades of the century. They included a Frenchman, JG Vanderheym, who accompanied Menelik on one of his expeditions to the south of the country. He reports, in his book *Une Expédition avec le Négous Ménélik* (Paris, 1896) that Menelik, who was by then Emperor, « begged him to come and photograph him ». Later in his memoirs Vanderheym recalls spending « a very interesting morning posing Empress Taytu (the Emperor's consort), and the princesses and ladies of the court, who had dressed in their most beautiful clothes ».

Another French traveller of photographic interest was Hugues Le Roux, who at the turn of the century took interesting pictures of the Ethiopian capital, as well as pictures of everyday Ethiopian life. He recalls, in his book *Ménélik et Nous* (Paris, 1902), that he used a French camera, a verascope Richard, which he describes as an instrument of « unique precision ». It enabled him, he says, to present the French government, French geographical societies, French chambers of commerce and, in fact, the whole of France, with a hitherto unknown image of the « real » Ethiopia.

Besides official portraits, this period witnessed the beginnings of «photographic reportage». This featured shots, for example, of Menelik watching the first steamroller working on Addis Ababa's roads, inspecting the construction of the Djibouti-Addis Ababa railway, or riding in the country's first motor car. Such photographs were to become increasingly prevalent in later reigns.

Though the principal photographers of this period were all foreigners, like those mentioned above, and many others, at least one locally-born but foreign-educated Ethiopian of this period is known to have developed a passion for photography.

123

< Photographer
HAIGAZ BOYADJIAN ©
*The court of Emperor
Haile Selassie.*
Dr Berhanu Abebe
collection.
New print by
Denis Gérard.

THE
BOYADJIANS

Bedros Boyadjian (father)
b. Dikranaguerde, Armenia
18 May 1868
d. Addis Ababa 14 May 1928

Haigaz Boyadjian (eldest son)
b. Alexandria, Egypt
24 April 1901
d. Addis Ababa 5 June 1941

Torkom (Tony) Boyadjian
(the second son)
b. Addis Ababa 1920
d. Addis Ababa 1987

Photographers
at the Ethiopian
Royal Court

Ethiopia's first professional
photographer was the
Armenian, Bedros Boyadjian,
who was nearing 40 when he
arrived in Addis Ababa in
1905. Initially part of the
entourage of an Armenian
priest, he set up as a photographer shortly after his arrival
and became one of the
Emperor Menelik's court photographers. He was succeeded in 1928 by his eldest
son, Haigaz, who photographed the Empress Zawditu.
Haigaz was in turn succeeded
by his younger brother
Torkom, known as Tony, who
became Haile Selassie's court
photographer.

He was Negadras Tesemma Eshete, who had studied in Germany in the early years of the 20th century, and was later also renowned as an intellectual, poet and wit. A biography in Amharic (the principal language of Ethiopia), which included some photographs he is believed to have taken, was long afterwards published by his son, in a monograph entitled *Semna Warqu. Tesemma Eshete* (Addis Ababa, 1985).

Despite royal enthusiasm for the camera, many of the uneducated populace were fearful of it and reluctant to be photographed. The British traveller Herbert Vivian recalls in his book, *Abyssinia* (London, 1901) that when he tried to snap a « delightful » Somali chambermaid, this «usually silent creature emitted a shrill scream, and fled». His compatriot, the ethnographer and big-game hunter, Percy Powell-Cotton, likewise states in his *Sporting Trip through Abyssinia* (London, 1902) that he aroused «a good deal of curiosity» when he tried to take photographs in Addis Ababa market. One girl, realizing that he was attempting to take her photograph, ducked and exclaimed, « By the Holy Trinity, tell me what he is doing? »

Notwithstanding the increasing prevalence of the camera in late 19th- and early 20th-century Ethiopia, it is interesting to recall that Menelik's resounding victory over the Italians at the Battle of Adwa on 1 March 1896, passed photographically unrecorded by either side. Photographs were, however, taken of the Emperor's victorious chiefs, as well as of the cannon which enabled him to achieve his historic triumph. It was due to the Adwa battle that Ethiopia withstood the European Scramble for Africa, and thereby preserved its ancient independence.

The early years of the 20th century witnessed the beginning of modernization in Ethiopia, and with it the opening up of the country to foreigners. One of those who arrived at this time, in 1904, was an Armenian photographer called Bedros Boyadjian, who became a naturalized Ethiopian and founded a dynasty of Ethiopian court photographers. He was followed, in 1909, by another Armenian, Levon Yazedjian, who was also much favoured at court, and in the following year by G Mody, an Indian from Gujarat. This period also witnessed considerable photographic activity by visiting European anthropologists, who took many photographs in a very impersonal style of various Ethiopian « racial types ».

The advent of photography was by now beginning to play a significant role in Ethiopian state-building. Hitherto a ruler might have made himself known outside his immediate vicinity by the display of his mule, horse or, more especially, his « negarit », or drum. After the coming of the camera, photographs of the monarch served a similar purpose by bringing the monarch, however distant, into public awareness.

The Boyadjians, court photographers

∧ Photographer BOYADJIAN FAMILY © ca. 1935
Portrait of Dikranuhi (Dickie) Boyadjian.
Dr Berhanu Abebe collection.
New print by Denis Gérard.

∧ Photographer BOYADJIAN FAMILY © ca. 1925
The Boyadjian family in Addis Ababa.
Dr Berhanu Abebe collection. New print by Denis Gérard.

∧ Photographer HAIGAZ BOYADJIAN © ca. 1927
Bedros Boyadjian.
Courtesy of the Armenian Community of Addis Ababa.
New print by Denis Gérard.

∧ Photographer BEDROS BOYADJIAN © ca. 1927
*Portrait of the Boyadjian children. Haigaz in the
centre, Lussentak on his right, Dikranuhi and
Torkom on his left.*
Dr Berhanu Abebe collection.
New print by Denis Gérard.

∧ *Portrait of Torkom (Tony) Boyadjian, ca. 1940*
Dr Berhanu Abebe collection. New print by Denis Gérard

∧ Photographer BEDROS BOYADJIAN © ca. 1913. *Portrait of Lussentak, younger daughter of Bedros Boyadjian.*
Dr Berhanu Abebe collection. New print by Denis Gérard.

125

Portrait photographers

∧
Photographer
BOYADJAN FAMILY ©
Ras Beru Wolde Gabriel.
Denis Gérard collection.

∧
Photographer
BOYADJIAN FAMILY ©
*Portrait of Merid Azmach
Asfawosene Haile Selassie
son of Emperor Haile Selassie,
d. January 1997.*
Dr Berhanu Abebe collection. New print by Denis Gérard.

Photography attributed to   >
BEDROS BOYADJIAN ©
*From right to left : Lidj
Iyasu, his father Ras
Mickael and Ras Hapte
Ghiorgis.*
Private Collection.

A photograph of one of Menelik's great state banquets reveals that by the time of his reign it was already customary to decorate the hall in the palace with many photographs of the sovereign and his consort, Empress Taytu. Portraits of Menelik, influenced by photography, likewise appeared on the Ethiopian national currency and postage stamps, both initiated in 1894. Menelik's portrait, and those of subsequent rulers, in one way or another also entered international consciousness, the effigy of the ruler being equated with the ethos of the country. While the advent of a ruler led to the widespread distribution of his or her photograph, this was followed by the rapid disappearance of those of his or her predecessor. The coming of photography also had a culturally important impact on Ethiopian funeral procedure. Hitherto it had been customary, during funeral processions, to display an effigy of the deceased and sometimes of his favourite steed, but in the case of persons for whom photographic portraits were available, these came to be used instead. One of the first such occasions was the funeral of Ras Mekonnen in 1906, when the priests of Addis Ababa are reported to have remained all day beside his portrait and catafalque. Half a century or so later, photographs were also placed on gravestones.

Menelik's death in 1913 after a long illness, and the succession of his young grandson, Lej Iyasu, was of no small

photographic interest. The accession was, however, characterized by a power struggle. This was intensified by the outbreak of World War I, in which the two sides, the Allied and Central powers, identified themselves with rival Ethiopian factions, thus adding fuel to the fire. Photography at this time rose to new heights of importance.

One of the most interesting early photographs of young Lej Iyasu, a particularly photogenic figure, was designed to enhance his support among the more conservative members of the society. The picture shows the child-like Iyasu wearing a lion's hair headdress, like that worn by mature warriors. No less significant is the fact his tutor, Menelik's trusted courtier Ras Tessema, who held the honorific title of Betwaddad, literally the monarch's « Beloved », is seated immediately beside him. The chief places a fatherly hand over that of his ward, thus signifying that Ethiopia's destiny is in tried, as well as youthful, hands. A painting with a not dissimilar theme was also painted at about the same time in the important church of St Mary, at Addis Alem, west

of the Ethiopian capital. Scarcely less interesting, politically, was a photograph depicting Iyasu kneeling in filial devotion beside his father, Ras Mika'el, the ruler of Wallo province. The latter nobleman has his hand on his son's head, to show his confidence in his offspring. The message is further underlined by what would seem to be Menelik's imperial crown, placed immediately behind the Ras.

Iyasu later came under bitter criticism for being seen in mosques and attending Muslim ceremonies. It was asserted that such action proved that he had abjured the Christian faith, the age-old faith of the Ethiopian monarchy, in favour of that of Islam. Widespread rumour, not confirmed by contemporary documentary evidence, claims that popular fear of the prince's apostasy was fanned by an even more politically important photograph or, as some claim, group of photographs. They supposedly depicted Iyasu dressed in Muslim costume. These pictures were allegedly not genuine, but « doctored » pictures devised by one of the country's early resident Armenian photographers, Levon Yazedjian.

<	Photographer LEVON YAZEDJIAN ©ca. 1916
*Lidj Iyasu posing in Muslim dress
in Harare with Abdulahi Ali Sadiq
and his family.*
Courtesy of Ahmed Zekaria,
Institute of Ethiopian Studies.
New print by Denis Gérard.

Sight of this work, or works, is said to have persuaded the Ethiopian Patriarch and high clergy to free the nobles from their earlier oath of loyalty to the prince. No such photograph, it should be noted, has ever been found.

The mystery surrounding the alleged fake photograph, or photographs, is compounded by the fact that an apparently genuine photograph of Iyasu, wearing a Muslim turban, exists. It was taken in Harar and shows him seated with a prominent Muslim city leader, Abdulahi Ali Sadeq, standing deferentially beside him. If this photograph is genuine, as it almost certainly is, what purpose could there have been, one may ask, in producing a « doctored » one? Was it because the photograph taken in Harar was unavailable in Addis Ababa?

Another politically significant photograph of Iyasu, taken by the said Yazedjian, was published in 1915 in the official Addis Ababa newspaper, Aimero. The picture is interesting in that it shows the prince, in Ethiopian nobleman's dress, wearing a cross - which would doubtless have done much to reassure Christian fears of Iyasu's alleged apostasy. Iyasu was, however, duly deposed in 1916 for treason against the Ethiopian Church, whereupon Menelik's daughter Zewditu was proclaimed Queen, and Ras Mekonnen's photogenic son, Teferi, became heir to the throne, soon afterwards being recognized as Regent. This resulted in a system of dual government, in

which power was divided between the two rulers, each with their own palace, court and government. Separation of power was symbolized, and vividly represented, in another politically revealing photograph in which Zewditu and Teferi are both depicted in positions of distinction, but seated quite apart from each other.

The importance of positioning in Ethiopian group photographs can likewise be seen in those of the nobility, who were often photographed with their followers and, in not a few cases, with their favourite firearm. A good example of this kind of picture is one taken by Bedros Boyadjian of an early 20th century chieftain, Dejazmach Geneme Delnessew. He is depicted in ceremonial dress, seated in the centre of the photograph, with his rifle and shield. Behind him are his warriors in military costume, all but one of them with lion's hair headdresses.

Teferi meanwhile soon emerged as the leader with responsibility for foreign affairs. Only too conscious of the propaganda value of the cameras, he was frequently photographed by visiting foreigners. In 1923 he succeeded in obtaining his country's entry into the League of Nations, and in the following year undertook an extensive and well-photographed tour of the more important European capitals, as well as Cairo and Jerusalem.

∧ Photographer
BEDROS BOYADJIAN © ca. 1911
*Dedjazmatch Geneme Diljnessaw
and his retinue.*
Rosa Terrefe collection.
New print by Denis Gérard.

State photography in Ethiopia reached new heights after Zewditu's death in 1930, when Teferi ascended the imperial throne and assumed the name Emperor Haile Selassie I. His coronation, an international media event, was widely photographed, notably by the prominent Armenian court photographer, Haigaz Boyadjian, as well as by many visiting foreign journalists and cameramen. Coronation pictures, which included portraits of the monarch and his consort, Empress Menen, group photographs of the Imperial Family, cardboard arches erected for the occasion and crowd scenes, accordingly appeared outside the country in many publications, among them *L'Illustration* and *Le Monde Illustré*, in France, *The Illustrated London News* in Britain, and the *National Geographic Magazine* in the United States.

Haile Selassie's brief prewar reign was well covered photographically by several resident Armenians, as well as by foreign journalists and other visitors from abroad. Their photographs captured the establishment by the Emperor of various new institutions. These included the country's first parliament, and modern schools and hospitals, as well as the Addis Ababa railway station, the terminal of the line to Djibouti. There were also shots of soldiers, the Emperor's bodyguard and police, all three in newly-introduced uniforms. Many such pictures appeared in Wilhelm Goldman's *Das ist Abessinien* and Ladislas Farago's *Abyssinia on the Eve*, both published in 1935, in Leipzig and London respectively.

This prewar period of development coincided with the coming to Ethiopia of a further half a dozen or so foreign photographers, for the most part Armenian, but including also one Greek, Alex Tsouklas. They included Abram Chabaz, Hrant Vararanian, and Piuzant Abouseifian, all of whom established studios in Addis Ababa's main commercial street, Ras Mekonnen Avenue.

Portrait photographers

>

Unknown photographer © 1916
Coronation of the Empress Zawditu.
Courtesy of Denis Gérard.
New print by Denis Gérard.

Several other photographers, also chiefly Armenian, also began taking cheap « instant photographs » in the capital's market area. The practice of tinting of black-and-white photographs in Addis Ababa also dates from this period.

The impending Italian fascist invasion was also photographically well documented. Photographers of this time depicted independent Ethiopia's woefully inadequate preparations to withstand the armed might of Fascist Italy, as well as patriotic young Ethiopians enrolling to defend their country's freedom and independence. No less significant was a photograph of the Emperor walking around the capital's principal place of worship, St George's Cathedral, with a rifle over his shoulder, thus visually symbolizing the fact that he would soon have to defend his country with gun in hand.

The Italians, for their part, took innumerable photographs of their vast war preparations and military build-up. They even took pictures of the poison-gas bombs they were soon to drop in Ethiopia - though these photographs, as a result of Fascist censorship, were not published at the time, and only became known 60 years later. Photographs of the effects of poison gas, as well as of the fascist bombing of Red Cross hospitals were, however, published at the time outside Italy, in JWS Macfie's *An Ethiopian Diary* (London, 1936), and subsequently in M Junod's *Warrior Without Weapons* (Geneva, 1982).

Photography was extensively used in Fascist propaganda. Italian publications of the period sought, through the camera, to depict Ethiopia as a land of barbarism, in need of Mussolini's self-proclaimed « civilizing mission ». Pornographic photography depicting naked young Ethiopian women was also produced to popularize Mussolini's African adventure among the young male population of Fascist Italy. These pictures, however, were later withdrawn when Fascist Italy developed a policy of virulent racism. Characteristic of this period was the Fascist photogravure journal *Difesa della Razza*, the front page of which on one occasion carried a reproduction of a sword separating a photograph of a Roman statue from one of a hook-nosed Jew, and a greasy and jewel-bedecked African woman of markedly negroid appearance.

During the ensuing Fascist invasion and occupation, photography was largely in the hands of the Italians, who took numerous pictures of their operations as well as of the destruction of Addis Ababa by looters, prior to their seizure of the city. After the establishment of Fascist rule, several Italian photographers established themselves in the capital. Many Italian photographic picture postcards of Ethiopia were also issued.

The Emperor had by then gone into exile in Britain, and was widely photographed there, as well as at Geneva, where he addressed the League of Nations in June 1936. His appearance at the League, the first and only one by a son of Africa, did much to enhance his status as an anti-Fascist and anti-appeasement leader, as well as a potential symbol of emergent Africa.

Fascist control of the country during the ensuing occupation, was effectively challenged in many parts of the country by the Ethiopian Patriots, who resisted the enemy throughout the occupation period. At least one Patriot, Lej (later Colonel) Tedla Mekonnen is known to have been in possession of a camera. Photographs of the Patriots were also taken by an adventurous Australian, Arnold Weinhold, who entered the country during the occupation. They were subsequently published in a *New Times and Ethiopia News* pamphlet entitled *Unconquered Ethiopia* (Woodford Green, Essex, 1940). Photographs of Fascist executions, beheadings and other atrocities taken by the invaders and found after the country's liberation, were later published in another such publication, Italy's *War Crimes in Ethiopia* (Woodford Green, Essex, 1946, reprinted Chicago, 1996).

Ethiopia's liberation in 1941 and the return of the Emperor opened a new era of progress. This was accompanied by the opening, or reopening, of many new institutions, and with this a dramatic expansion of photographic reportage, which was largely supervised by the state Ministry of Information. This period also witnessed a considerable expansion of education and the despatch of many more students for study abroad. The growth of education led to the emergence of the first truly Ethiopian court photographer, Yohannes Haile, and of his assistant, Tesfay Tekwame.

∧ Photographer BOYADJAN FAMILY ©
Ras Habata, his retinue and gun-bearer.
Denis Gérard Collection.

Numerous photographic postcards were issued by the Ethiopian Tourist Organization, and others. Images of the country gained increasing currency after Addis Ababa became the Headquarters of the United Nations Economic Commission for Africa, UNECA, and of the Organization of African Unity, OAU. Increased photographic activity was accompanied by the emergence of several modern-trained Ethiopian professional photographers. They were engaged mainly in taking portraits, partly because the political and social climate and the paucity of newspapers discouraged private involvement in photographic reportage.

One of the best-known postwar studios, Photalité, was established in the then newly-developed southern area of the city near the National Theatre by an Italian, Carlo Riegler, in 1953. This was the first place in Addis Ababa to introduce Agfacolor, Feraniacolor, and Kodacolor. He was succeeded by two other Italians, Franco Concovo in 1963, and Antocio Zusci in 1971. After the Ethiopian Revolution of 1974 the firm was taken over by the Yusuf Abdurahman family, an Ethiopian family from Harar.

Other studios of repute, which came into existence somewhat later, included Studio George, founded by an Armenian, George K Mekjan, which was replaced by Studio Jiro, run by another Armenian, Jirary K Mekjan; and two Ethiopian-owned studios, Photo Berhan and Photo Speedy.

The political importance of photography was recognized not only by the Emperor, but also by his opponents. Immediately prior to his overthrow in September 1974, the ruling military government used state television to discredit the monarch among the populace. They did this by showing Jonathan Dimbleby's film of the famine then raging in the north of the country, interspersed with scenes of court luxury. Fake photographs of the Emperor in compromising situations with white women were also sold privately at street corners.

During the last quarter of a century or so Ethiopian photography has come of age, with a veritable explosion of photographers, photographic studios, and photograph-taking.

131

Portrait photographers

The number of photographic studios, by now almost entirely Ethiopian-run, has significantly expanded, and they are often crowded with customers. Most studios are busy taking portraits, photographs of family and other occasions, and passport photographs. Some shops, however, are concerned only with developing colour films and making prints. Most studios produce colour photography, but at least two, Yohannes Haile and Photo Jiro, prefer black-and-white. Despite the advent of colour photography, several photographers still also tint photographs, and report has it that many Ethiopian women, who make little use of makeup on their faces, are not displeased to see their portraits tinted.

It has become common for Ethiopians to take photographs of weddings, baptisms, graduation and other family and social occasions. Development of photographs in Addis Ababa is cheap by world standards: a 10 x 15 cm colour print costs the equivalent of only 20 US cents. Photographers are almost always to be found at « wedding parks », where newly-marrieds celebrate with their guests, at Addis Ababa Restaurant, at the airport and at the small lion zoo. The shooting of passport photographs has become a small industry. More and more private Ethiopians possess cameras. Computer developing and printing in local studios has become widespread. There is also at least one camera-repair shop near the Old Post Office. Founded around 1940 by Varush Bagdessarian, a member of a technically-minded Armenian family, it has been run since 1981 by Magher Hassen Keval, an Indian, whose family has lived in Ethiopia for four generations.

Photographic studios are to be found also in most regional capitals, among them the railway town of Dire Dawa. The first studio there was reputedly established by the Armenian, Abram Chabaz, and later run by an Indian, Omar Ibrahim Keval. Though still far less numerous than painters, whose numbers have been swollen by the existence of a School of Fine Arts, several professional Ethiopian photographers have emerged. Their work for the most part tends to be formal, and is only on rare occasions highly imaginative. Current photographers, in addition to Yohannes Haile, include Bezabih Abitew, who specialized in sports photographs, Eyobel Zerfa, Negash Wolde Amanuel, Kebede Bogale, Solomon Bekele, Endreas Getachew Kassaye, Khalil A Khalef, and Getachew Erko, who began his career as a cameraman. At least three photographers are also to be found among the Ethiopian diaspora: Shimeles Desta, a former employee of the Ministry of Information in England, and Balcha, Tesfaye, Andargé, and Gediyon Kifle, in the United States. Several of the above photographers have gained, or are gaining, a national and international reputation.

Ethiopia's remarkable beauty and that of its inhabitants is, through photography, being increasingly recognized throughout the world.

Richard Pankhurst & Denis Gérard

Bibliography:

Brunetta, GP and Gili, JA. 1990. *L'ora d'Africa del Cinema Italiano* (Rovereto).

Goglia, L. 1985. *Storia Fotografica dell'Impero Fascista 1935-41* (Rome and Bari).

Hirsch, B and Perret, R. 1989 *Ethiopie Année 30* (Paris).

Pankhurst, R. 1976. *The Genesis of Photography in Ethiopia and the Horn of Africa* in The British Journal of Photography. Nos. 41-4.

Pankhurst, R. 1992. *The Political Image: The Impact of the Camera in an Ancient Independent African State*, in E Edwards, Anthropology and Photography 1860-1920. Connecticut and London: New Haven.

Pankhurst, R and Gérard, D. 1996. *Ethiopia Photographed: Historic Photographs of the Country and its People taken between 1867 and 1935* (London).

Triulzi, A. 1989. *L'Africa dall'Immaginario alle immagini* (Turin).

Triulzi, A. 1995. *Fotografia e Storia dell'Africa* (Naples).

UNKNOWN photographer © /\
Ethiopian patriots during the Italian occupation. (They had taken an oath not to cut their hair.)
Courtesy of Richard Pankhurst.
New print by Denis Gérard.

Photographer BOYADJAN FAMILY © >
Ethiopian nobleman dressed as a warrior.
Denis Gérard Collection.

Tinted portrait photography in Addis Ababa

Guy Hersant

One characteristic of Ethiopian photography is the retouching of portraits, a practice introduced by Armenian immigrants. The facial features are highlighted with ink, to which are added areas of flat tint and matching backgrounds. Even today these portraits are used as models by street photographers working in colour.

Armenians have lived in Ethiopia since the 14th century. Their skills have always been appreciated by Ethiopia's long line of hereditary rulers, while their influence has marked many aspects of the country's civilization, including its religious life, literature and architecture. During the 19th century, Armenians were instrumental in the progressive modernization of Ethiopia, where they excelled in fields such as mechanical engineering, printing and photography. Emperor Menelik II employed the Armenian Boyadjian as his official court photographer. His son, following in his father's footsteps, became one of Haile Selassie's portraitists.

After Haile Selassie's return to Ethiopia from exile in Great Britain in 1941, a new influx of Armenian immigrants arrived in Addis Ababa.[1] Among them were professional photographers who were directly employed by the Emperor or occupied administrative positions in his government. Others opened studios situated on the capital's main commercial thoroughfares. There were also a few Italian photographers; the most active Italian-owned studio was located across the street from the municipal theatre.[2]

Armenian photographers were known for their skill in retouching and hand-colouring portraits and were equipped with the latest products and equipment. They also trained their Ethiopian employees in retouching techniques and film development. In time, Ethiopians established their own studios in many of the popular quarters of Addis Ababa and the city centre, while others acquired the studios of their former employers who had left the country during the Armenian exodus of 1974.

Guy Hersant was born in France. After seven months in Bamako as an assistant in Michel Thuillier's La Croix du Sud studio and an encounter with Malick Sidibé, he began his career as a professional photographer. In 1993 his book, *L'Africaine*, was published by Éditions Filigranes. He is also the author of a documentary film on photography in Guinea.

1. In the early 1970s there were approximately 1 500 Armenians living in Addis Ababa. The rise to power of Derg in 1974 provoked a massive exodus of this community. Today, the entire Armenian population of Ethiopia is probably no more than 100 individuals.

2. Mussolini's troops occupied Ethiopia from 1936 to 1940 and forced Haile Selassie into exile in Great Britain. After their departure, certain Italians chose to remain in the country.

<

Photographer BOYADJIAN FAMILY ©
Tinted photograph from the mid-20th century. The retouched portrait.
Dr Berhanu Abebe collection.

Portrait photographers

Under the governments of Derg and the dictator Mengistu and until 1991, the country's serious economic and political problems had an adverse effect on the business activity of the studios. The economic crisis limited the availability of modern colour negative film and, in certain cases, favoured the survival of traditional methods of colouring portraits by hand.

In the last four or five years, following a wave of liberalization, itinerant photographers have appeared in the streets of Ethiopia's principal cities. Although generally untrained and equipped with mediocre cameras, they occasionally produce excellent results. The poses, composition and treatment of colour in their portraits are similar to those displayed in the windows of studios, which are in fact their sole source of stylistic reference.

Once established in their own studios, Ethiopian photographers rapidly transformed the techniques that they had learned from their former Armenian employers and adapted them to their own tastes. The often sombre tones favoured by the Armenians gave way to bright unmixed colours applied to clothing and backgrounds. The quality of retouching was less subtle, while facial expressions were accentuated. It was also difficult to procure modern photographic equipment and materials. Negatives rarely exceeded 6 x 6 cm, which made both full-length poses and retouching difficult. The size of the finished portraits was generally no more than 18 x 24 cm.

Today, the majority of Addis Ababa studios offer portraits in black-and-white or colour, with the latter dominating the market. A few studios work exclusively in black-and-white, and in the more modest quarters, some still carry on the tradition of hand-coloured portraits.

RETOUCHED NEGATIVES

The retouching techniques practised by most Ethiopian studios consists of using a fine lead pencil to shade in unwanted elements on the emulsion of a negative treated with linseed oil. Using a magnifying glass, the retoucher delicately fills in clear areas on the negative which would otherwise appear as unwanted wrinkles, scars or other physical defects.

RETOUCHED PHOTOGRAPHS

Retouched negatives are generally printed on matte paper. Finished prints are also sometimes retouched by using a razor to remove a portion of the surface emulsion to correct for shadows or residual imperfections in the original negative. Lighter portions of the print are modified by using a pencil to gradually shade the area until it merges with a darker section. When skilfully practised, the technique permits the harmonization of contrasting light and dark tones and creates a striking sculptured effect on the subject's features.

HAND-COLOURED PORTRAITS

Hand-coloured portraits are produced by using a fine brush to apply transparent inks to a slightly underexposed black-and-white print, while crayons are used for larger facial areas and backgrounds. Photographs coloured in this manner are normally sprayed with a fine layer of gum arabic, which dries into a transparent protective coating. The technique was nevertheless rarely employed by Armenian photographers, and is never encountered in the work of their Ethiopian successors.

Guy Hersant, October 1996

NEGASH WOLDE AMANUEL

ETHIOPIA
b. Wollo, Ethiopia 1931.
– d. Addis Ababa 1988

Negash Wolde Amanuel was born in Wollo, Ethiopia, in 1931. After studying at the New York School of Photography, he began working for the Ethiopian Tourist Commission in the late 1960s. He later trained as an advertising photographer in Hamburg. Returning to Ethiopia, and despite a political climate hardly favourable to cultural activities, he opened his own studio and worked there until his death in 1988.

Photographer NEGASH WOLDE AMANUEL ©   >
Old Ethiopian man.

PHOTO JIRO

Ethiopia

Facing the former post office in the Piazza neighbourhood, the Jiro Photo Studio belongs to the older generation of establishments opened by Armenians after Haile Selassie's return from exile. One of them, Georges, founded and ran this studio from 1945 to 1955, before selling it to another Armenian, Jirary K. Mekjan (Jiro), whose name today's establishment still bears. Georges and his successor were remarkable photographers, displaying complete mastery of all the techniques used by the great European portraitists of the time. Addis Ababa notables and members of the bourgeoisie thronged to a studio whose clientele also included rich businessmen passing through the capital. In 1974, after handing on the business to Almaz Sharow, who had been working with him for him six years, Jiro packed his bags for Canada, where he still lives. Almaz Sharow continues to run the Jiro Studio, now almost exclusively limited to producing black-and-white identity shots.

Photographer
JIRAYER K. MEJAN © ca. 1990
Tinted photographs.
Photo Jiro collection, Addis Ababa.

PHOTO ADDIS ZEMEN

Ethiopia

Photographer
ATO KEBEDE GUEBRE MARIAM ©
Ethiopian Abouna (priest).
Young Lady from the North.
Photo Addis Zemen Collection, Addis Ababa

Portraits and scenery

Tobias Wendl

The British policy of « Indirect Rule » enabled Africans in the territories colonized by Great Britain to learn European techniques earlier than others, so that the Ghanaians were familiar with photography from the turn of the century. The arrival of the box camera in the 1920s speeded up the democratization of photographic techniques, and the Ghanaians adopted photography for themselves - initially by touching up photos, then through photo-montage and finally in the form of painted scenery that played a part in Ghanaian social life, notably thanks to the room divider, which can be seen as scenery in praise of consumer society. All these photos operated as codes in a society in which the image one projected was very important.

*If you don't photograph yourself
and you die, you have died forever.
Nobody will remember you, nobody will know you!*

Although it is difficult to date the origins of photography in Ghana precisely, it was nevertheless practised here earlier than in neighbouring countries, particularly the former French colonies of sub-Saharan Africa. This precocity can be ascribed to the British colonial doctrine of Indirect Rule, which encouraged the training of local support staff (including photographers) to assist the British colonial and commercial administrations. The specific characteristics of the Gold Coast, with its rich natural resources and booming local economies, also played an important role in the early development of photography. Nowhere else in Africa was there as much business activity as on the appropriately-named Shopping Street, Accra's main commercial thoroughfare. Well-established maritime trade routes connected Freetown and Luanda with other ports along the Gold Coast, which early took on a distinctly cosmopolitan atmosphere. In the 1850s, the first photographers to arrive in Ghana were Europeans equipped with daguerreotype cameras. This initial wave of pioneers later included a scattering of local African and African-American photographers whose names and precise origins remain unknown.

*Joseph K. Davies a studio
photographer of Saltpond[1], Ghana*

Tobias Wendl, anthropologist and film maker, teaches at the African Studies department at Munich University. He has been studying Ghanaian photographers for many years. He and Nancy du Plessis made the documentary *Future Remembrance - Photography and Image Arts in Ghana* (1998). He was also co-commissioner, with Heike Behrend, of the exhibition, *Snap me One! Studio Photographers in Africa* (Munich 1998) and co-wrote the book of the same name, published by Prestel.

1. Tobias Wendl and Nancy du Plessis. 1997. *Future Remembrance. Photography and Image Arts in Ghana.*

< Photographer ERICK P LUTTERODT ©
*Portrait of a Methodist priest,
Accra, ca 1910.*

Portrait photographers

After disembarking from steamships in the principal ports along the coast, they made their presence known through advertisements in the local newspapers. Working in temporary studios for the period of their stay (usually a few weeks), they displayed examples of the « new art of photography » to the astonished inhabitants before having them sit for their own portraits.[2]

EARLY URBAN STUDIO PHOTOGRAPHY, 1880-1940

The invention of photosensitive glass-plates, which replaced the earlier and complicated colloidal technique, had a profound impact on the photographic activity of the period. A new era began, marked by the opening of the first permanent photographic studios in the cities of Africa's principal commercial ports. Many of these early photographers were of mixed origin, often the offspring of a European father and an African mother. As products of two distinctly different cultures, they seemed destined to practise a technique invented in one culture, within the geographical context of the other. Among the best known were N Walwin Holm and Gerhardt Lutterodt, whose respective grandfathers were English and German. The lives of both men were marked by an extreme mobility, as well as a profound personal involvement in Gold Coast society. Holm opened a studio in Accra in 1883, and in 1897 became the first African member of the British Royal Photographic Society. After spending seven years in England, he returned to Africa and practised law in Lagos. Lutterodt, who had probably purchased his first camera on a visit to Germany, began his career as an itinerant photographer between Freetown and Duala in the 1870s. After having trained his nephew, Freddy Lutterodt (1871-1937), and his son, Erick (1884-1959), he retired to a plantation which he had acquired in Fernando Po. The two young men pursued their photographic careers in Accra: Freddy opened his Duala Studio in 1889, followed by Erick's Accra Studio in 1904. Both studios, located near Accra's main post office, rapidly became important centres of early urban photography[3]. Nearly all of the « third generation » of Ghanaian photographers trained with one or the other of these two men, including Bright Davies, Dam Darko, Harry Dodo and Alex Acolatse, who opened a studio in Lomé in 1900.[4]

Unfortunately, few examples of late 19th-century glass-plate photography exist today, the majority having been destroyed by the effects of humidity on the fragile layer of silver bromide, or simply discarded when the early studios closed in the late 1940s and early 1950s. Nevertheless, some of the early photographs taken by Freddy Lutterodt and JAC Holm are reproduced in Allister Macmillan's The Red Book of West Africa, published in 1920.

Other examples can be found in family albums dating from the period, in picture-postcards and in the framed portraits that still adorn the homes of the wealthy in Accra, Cape Coast or Sekondi.

During the early colonial period, having one's photographic portrait taken was an important event reserved for members of the privileged classes. The style of these portraits was rigid and distinctly Victorian, for in addition to the European artistic tradition governing portraits in general, the photographic techniques of the period required the subject to maintain the same position for several minutes. The images also mirrored a rigid social order in which the subject's social position was infinitely more visible than his or her personality. The poses, difficult to maintain and manifestly uncomfortable, were further complicated by uniforms and ceremonial attire often worn by the subjects. One of the unstated purposes of these portraits was to provide visible proof of often newly-acquired wealth and social standing. According to Gisèle Freund,[5] they were invested with the all the codes and traditions governing self-representation during the period of British colonial rule.

Prior to World War I, a handful of African photographers were established in the principal cities of the Gold Coast. Others would later open studios further inland in mining centres such as Aboso, Tarkwa and Obuasi and the newly-prosperous cocoa-producing regions of Kumasi and Koforidua. Their cameras were generally European or Japanese models using glass-plate technology and often lacking automatic shutters. The photographs were taken by removing the camera's lens-cap and exposing a photosensitive glass plate (usually a « full plate » of 18 x 24 cm and occasionally a « half-plate » format of 13 x 18 cm). After being developed, the image was often retouched by hand. Prior to electrification in the 1920s, prints were obtained by exposing a sheet of photosensitive paper to either natural or candle light.

More than anything else during this period, a photographer's reputation was based on his retouching techniques. As portrait photography became more popular, retouching developed into a system of precise aesthetic conventions that governed the representation of each social class.

THE AESTHETICS OF RETOUCHING

A close examination of the manner in which photographic negatives were retouched during the first two decades of this century reveals a coherent system of aesthetic imperatives common to the period. The techniques, which are still practised today, were first developed in Europe.

James K. Bruce-Vanderpuye

Ghana
b. Accra, Ghana 1901 – d. Accra 1989

James Bruce-Vanderpuye opened the Deo Gratias Studio in 1922 in the Jamestown quarter of Accra and began photographing class reunions, marriages, funerals, and official events. During the period of civil unrest in 1949, he photographed scenes of police brutality in Accra. Later in his career, Vanderpuye shot advertising photographs for oil companies like Shell and Mobil, and worked on advertising campaigns for a number of other European firms. Given the lack of organization of his photographic archives, examples of his work during this period are unfortunately rare. Other important but unpublished photographs include a series of portraits of the « Big Six » - the six national leaders who led Ghana to its independence.

Photographer FAK AWORTWI © >
An Ayefor (an initiate who represents the ideal of female beauty) and her Abawa (assistant), ca. 1950.

Photographer
JAMES K BRUCE-VANDERPUYE © V
Wedding in Accra, ca. 1955-1960.

2. A typical example was the *Accra Herald*, founded by Charles Bannerma. See also: *A Summary History of the Ghana Press, 1822-1960*. Ghana Information Service, Accra.

3. The two cousins started out as itinerant photographers. On several occasions between 1909 and 1913, Erick was officially honoured for his work in the Cameroon by the German colonial governors, Hernicke and Jeager. Freddy worked as the official photographer to the British governor during the latter's voyage through Togo and the Ashanti region in 1919-20.

4. Philippe David's. 1993. *Hommage à un des Premiers Photographes Togolais: Alex A Acolatse, 1880-1975*. Lomé, Éditions Haho.

5. In *Photographie und Gesellschaft*, 1976.

Portrait photographers

As an even earlier influence than pose, composition or painted backgrounds, retouching determined the specifically « African » quality of these images. In Ghana, retouched skin became magically lighter; wrinkles were erased and disappeared. The ideal portrait was characterized by a harmonious progression from shadow to light. After being skilfully retouched, the subject's features were smoothed and his or her specific personality disappeared behind a conventional mask of idealized features and expressions.

The practice of lightening the subject's eyes (particularly around the iris) is also specifically African. « Whiteness » of the eyes was seen as a sign of health and intelligence. At the other extreme, bloodshot eyes were associated with sorcery and evil. Retouched faces appeared more relaxed, rounder and smooth-featured: in short, youthful and appealing. As in the plastic arts at the time, all traces of age or ill-health were banished.[6] Even necks, arms and shoulders were embellished; prominent collarbones, suggestive of hunger and poverty, were retouched, as were the contours of veins on bare arms. The subject's neck was often enhanced with folds of fat, an evidence of wealth and beauty; the same particularity - known in Anglo-Ghanaian as « wrabbles » - was also employed in the plastic arts. The retouching of ritually-inflicted scars was essentially a question of the personal choice of both the photographer and his subject. Although some photographers considered them as primitive throwbacks to the tribalism of the northern regions, others left them in the finished portrait.

SEKONDI AND THE « NIGERIAN CONNECTION »

After Accra, designated by the English in 1876 as the seat of their colonial government, the Cape Coast port town of Sekondi played the second-most important role in the history of photography in Ghana. The birthplace of « High Life » music, a centre of the latest fashions and fads, the first electrified city of Ghana and a railroad hub between Kumasi and the mining towns of the interior, Sekondi long had the reputation of being the most cosmopolitan city of the Gold Coast. Photographers such as WC Enchill, Joseph E Ansa, J Fritz Plange and Ben Adetundji had studios in Sekondi. Others, such as FAK Awortwi, had either come there from Nigeria or were the offspring of Nigerian immigrants to Ghana. This oft-recurring connection to Nigeria was no accident: the colonial administration considered Lagos to be an integral part of the Gold Coast until 1866. It also explains the origin of the tradition of painted backgrounds in Ghanaian photography.

The celebrated photographer Steven Abiodu Thomas (ca.1902-1989) was the undisputed master of the painted photographic studio background. The son of a Ghanaian mother and a Liberian father, Thomas began as a photographer's assistant in Lagos. He later moved to Ghana and became, with Alex Osei (ca.1905-1985) and Simon de Venos-Quaye, one of Sekondi's most popular photographers. Inspired by the studio backgrounds that appeared in the photographic catalogues distributed by English firms (a voluminous correspondence with one of them, Pemberton Brothers of Blackpool, was discovered among his papers after his death), Thomas began faithfully copying them. He would later replace certain details and introduce others, in keeping with local tastes. The backgrounds were so successful that photographers from Sierra Leone, Liberia, the Ivory Coast and Upper Volta (Burkina Faso) travelled to Sekondi to purchase them directly from Tommy's Paramount Studio. More than anyone else, Thomas was instrumental in creating the distinctive stylistic unity of studio backgrounds in West Africa, while also paving the way for the specifically « African » qualities of the photographs themselves.

THE BOX CAMERA AND THE DEMOCRATIZATION OF THE IMAGE

In the 1920s, a large, wooden device began to appear on the streets of Ghana's cities and villages. Officially known as the box camera, it was also diversely referred to as the « Gold Coast Box » and the « Wait and Get » camera. The originality of the box camera was that it incorporated its own system for developing and printing film. After taking a picture, the photographer could develop, retouch and print the negative by means of a miniature laboratory installed within the camera itself. The origin of what at the time was considered a simple and efficient process for producing « instant » photographs is unknown, but variations of the basic theme appeared in Europe, India, South America and North Africa. In Ghana, a new and popular fashion was born: people of modest means could have on-the-spot portraits taken by an itinerant photographer. It was the first step in the democratization of the photographic portrait, which until then had been reserved for the upper classes. Yaw Nkrabeah, a Kumasi manufacturer of box cameras, was also a seasonal itinerant photographer. From 1938 to 1965, he regularly travelled through West Africa, photographing people and selling his cameras. It was a profitable activity, particularly in the French colonies, where identity photographs were increasingly demanded by the local authorities.

PHILIP KWAME APAGYA

Ghana
b. Sekondi, Ghana 1958
– lives in Ghana

After training in his father's studio, he opened Normale, his own studio in Shama, in 1982. Following the colour revolution in the late 1980s, he worked as a travelling photographer for a while in the Sassandra region. He also studied photojournalism at the Ghana Institute of Journalism in Accra. In early 1990 he started creating fantastic painted backdrops that revolutionized studio photography.

Photographer >
PHILIP KWAME APAGYA [copyright symbol]
Decorative backdrop representing
Accra International Airport, ca. 1996.

6. Jean Borgatt. 1990.
Likeness and Beyond.

146

JAMES K BRUCE-VANDERPUYE AND THE EMERGENCE OF PHOTOJOURNALISM

The number of studio and itinerant photographers in Ghana steadily increased until the end of World War II. During the same period, smaller and more technologically-advanced cameras became available along with standardized pre-packaged rolls of film. The 1940s were also marked by the birth of nationalism. Kwame Nkrumah and Joseph Danquah launched the movement for national independence in 1947, following the United Gold Coast Convention in Saltpond.

James Bruce-Vanderpuye (1901-1989) was one of the photographers who documented many of the major events of the period. In 1922, he opened the Deo Gratias Studio in the Jamestown quarter of Accra and began photographing class reunions, marriages, funerals, and official events. When not in his studio, he often took to the streets with his camera. During the period of civil unrest in 1949, he photographed scenes of police brutality in Accra, in which Cornelius Adjetey and two other demonstrators died. More than simple images of the period, Bruce-Vanderpuye's photographs were also stylistically innovative. Spontaneous, unposed and dynamic, they captured the instant in much the same manner as American news photographs in the 1940s. Later in his career, Vanderpuye shot advertising photographs for oil companies like Shell and Mobil, and worked on advertising campaigns for a number of other European firms. Given the lack of organization of his photographic archives, examples of his work during this period are unfortunately rare. Other important but unpublished photographs include a series of portraits of the « Big Six » - the six national leaders who led Ghana to its independence.

Vanderpuye considered himself more of a studio photographer than a photojournalist. When the South African magazine Drum published a special edition on Ghana, he declined to submit any of his work. His colleague Ghana Christian Gbagbo was commissioned to photograph the conference of the Pan-African Union which took place in the capital, as well as a photo-documentary on Accra's young rock-and-rollers, entitled Tokyo Joes and Teddy Boys. The images that resulted are considered to be classics of photojournalism.

THE GOLDEN AGE OF STUDIO PHOTOGRAPHY (1950-1980)

The period from 1880 to the 1940s represents the initial phase of photography in Ghana, in which most of the work took place in studios. The next phase, from 1950 to 1980, can be said to be the golden age of black-and-white photography.

In 1957, Ghana was the first African country to gain its independence. More and more cities were connected to the national electricity grid, and the economy leapt forward thanks to the export of cocoa. Signs of new progress and prosperity began appearing: an improved road system, increasing numbers of private automobiles and the construction of modern buildings.

Portrait photographers

Segor, Rolleiflex and Yashika cameras were readily available on the market, as well as reasonably-priced enlargers. The tastes of the public also began to change. People no longer wanted just identity photographs or ordinary portraits, but also what came to be called « fun pictures » - images which were taken simply for the pleasure of being photographed. People went to studios more often, both individually and in groups, for souvenir photographs. They became increasingly aware of the value of photography as a means of capturing special moments in their lives - moments which could be re-experienced in images. Even the names of some studios - such as Mma Mhwe Nde (Don't just think about today) - expressed the concept of the photo-souvenir. At least one studio - and in some cases, many - could be found in every town of southern Ghana. Despite the competition there was enough work for everyone and profits remained at an acceptable level. Given the demand, some photographers expanded their activities through partnerships or took on new assistants and trainees. Many studio-owners became wealthy in the years between 1950 and 1970: even today, their luxurious automobiles and villas testify to the profitability of the profession during this period.

NEW MODES OF SELF-REPRESENTATION

As photography progressively became an integral part of daily life and social identity, photographers were increasingly called upon to immortalize celebrations, ceremonies and important events. Enlarged and framed under glass, portraits hung like icons in living-rooms, celebrating the impossible ideal of the picture-perfect family. Although stylistically similar to advertising posters, they rapidly became objects of veneration, replacing the traditional clay statuettes used in ancestor-worship.

Photo-albums became veritable illustrated biographies, offering a reassuring image of their owners through the multiplication of their idealized likenesses. The photo-album also gave rise to a new ritual: it was presented to first-time visitors to the home, as if to symbolically introduce them into the family circle. This phenomenon perfectly illustrates the importance of the role played by the photographic image in a culture where the ritualized representation of the individual was an integral part - and art - of daily life.[7]

Still another practice in the ritual of self-representation would later emerge: the exchange of personal portraits. Individuals began giving (or sending) photographs of themselves as a means of creating their symbolic double. The photographic portrait began to take on a life and significance of its own, serving as tangible proof of friendship, love, one's own modernity and social status. The exchange was governed by a subtle system of rules based on notions of proximity and distance.

The farther away a person was, the greater was the need to send him or her a photograph. Inversely, a lesser distance reduced the need for sending a image of oneself. If the relationship between two individuals was of a conflictual nature or characterized by widely different social status, photographs were not exchanged - a precautionary gesture based on the fear of their providing a support for malefic rituals.

Conversely, the unexpected encounter between two old friends often resulted in a visit to the photographer to immortalize the event. The return to health after an illness was commemorated by a photograph of the person surrounded by fresh flowers. An individual suffering from psychological distress would be photographed in the hope of exorcising his or her problem to the point of being liberated from it permanently; it would not be misplaced to qualify this practice as a veritable form of « photo-therapy ».

THE SYMBOLIC LANGUAGE OF GESTURES

An entire system of codified photographic gestures thus emerged, whose significance could easily be interpreted by anyone familiar with their symbolic meaning. For example, a man photographed raising his forearm in the presence of a woman signifies « she is my lover! ». Other gestures allude to adages and proverbs: a hand extended upward signifies « Gye Nyame, except God » (God alone is untouched by all that we may do or say). Pointing a finger towards one's eye means that the person is aware - or has personally witnessed - a specific event or incident. In another example, in this case a photograph taken by Philip Kwame Apagya in 1996, a woman with several children at her feet is gazing upward toward the heavens. For the initiated viewer of the scene, the meaning is clear: the woman is expressing both the passage of time, and with its passing, her desire for additional children.

THE LANGUAGE OF TEXTILES

In Ghana, photographers often worked hand-in-hand with local tailors. Both activities were based on appearance, and both photographers and tailors were experts in the creation of the self-image.[8] For the Ghanaian photographer as much as for his client, smartly-styled clothing was an essential element for a successful photo. It was not uncommon to find photographic studios and tailor shops facing each other on the same street or even located in the same building. Many tailors also conducted second professions as photographers, particularly during holiday periods, when the demand for photo-souvenirs was strong.[8] Beyond the importance of clothing in photography, there was also the phenomenon of commemorative textiles. In Ghana, as in other West African countries, special events were often associated with specially-designed textiles.

Photographer >
PHILIP KWAME APAGYA ©
Decorative backdrop representing Manhattan, Shama, ca. 1995.

7. Jean-François Werne. 1993. *La Photographie de famille en Afrique de l'Ouest.*

8. In this context, it is interesting to note the similarities between advertising illustrations for tailor-hairdressers and photographers in West Africa.

Portrait photographers

Every year, a great number of such textiles were created in association with religious, civil or institutional celebrations and anniversaries. The fabrics were printed with designs and texts expressive of a common bond to a specific social context. Even today, the association of textiles and text is an essential characteristic of Ghana's extremely ritualized funeral ceremonies.[9] Here, it is less a question of a specific « uniform », than the uniformity of expression: clothing cut from the same specially-printed cloth, bearing the same text and addressing a specific event: the disappearance of an individual from the community. The chaos and loss represented by death is exorcized by the funeral ceremony, which in turn is immortalized - preserved in the collective memory - by a photograph.

Depending on the ceremony or event, clothing and textiles can also express other commonly-shared sentiments or observations pertaining to daily life, ranging from « A mighty tree has fallen » to « Only parents know what their children will eat in the evening ». The bonds between husbands and wives (or mothers and children) are symbolically expressed by clothing made of the same fabrics.

The photographer Francis Honny was a master in the art of the symbolic language of textiles and clothing. In one of his photographs of a couple, their clothing contains silent commentaries which, although symbolic, are as obvious as photo-captions. The man's outfit is tailored in a fabric known as « Kotoka Pencil », in reference to General Kotoka, the political leader who seized power from Kwame Nkrumah in 1966. The patterns of the woman's skirt refer to a somewhat fatalistic local proverb, namely, « If matrimony was like a groundnut, we would have opened it up to see what it was like before getting married ».

Many of the portraits taken during the golden age of black-and-white photography contain similar sub-texts and symbolic allusions carried by clothing deliberately chosen for that purpose, but whose meaning was accessible only to those familiar with the proverbs or specific social contexts to which it alluded. Less often, but also based on the same principle of symbolic or allegorical commentary, women were photographed in special hairstyles.

The archives of Ghanaian photographers contain many such examples of image-based metaphor and symbolism. Photography integrated this hidden language, so characteristic of Ghana and the rest of West Africa, which manifested itself in textiles, hairstyles, the position of the hands, the arrangement of clothing and a multitude of other details.

THE PHOTOGRAPHER AS KING-MAKER

The photographic studios of Ghana were often equipped with their own dressing-rooms, wardrobe collection and clothing accessories. If neck-ties and jackets were staple items, there were frequently other more unusual accessories, such as traditional Kente-cloth scarves, ceremonial sandals of the type worn by tribal chiefs, hats, watches, umbrellas and even swords. Alfred Six, a photographer who studied at the New York Institute of Photography before opening his own studio in Kumasi, describes himself as a « king-maker ». Six possesses all the accessories necessary for transforming ordinary citizens into traditional chiefs or kings, and women into *ohemmaa* (queen-mothers). For the Ashanti, the period between the death of the queen mother and the arrival of her successor is marked by a frenzy of « photo-wannabes »: women of all ages and social condition have their portraits taken in the traditional royal attire of an Ashanti queen. Observing this phenomenon, astute young photographers such as Philip Kwame Apagya have equipped their studios with the appropriate backgrounds, including the traditional royal umbrella of the Ashanti kings. Such personal metamorphoses are typical of Ghanaian photography today, and were probably even more prevalent in earlier years. They reflect the desires and fantasies of the inner self, and offer a temporary escape from the reality of lesser destinies and social conditions. Beneath a surface whose apparent realism belies the presence of metaphor and the yearnings of the popular imagination, is the manipulation of the self-image. In Ghana, photography is not the expression of reality. Unlike European photography, it does not attempt to reveal or highlight social realities but on the contrary, transposes them to another, more imaginary and abstract, level.

NEGATIVES, GHOSTS AND PORTRAITS OF THE DEAD

In Africa, photographers initially encountered strong resistance to their work, owing to a commonly-held belief that being photographed could lead to losing one's soul or being harmed through black magic. An early expression for the camera was « the machine that traps shadows »; negatives were referred to as *saman*, or « ghosts of the dead ». Using light and film, the camera « captured » the person and produced his or her photographic double. The negative made invisible things visible, revealing what appeared to be the subject's « ghost » in an allusion to - and prefiguration of - his own death. Even today, this underlying association with mortality discourages many older people from being photographed.

Photographer >
PHILIP KWAME APAGYA ©
Decorative backdrop of a « room divider », Shama, ca. 1996-97.

9. See Kwame Arbin's *The Economic Implications of Transformations in Akan Funeral Rites in Africa* 64/3, 1994.

10. James Van Der Zee. 1978. *Harlem Book of the Dead.* Also see Jay Ruby's study of the social history of post-mortem photography. 1995. *Secure the Shadow. Death and Photography in America.*

Similarly, pregnant women avoid the camera - even going to the extreme of categorically refusing simple identity photographs. To do otherwise would be tantamount to running the risk of exposing both the mother and her unborn child to any number of potential dangers. Photographers also put themselves in danger when taking a memorial picture of a person on his or her deathbed, or during a funeral. The dead person's ghost is thought to be hovering about the corpse - and if provoked, capable of violently turning against the « aggressor ». For the photographer, the risks run from being blinded to the destruction of the negative; it is for this reason that they implore protection by means of ritualized libations and offerings to the spirit of the dead. In Ghana, the widespread custom of arranging the corpse upon a sumptuously-decorated funeral bier - generally rented for the occasion - is a Victorian heritage dating from the British colonial period. In its current form, the practice has undergone certain modifications: the decorative elements of the bier now include photographs of important moments in the deceased person's life. The corpse's clothing is changed several times during the ceremony, further emphasizing the impression of a rite of passage.

The portrait of the family and friends in mourning and grouped around the funeral bier is always the most dramatic moment of the ceremony. The sheer number of these images in photographic archives attests to their widespread use both as a substitute for and as a souvenir of the deceased. They also serve as visible proof that the funeral service has been duly carried out. This Victorian custom of funerary portraiture - like many other Ghanaian practices and traditions - can also be observed in photographs taken in Harlem by James Van Der Zee.[10]

THE MAGIC OF PHOTO-MONTAGE

Photo-montage was another technique that appeared during the golden age of black-and-white photography. Effects of double and even multiple exposures were created by selecting elements from other photographs of the same person to produce a new and composite image. For the public, photographers were like magicians, and it was no coincidence if the word itself often appeared in the names of their studios, such as the Magic Photo Studio or the Mr Magic studio.

Portrait photographers

The exchange of bodies and heads was among one of the most frequent practices; it was used to create full-length funerary portraits in the absence of pre-existing head-to-toe photographs of the deceased. The technique was simple, and consisted of sizing up (or down) the dead person's identity photo to correspond to the proportions of another person's body. It was often the ideal solution for the family of the deceased, since in Ghana there is a saying which goes: « No funeral without a full-length photo! ». Villagers and migrant workers also often requested this technique: since they often lacked appropriate clothing, they resorted to the illusion of having their visage appear on the body of an elegantly-dressed person. Some of these photographs were so crudely done as to appear as the obvious falsifications that they were; others were more subtle. At best, and practised by a master, the technique was impossible to detect.

The effects obtained could be endless, and each studio had one or more speciality, such as newly-wed couples appearing on a television screen, or one's portrait in a bottle. Others associated two different poses of the same person in a sequential context: a man seated, reading a newspaper and having his cigarette lit by his double; in another, both the person sitting for his portrait and the photographer behind the camera are identical. For many people, images such as these were associated with magic. For the photographers, they were simply the proof of their talent and expertise.

The multiplication of the same person's image on the same print - a form of two-dimensional « cloning » - was and still is practised in Ghana as well as in Kenya and Nigeria. In Ghana, however, multiple portraits are not associated with the cult of twins, as in Nigeria (see Sprague, 1978). According to Walter Benjamin, such photographs can be considered as a meta-image illustrating the technique of image-multiplication as an end in itself.

THE ERA OF « ONE-MAN-THOUSAND » (1980 TO THE PRESENT)

In the 1970s, a political and economic crisis in Ghana resulted in the near-paralysis of photographic activity. By the mid-1980s, the situation had improved, but the introduction of colour film and fully automatic processing laboratories progressively replaced the demand for hand-developed black-and-white film. People increasingly turned to the new laboratories for film development and prints. As their owners, who were generally well-funded Korean, Chinese, Indian or Lebanese businessmen, expanded their activities to include photography, the traditional studios were forced to close. The situation in Ghana began to resemble what had occurred in Europe following the Second World War, but with one important difference: wide-scale amateur photography was a rare phenomenon.

Itinerant photographers also reappeared during this period. Although a few also worked as agents for the colour laboratories, their professional activity was generally low-volume and modest: possessing only one camera, they travelled from place to place offering their services.[11]

For Ghanaian photographers, a new and difficult period began, often referred to as the « one-man-thousand ». It is an expression which evokes a local fish so small that a thousand of them are needed to satisfy one's appetite. In essence, it meant that with their profit-margins substantially reduced and totally dependant upon the owners of the major film laboratories, photographers had to considerably increase the volume of their work in order to survive.

PHOTOGRAPHS OF SOCIAL EVENTS AND PHOTOGRAPHY AS A SOCIAL EVENT

Photography in Ghana underwent several transformations in the 1990s. Colour film became less expensive to purchase and develop, the format of prints was reduced and more people began taking snapshots. At the same time, traditional studio photography gave way to the informality of outdoor settings and poses, and the photographing of social events became fashionable to the point of excess.

The Ghanaian people have a deeply-rooted enthusiasm for festivities. Photography, and more recently video, occupy an integral place within this tradition today. For Ghanaians, photography has become an indispensable element of festivities, celebrations and ceremonies, for it is felt that photographs highlight and immortalize such events. The photographs are almost always in colour, the obvious means for capturing the richly-coloured party-clothing worn by Ghanaians.

Today, such events increasingly serve to honour « big men »: Ghana's rich and nouveau-riche. The objective is purely self-representational: the display of one's power, celebrity and prestige. The overall phenomenon has become so prevalent that it may well take on the characteristics of a social syndrome: it is already referred to as « big manism » or « big mania », and at a certain level of society, people who cannot afford to hire a photographer avoid giving parties in order not to lose face. Photographs are offered like food and drink; their quantity and quality serve as an indication of wealth and social status. For the participants, they fulfil a double objective: on one hand, they constitute the tangible proof of their presence at the event; on the other, they represent a prestigious token of esteem given by their host.

Photographer
PHILIP KWAME APAGYA ©
Self-portrait as a dignitary.
Shama, ca. 1996.

11. With one notable difference, the situation in Ghana is similar to that of the Ivory Coast (see Jean-François Werner, 1996). In the latter country, however, political antagonism exists between the older studio photographers who are often Nigerian nationals and the young itinerant photographers, citizens of the Ivory Coast.

THE LANGUAGE OF BACKDROPS

Desirous of adding supplementary interest to their photographs, studio photographers have rediscovered and renewed a long-standing Ghanaian tradition: that of the painted background. Like other accessories, backgrounds are a heritage of European photography and constitute an intermediate phase between painted portraits and portrait photography. In Ghana, however, the painted background became an original art-form in itself. The first backgrounds were initially characterized by the representation of draped curtains and classic columns, stairways, pedestals or richly-appointed rooms whose half-opened windows gave onto a distant city or a pastoral scene. During the 1940s, artist-photographers such as Steven Abiodu Thomas broke away from the established colonial models and created backgrounds whose styles corresponded more closely to the tastes of their clients. Since that period, photographers and painters have constantly renewed their themes: their subjects and decoration constitute a reflection of passing fashions and specific periods of Ghana's contemporary social history.

Among the earliest subjects were painted references to Ghana's newly-electrified cities. The emergence of light from immemorial darkness - previously unimaginable for villagers who perceived it as a miracle of modern civilization - was symbolized by the image of one or more street-lights. As photography itself increasingly reflected the modernization of Ghana, street-lights were replaced by high-tension lines and pylons.

Cities were represented by stylized skyscrapers, imposing buildings and fanciful freeways with their cloverleaves and access ramps. Calendar illustrations featured painted representations of the Manhattan skyline or various interpretations of Abidjan's Hotel Ivoire. The backgrounds used in village or rural studios often represented the facade of a well-known bank (in general, the Ghana Commercial Bank). This was also a reflection of the population's progressive awareness of another aspect of modernity: a money-driven economy.

The majority of painted backgrounds representing urban themes contain dream-like images of houses, streets, automobiles and public gardens. Airports began to appear in the 1970s: less as a place for arrivals and departures than as another symbol of modern life, linking Ghana with the rest of the world. In general, the scene would represent an aircraft with a loading ramp against its open door in the foreground, and hangars, a control tower and other aircraft taking off or landing in the background. An « International Airport » signboard was usually included, along with visual references to Accra or Abidjan and occasionally Moscow, Dusseldorf or Paris. The scenes were initially painted in black-and-white; the introduction of colour film in the 1980s marked the arrival of coloured backgrounds. Two other major innovations which occurred during the period were the increasing realism of the scenes depicted and the introduction of certain possibilities of interaction between the individual being photographed and the scene itself.

Portrait photographers

The « Room Divider » was and still is an extremely popular background. Here, the individual posed in front of a painted representation of a showcase-like cabinet filled with everything that the ordinary person dreamed of possessing: a television, a tape-recorder, a videorecorder, a telephone, an ornamental clock, books, videotapes, elegant glassware, statuettes in fine porcelain, bottles of whisky, china vases and electric fans. The scene was completed by a refrigerator, often opened to display a veritable cornucopia of food products. The backgrounds presented these items like so many trophies, in the middle of which the person being photographed appeared like the king of an idealized society of mass consumption. The scenes were represented realistically and offered numerous possibilities of interaction: the person being photographed could appear to be pressing the button on a painted electric fan, turning on a television, opening a refrigerator or even offering a drink to an invisible guest. Other scenes represented a living-room, complete with a sofa, coffee-table and armchairs, or a modern and generously-appointed kitchen.

Philip Kwame Apagya, a photographer and background artist known for his realism and use of bright colours, qualifies his early years in the profession as « an unbelievable success. It was like a jet taking off: people saw the backgrounds and said 'How beautiful! A roomful of precious items! Whose house is it?' When I told them that it was taken in a photographic studio, they all wanted to know whose it was, and when I told them it was mine, they came for their own portrait. »

Nelson Ankruma Events, another photographer known for his innovative studio backgrounds, relates this story: « One day a woman arrived in my studio and had herself photographed in front of the 'room divider'. Her husband became furious when he saw the photo, for he was convinced that it was taken in another man's living-room - certainly that of her lover. When she tried to explain that it was simply a studio photo, her husband insisted on coming here to see for himself! »

Although the « room divider » is probably still the most popular background today, the number of other themes continues to increase steadily. Among them, is the facade of an imaginary villa, generally a two or three-storeyed building similar to those found in Accra's wealthier residential neighbourhoods. An exterior staircase often leads to the first floor; a portion of the roof is given over to a terrace; there is a television antenna, and more recently, a satellite dish; in the background, often an automobile and swimming-pool. The villa is surrounded by a wall and accessed by a doorway. « Visitors » are often photographed at the entrance, ringing a painted doorbell.

As urban contexts increasingly became part of the daily life of many of Ghana's citizens, images of villages and nature began to appear on studio backgrounds.

The representation of nature was limited to landscaped parks and highly-domesticated gardens rather than virgin forests. Other themes refer to technological progress, historical sites and the modernization of Ghana's urban infrastructure: the Adouri Bridge on the Volta, Nkrumah's tomb, the ancient forts of Elmina and Cape Coast, the new National Theatre of Accra and numerous versions of Kwame Nkrumah Circle, the animated hub of the capital and centre of the city's night-life.

THE ILLUSION OF REALITY AND THE REALITY OF ILLUSIONS

Certain studio backgrounds also feature motto-like phases whose messages are like veritable photo captions: « 99 steps to heaven », « Accra sweet but no family », and so on. The origin of these often wry observations concerning existence is probably the rich oral heritage of Akan proverbs used by the spokesmen of the tribal chiefs for important speeches. The same types of phrases can be seen on Ghanaian buses and taxis, for example: « Observers are worried! »

Phrases such as the above contain several semantic levels of signification, expressive of the frontiers between illusion, desire and reality. In the same manner, it is precisely through the lines of fracture with «normal» reality that the universe of Ghanaian photography reveals all its richness and multiplicity. In Akan, the word « reality » (nokwar) belongs to a semantic class of objects which are invisible to the naked eye. In this sense, reality is not important to Ghanaian photographers insofar as they are more interested in the exploration of the mysteries of exterior appearance.

Their photographs are at the same time surrealist and hyperrealist works constructed around a system of surprises and ruptures with reality. By their double celebration of the « illusion of reality » and « the reality of illusion », they provide a vehicle for the unexpected and trouble the observer. Within the context of artificial reality, individuals are photographed before totally falsified backgrounds whose hybrid array of items symbolizing modernity permits them to transcend their ordinary identity and achieve an allegorical level of existence. Many of these backgrounds are characterized by an interpenetration of the real and the unreal, such as placing one's foot on the step of a painted staircase, one's hand on an equally false banister of a painted villa, and other « appropriate » actions or gestures within a totally artificial context. The illusion is heightened by the use of a system of artificial lighting which accentuates the integration of the subject within the painted background.

In terms of their larger significance, the works of the younger generation of Ghanaian photographers who have followed in the footsteps of Philip Kwame Apagya and Nelson Ankruma Events represent much more than a social history in photographic images.

Bibliography:

Kwame Arhin. 1994. The Economic Implications of Transformations in Akan Funeral Rites. Africa 64/3.

Heike Behrend & Tobias Wendl. 1997. African Photography, New York, Simon & Schuster, The Encyclopedia of Subsaharan Africa. John Middleton.

Walter Benjamin. 1963. Das Kunstwerk im Zeitalter seiner technischen Reproduzierbarkeit. Frankfurt/Main, Suhrkamp.

Borgatti, Jean (Ed.). 1990. Likeness and Beyond. Portraits from Africa and the World. New York, The Center for African Arts.

Philippe David. 1993. Hommage à un des premiers photographes togolais : Alex A. Acolatse. 1880-1975. Lomé, Éditions Haho.

Okwui Enwezor. 1996. A Critical Presence. Drum Magazine. New York, The Solomon R. Guggenheim Foundation In/sight. African Photographers, 1940 to the Present.

Gisèle Freund. 1976. Photographie und Gesellschaf. München, Rogner & Bernhard

Allister Macmillan. 1920. The Red Book of West Africa. London, Frank Cass.

Jay Ruby. 1995. Secure the Shadow. Death and Photography in America. Cambridge,. MA: MIT Press.

Anthony Sampson. 1983. Drum ; An African Adventure and Afterwards. London, Hodder & Stoughton.

Stephen Sprague. 1978. Yoruba Photography ; How I see the Yoruba see themselves. African Arts 12/1.

Tobias Wendl. 1995. Afrikanische Reklamekunst. 23-minütiger Dokumentarfilm (Betacam-SP), Distribution: IWF Gottingen.

Tobias Wendl. 1996. Why they don't see what they could see. The perception of photographs from a cross-cultural perspective. Anthropos 91/1.

Tobias Wendl. 1997. *Allegorien des Selbst. Zu Geschichte und Praxis der indigenen Fotografie in Ghana*. In: Indigene afrikanische Ethnographien, Heike Behrend & Thomas Geider (Eds.), Kolpe, Koln.

Tobias Wendl & Nancy du Plessis. 1997. *Future Remembrance. Photography and Image Arts in Ghana*. 55-minütiger Dokumentarfilm (Betacam-SP). Distribution: IWF Gottingen.

Jean-François Werner. 1993. *La photographie de famille en Afrique de l'Ouest. Une méthode d'approche ethnographique*. Xoana 1/1.

Jean-François Werner. 1996. *Produire des images en Afrique: l'exemple des photographes de studio*. Cahiers d'Etudes africaines 141-42.

Jean-François Werner. 1996. *Profession photographe : un étranger peut en cacher un autre*. Abidjan, Actes du Colloque GIDIS-CI.

James van der Zee. 1978. *Harlem Book of the Death*. New York, Morgan & Morgan.

Photographer
PHILIP KWAME APAGYA ©
*Room divider painted scenery,
ca. 1995-96.*

Certain parallels can be drawn between their work and that of the American Pop Artists of the 1960s and 1970s. By placing them outside their normal context, they integrated images of products of the consumer society into their works, which were then often replicated in series in much the same way a photographer produces a series of prints. These similarities have their common origin in 20th-century consumerism which has pervaded much of the planet.

« Pop-Ghanaian » photography constitutes a precise demonstration that the power of attraction of material goods increases proportionally to their absence. By transforming this universe of objects into a world of icons, it creates images which are also highly significant works of art.

The phrase « Observers are worried! » reveals a conception of reality in Ghana in which there is much more than meets the naked eye, and where the acceptance of the ambiguities, paradoxes, illusions and multiple facets of existence is accepted as a basic fact of life. This conception is mirrored in much of the language of daily life, rich in proverbs whose meaning and interpretation are also multiple.

The expression *Kasa mbranyl* signifies the act of using highly-codified proverbs, idiomatic phrases and words with hidden meanings to create several levels of signification: one voices one's opinion, but one expresses it indirectly. This fundamental multidimensionality of the spoken word (mbebusem) also extends to the world of objects, of which the photographic image is a part. In this sense, any attempt to interpret Ghanaian photography within a purely Western framework of reality can only result in one's becoming a rather « worried observer » oneself.

Tobias Wendl

John Kiyaya

Tanzania
b. Kassanga, Tanzania ca. 1970
– lives in Tanzania

John Kiyaya was educated in mission schools. The deciding factor in his choice of career was his meeting with the French writer, Jean Rolin, who gave him a camera so that he could finance his studies by taking portraits. John Kiyaya mainly photographs the people living on the shores of Lake Tanganyika, where he was born. While he works as a photographer, he is also studying journalism in Dar-es-Salaam.

Photographer JOHN KIYAYA ©1992

John Kiyaya Kasanga 1992.

Photocomic: a Sapeur from Brazzaville

Arca, a young man from Brazzaville who is an inveterate Sapeur (member of SAPE – the Society for the Advancement of People of Elegance) is dressing for the evening in his dingy studio apartment in Kinsoundi, a working-class neighborhood on the outskirts of the capital.

Dressing up smart is what really turns me on.

« You know, man » he says, rubbing on skin cream, « war just isn't my thing. I manage to find the money to eat and hang out in videobars. »

We take the bus out to Moukondo, a distant suburb northeast of the city. « You know, since the war, nobody's having any fun in Bacongo anymore: all the Sapeurs hang out in Moukondo now. » At Moukondo, we get off the bus in the pouring rain. « Rain! Just what I needed to ruin my night. » The rain stops. The lights of the Nzaba, the club we're headed for, appear a short distance up the road. Arca starts walking faster. « That's where I won my first prize for the best-dressed Sapeur. Everybody knows me there: I'm a real star ! » he confides triumphantly. As we pass through the door, he begins radiating charm, proudly showing off his clothes.

He disappears into his room and returns with his outfit for the evening. « I scored these off a guy just back from Paris, » he says with a broad grin. And adds as if in afterthought : « I have to give them back tomorrow morning. » He dresses slowly, putting on each item with infinite care. « I love this, man, I just love it! » he says repeatedly. « Hey, you gotta give me the pictures as soon as they come out in your book. You won't forget, right? I'm gonna make posters of out them! »

Arca checks out the scene, saluting his admirers and joining a group of friends and their girls. Coloured lights illuminate the interior, rumbas play in fast and slow tempos and rivers of Ngok (Congolese beer) are being downed by the customers. Seeing my camera, one of Arca's friends plants himself squarely in front of the lens, waving his passport and plane ticket to France like a flag : « Look man, everything but the visa... ! »

Such are the nights and dreams of the young Sapeurs of Brazzaville: lives spent attempting to attain the often-unreachable dreams of an improbable ideal.

Text and photographs by FRANCK BITEMO © Les rêves d'Arca un Sapeur de Brazzaville, Congo, 1998.

Studios in the Congo

Sophie Erlich Mapaka

Foto yo otikela ngai na libongo
Na kati ya motema, ekoma nde elili
The photograph you gave me at the station is now a picture that lives in my heart.
Lutumba & OK Jazz

In the euphoric post-independence years of the 1960s, photography was going full steam ahead and studios - André Déposé, Pierrot, Dekoum, La Lune and others - were opening up all over Brazzaville, Poto-Poto, Moungali and Ouenz. Since few people had cameras at the time, you had your photograph taken alone or with the family, or you went out and hired one of the itinerant photographers who toured the neighbourhoods with his camera slung over his shoulder, shouting « Foto ! Foto ! » Young, snappy dressers came along to get their latest sartorial acquisitions immortalized on glossy paper. Until the late 1980s the Main Bleu (Blue Hand) bar was packed out for the « concours d'élégance » (style contests) that were featured several times a week. You might see a young man in a suit astride the moped that symbolized his success, a teenager in bell-bottoms holding his friend's hand by the fingertips, a kid in spanking new football gear. A country's entire memory is there in these black-and-white portraits that have survived - but for how long? - successive changes of government and the hot, humid climate of Equatorial Africa that makes it so hard to keep photos intact. The Studio André Déposé was all the rage then, with painted backdrops that meant you could pose in front of the Eiffel Tower or the Arc de Triomphe. The photographer learnt his trade as he went along, starting as an apprentice working for a master. A few names spring to mind: Pilo, one of the doyens of Congolese photography, who now sticks strictly to running his hotel in the southern part of the city; Simon Kinioumba, known as Simarrot; André Ngouami from the André Déposé Studio and Pierre Ngouala from the Pierrot Studio in Ouenze.

In 1969 the Congo's growing rapprochement with the Soviet Union led to the adoption of a Marxist regime. Many Congolese students who were given grants to study in the USSR came home with cheap cameras. Photography at the time was a propaganda tool, with the news being covered by official photographers. Albert Nkouka worked for the state press agency until the end of the one-party period; even now he never goes out without his ageing Canon and has thousands of photos in his studio on OAU Avenue in Bacongo. Born in 1945, Alphonse Kina was a sports reporter for *La Semaine Africaine* (African Weekly) from 1968 to 1987, opening his studio in Poto-Poto in 1970. Abel Nkombo (1940-1996) worked for a time in Pointe-Noire.

Then everything seemed to come to a halt in the late 1980s, with the Congo reeling from the shock of the oil crisis: in 1985 almost three-quarters of the country's resources had come from petroleum.

In 1991 the National Conference put an end to the one-party state. A liberated press put the printed word ahead of the image and the new newspapers, bereft of financial resources, were marked by extreme visual poverty. Regarded as mere illustration, the photograph was pushed into the background.

« At the time I could earn up to several hundred thousand francs CFA a week », André Ngouami confided to me in his Ouenze studio (CFA francs being the currency of Francophone Africa); but when you look at the dilapidated state of today's city, it is hard to believe in that golden age when money flowed freely. Now nothing remains but thousands of negatives stored in boxes; and in his studio André Ngouami now takes practically nothing except identity photographs. Lots of households have small automatic cameras or camcorders, and photographers are only called in for such major occasions as weddings, baptisms and wakes.

Today you can have a colour portrait taken for only a few hundred francs CFA by the photographer-reporters you see at all official ceremonies. They use mainly colour negative stock that is then handed over to small studios - often no more than wooden shanties - in Bacongo, Poto-Poto, Moungali and Ouenze. These studios are, in fact, only intermediaries, since they themselves have no laboratories. It is extremely difficult to take pictures in the street, even for the Congolese, and photographing a building or some architectural detail can lead to confiscation of your camera. Spy-paranoia or the outcome of 20 years of one-party government? It's more complicated than that. In these times of crisis the disinterested gesture no longer exists. Photography without a clear reason always seems suspect. Taking someone's picture means stealing part of his or her soul, and more so in the Congo, perhaps, than elsewhere: Ndoki the sorcerer needs a picture of the chosen victim before going to work and photographss have become part of his stock-in-trade. In such a difficult context the new generation of photographers is finding it hard to get a foothold: every photograph you take needs to be sold, and gaining access to a colour laboratory is all but impossible.

And yet a few new names are emerging. Jéhu Olivier focuses on musicians and artists he knows well, he himself being the singer in a rap group. Désiré Loutsono, better known as Kinzenguele, photographs Congolese artists and intellectuals for the New Art Association. Arsène Nguengo Ngouma works for *La Semaine Africaine*. Franck Bitemo, journalist at the Press Resource Centre, likes to portray Brazzaville society.

A retrospective exhibition of Congolese photography was scheduled to open in Brazzaville on 15 June 1997 but war broke out on 5 June 1997.

Sophie Erlich Mapaka

A short history of photography in Kenya

Heike Behrend

Kenya's first studios were opened by photographers of Indian origin. After an initial period during which their clientele was made up largely of Europeans and wealthy Indians or Africans, and their work limited to reproducing the archetypes of Victorian photography, they developed an aesthetics mingling their own traditional culture, the British colonial heritage and local demands. The result was an original style which lives on in the diversity of indigenous photography in Kenya today.

For centuries, the east coast of Africa was the centre of a dense network of trade and commercial exchanges with Arabia, Persia, India and Indonesia. At the same time, the region also conducted trade with countries located within the interior. East Africa's unique geographical situation from early on favoured the emergence of a hybrid modernity within the towns along its coast (Middleton, 1992).

Photography began to develop in East Africa during the early period of European colonization. In 1868, AC Gomez, an Indian from Goa, opened a photography studio in Zanzibar (Monti, 1987). Portrait photography developed here much in the same manner as in India or Europe, but also grew out of ethnographic photodocumentation undertaken for various colonial administrations and portraits of members of various royal courts (MacDougall, 1992; Gutman, 1982; Pinney, 1997). Established along the East African coast, Indian photographers perpetuated their own stylistic traditions which then, as today, differentiate the region from West Africa.[1]

European colonial administrations used photography to identify and classify the peoples subjected to their rule. The Indian traders who had been active on the East Coast for centuries also saw photography as an instrument of power for those who could master the technique.

Heike Behrend is a professor of ethnology at the Institute of African Languages and Culture in Cologne, Germany. She is currently preparing a book on war and religion in Africa, as well as a study on popular photography in Kenya. She is the author of numerous articles and books, including *La Guerre des Esprits en Uganda: Le Mouvement du Saint-Esprit d'Alice Lakwena*, Paris, L'Harmattan, 1997 and *Love à la Hollywood and Bombay: Kenyan Post-Colonial Studio Photography*, Paidenwa, 1998.

1. The Indians of Kenya, unlike the indigenous African population, were favoured by the British colonial government. A system of *de facto* apartheid prevented Africans from creating their own businesses and accessing new forms of technology.

< Photographer
SAMMY BIG SEVEN STUDIO © 1995
Likoni, Mombasa, Kenya.

Portrait photographers

They thus attempted to assimilate this « power » by refusing to be photographed themselves, and by their progressive monopolization of photographic activity itself, thereby creating a commercial and stylistic hegemony which served their own needs.

In the early 1890s, ARP de Lord, CAW Grün, EC Dias and JB Couthino - the latter two originally from Goa - opened photographic studios in Zanzibar. C Fernandez and C Vicenti established studios in Dar es Salaam. The aforementioned Grün and Couthino also set up branches in Mombasa, which was the site of William Young's Dempster-Studio as well. Young, who was the official photographer for the Uganda railways administration, documented the construction of the line connecting Mombasa to Kampala and opened a studio in Nairobi, the future capital of colonial Kenya, in 1905.[2] Other photographers, including TA Costa, DV Figueira and AH Firmin, also opened their own studios in Mombasa during the same period.

At the turn of the century, the majority of the towns along the coast and within the interior of East Africa had one or more photographic studios. These studios operated within a highly cosmopolitan urban context, characterized by a mixture of foreigners of oriental and occidental origins whose cultures and traditions were entirely different from those of the local African population. The clients of these studios were Europeans and Indians, along with a few members of the local African elite. In addition to portraits, the studios created a series of postcards whose images, as they circulated around the entire planet, reinforced the idea of Africa as a continent of racial stereotypes and « local curiosities ».

During this period, the majority of Kenya's studios imitated Victorian stylistic conventions regarding accessories. Subjects were photographed in front of false plaster columns, draped curtains, tapestries, artist's easels and palm trees. The paradox of these often lugubrious settings, aesthetically situated somewhere between a torture chamber and the throne-room of a mad king, has been marvellously described by Walter Benjamin.[3] In time, Africans opened their own studios and developed their own styles adapted to the demands and tastes of their local clients. The colonial and postcolonial eras witnessed the development of a variety of popular traditions concerning the photographic portrait.

In 1918, the Indian CD Patel opened the celebrated Patel Studio in Mombasa, where he immortalized many of the city's leading personalities during the colonial period. Born in 1886 in the Indian province of Gujarat, Patel located his first studio in the old section of Mombasa before moving to Nkrumah Street in 1928.

The studio was so successful that it became necessary to enlarge it in 1933.[4] Its clients were mainly members of Mombasa's upper classes, including the colonial governor. Upon his retirement in 1942, Patel sold his studio, which closed in the 1950s. After returning to India, his two sons set up the Bombay Photo Stores in Calcutta.

NV Narandar Parekh, whose grandfather also came from Gujarat, founded the Parekh Studio in the late 1940s. In addition to traditional Victorian portrait photography, he also created what he termed « film-style-photography », in which couples were photographed in a romantic manner similar to that of Hollywood and Bombay movies. Parekh's initial clients were mainly wealthy Indians, Arabs and Swahilis. In the 1960s and perhaps earlier, he began photographing less affluent people, including migrant workers from the interior of the country who had found jobs on the coast.

The « Africanization » of portrait photography also dates from the 1960s. In the majority of photographic studios frequented by the less affluent portion of the population, the painted backdrops represented urban landscapes or bucolic scenes from the Kenyan countryside. Parekh's approach was somewhat more minimalist: his backgrounds consisted of a neutral-coloured backdrop with the occasional use of a draped curtain and props such chairs, plastic flowers or a small table. The stylistic domination of the West, which had long governed poses, clothing and the use of European accessories, gradually gave way to a more local and highly African approach. In 1983, Parekh sold his studio and moved to London.

In 1880, Baghat Singh travelled from Lahore, the capital city of Pakistan, to Kenya, where he established a profitable business manufacturing and selling carriage wheels to British colonists. In the 1950s, Ram Singh, one of Baghat Singh's sons, who was originally destined for a career in finance, took over a photographic studio created a few years earlier in Nairobi by his brother. The Ram Singh Studio was immensely successful; many of its clients were members of the pro-nationalist East African liberation movement, including political leaders such as Jomo Kenyatta, Julius Nyerere and the union activist, Tom Mboya, who would later be assassinated.

In 1962 the studio was taken over by Ram Singh's son, who renamed it Studio One. In the late 1960s he went to Hamburg to learn the techniques of colour photography (Behrend and Wendl, 1997). Studio One was able to survive the economic crisis that closed many of its competitors owing to its mastery of colour photography.

OMAR SAID BAKOR
Kenya
b. 1932 – d. 1993

The Studio Bakor was founded by Omar Said Bakor in Lamu in the 1960s. Bakor's family was originally from Yemen. An inspired self-taught photographer, Bakor worked as an itinerant photographer for ten years before amassing enough money to open his own studio. In the course of his career, he developed a highly personal style of photo-montage and composite portraits in the tradition of magic realism and surrealism.

Photographer
BAKOR STUDIO © ca. 1970
Man with two heads, Lamu, Kenya.

2. Monti. 1987. 172.

3. Benjamin. 1977. 375.

4. Patel's son, Jayar, stated in a letter that his father established the first film development laboratory in Mombasa.

Portrait photographers

In 1990 the studio was purchased by Kenneth Kamau, who is still its owner; Kamau's father had previously worked for Ram Singh before opening his own studio.

In the course of an interview in Nairobi in August 1996, Kenneth Kamau commented on the enormous popularity of photography among present-day Kenyans. On payday at the end of every month, his studio is besieged by smartly-attired men, women with new outfits and hairdos and entire families dressed in their best clothing: their portraits are offered as tokens of esteem to friends and loved ones. According to Kamau, on holidays such as Christmas « people go mad »: having one's portrait taken is an integral part of the festivities. The photographs are later kept as souvenirs or given to friends. Marriages and birthdays are unthinkable without being photographed; in effect, the photographer's presence is indispensable for every important event of one's life.

Kenneth Kamau also said that during funeral ceremonies in certain areas of Kenya - particularly in the central provinces - a portrait of the deceased is placed on the coffin. In former times, coffins were generally opened to allow mourners to say their farewells. But since the custom often provoked highly emotional scenes of grief and hysteria - especially among women - a photograph now replaces the actual person and the coffin remains closed. For Kenneth Kamau, this represents progress over the former tradition, insofar as it allows mourners to control their feelings by distancing themselves from the full force of their emotions via a symbolic substitute for the loved one (Norbert Elias: 1969).

The Studio Bakor was founded by Omar Said Bakor (1932-1993) in Lamu in the 1960s. Bakor's family was originally from Yemen. An inspired self-taught photographer, Bakor worked as an itinerant photographer for ten years before amassing enough money to open his own studio. In the course of his career, he developed a highly personal style of photomontage and composite portraits in the tradition of magic realism and surrealism as he sought, in the words of his son Najid Omar, « to create strange effects, and simply to have fun ». Other photographs by Bakor illustrate the history of Lamu, and some of these minor masterpieces were sold to tourists in the form of picture postcards.

In the 1980s, the crisis provoked by the transition from black-and-white to colour photography resulted in the closing of many studios. The resulting vacuum was filled by the emergence of a new profession: that of the street photographer. Street photographers generally use unsophisticated flash cameras and develop their film and prints in a laboratory which offers them a discount in exchange for the volume of their work and their unwavering allegiance to the specific brand of film sold there.

In the majority of Kenya's cities and towns today, street photographers can be seen taking the portraits of visitors (generally African tourists) in front of local museums, monuments and historical sites. On any given day, for example, numerous visitors to the Kenyatta Conference Centre have their portrait taken before this symbol of the modern African state. A number of different poses are possible: one of the most popular consists of emphasizing the sheer size of the building in relation to that of the person having his or her picture taken. Images of this type can also be interpreted as mute criticism of post-colonial politics, in which the ordinary person is symbolically oppressed by the imposing volume of the monument.

Street photographers also photograph ordinary citizens, who often request their services for marriages, birthdays and other important family celebrations. Since their prices are significantly lower than those charged by the studios, a bitter professional rivalry has gradually emerged between the street photographers and their better established colleagues. The profession is exercised principally by young men: for many of them, their activity is seen as a means of amassing enough money to open their own studio.[5] If a few women have succeeded in establishing themselves in the same profession on the west coast, the strictures of Islam regarding the separation of the sexes limit their activity to photographing other women. Equipped with either traditional or video cameras, they film members of their own sex during marriage ceremonies and other celebrations (Behrend, 1998).

In conclusion, it can be asserted that photography occupies a solidly established position in contemporary Kenyan culture. It continues to document personal and social history and has an integral place in funeral rites and ancestor worship. It is also used to both heal and hurt (particularly in the practices associated with love-magic), serves as a tangible souvenir of celebrations and special events and is the object of exchange and gift-giving. Men and women of every social class use it as a means of exploring a complex system of multiple identities. The purpose of such photos is less to capture an objective exterior reality than to reflect a new and modern vision of one's existence in the world, a vision which at the same time offers a flattering image of one's social position. Naïvely, yet profoundly, it plays upon the most positive aspects of a series of dynamic and modern social identities, as opposed to all that is considered old-fashioned, static and « traditional ».

Heike Behrend

Bibliography:

Bedrend, Heike. 1998. *Feeling Global*. The Likoni Ferry Photographers in Mombasa, Kenya.

Bedrend, Heike. 1998. *The Appropriation of Western Tourist Spaces : The Likoni Ferry Photographers in Mombasa/Kenya : Photography's Other Histories.*, Chris Pinney et Nicolas Peterson editors., Canberra, in preparation.

Photographer >
BAKOR STUDIO © ca. 1975
Man sitting on the moon, Lamu, Kenya.

5. In the early 1990s, a group of young street photographers - most of them from the western provinces of central Kenya - moved into the Likoni quarter in Mombasa and set up makeshift studios there. Their astonishingly imaginative painted backdrops, representing naïve visions of a modern, multicultural and cosmopolitan Africa, delighted their clients who, like them, were migrant workers who had moved from remote rural regions to the capital (Behrend, 1998).

SAMUEL FOSSO

Central African Republic
b. Cameroun 1962 –
lives in Central African Republic

After a long and punishing odyssey that took him from Cameroon to Nigeria, Samuel Fosso settled in Bangui at the age of ten. He became an apprentice photographer in 1975, but wasted no time in setting up on his own. From the age of 16 he used the spare moments between sessions in his studio to take self-portraits, alone or with friends - a self-regarding stance that is exceptional in Africa. He sets the scene meticulously through his use of clothing fashion and the backgrounds he creates in a studio that changed its name several times - Studio Confiance, Studio Gentil, Studio Hoberau - before becoming Studio Convenance.

Photographer SAMUEL FOSSO ©
Self-portraits, ca. 1970.

Gaston-Paul Effa

So long forgotten...

I don't think he read a single book throughout his long life. I can't say that he even knew how to write. There was no link between him and literature, nothing, not even distant or vague, no appeal: literature was an unknown, possibly absurd, unattainable world of no interest to him whatsoever.

The naïve need to describe - describe what? To express? No, not even that ... and express what? I do not know why I suddenly thought of my paternal grandfather again. It must be because of the long-forgotten photograph that I've just found in an old box.

My grandfather was 80 when I left for France. I was not yet 16, and he gave me this photograph to remember him by.

My father had recently refused to inherit a totemic bag: he was moved and troubled by the veiled reality that he wanted, but refused, to discover. Despite his polygamy, my father had just converted to Christianity and could not accept all the taboos that went with the responsibility of succeeding my grandfather, witchdoctor of the Béti tribe. This obscure and unbearable responsibility, which required a lifetime of worthiness, entailed not eating manioc and yams, the staple foods in Cameroon, not sleeping with a woman during a waning moon, not getting wet in the rain and not being able to wash any part of your body except your hands and face ...

I would not be so fascinated and stubbornly attracted by this image of my grandfather if it hadn't made me feel helpless from the start, if it hadn't remained so foreign to the end.

How can writing be the instrument and location of a fable, when life and the world are themselves that enigmatic tale, that impenetrable world where I vainly wait for the smallest fissure to open and let me in, yet every attempt leaves me that much more dazed and bruised.

On 4 August 1982, my father told me that my grandfather had been found dead, sitting against a tree in the pouring rain. His totemic bag, burnished and polished with a crow's wing, had disappeared, breaking the closed circle of the tribe and releasing the essence of a community without name.

How I would like to know what happened that day, I who for so long had placed so much importance on a state of wakefulness, consciousness, rejecting this obscure, distant spring welling up inside me. I had always refused to hear its muted bubbling, inhale its suffocating mystery; how could I have suspected that I had no choice but to be faithful to my grandfather's ravaged destiny?

Gaston-Paul Effa
Langatte, 14 September 1997

The awakening of a vision

L'éveil d'un regard

Before independence, African photographers were commissioned to do portrait work only, while photography of architecture, daily life and landscapes remained in European hands. After independence many European photographers left and a new generation of African reporter-photographers arrived on the scene, helped by new techniques like flashes and small and average formats. Some portrait photographers left their studios and went out to photograph society, parties, weddings and christenings. They showed an Africa enjoying itself in bars and restaurants, while another Africa took to the streets to display the joys of independence and the first disappointments of its fledgeling states.

Young people were particularly fond of seeing themselves in photographs that looked just like the ones flooding in from the countries up North. Photography was the most appropriate modern medium for showing they belonged to the world. Abandoning the poses of portrait photographs, the Africans started forging a new image of themselves that they could finally recognize. Other photographers also discovered the landscapes and traditions of their country, and realized the urgent importance of immortalizing them.

Photographer PHILIPPE KOUDJINA ©
Bar by night, Niamey, Niger, ca. 1965.

PMSL & JLP

Photographer PHILIPPE KOUDJINA ©
The accordionist: night in Niamey, Niger ca. 1965.

Philippe's nights in Niamey

PHILIPPE KOUDJINA

In Niger it's summer all day, every day. And at night the heat is still there. In Niamey, ringed by the barren Sahel, where the majestic Niger flows by on its way to the sea, parched in summer and spread like a gleaming mirror in winter, hot nights in cool nightclubs are the world of Philippe Koudjina, photographer-reporter covering Niamey-by-night since 1962. This was the golden era of Independence, of the sheer joy of finding freedom, of pride in being African. And in the heat of the night the frantic young cut loose to the sound of Afro-Cuban rumbas from Zaïre and the twist from Europe.

When Philippe (Koudjina, that is, the photographer) isn't around, everyone wants him; and the feeling of having missed out torments him until the next morning, when he makes himself a promise not to forget the night to come. Who doesn't know Philippe Koudjina, photographer of the night, photographer of hearts beating as one and never to be parted? When he arrived in Niger, led by the luck of his job as a surveyor, the Togo-born Beninese was already hooked on photography. And one day in 1959 he opted for Niamey, for its nights and for the photography he was to practise to the exclusion of all else.

Not as a studio photographer like Mama Casset, Seydou Keita or Cornelius Augustt Azaglo, but as a photojournalist, the kind who is out in search of life, day and night. Nonetheless, 1972 saw him set up in a studio for a few years, as fashion dictated. And all the petit bourgeois of Niamey wanted their photographs taken against a « futurist » urban backdrop, under glaring lights, posing proudly in their finest attire even if it meant borrowing a tie to show off in. Photographs that were still in black-and-white then, photographs to be given to parents or close friends and then pinned up on a bedroom wall. Photographs that commanded respect and showed that you counted for something in your neighbourhood.

Everyday life was hard and even if you cheated a little at photograph time, it made an impression and proved you were the worthy bearer of your father's name - important in a country where society is based on family lines. Philippe Koudjina was there for all the big events, all the parties especially, in the early days, those given by French servicemen, who could easily afford to have their picture taken - and all the nights, with his old out-of-synch flash camera: nights of the beer-drinking lady accordionist and the languorous lovers of Harry's Bar, nights of the local youngsters crowded round the record-player at the Tropicana, while the old folks met in the concession yard with its white neon lights.

Niger at Independence time was a uranium-rich country where life was good, where all the big French stars gave concerts - Claude François, Adamo, Johnny Halliday. Pier Paolo Pasolini and La Callas came through looking for locations for *Medea* in 1969. And every time Philippe Koudjina was on the spot. He caught them at the airport, no doubt not really knowing who they were, but getting La Callas just right, the diva of five continents, followed by a Pasolini struggling with the luggage. In the same way Philippe Koudjina caught thousands of passing faces. With his wealth of good humour and feminine conquests, he was materially wealthy as well, he owned a house and a car. Those were the glory days. The last days before colour and the pitiless competition of photography made easy.

Now he's disabled and makes a living slogging around on foot. No furniture in his two rooms in a small concession: just trunks full of negatives piled up any old how, still there as if to bear witness to his past splendour. There's no humidity in Niger, no tropical fungi, just the fine dust that gets into everything and scratches pictures until they disappear. Today 24 x 36 cameras, updated when and if he's got the money, have taken over from the handsome Rolleiflex 6 x 6s, the Polaroid and the view cameras of his early days.[1]

To put the seal on his success he opened his studio in 1972: a studio that - like so many others - would close a few years later with the invasion of colour and cameras for all, and above all the competition that grew tougher by the day in a context of no money, no work and nothing to do.

Yet he never gave up his nights. Today, the early hours find him there among the multitude of youngsters for whom itinerant photography is a means of survival, waiting for the minilab to develop his night pictures and using the time to catch up on some sleep.

Then, prints in hand, he heads for the market to buy the midday meal his very young wife - women, always women - will prepare; the meal he will share with his three young children amid the heat and dust of the wood fires. After the afternoon siesta - his only real night-time - he sets off again, photos and camera in hand, his leg bandaged, his gait lopsided, out to tempt those he caught the previous night, plunging back into bars, restaurants, clubs, mean streets, at the end of a life of drink and drugs, back into his own life, his real life, the one that most people prefer to pass over in silence.

JLP & PMSL

1. View camera : a large format camera with a ground glass screen for viewing.

PHILIPPE KOUDJINA

b. Togo 1940 – lives in Niamey, Niger

Photographer PHILIPPE KOUDJINA ©
Night in Niamey, Niger ca. 1965.

The extraordinary chronicler of the crazy Niamey night-life of the Seventies, he is today an
independent, itinerant photographer who takes pictures in bars and night-clubs.

DEPARA

*Democratic Republic
of Congo*
*b. Kbokiolo, Angola 1928
– d. Kinshasa 1997*

A shoe-repairer until 1953, Depara took up photography in 1950, the year he got married in Matadi. To record the event he bought himself a little Adox camera. Back in Kinshasa in 1951, he tried to combine photography with odd jobs - fixing bicycles and cameras, buying and selling scrap metal. The subject of his photos was the singer Franco and music from Zaïre: at the time Kinshasa was a music centre where Zaïre-style rumba and cha-cha played all night. Depara opened his studio, the Jean Whisky Depara, at 54 Kato St and around 1954 became Franco's official photographer: the singer had spotted his work and invited him along when he was performing, especially in Mokalia. The photos taken from his bicycle date from this period. By day he frequented the city's nganda (bars): the Kwist, run by a West African, the Okay Bar on Itaga Street and the Sarma Congo, a Belgian store - now the People's Co-op - that had its own bar. At night, alone and with his flash camera slung over his shoulder (« like a bow », as he put it), he toured the fashionable clubs: the Afro Mogenbo, the Champs-Elysées, the Djambo-Djambu, the Oui, the Fifi, the Show Boat. Outside Itaga Street the most « in » spot in 1955 was the Kongo Bar on Tshoapa Street, now a church, along with the Opika (intersection Kabambaré and Bokassa Streets) and the Bingabar on Lake Moéro, in the Barumbu neighbourhood. The atmosphere was crazy, selling photos was easy. While keeping up his night work, he took photos by day in his studio until 1956. He was an official parliamentary photographer from 1975 to 1989, when he retired to devote himself to fishing and building pirogues.

Photographer DEPARA ©
Depara, self-portrait, ca. 1960.
Depara, self-portrait, ca. 1960.

Photographer DEPARA ©
Portrait of Franco, 1956.
Portrait of Franco, 1956.
Franco's first concert with OK Jazz, 1954.

Photographer DEPARA ©
Kinshasa swimming pool.
Young kids.
At the wheel of an American car.
Young girl in field.

MALICK SIDIBÉ

Mali
b. Soloba, Mali 1936
– lives in Bamako

Malick Sidibé began his studies at the Bamako Institute for the Arts in 1952 and in 1956 French photographer Gérard Guillart taught him photography in his shop in Bamako, using a Brownie Flash. Later he opened his own studio, doing industrial work and photographing the youth of Bamako in their leisure moments: he was drawn by their relaxedness and their attempt to distance themselves from the traditional rules of family life in Mali. He enjoys a reputation as a camera repairer and is currently president of the GNPPM, the Malian Professional Photographers' Group.

Photographer MALICK SIDIBÉ © 1970

Photographer MALICK SIDIBÉ © 1970

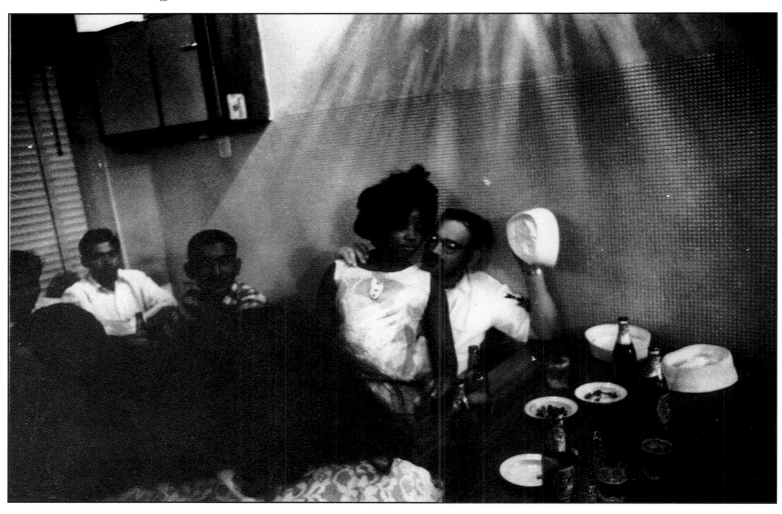

RICARDO RANGEL

Mozambique
b. Maputo, Mozambique) 1924
– lives in Maputo

Ricardo Rangel is of mixed African, Greek and Chinese stock. From 1952 to 1984 he worked for various press organizations and in 1983 founded the Photography Training Centre, where almost all Mozambique's photographers went to learn their trade. The photographs shown here are part of his coverage of Araujo Street, a nocturnal haunt of sailors of all nationalities passing through Maputo in the 1960s.

Photographer RICARDO RANGEL © 1960
Our nightly bread.

BILLY MONK

South Africa
b. Cape Town, South Africa 1937– d. Johannesburg 1982

Billy Monk died on 31 July 1982 in Johannesburg, struck down by two bullets in the heart. He was a photographer and, according to his friends, a gentleman. He worked by night as a bouncer at the Catacombs, a club in Cape Town, and sometimes by day as a diamond prospector. All that remains today are one or two self-portraits showing his broken nose and his pictures from the 1960s and 1970s. Armed only with a 35 mm lens on a Pentax body, a few rolls of black-and-white Ilford film and a feeble flash, Billy Monk

brought a tragic but in no way indulgent sensibility to bear on the nocturnal world. He photographed his fellow human beings with no social or documentary intent, simply selling his pictures to their involuntary subjects: drunken sailors, prostitutes in love, worn-out transvestites, laughing dwarves, passionate lovers. On 31 July 1982 Billy Monk thought he might hitch a ride to Johannesburg to see the exhibition of his photos at the Market Gallery. An unforeseen encounter decided otherwise.

Photographer BILLY MONK ©
In the night.
Cape Town, ca. 1968.
Courtesy of the
South African National Gallery.

MOHAMED ABDALLAH KAYARI

Djibouti
b. Djibouti 1929 – lives in Djibouti

Mohammed Abdallah Kayari belongs to the first generation of Djibouti photographers. He learnt photography at the Ullman studio in 1950, then at the Tran Quan Studio in 1953, working as a laboratory technician and taking wedding photographs, identity shots and still lives. In 1962 he began as a photographer with the national weekly *La Nation*. Both as an eyewitness and as a custodian of Djibouti's memory, Abdallah Kayari has been casting a wry eye over the port, the Afar region and his home city for almost a half-century now. He also takes family portraits.

Photographer
MOHAMED ABDALLAH KAYARI ©
Djibouti.

The official agencies

Les agences officielles

The wave of independence in the 1960s and the socialist ideologies adopted by some African countries gave rise to numerous official press agencies, some of which were based on former colonial bodies, like AMAP in Mali, ONICEP in Nigeria, Congopresse in the Democratic Republic of Congo, the Onacig and Sily-Photo in Guinea, ANTA in Madagascar and A Foto in Angola. A highly structured network of photographers covered official events and visits by heads of state and political or administrative VIPs. Images were by far the best way of asserting that the administration of the state, now liberated from colonialism but nonetheless shaped by it, really was the work of its own inhabitants. The new rulers had to project a public image of a leader who was representative of society. The official agencies were there to promote the official version of the role of the administration, of the new nation and of the politician guiding it for the benefit of all. In the initial enthusiasm of Independence, this official photography was eagerly embraced by both photographers and the people, but everyone soon realized its limits, governed as it was by the growing autocracy of a power to which the people felt increasingly subjected. As a result, the veracity of images was increasingly questioned. Official agency photography could not go on hiding the reality of the people indefinitely. It started to decline in the 1970s, but the structure of the agencies was not disputed. Consequently, many of these agencies still exist today, but without finance or activity.

PMSL & JLP

Photograph
AMAP / ANIM ©
President Nkwame Nkrumah
on a state visit to Mali,
ca. 1960.

AMAP/ANIM

Mali

Created at Independence and based on a previous colonial body, the ANIM (National Malian Information Agency) grew under Modibo Keita, followed by Moussa Traore, with help from the Eastern bloc. Some of the staff were trained in the former East Germany and Czechoslovakia. The ANIM became the AMAP (Malian Press and Publicity Agency) in 1992. It used to employ 15 photographers posted in every region of Mali; today there are only six. The 6 x 6 mm and 24 x 36 mm archives are kept at the agency, whose activities are today much more limited.

∧ Photograph
AMAP/ANIM © ca. 1960
Demonstration in the streets of Bamako.

< Photograph
AMAP/ANIM © ca. 1960
Malian and Vietnamese women parade in Bamako.

Photograph >
AMAP/ANIM © ca. 1960
President Modibo Keïta.

Photograph AMAP/ANIM © 1991
The Bamako events.
The fall of Moussa Traoré.

SYLI-PHOTO - ONACIG

Guinea

At the time of Guinean indepedences in 1958, the colonial photographic collection was attached to the Ministry of Information and Ideology. In 1961 the Agency Syli-Photo was set up, working for the state under the supervision of President Sékou Touré . Very soon it owned dozens of photographic studios in Conakry and in the large towns in Guinea. The collection was methodically catalogued without mention being made of the photographers' names. On the death of Sékou Touré, the agency was more or less abandoned before being incorporated into ONACIG (National Board of Guinea Cinema) in 1986. The photographic collection, much of which has now come to light, is of prime importance as a witness to the important events of the last 30 years in Guinea. Syli-Photo - ONACIG has slowed down its activities considerably since 1986.

In the time of Sékou Touré

Guy Hersant

As soon as independence was declared, Sékou Touré's Guinea took control of the former colonial photographic service. With a staff trained by a Czech photographer, Syli-Photo became a veritable press agency with a monopoly over nearly all photography in Guinea for several years. The agency's job was to document the actions of the government and its supreme leader. The first Korean colour laboratory opened in Conakry in 1985, a year after Sékou Touré's death.

In 1958, Guinea was the first country of the French colonial empire in West Africa to attain independence. After Sékou Touré's legendary « No » to De Gaulle, and until his death in 1984, the « Supreme Guide of the Revolution » presided over the destiny of the Peoples' Republic of Guinea, Africa's first socialist state.

The government rapidly took over the photographic service of the former French colonial administration in Conakry and integrated it into the newly-created Ministry of Information and Ideology. Ten men and women were recruited and trained as photographers by Mr Loubo, who directed the government's photographic and cinema services until 1965.

In 1961, the service was restructured along the lines of a press agency and renamed Syli-Photo. Government-run and -controlled, one of its first actions was the expropriation of the network of French-owned photographic studios in Conakry and other principal cities of the country. In general, the studios were allowed to continue their former activity of producing portraits and identity photos, while enjoying a de facto monopoly in the sales of film and photographic supplies in the country.

< Photograph
SYLI-PHOTO - ONACIG © 1962
Presidents Léopold Sédar Senghor and Sékou Touré during the Senegal-Guinea conference in Labé, Guinea.

∧ Photograph SYLI-PHOTO - ONACIG © 1963-64
Algerian President Ben Bella during a state visit to Guinea.

Photograph SYLI-PHOTO - ONACIG © 1964 ∧
Ivory Coast President Houphouët-Boigny during a state visit to Guinea.

From 1961 to 1967, Mustapha Wally, a photographer of mixed Guinean-Senegalese origins, served as Syli-Photo's director. Wally had been trained in photography at the Agfa School in Hamburg; his wife, an East German, was put in charge of the agency's archives. Although the negatives were carefully captioned and classified, the names of the photographers were never noted. Today, it is impossible to determine the identity of the photographers who took them.

By the 1960s, Syli-Photo had attained a highly professional level of operation, while talented photographers such as Amadou Bah, Élisa Camara, Samoura and Wouly Barry contributed to the agency's reputation for excellence. In 1962 the government opened a photography school directed by the German photographer, Kurtlinger. Although the school closed two years later, it nevertheless trained 22 new photographers, most of whom were assigned to other cities with the objective of creating a national network of Syli-Photo photographers.

The Syli-Photo staff covered every aspect of politics, culture and sport in the country. Mass meetings, sumptuous receptions for foreign dignitaries, official inaugurations and the public appearances of President Touré were amply documented by their cameras. They often accompanied the President or members of his government abroad, were assigned to research projects by visiting experts, and produced photographic illustrations for reports, books and periodicals. For purely ideological purposes, Syli-Photo photographers were also allowed to film the prison camp of Boiro and the hangings of criminals. Other and more specialized activities included aerial photography of strategic and industrial sites and the documentation of various infrastructures. The agency's photographers were constantly active on assignments both nationally and abroad. Certain staff members, exhausted by the workload and frenetic pace or, like Wouly Barry, sickened by the acts of repression they had had to photograph, simply resigned and took up activities such as commerce, farming or studio photography.

In 1976, Amadou Bah died in a motorbike accident after a photo session at the presidential palace. But there was no shortage of replacements and new photographers, such as Alpha Bacar Diallo and Laye Camara, joined the agency. All the Syli-Photo staff members who were active during this period describe it as one in which work was interesting and plentiful and photographers had generous financial means and the latest equipment at their disposal. Today this is no longer the case.

President Touré was particularly cordial toward « his » photographers, and often took a personal interest in their work and family life. He was so approachable that on the occasions when he travelled abroad, foreign photographers, used to stringent security measures for heads of state, were astounded by the proximity and familiarity accorded to members of the Guinean press. This did not prevent several of these photographers, including Amadou Bah and Wouly Barry, from being imprisoned in Camp Boiro after the events of 1970. Liberated after completing their sentences, they had little choice other than to return to the waiting arms of their « benevolent » dictator-president.

Of the 26 years of Syli-Photo's continual activity, little - in terms of archival material - remains today. After Sékou Touré's death in 1984 and until the founding of the Third Republic in 1986, little effort was made to preserve the work of the agency's photographers, which over the years was subjected to vandalism, looting and the destructive effects of the tropical climate. The work of the studio photographers has fared little better: when not abandoning the photographs and negatives to destruction by their successors or descendants, most of them simply disposed of the images that they had amassed during the 30 to 40 years of their professional careers. The remains of the Syli-Photo archives are stored at the headquarters of the ONACIG (*Office National du Cinéma Guinéen*). To the dismay of Mr Souma, the director of the photography department, the majority of the negatives have been haphazardly thrown into cardboard boxes and appear to have been completely ruined by the effects of humidity.

Only the 6 x 6 cm black-and-white negatives dating from 1960 to 1963, which were carefully placed in individual cellophane envelopes by the conscientious Madame Wally, have survived the destruction.

The archives, although incomplete, testify to the professionalism and industry of the Syli-Photo photographers. The images are often artistic and vibrant, occasionally amusing, and have an enormous historical value. Given the lack of liberty during the Touré years, unposed and spontaneous street scenes or images of village and neighbourhood life are markedly absent. Instead, the Syli-Photo photographers documented the birth and infancy of Africa's first socialist government, including the pompous celebrations of its political leaders, eager to be immortalized on film. Although this type of state-commissioned photography was a familiar product of the Eastern European countries during the same period, the Syli-Photo images are permeated by a carefree and typically African enthusiasm whose charm and impertinence make them extremely engaging.

For a more intimate vision of Guinea during the reign of President Touré, one must turn to the independent photographers. Although the majority were rarely allowed to venture beyond the confines of their studios, a few of them, mostly established in small towns in the interior of the country, nevertheless captured numerous scenes of the spontaneous daily life of their fellow-citizens. This was the case of Zacharia Kaba, a photographer of Kankan who, although retired since 1990, has preserved the greater part of his archives. Some of them, composed of entire rolls of negatives covered with an impressive layer of dust, hang suspended from wires that crisscross his former darkroom.

Mamadou Barry, a charming and aged photographer, continues to produce portraits and identity photographs in his little studio in a popular quarter of Kankan. Stubbornly opposed to the politics of Touré, Barry never used his talent to extol the glories of the regime.

Although he began his career in 1955, he has only preserved six or seven 13 x 18 cm negatives of his remarkable work. In Kouroussa, another locality in Upper Guinea, Alpha « Agfa » Diallo travels through the bush on his bicycle for weeks at a time during the dry season before returning home with his new stock of identity photographs for the government. Although active for many years, Diallo is another of the many photographers who has never kept archives. The traditional activities of the studio photographer have diminished dramatically with the passage of time. Aside from rare members of the previous generation, such as Mamadou Barry (who still likes to work in black-and-white despite the difficulties of obtaining film and development chemicals), the young photographers who have succeeded them continue with portrait and family photography using colour negative film. Often inexperienced and ill-equipped, they all have their film processed in one of the 20 rapid-development laboratories (ten of which are in Conakry) owned by South Koreans. The latter, through their domination of the market, exercise a phenomenal monopoly over the photography-related economy not only of Guinea, but also of much of West Africa.

The transition from black-and-white to colour, made obligatory by the mechanization of film processing and the monopoly of the development laboratories, in conjunction with the long period of cultural and technological isolation imposed by the socialist regime, has resulted in the semi-stagnation of Guinea's collective and individual creative energies. Photographers are among those who suffer from this most: some have attempted to organize unions or professional associations but, since they lack the information and financial means to do so, little has so far been accomplished. Official institutions such as the ONACIG, the National Museum and the Ministry of Culture, increasingly aware of the factors weighing upon the preservation and development of the country's photographic talent and heritage, have taken steps to preserve existing archives and favour the training of new photographers and the development of new careers.

Guy Hersant

Tierno Monenembo

Portrait of my grandfather

In 1960, my father stumbled across a yellowing photograph eaten away by mould while looking for some forgotten item in the archives of the National Research and Documentation Institute of Guinea (INRDG): the most eminent figures of Porédaka, our native village, gathered together and immortalized by a camera lens! Many were already nearly adults when a column of French soldiers and Sudanese infantrymen, led by Captain Müller, beat the Almamy Bocar Biro, the last king of Fouta-Djalon (the last independent kingdom in West Africa, as far as I know). So this photograph is not just a family relic, it's an historical document! It was taken around 1930, most probably by an ethnologist. But my father had never seen or even heard of it before. As far as he knew - and his investigations would later prove him right - none of his brothers or cousins had a copy of it. He had discovered it in a drawer, hidden between old maps of French Guinea and various monographs on the habits and customs of the different peoples in the region: Bagas, Nalous, Kissis, Peuhls, Malinkés, etc. A small card stapled to the photograph read: « Portrait of Fouta Djalon dignitaries (village of Porédaka) ».

He quickly made some copies of the photograph and distributed them to all his relatives. It was a major event! That year, my father had started retracing the family tree back to the 17th century, when our ancestors were said to have left Macina, the Niger loop, headed for the grassy high plateaux of Fouta-Djalon. He had already collected several accounts from griots (travelling poets, musicians and folk-historians) and old men, a few old notices written in Peuhl or Arabic, and created a noteworthy photograph library with his old Agfa bellows camera. Then this photograph appeared out of nowhere, like a gift from the gods! But that wasn't the biggest surprise. After all, he had accidentally discovered a photograph of the Almamy Bocar Biro a few years previously. He had no idea that Mr Nièpce's funny little machine had already toured the world (including the African mangrove swamps, no less). No, the surprise was that his own father, Thierno Macka (the guy with a black cloak, hat slightly askew in the second row, sixth from the right) had let himself be snared by the cheeky little contraption.

To think that he had tried all kinds of tricks and ruses to get a photograph of his venerable father, to no avail! The latter would invariably declare that he would not give his face over to the heathen white man's abominable, bewitched object.

- There's nothing magical about it. It's simply shadows and light.
- That's just the point. If it's not magic, then I'm not interested. There's no point creating an uglier version of my nostrils and my eyebrows without being able to depict my fits of anger and my dreams!

How the devil did he end up in that photo? It's hard to imagine a squadron of infantrymen forcing him to pose at gunpoint. It would be more plausible to speculate that he must have been tricked. For example, someone might have brought along a griot to sing his praises while the photographer pressed the button. Or a marabout (holy man) might have gathered everyone together under the pretext of blessing the clan. Unless he grudgingly agreed to do the same as everyone else, for once. For my dear grandfather was not an easy man. He would get into a huff over nothing, didn't give a damn about orders from above and never followed other people's advice. In fact, he owes his modest position in the photograph to his bloody-minded nature. If he had been a little more accommodating, he would have been sitting in the front row in the chief's seat, with all the trappings: turban, talisman, stick et al. That position was rightfully his. But the colonial governor preferred his cousin, Alpha Saliou (the funny one sitting in the middle of the row). He had attained the rank of sergeant during the First World War for slaying Germans in the quagmire of the Ardennes. Whereas my grandfather had not only refused to join up, he had also threatened to burn down the school, and paid his taxes only under extreme duress.

This state of affairs was the basis of a memorable quarrel (that still stands between the two families today, though in much milder form) about which the Peuhls know the full story. My grandfather drew his sabre and called God and his loyal followers to witness: « Tell this usurping dog to return what is owing to me.

Otherwise I will slit his throat or burn down the village ». The elders had to use every ounce of their patience and tact to bring him to reason. One shrewd politician, Alpha Saliou, offered his most beautiful sister in marriage. A girl was born from this union, my aunt Aye-Sira, whose husband's name I would later bear.

Yet there was still more drama to be played out in the village. The man behind the ruckus was also a sergeant: anyone would think the infantrymen had come back to the village with the intention of carrying on the war they had left behind them. His name was Thierno Amadou, and he was an elegant medical student. He is not in this photograph, but he loved showing off for the camera. There were several photographs in the village of him grinning happily, with his cap, gabardine overcoat, gaiters and boots. He is remembered as the first man in the village to have brought back Roberval scales and a bicycle. He was as modern as my grandfather was archaic. While the former was happy to chatter about Notre Dame and the Eiffel Tower, Bordeaux and Sedan, the latter took a train once in his life, from Mamou to Conakry. It was a coal-fired train that made him cough and covered his clothes in smoke and dust. He kicked up a right rumpus, complaining that he had been made to pay to travel in a boiler when he could have taken his horse, a means of locomotion that did not belch smoke or ask you for your ticket but that travelled just as fast. Unfortunately, there was no local Nadar[1] to capture this lively scene on film at the time.

Nonetheless, a sweet young thing ended up falling in love with Thierno Amadou. They got married and had two children (my uncle Siddi and aunt Malado). The scandal split the village into two antagonistic fractions who nearly battled it out with guns and knives. Paradoxically, I owe my birth to this quasi-Shakespearean tragedy. To calm things down, the elders decided to offer one of Thierno Amadou's daughters, my future mother, to one of Thierno Macka's sons, my future father.

My maternal grandfather died in 1983 aged 95. I never knew my paternal grandfather. He died when I was three months old. Which means that I « ate » him to find the strength to be born, just like I « ate » all the old men in the village who passed away that year. I don't apparently bear much physical resemblance to him, except for his slenderness, his slim fingers and flat fingernails. I look more like my paternal grandmother, the famous Néné Mbo, to whom I owe my unpronounceable, primitive assumed name. But I am told I have his character: edgy, cantankerous and incorrigibly indecisive. And that, as my wonderful grandfather used to say, cannot be seen in a photograph.

Tierno Monénembo
1. A famous French photographer.

∧ Photograph
CONGOPRESSE © ca.1950
*Urban police in Léopoldville
(Kinshasa).*

Photograph
CONGOPRESSE © ca.1950
Tannery in Léopoldville (Kinshasa). >

Photograph
CONGOPRESSE © ca.1950
*Bushi dairy, Kabare,
Kivu province.* >

< Photograph
CONGOPRESSE © ca.1950
*Provincial Police Training School,
Lufungula camp in Léopoldville
(Kinshasa).*

CONGOPRESSE

Democratic Republic of Congo

Congopresse was the official agency of the Belgian Congo in the days when the territory, one of the largest, richest and most densely populated in Africa, belonged to the King of Belgium. The process of colonization was particularly harsh and violent, yet every means possible was used to make it look beneficial.

Congopresse's images, transmitted throughout the world as documentary photographs of Belgian Congo, showed an Africa brought firmly under the yoke of the police and their Dobermanns, but also a «happy» Congolese population in its moments of leisure. When independence came, the fleeting emancipation so painfully led by Patrice Lumumba did not free the country from dictatorship. Congopresse has greatly reduced its activity since 1970.

∧ Photograph
CONGOPRESSE © ca.1950
*Photographer Jean Nsuka in
Léopoldville (Kinshasa).*

< Photograph
CONGOPRESSE © ca.1950
*Swimming pool at the Général
Ermens Sports Park,
Léopoldville (Kinshasa).*

Photograph ∧
CONGOPRESSE © ca.1950
Léopoldville (Kinshasa).

Photograph >
CONGOPRESSE © ca.1950
*Athletics competition in Léopoldville
(Kinshasa).*

A Foto

Angola

The Angola Information and Tourism Centre, CITA, was founded in 1949 in Luanda when the famous slogan «Let's go and discover Angola» was announced. The photography department launched a huge campaign to record all the aspects of Angolan daily life: portraits of Portuguese colonists, traditional chiefs and Angolan peasants, gravestones of dignitaries, ritual or official ceremonies, traditional dances, the Luanda carnival, landscapes, etc. The CITA ceased to exist in 1975 when Angola gained its independence. The Information and Propaganda Department (DIP) of the MPLA, created in 1977 under the authority of the Ministry of Information, recovered the CITA collection. As its name suggests, the DIP served the authorities and its mission was to promote the government's image in covering the war against UNITA, the trials of captured English and South African mercenaries, state visits from Soviet Bloc leaders, and presidential tours. In 1981 the DIP changed its name to En Foto (National Photo Enterprise). Following attempts at national reconciliation and the first elections in 1991, En Foto was privatized and became A Foto. The agency diversified and branched out into advertising, industrial and tourist photography, birthdays, weddings, banquets, portraits in people's homes, sporting events and postcard publication. A Foto has four contract photographers, a colour and black-and-white developing and copying lab, and the archives of its predecessors. The archives contain over 150 000 prints taken by a hundred anonymous Portuguese and Angolan photographers, arranged by subject in filing cabinets, which retrace nearly half a century of Angolan history.

Photograph A FOTO © 1958 ∧
Soba – traditional authority – during an official ceremony in Moxico.

Photograph A FOTO © 1953 >
Portuguese colonist couple in Lubango.

Photograph A FOTO © 1953 ∧
*The Maréchal Carmona native
association in Luanda.*

Photograph A FOTO © 1958 >
*Soba – traditional authority–
with his secretary in Benguela.*

FTM Agency

Madagascar

The French colonists set up an IGN (Institut Géographique et Hydrographique Nationale) branch in Madagascar in 1896. Military land surveyors and engineers travelled the country to set up infrastructures. What would later become the FTM was the Madagascan geographic service (SGM) at the time. In the 1950s, this military mission turned into a social and economic one and the geographic service compiled basic maps for work on main roads. When Madagascar gained independence in 1960, the Geographic Service continued to be a branch of the IGN. In 1974, the Madagascan state took over the Geographic Service and turned it into the FTM (Foiben Taosarintanin'I Madagasikara). The photographs taken between 1896 and 1905 all come from the military missions; the others are currently stocked at the Anta agency. The photographs were taken by French and Madagascan photographers who accompanied the various missions, but nobody knows what their names were. The FTM currently handles aerial shots, photogrammetry and orthophotography (techniques used in mapping and surveying), but its main activity is focused on the creation of tourist and thematic maps of the country.

∧ Photograph FTM © 1901
Foreground left:
Foreground left: Tsimanandrafozana Kamany, son of Toera the Sakalava king, who later became governor of Menabe for over 50 years. Centre: Havana, his tutor, after the king's death in 1897. These warriors fought the French to defend the Menabe province.

< Photograph FTM © 1898
Two young thieves being clapped in irons in Tananarive.

Photography FTM © 1902 >
A leper from Ambohidratrimo.

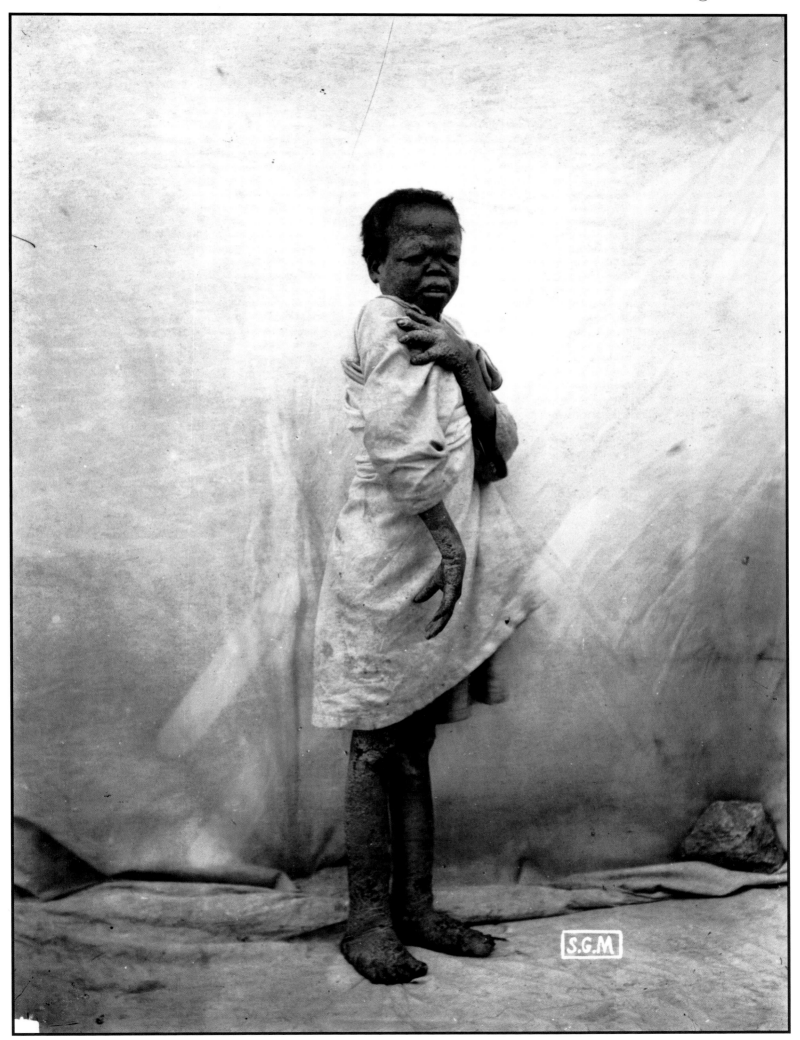

S.G.M

Michèle Rakotoson

MY UNCLE, MY MEMORY

(referring to the photograph The rebels of 1947 from the ANTA Agency)

- I think it's my uncle ...

She is looking at a photograph taken during the 1947 rebellion. An unknown photograph. With unknown people. But she has a strange impression that this is a face she has seen, or made out before.

The adored uncle around whom myths have been woven. The son who took to the forest to follow the woman he loved, a beautiful young girl, 15 years old, who became his love, his whole life, the pretext for discovering the life of the abandoned people who lived there, then the rebellion, 1947 ...

A myth.

- I'm sure it's my uncle.

She smiles, giggles, laughs at herself ...

- Your ego will catch you out one day ... You see yourself everywhere, and when it's not you it's your family ...

But the snigger fades away. She definitely recognizes him. He had the same pale colouring, almost Asian, and he must have had that posture, those clothes. He had been on the way to becoming a dentist in the mid-1940s in Antananarivo, then fled to the forest, looking for an ideal, met his ideal, and paid the price ... a high one ...

A song wanders through the depths of her memory, a tune ...

Ramatoa an ...

Zany foko, lasanao

- Woman, you who have carried my heart away ...

That's what photographs are for, for holding time still, possibly for identification. This photograph is beautiful. He is standing, a little taller than his companions, who have a somewhat rougher appearance. He is lighter-skinned, westernized. The neo-colonial clichés work well here: he is the civilized native who will lead his people out of darkness to victory. «The uncle» even begins to look like the personification of Victory. To make this leap is easy, but its logic does not stand up to analysis. The photograph was taken in Moramanga, in 1947. The massacres had started there when the soldiers opened fire on the train carriages where the rebels had been locked up. Torturers sometimes lack imagination, or maybe they are just loyal to their methods. Fleeing the European courts in 1946, they took the death-train principle with them ... And the fair-skinned man is a rebel leader, like her uncle.

She decides that it is him. Her favourite uncle. You create your own memory, your own personal mythology: history is only recognizable when it talks about oneself. This man is her uncle, her childhood obsession. The man who never said a word, who told her about the camps once, and only once.

It was a nightmare, you know, he had said. Absolute horror. We had nothing to eat but manioc, and they used to throw excrement into it before we ate it. We were hungry, we made do with wiping it off. And then there was ...

The uncle had said no more. One day she was told he had died. Never had the time to ask him questions about that time, made do with remembering his anger, his rebellion, his sighs. What happened? Why the silence?

A childhood spent in the shadow of silence ... from the father, from the uncle, these men who came back muted ... The uncle who had never been able to return to the town, to his own people, the uncle who chose the forest ... as though the rebellion meant he could no longer see anyone at all.

She looks at the photograph and decides it's him. A way for her to break the silence, history's silence, her uncle's, her father's silence, get away from the shadowy areas, understand, bid farewell to the anger and the hatred ...

She looks at the photograph, thinks of Vatomandry, the holidays, the farm workers over there. She smiles in relief. The decision has been made. She is going to rebuild her memory little by little, find a coherency at last. The story is no longer just words, it is now hers, there are faces to it, the uncle's silence is being filled, the shadows are melting away and facing the cries, the memories are becoming her own.

- It's my uncle, she says to herself.

And tears up the photograph.

Michèle Rakotoson

ANTA

Madagascar

The agency was set up in 1928 but only really took off in 1946 when the photographic information service was set up. With the birth of the *Revue de Madagascar*'s publication *Red and Gold*, a policy of systematically archiving its numerous photos became essential. The events of 1947 speeded up organization of the agency, including the installation of the photolab in the district of Ambohidahy. From 1957 the new cinema department gave the Agency many news and current affairs documents. When independence came, the photographic information service at the time assembled all the photographs of official ceremonies: visits of foreign heads of state, inauguration of the stadium, arts prize ceremonies. The disappearance of the *Revue* and the *Madagascar Bulletin* in 1974 considerably slowed down the service. ANTA is now seeking new legal status.

∧ Photograph ANTA © 1947
Derailing of a locomotive.
Attack during the 1947 rebellion.

Images of reality

mages du réel

One of the big question marks with regard to African photography is the almost complete lack of photographs depicting social and political reality, with the exception of a few individuals and certain countries like South Africa and Kenya, which seem to be special cases. State agencies towed the official line of autocratic powers and seriously undermined the credibility of photography, which no longer represented social reality. However, this must be seen in the context of the editorial poverty of most African countries. The proliferation of publications specializing in analysis and commentary in the 1980s and 1990s could have created an opportunity for social photography, but in fact only official newspapers and publications close to the government had the economic means to print photographs. Publications expressing independent opinions probably did not feel the need to publish photographs, and when they did, the quality was so poor the photographs could barely be made out. Yet is it therefore possible to conclude that the media and photographs played no part in the democratization, where applicable, of Africa?

The examples in southern Africa of the Frontline states at war - Mozambique, Zimbabwe and Namibia - and of the anti-apartheid struggle in South Africa, show that there is «no reality without an image». These courageous examples of photography were weapons of the people, often triumphing by showing the world at large images of revolutionaries at war, massacres and inequality. This militant photography, in the cause of which some heroic photographers fighting for human rights died, was accompanied by photography that depicted the banality of another, less spectacular reality - that of daily life as it was truly lived, whether in poverty or affluence. These photographers felt a strong need to reveal society the way it was and the way they experienced it. They operated on the fringes and often worked in very difficult, if not impossible, economic conditions, producing photographs taken in the homes of people from all walks of life, photographs of social outcasts, and photographs of rural, urban and architectural environments.

Photographer
JOHN MAULUKA © 1980
Independence day in
Zimbabwe.

PMSL & JLP

223

The press in Kenya

Sébastien Porte

Kenya has a long tradition of print journalism.[1] Although often associated with foreign interests, the Kenyan press is today considered to be both relatively independent and representative of a diversity of viewpoints. There are two principal daily newspapers in the country: *The East African Standard* and *The Nation*. The first has existed for nearly a century, while the second appeared after Kenya's independence. Other periodicals include those affiliated with the government and a small number of low-circulation periodicals of the alternative press.

Sebastien Porte holds a degree in political science and is a journalist. From 1996 to 1997, he was a cultural attaché at the French Embassy in Kenya.

THE EAST AFRICAN STANDARD

Founded in 1902 by an Asian who had made a fortune out of the construction of a railroad between the coast of the Indian Ocean and Uganda, *The East African Standard* is East Africa's oldest daily newspaper. From its very beginnings, it was an ally of colonialism. Its founding dated from the period when the British, aided by workers imported from India, began to construct railroads and reinforce their control over the region. In 1910, *The Standard* was purchased by a consortium of English colonists. Its headquarters were transferred from Mombasa to Nairobi, a new city on the edge of the Rift Valley. In 1923, it absorbed its principal competitor, *The Leader*, and began publishing local editions in Tanzania (1930) and Uganda (1953). After the decolonization of Kenya, the paper was sold to the British Lonrho Group in 1970. As a foreign-owned (and specifically British-owned) newspaper, *The Standard* adopted an editorial position which reflected the opinions and interests of its white readership, while its style was similar to that of English tabloid papers such as *The Sun*. Today, *The Standard* is principally owned by Kenyan nationals. In 1996 it was purchased by elements reputedly close to the Kenya African National Union (KANU), the political party of President Daniel Arap Moi, who has been in office since 1978. *The Standard*'s daily readership is currently estimated at approximately 65 000.

Photographer >
KHAMIS RAMADHAN © ca. 1990
Demonstrations.

1. *The East African Standard* and *The Nation*, Kenya's two most popular high-circulation newspapers, are modelled on Anglo-Saxon dailies. Their readership includes the populations of east and southern Africa.

Images of reality

THE NATION

If the origins of *The East African Standard* are rooted in colonialism, those of *The Nation* are directly linked to the postcolonial period. Even today, however, much of *The Nation*'s capital is still foreign-held: *The Nation Newspapers Company Ltd* was created in 1958 by the Aga Khan and his private secretary, Michael Curtis, who had been trained in modern press management techniques in Europe and the United States. After Kenya's independence in 1963, a new generation of local African journalists began working for the paper, several of whom, such as George Githii and Hilary Ng'weno, would eventually occupy the position of editor-in-chief. *The Nation* was also quick to adopt the latest in technological progress. It was one of the first newspapers outside the United States to be printed on web offset presses in 1960 and adopted the technique of photo-composition in 1972. Colour illustrations appeared in early 1997, a year after those of *The Standard*. In 1968, *The Nation*'s circulation began to surpass that of *The Standard* and it became East Africa's most widely read newspaper. Its circulation increased from 57 000 in 1971 to 200 000 in 1990. With its four leading titles (*The Daily Nation*, *The Sunday Nation*, *Taifa Leo*, a Swahili daily and *The East African*, created in 1994), the Aga Khan's press group is at present Kenya's largest.

THE KENYA TIMES

The Kenya Times, the country's third-largest daily newspaper, was launched in 1983 by President Moi's political party, the only official party in Kenya from 1982 to 1992. The paper was established to replace *The Nairobi Times*, Hilary Ng'weno's weekly, judged to be too critical of the government. Openly favouring President Moi's politics and extremely critical of his opponents, *The Kenya Times* was the quasi-official organ of the government: its directors and editorial staff were hand-picked by Moi himself. In 1987, the paper came under joint ownership of the Robert Maxwell Group. Less than ten years later, *The Kenya Times* ceased publication of its Swahili edition and today appears only in English.[2] As for the remaining titles of the Swahili rural press, most have today ceased publication after vainly attempting to attract a permanent readership in the late 1980s.

Despite its nationalistic ambitions, the daily press of Kenya never achieved the autonomy from non-national influence desired by the government. For purely nationally-controlled publications, one must turn to Kenya's weekly periodicals.

MAGAZINES

To ensure their interests - principally advertising sales and the avoidance of conflicts with the government - the groups that own Kenya's two leading daily newspapers have adopted moderate editorial policies characterized by political neutrality. Since both papers have also adopted a policy of using articles supplied by Western press agencies, their readership is principally composed of the urban English-speaking segment of the population.

By contrast, the weekly periodicals, which are generally locally owned, have preserved their independence and editorial freedom - often being critical of the established order. The first example of alternative journalism in Kenya was *The Weekly Review*, founded by Hilary Ng'weno in 1975, which specialized in political analysis and commentary. After resisting years of political and financial pressure - despite the initial support of the Kenyan government - *The Weekly Review* enjoys a wide readership both in Kenya and abroad.

Society and *Finance* are two political magazines close to the opposition parties. Along with the *Nairobi Law Monthly*, a law review launched in 1987, these publications campaigned for the end of a single-party system in Kenya. As a result of various political pressures, their publication has become erratic; other titles, such as *Beyond Magazine* or the *Financial Review*, were simply banned in 1987. Among other economic and financial periodicals are *The Economic Review* and the *Business Chronicle*, the latter title being the main competitor of *The East African Standard*.

Today, Kenya's highest-circulation weekly is Kenneth Matiba's *People* magazine. Created in 1994 by Matiba, the leader of the Ford-Asili party, *People* is the voice of the opposition. If, as planned, it becomes a daily publication, it may well supplant the pro-government *Kenya Times*. More recently, *The Evening News*, launched in 1997, is an evening paper that appeared following President Moi's re-election in December of the same year.

A TENTATIVE EMERGENCE OF FREEDOM

Although the current wave of democratization appears to have weakened Kenya's long-standing tradition of overt censorship and physical and political coercion of the press, more hidden forms of control still exist. In general, however, the owners and editorial staff themselves exercise a prudent form of self-censure to avoid open conflict with the government.

Photographer >
KHAMIS RAMADHAN © ca. 1990
Demonstrations.

2. Unlike Tanzania, where Swahili has been preserved as the official language at every level of society, Kenya has always accorded a privileged position to English. Swahili is spoken by most of the country's population, although numerous local dialects have tended to detract from its use.

3. In its 1996 report, the watchdog association Reporters Sans Frontières identified several cases of harassment and interference with the liberty of the press in Kenya. The report also documents the experiences of journalists - including the photographer, Jacob Waweru - who have been victims of police harassment or physical aggression by militant members of the KANU and members of the government security services.

After the transition to a multiparty system in 1991 and the organization of the first free elections the following year, the situation of the press in Kenya has clearly improved. Although it was considered relatively unrestricted in the African context of the 1960s and 1970s, the Kenyan press increasingly suffered from government interference and the limiting effects of the one-party system after the attempted coup d'état of 1982. The situation worsened during the years that followed, with numerous attacks against freedom of the press and liberty of expression. Journalists were harassed, arrested and interrogated, and certain periodicals were forced to cease publication. During the same period (1982-83), the pro-government *Kenya Times* was launched, while editors such as Githii of *The Standard* and Rodrigues of *The Nation* were replaced by individuals less critical of the government.

Although the transition to democracy has not resulted in the massive creation of new titles, there is already a relatively abundant choice of periodicals in Kenya, the majority of which are no longer the object of direct censorship. For news photographers, police harassment and intervention has significantly diminished, with the exception of occasional interference by the GSU, a special unit assigned to important political events.[3]

Despite the explicit guarantee of liberty of the press as stated in article five of Kenya's constitution, the government still possesses an important legal arsenal for silencing critics (anti-insurrection and censorship laws, legislation for the protection of state secrets and public order, and the exclusion of journalists from sessions of parliament). There are also indirect methods of control, including economic pressure, arbitrary taxation, the threats to potential advertisers and the

corruption of editors and journalists: in Kenya, the preferred method is the carrot rather than the stick.

The strategy of the mainstream Kenyan press is to placate the authorities by exercising self-censorship, for experience has proved that it is wiser to suggest ideas between the lines than to risk censorship or even arrest for overtly writing about them. Editors generally preserve a semblance of liberty by carefully selecting the articles and photographs appearing in their papers - rather than having the authorities do it for them. The result is the often-criticized political conservatism and neutral tone that characterizes the major dailies.

The period preceding the national elections of December 1997 provoked a resumption of tension between the Kenyan press and the government authorities.

Images of reality

As early as January 1996, the proposal of yet more laws destined to further limit freedom of the press resulted in a wave of protest both in Kenya and abroad. The new legislation called for the application of a «code of good behaviour» for journalists and the press. Only those adhering to the code would be eligible for official accreditation by the Press Council, which also had the power to inflict a series of punishments (ranging from the loss of official accreditation to fines and prison sentences) to both local and foreign journalists. Owing to the public outcry and pressure from the exterior, the Attorney-General of Kenya was forced to abandon the project less than a month after it had been announced. Nevertheless, the thinly-disguised purchase of *The Standard* in 1996 by a consortium close to President Moi, was far from innocent, given the context.

During this period, public protest increased; as the date of the elections approached, university students demonstrated, the opposition campaigned for democratic and constitutional reforms and the press became more outspoken in its criticism of the government. As the tension mounted, the situation degenerated into a series of violent confrontations which culminated in the incidents of 7 July 1997, in which more than 20 demonstrators were killed. The following morning, the daily newspapers published colour photographs illustrating the violence of the government's repression of the movement, including the massacre of participants who had sought refuge in a church. Not surprisingly, the local government-run television stations accorded limited coverage to the event.

THE EMERGENCE OF KENYAN NEWS PHOTOGRAPHY

Although much progress remains to be made and its identity is still embryonic, news photography in Kenya is currently undergoing a promising transformation with the arrival of a new generation of talented and courageous photographers.

For a variety of cultural and economic reasons common to both the Kenyan press and its readers, the country's newspapers tend to consider photographs as being of secondary importance to printed text. Considering the importance accorded to the photographic image elsewhere in the world, it would be an exaggeration to say that the Kenyan press has attained the same level: relative to other African countries, however, the quality of Kenyan news photography leaves nothing to be desired, being surpassed only by that of South Africa, with its uniquely dynamic and prolific press. Both economically and politically, the « New South Africa » is emerging as a model for its neighbours, and one which is perhaps even more attractive than that offered by North America or Europe.

Over the last few years, a new generation of highly professional news photographers has begun working in the Kenyan press.

Unlike press photography in the 1980s, their work is characterised by a spirit of innovation, creativity and dynamism - occasionally to excess. Their coverage of political events has little in common with the previous tradition of insipid official images immortalizing handshakes and artificial smiles. Today, Kenyan photographers no longer work at a safe distance from events, and they accept the risk of taking photographs which may never be published.

Despite the frequent use of archival material or photos supplied by Western press syndicates, papers such as *The Nation* and *The Standard* each day publish photographs taken by local photographers to illustrate local news stories. Agency photos serve as important models for Kenyan photographers, as do more generally the foreign journalists and international media chains present in Nairobi. A number of Kenyan photographers readily admit the influence exercised over them by the American and European press, which they often consider as being both a model and a source of inspiration.

Besides these external influences, Kenyan journalists and photographers have limited means of acquiring their professional skills other than at the University of Nairobi's School of Journalism (which has existed only since 1970) or the Kenyan Institute of Mass Communication (for those interested in pursuing a career in radio, film or television). The majority of the (approximately 30) Kenyan press photographers working for the three leading daily papers have never received professional training and gradually learned their craft through hands-on experience.

The current limitations in professional training, the lack of contact and exchange with Western colleagues, the absence of a clearly-defined professional status and, above all, the absence of an association to defend the liberty of the press against the onslaughts of the government, are among the unfortunate realities of Kenyan journalism today. The situation of freelance photographers is particularly unenviable: the market value of a photograph published on the front page of *The Nation* is approximately five US dollars. The same photographer is also more vulnerable to police harassment and political coercion than staff photographers for one of the established dailies.

In addition to these severe drawbacks, professional photographers also suffer from limited budgets for covering events, and are further hampered by often obsolete equipment and the mediocre quality of the reproduction of their work in the press. Much progress remains to be accomplished before press photography in Kenya can fulfil the promises offered by its potential for excellence.

Sébastien Porte

KHAMIS RAMADHAN

Kenya
b. Nairobi, Kenya 1965 – lives in Nairobi

Khamis Ramadhan has been interested in photography since he was eleven. His interest in images led him to become a researcher. Since 1992 he has been working as a freelance photographer and his photographs are published in African papers in Europe and East Africa. Kenya is the second most important press centre on the continent, after South Africa, and a large number of high-circulation publications exist in the region. The multiparty system and a series of democratic elections in the country sparked off tighter control of freedom of the press by the ruling powers, but the mobilization of the democrats and violent demonstrations have ensured a certain amount of freedom, mainly guaranteed by the fact that newspapers censor themselves.

Photographer ∧
KHAMIS RAMADHAN © ca. 1990
Demonstrations.

> Photographer
> ALEXANDER JOE - AFP © 1997
> *Demonstrators grappling with the police at the Anglican Cathedral in Nairobi.*

ALEXANDER JOE

Zimbabwe
b. Harare , Zimbabwe 1951
– lives in Nairobi

Alexander Joe started photography in 1975. He worked for the *Rhodesian Herald* and covered the war of independence in Zimbabwe, then the war and famine in Mozambique. In 1982 he set off to try his luck in London. He covered the miners' strike and the war in Northern Ireland for the *Guardian*, the *Times* and the *Daily Mail*. He joined the Agence France Presse (AFP) in 1985 as a freelancer in Harare, before becoming a permanent East Africa correspondent and settling in Nairobi in 1991. He has covered the famine in Ethiopia, the fall of two Ugandan governments, the coronation of the King of Swaziland, the war in Angola, the ousting of the « Red Terror » regime in Ethiopia, the war and famine in Somalia, two coups d'état in the Comoro islands, the strike that brought down the Ratsiraka government in Madagascar, the liberation of Nelson Mandela, the first multi-party elections in South Africa, the genocide in Rwanda and Burundi and most recently, the plight of refugees in Zaïre.

Photographer ∧
ALEXANDER JOE - AFP © 1998
Demonstrations in Nairobi.

Camerapix

Roger Barnard

When three hijackers ended the life of 175 passengers on Ethiopian flight ET961 on 23 November 1996 off the Comoros Islands, the crash-landing also killed Mohamed Amin, one of the most remarkable men to come out of Africa. Mohamed, already an internationally renowned news cameraman, once again became front-page news. Typically, he went down fighting, urging passengers to stand up and take on the hijackers, although nobody did. It was a sign of great courage: he was not going to sit idly by when there was even a slight chance something could be done to save the situation.

Running away from danger was not his style. When he died at the age of 53, Mohamed's body had acquired a certain textured look. He had lost an arm in an explosion, been beaten up, tortured, shot at, and injured in several car crashes: he was definitely not in pristine condition. But none of these body blows had blunted his razor-sharp mind. Indeed, it was his resolute determination to succeed which characterized his life and brought him so many plaudits and rewards. His ability to overcome bullying bureaucracy and petty officialdom was legendary. Meticulous planning was the hallmark of all his assignments and he carried with him a contacts list that was the envy of every self-respecting journalist. Through this combination - plus a God-given gift known as « Mo's luck » - he triumphed where many failed. He was admired by colleagues as the consummate professional, but it was an admiration tinged with envy when, time and again, Mohamed would get the exclusive pictures that kept him at the top and denied others the glory.

Mohamed Amin was a workaholic who demanded no less from anyone he employed. At his Nairobi-based media company, Camerapix, he worked seven days a week, usually 12 to 14 hours a day, often rising at two or three in the morning so he could work undisturbed. For anyone who was employed by him and had a life outside Camerapix, this was a hard act to follow. He was undeniably charming. It was his secret weapon. When Mohamed wanted something resolved he would explore all normal channels and, if that failed, reach for the magic contacts book. If that did not do the trick then he would turn on the charm. It flowed like a river in spate, and it worked on everyone, beguiling men, women, petty bureaucrats, politicians, heads of state, gun-toting guerrillas, despots and dictators.

He was often unassuming but not especially modest and an autobiography was in progress at the time of his death, his way of making sure that there would be a lasting record of his considerable achievements. Of these, the greatest was his photographic coverage of the Ethiopian famine of 1984 when, by bringing the plight of millions of starving people to the attention of the world, Mohamed indirectly initiated the greatest act of giving ever and earned himself and BBC colleague, Michael Buerk, awards and accolades from all over the world.

Roger Barnard is a journalist for Camerapix, an agency with offices in London and Nairobi, Kenya, which was founded in 1969 by Mohamed Amin, Brian Tetley and Duncan Willetts. Photographs and editorials cover news and tourism in southern Africa.

< Photographer
MOHAMED AMIN - CAMERAPIX ©
1989
Prisoners at Tigray during lthe war between Ethiopia and Eritrea.

Images of reality

Mohamed Amin, born on 29 August 1943, sold his first pictures at the tender age of 15, launching himself on a career initially as a photographer, and later as an award-winning cameraman. He was regularly first with the news from the trouble-spots in East Africa and the Middle East. Often this put him in conflict with authorities, and on many occasions he risked his life, but a combination of his own negotiating skills - and perhaps a dash of « Mo's luck » - always saw him through. Anyone following Mohamed Amin's career will know how closely his life was interwoven with those of his two friends and colleagues, Brian Tetley and Duncan Willetts. Together they formed a triumvirate which produced a phenomenal volume of high quality work, putting Mohamed's company, Camerapix, at the forefront of African and international media companies. He met Tetley in Nairobi in 1969 and Willetts eight years later. After they joined forces, Camerapix gradually expanded into publishing, a venture which grew over the years into a major force in travel and tourism. In a portfolio of some 40 titles produced by Camerapix, Tetley either wrote or edited the text and Amin and Willetts took virtually all the pictures.

Mohamed's first venture into publishing had been a photographic tribute to the late Tom Mboya in 1969, and several other books followed, but Pilgrimage to Mecca, the first of his large format, high quality coffee-table books, published in 1978, saw Camerapix move increasingly into book publishing. *Cradle of Mankind*, *Journey Through Pakistan*, *Journey Through Kenya*, *Run Rhino Run* and *Ivory Crisis* soon followed, and new titles were added every year, all meticulously produced with superb photography and high quality prose. 1989 saw the first of the *Camerapix Spectrum Guide* series, with *Spectrum Guide to Kenya*. The series is being steadily enlarged and updated to this day. More reference books than simply a travel handbooks, the beautifully illustrated and highly informative *Spectrum Guides* highlight countries in Africa, the Indian Ocean, the Indian subcontinent and the Middle East. *Spectrum Guide to Uganda* and *Spectrum Guide to the United Arab Emirates* are the latest titles to be produced. Many Camerapix titles have been translated into French, German, Italian, and other languages.

The events which brought about the Ethiopian famine of 1984 add up to a catalogue of despair seldom equalled in the annals of global disasters. Mohamed Amin's pivotal role in focusing world attention on the plight of starving millions must be seen as a landmark in the turbulent history of the continent. It wasn't simply a case of being in the right place at the right time, for Mohamed had fought for months for permission to visit the relief camps. Had he not been so determined, the brutal facts might never have been exposed. If Mohamed had not acted when he did in the way he did, millions more men, women and children would have starved to death. The news reports which Mohamed produced, with Michael Buerk's commentary, rocked the world. Buerk still finds it hard to recall those tragic scenes: « It was like walking into a scene from the Bible. I had never seen anything like it before, nor have I since. There were all these people, thousands of them sitting around waiting either to get food or die. I felt completely helpless; all they wanted was food and there was nothing we could do about that, so we did the only thing we could and filmed it. Mo knelt down and let his camera pan around these quiet people without disturbing them, then we'd move on. The scale of it was almost impossible to comprehend. »

With rare candour, Mohamed admitted: « Ethiopia changed me. Until then I had been able to go into any situation, no matter how awful, and switch off. I could remain at a distance from the subject, not get involved. My job is to act as an unbiased observer, to report what I see without making judgements. But this was different. You can't remain untouched when there are people dying as far as the eye can see, especially when so many of them are children. Some of those scenes I filmed really choked me up, though I tried not to show it. I don't think I have ever felt so helpless. »

Later, in the newsrooms of the world, hardened newsmen and women stared transfixed at these haunting images. They moved the world, and the subsequent international relief effort by individuals and governments raised hundreds of millions of dollars in aid. Three million people could have perished in the famine but in the event, through intervention, the death toll was reduced to one million.

In 1991 « Mo's luck » almost ran out when he nearly lost his life in a huge explosion in Addis Ababa. His left arm was so severely injured in the blast that it had to be amputated and his colleagues thought that it spelled the end of the career of Africa's leading cameraman. However, they reckoned without the tremendous determination of the man. A few months later, with a new bionic arm especially made in the USA, Mohamed was back at work.

It was not generally known that, following the accident, Mohamed was in constant pain from a plate inserted into the top of his arm to hold fragmented bone together. For the rest of his life he frequently returned to hospital for treatment and to try to alleviate the suffering. In the many interviews for newspapers, magazines and TV Mohamed gave after the accident, he never once mentioned this fact.

Roger Barnard

235

JOHN LIEBENBERG

South Africa
South Africa, Johannesburg, 1958 – lives in Johannesburg

John Liebenberg was born in Johannesburg in 1958. His parents could not afford to educate him, so he was brought up with his little sister in an orphanage. When he was 14 his uncle gave him a camera. As a white South African, he was enlisted in 1976 into the South African army which was fighting the MPLA and SWAPO in Namibia and Angola. Deeply marked by the atrocities of war, he returned to Windhoek in Namibia after his military service. He became a photographer-reporter with the «Reds» for the newspaper *The Namibian*, and for Reuters. When apartheid and the war ended, Liebenberg waited for Nelson Mandela to become President before returning to Johannesburg. He now continues his work as a free-lance photographer-reporter throughout the frontline region where, sadly, the war is not quite over yet. He also covers Angola, as seen in these photographs, and the increasing numbers of destitute and outcast people in the townships.

«Have you been to Oshakati ... the Oniimwandi camp?
Have you heard the cries of the guerrilla fighters, locked up and tortured?»
For many years, Namibia was ripped apart by its colonial history, torn between Germany, Portugal and England, Angola and South Africa, right up until independence on 21 March 1990.
Excerpt from the book *Namibia*. 1994. Photographs by John Liebenberg and seven other photographers. Soleil Collection, Éditions Revue Noire.

Photographer
JOHN LIEBENBERG ©

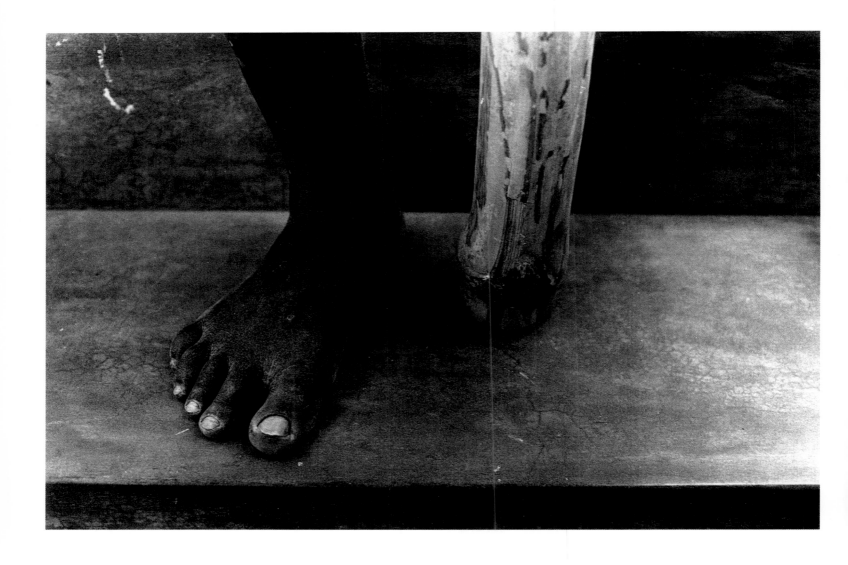

Chronicles of war

Simon Njami

The first evidence of photography in Mozambique dates back to 1873. The most renowned studio, run by the Lazarus brothers, was set up in Lourenço Marques (now Maputo) in 1899. The first photographs of local people were driven mainly by the European thirst for discovery so characteristic of the time: anthropometric visions that portrayed the stereotyped « noble savage » which Europe expected. It was not until the 1920s that photographs appeared regularly in the press, but newspapers started hiring professional photographers only after the Second World War.

In the early 1960s, Mozambique embarked on a war for independence that dragged the country into a cycle of violence, limiting photography to ideological propaganda. In 1964, the Mozambique Liberation Front, Frelimo, founded two years previously, launched a guerrilla war against the Portuguese. Photography became a weapon on both sides: photojournalism ruled, with its daily accounts of the fighting. Alongside the official press, three opposition journals were established: *A Voz do Moçambique*, *A Tribuna and Tempo*, set up later on, in 1970.

In 1964 the photographers Ricardo Rangel and Kok Nam worked for the Diario de Moçambique in Beira, the second largest city in the country. The content of these photographers' images set them both apart from their colleagues: they were committed to imbuing their photographs with a meaning that went beyond the direct narration of events. They always integrated background and social realism with the hopeless poetry of a country in the clutches of war. Ricardo Rangel shot most of the «Pão Nosso de Cada Noite» (Our Nightly Bread) series during this period. In 1968, Kok Nam (who started his career in the late 1950s as a commercial photographer) exhibited the results of his work alongside the Mozambican Armed Forces (FPLM), entitled « A Juventa pela Libertade » (Young People for Freedom). He portrayed the reality of young people fighting for what they considered to be a just cause.

Photographer RUI ASSUBUJI ©

RUI ASSUBUJI

Mozambique
b. Cabo Delago, Mozambique 1964
– lives in Maputo, Mozambique

After working as a cameraman for Mozambican television, Rui Assubuji studied at the Photographic Training Centre in Maputo. In 1991 he published a book, *Pa Ublie. Diaro di campo* 1990, a work of photoreportage on seasonal workers hired for the tomato harvest at the Villa Literno in Italy.

Photographer RUI ASSUBUJI ©

In 1970 Kok Nam and Ricardo Rangel participated in the creation of *Tempo*, a weekly journal that was the first to devote a full page to photography. Rangel was initially in charge of the page, before passing the job on to the younger Kok Nam. Independence was declared in 1975 and Samora Machel, leader of the Frelimo, became President of the Republic. Influenced by Soviet thinking, the new government signed a 20-year friendship and cooperation treaty with the USSR in 1977. In 1979, the Resistencia Nacional Moçambicana (Renamo) launched an anticommunist counter-revolution, supported by South Africa. Mozambique plunged back into the horrors of war and photographers were once again forced to take sides. The Frelimo government carefully controlled all images produced and State propaganda superseded Portuguese propaganda. Photography became so important that in 1981 the Mozambican Photography Association was established, with the support of President Samora Machel. Two years later, the Centro de Formação Fotografica (Photographic Training Centre) was opened with Italian cooperation. Its aim was to train young people in photographic techniques. It was run by Ricardo Rangel.

In 1994, Joaquim Chissano, who had taken over from Samora Machel after the latter's death in a plane crash, signed an agreement with the Renamo rebels. Peace, albeit fragile, seemed to have returned at last. The photographs of the younger generation, whether trained by Ricardo Rangel's Centro de Formação or not, reflected this reality. It was now up to these young photographers, most of whom were born in the early 1960s, to take stock of 30 years of war. Sergio Santimano, Rui Assubuji, José Cabral and Naita Ussene, to name but a few, became the spokespeople for society's rejects, the maimed, the people known locally as the deslocados (the displaced). Their photographs, like those of their elders, recount the mixture of poverty, joy and pain that make up the daily life of a people for whom the future can only be a huge question mark. Only once everything has been worked out and settled will a new photography come to light in Mozambique - one that is finally free of these obsessional, desperate images, which nonetheless hold a glint of hope for a new life waiting to be lived.

Simon Njami

242

The development of photography in South Africa

Kathleen Grundlingh

Photography in South Africa developed along the same lines as in Europe, illustrating all the classic themes. However, at the end of the Fifties photography, formerly reserved almost exclusively for whites, became a weapon for the white and black photographers who wished to fight apartheid with documentary photography which would show the whole world the horror of the regime. Since the first multiracial elections in the Nineties, South African photographers have needed to redefine their role and have been faced with a creativity crisis in the search for their African identity.

In many respects the development of photography in South Africa mirrors similar developments in Europe and other parts of the world. Three separate yet interrelated aspects of photography are common to the development of the medium in the first quarter of this century: the rise of the amateur photographer, the abandonment of romantic pictorialism for realism and the rapid growth of documentary photography.

One of the pioneers of photography, John Frederick Herschel[1], moved to the Cape of Good Hope in his early adulthood to continue his father's pursuit of a comprehensive survey of the stars in the Southern Hemisphere. It is believed that he became interested in photography before his arrival and continued his experiments during his stay. By the time Herschel returned to England, Daguerre had mastered the art of permanently fixing the images made by the camera obscura. Eleven weeks after the official announcement in Paris (1839) of the Daguerre process, the first pictures were taken in Africa. At the time it was fashionable to travel, and with the introduction of the steamship it became possible to visit remote continents with relative ease. For the Europeans, Africa was unexplored territory ready to be mapped and colonized, and Livingstone was the first traveller-explorer in Africa to use photography to document his journey.

1. John Frederick Herschel, son of astronomer Sir William Herschel, was born in Buckinghamshire, England, in 1792. Regarded by some as one of the fathers of photography, he was made a baronet and buried in Westminster Abbey near Sir Isaac Newton's grave.

Kathleen Grundlingh was born in Johannesburg in 1960. After studying at L'Accademia dei Belli Arti di Pietro Vannucci in Perugia, Italy, she completed a postgraduate degree in Fine Art at the University of Cape Town. She has since been working at the South African National Gallery as Curator of Photography and recently as Head of the Curatorial Department. Since the mid-1980s she has been involved in many national photographic projects that have been designed to stimulate the interest in and underscore the importance of photography within the arts. Together with other curators, she is currently researching the development of photography in southern Africa in preparation for an exhibition titled *The Story of South African Photography*.

Images of reality

The use of the wet collodion process[2] became possible after Daguerre's death, but the medium was very difficult to master in Africa. Early explorer diaries tell of the damaging heat and dust, the overexposure of plates owing to the harsh African light, the detrimental effects of high humidity, the difficulties of obtaining clean water and the strong winds that disturbed carefully balanced tripods. Processing was done at night, usually in an ox wagon covered by blankets and skins in an attempt to block out the rays of the moon and the flickering firelight. Invariably these attempts were a dismal failure. Without taking these complications into account, David Livingstone dismissed his brother Charles as a useless photographer.

The introduction of the dry plate allowed the use of smaller hand-held cameras and gave birth to the era of the amateur photographer. These amateurs formed clubs which stimulated the rapid increase in the range and number of photographic journals. The first camera club meeting was held in Kimberley in 1890; the Cape Town Photographic Society was addressed by Sir Benjamin Stone[3] in 1894 and by 1895 there were eleven societies that regularly exchanged information and ideas. At the time these were the only photographic societies in Africa apart from two in Algeria (one in Constantine and one in Oran). In 1896 the first National Salon was held in Cape Town.

By the turn of the century images of war had become very popular at lantern shows in both Britain and South Africa and the role of photography as a medium of propaganda was recognized. The war correspondent HC Shelley, who accompanied Churchill to South Africa during the Anglo-Boer War, crusaded against the artistic impressions of battle that were often constructed from hearsay and at a location far removed from the site of the action. He championed the use of documentary photography that could capture an image of an actual event, thereby revealing the « truth ». He developed the use of balloons which carried a battery of cameras high over the hilly and bushy terrain that kept the Boers[4] hidden. These images taken at the battlefront captured the imagination of the British public and were mounted for use in opera-glass viewers and sold for a penny.

« Pictorial » photography as a genre was firmly established in Britain by the Royal Photographic Society and the Linked Ring[5] and, together with the American Photo-Secession[6], they organized the first major photographic exhibition in Cape Town in 1906 when 629 images were exhibited. The exhibition was considered the finest of its kind in the Southern Hemisphere. As a result, the portrait was overshadowed by the new trend of photographing landscapes and outdoor scenes.

The amateur snapshot gained momentum. Arthur Elliot's[7] work remains a testament to the time and a valuable historical document of early Cape architecture and its surrounds. Sir Benjamin Stone's visit and that of Alexander Keighley[8], a highly respected British photographer who travelled the length and breadth of the country in 1939 promoting photography as an art form, had a profound effect on the spread of the «pictorial» movement which reflected the established European trends.

The encroachment of colonialism also saw the introduction of Europe's fascination with the making of detailed records about people who were perceived to be different. This practice, and the obsession with the insights that physiognomy might provide, was seen in the work of August Sander[9], who meticulously documented various « types » within his own culture. A similar project was undertaken by AM Duggan Cronin, a pioneer of anthropometric photography in South Africa. Acclaimed as one of the country's foremost photographers, he aimed to document the cultural, social and economic life of all the various indigenous inhabitants of Southern Africa. These works were exhibited in Wembley at the SA Pavilion in 1924, and were contextualized by maps showing the location of each grouping. The images were described in Britain as some of the finest « native » studies yet seen. He wrote: « Year by year the Natives were becoming more and more civilized and any delay in the work would mean that valuable records of the Natives in their primitive state would be lost for all time »[10].

Running parallel to the almost exclusively white camera clubs which exhibited regularly over the years at various national and international salons was the slow growth of the use of documentary photography by black photographers as a means of political resistance. This genre would become the vehicle for some of the strongest photographic work produced during this century in South Africa. While the salons exhibited work in the conservative pictorialist style, by the late 1950s the Progressive Photographic Society had been established in Johannesburg as the only forum for black photographers. But it was *Drum* magazine that was to show the best of black photographers' work. With the entrenchment of the Afrikaner Nationalist government and its apartheid politics, *Drum* became one of the first magazines to exert subtle political pressure. Its strategy was not to confront but to expose in ways that kept within strict boundaries. Jurgen Schadeberg[11], an immigrant from Germany, established the photographic department and under his guidance most of the country's top black photographers emerged. He was highly regarded by his protegés, who valued his critical approach and worked long hours to achieve the best results possible.

2. Collodion, discovered in 1847, was originally used in the treatment of wounds. A clean glass plate was coated with a solution of iodide and collodion and made light-sensitive by soaking in a bath of silver nitrate under an orange light. The plate was exposed in the camera while still wet and immediately developed in a darkroom by pouring pyrogallic acid over the image.

3. Sir Benjamin Stone, a wealthy businessman, was President of the Birmingham Photographic Society and founder of the British National Photographic Record Association.

4. Boers: Afrikaans, literally, farmers, Dutch-descended opponents of the British in the two Anglo-Boer Wars between 1880 and 1902.

5. In 1892 photographers in Britain founded an association called the Linked Ring in response to the sharp-focus traditionalists of the time. The organization staged international exhibitions between 1893 and 1909.

6. The Photo-Secession society was founded in America by Alfred Stieglitz in 1902 to promote photography as an art form. He was elected to the Linked Ring in 1894.

7. Arthur Elliot (1870 - 1938) was born in New York. He emigrated to the Cape in his early adulthood and specialized in recording early Cape history. A collection of 10 000 negatives make up the Elliot Collection, which is housed in the Cape Archives, Cape Town.

8. Alexander Keighley (1861 - 1947) concentrated mainly on landscape photography and portrayed the British countryside in idyllic terms as a sacred land where all was transformed into the beautiful and spiritual.

9. August Sander (1876 - 1964) was a portraitist and industrial photographer whose major project was *Man of the Twentieth Century*. Walter Benjamin considered Sander's subsequent publication, *Face of Our Time*, to be an « atlas of instruction » or a training manual to sharpen one's « physiognomic awareness ».

10. Dr AD Bensusan. 1966. *Silver Images: The History of Photography in Africa* (Howard Timmins) p. 104.

Photograph BOB GOSANI / DRUM © ∧
The Americans. Drum Magazine. Sophiatown, November 1954.

Photography DRUM © >
ca. 1955.

> Photographer
JURGEN SCHADEBERG / DRUM ©
Jazz in South Africa.

> Photographer
BOB GOSANI / DRUM ©
Guildy Blood.
Johannesburg, July 1956.

< Photographer
BOB GOSANI / DRUM ©
Maligned Tsotsis
Sophiatown, January 1954.

Jointly their work forced the government to address particular issues and initiate various commissions of enquiry, one of which focused on the convict labour system.

The magazine also became a vehicle for the positive expression of the black urban experience. This period was regarded as a renaissance in black culture and as the golden age of black journalism. The end of the Second World War saw the rise of a general sense of optimism and a feeling that South Africa was part of a larger international community. The 1950s were marked by the rise of enormous creative talent on the part of writers like Can Themba[12] and photographers like Bob Gosani[13], Peter Magubane[14] and Alf Kumalo[15], and it also saw the most powerful black political leaders of the century come to prominence. As the government cracked down on the free association of individuals, the shebeen became the hub of creative energies and its essence was captured by the *Drum* photographers. It is indicative of their lifestyles that Bob Gosani's motto was: « Live fast, die young and have a good-looking corpse ». Willie de Klerk, who joined *Drum* as a photographer in 1960, recalls his experience as follows: « It was exciting working for the magazine. *Drum* had the guts to print and publish. They attacked anything that attacked the people. But we were frustrated by much of what we had to deal with - the bad pay, the government not wanting to listen, the outside world not taking notice. This eventually got to all those newsmen, some turning heavily to drink. You'd find that while they got the stories, got the pictures, they would not be accepted. But if it were a white photographer, the whole world would know about it. »[16]

This upsurge in creativity was considered marginal by the white establishment and with the entrenchment of draconian apartheid laws it gradually dwindled, finding a new outlet in the documentation of the brutality of the state. Images of the forced removals[17] of Sophiatown and the massacre at Sharpeville[18] were seen across the world. As a result, photographers like Eli Weinberg, Ernest Cole and Peter Magubane were forced underground or into exile. Many black photographers were banned and imprisoned. The hardships they suffered are mirrored in the experiences of Eli Weinberg. Weinberg was born in Latvia in 1908 and emigrated to South Africa in his youth. He worked as a professional photographer and documented his involvement in and the gradual growth of the trade union movement over a period of 20 years. He was detained for prolonged periods during the state of emergency declared in 1960, held prisoner for seven months in 1964, and subsequently sentenced to five years' imprisonment. After his release in 1970 he was immediately placed under banning orders and in 1976 he left the country on the instructions of the ANC. He was given asylum in Tanzania. On his escape from South Africa the bulk of his negatives were destroyed. His book, *Portrait of a People*[19], though banned and the mere possession of which meant imprisonment, became a touchstone for the legions of documentary photographers who followed. He died in exile in Dar es Salaam in 1981. Ernest Cole[20], who died alone and destitute in New York, left a similar legacy in his book, *House of Bondage*[21]. Other events of historical importance were covered by Peter Magubane, among them the 1960s Sharpeville Massacre, the 1965 Women's March on Pretoria and the Treason Trial.

11. Jurgen Schadeberg was born in Berlin in 1931. After working as an apprentice photographer in Germany he immigrated to South Africa in early 1950 and was employed as chief photographer for *Drum* magazine. A retrospective exhibition of his work was held at the South African National Gallery in 1996.

12. Dorsay Can Themba (1924 - 1967), a highly talented writer, won a Drum short story competition in 1952. He later joined *Drum*, eventually becoming assistant editor at the magazine.

13. Robert 'Bob' Gosani (1934 - 1972) started working for *Drum* as an apprentice photographer in 1952. He was later recognized as one of the country's top photographers.

14. Peter Magubane (b. 1932) joined *Drum* as a driver and messenger in 1955. He started taking photographs while out on assignment with the photographers, eventually becoming chief photographer for the magazine.

15. Alf Kumalo (b. 1930) started his career in journalism in the 1950s working for the newspaper *Bantu World*. After he took up photography his images rapidly gained recognition and were in much demand.

16. From an unpublished interview with Gordon Metz, Mayibuye Centre, May 1994.

17. Black people were forcibly removed from land allocated to white people.

Photograph DRUM © >
Drum Magazine.
Balancing act.
Johannesburg, December 1954.

Photograph DRUM © >
Drum Magazine.
All-Male Moffie
Cape Town, September 1955.

< Photographer
JURGEN SCHADEBERG / DRUM ©
Boxer, ca. 1955.

In 1963 he became the first black man to exhibit photographs in South Africa. He was often arrested for being in possession of a camera and at times had to resort to concealing it in a loaf of bread or an empty milk container in order to take pictures. He suffered many years of abuse at the hands of the police. In detention he was brutally tortured and held in solitary confinement; he was banned for five years. Yet he was never convicted of any crime. Two other pioneers of the documentary school were Leon Levson[22] and Ranjith Kally[23]. All these resistance photographers had at some stage worked for Drum magazine. Among them they documented the lives of the disenfranchised, the hardships of migrant worker hostel life, the growth of the trade unions and political leaders, the influx of rural people to urban centres, the establishment of squatter communities and the hardships endured by the miners. Although disenfranchised themselves, their work became a monument to the dispossessed. These photographers, who bore the brunt of the system, suffering banishment, exile and imprisonment, managed to document the enduring spirit of a people who believed that in the end they would overcome. They also laid the foundation for a second generation of documentary photographers who came to the fore in the 1980s and who saw the results of the work started so many years earlier.

In the 1970s many photographers and writers were no longer able to support journalistic « neutrality » and committed themselves to the struggle. The camera, the pen and the canvas became instruments of war. Creative energies joined forces and artists and intellectuals became involved in grassroots work within their communities, handing on much-needed skills in the process. Cooperatives like Afrapix[24] were established and were instrumental in unifying creative talent, providing photographers

with support and a strong community base. Photographers like Omar Badsha[25], Peter Magubane and David Goldblatt[26], greatly influenced the style that developed. Although David Goldblatt did not document South Africa at the battlefront, his images forced many South Africans to take a cold, hard look at their society. He concentrated his efforts on searching out the essence of South African society, looking with extraordinary clarity at seemingly innocent everyday moments, and revealed in the inconspicuous detail all the complexities of the nation. His distinctive style influenced many of the younger photographers, who looked to him for criticism and advice.

Among the younger generation who emerged to document the defiance campaigns and broader resistance movements we find names like Paul Weinberg, Chris Ledochowski, Lesley Lawson, Rashid Lombard, Gideon Mendel, Santu Mofokeng, Cedric Nunn, Guy Tillim, Anna Zieminski and many others[27]. Two publications in the late 1980s marked important milestones in the work of these photographers: *South Africa: The Cordoned Heart*[28] and *Beyond the Barricades*[29], which showcased the resistance movement within the country. Together they depicted one of the longest and most violent periods of resistance. At the time, to take pictures in «unrest» areas without police permission was a criminal act and those breaking the censorship laws faced up to ten years' imprisonment. These photographers documented the huge uprising of popular resistance and the subsequent state backlash. The camera became a voice and a weapon for those denied basic human rights and was instrumental in bringing atrocities perpetrated by the state to the attention of the international community. The camera was accused of being an instrument of insurrection and of furthering terrorist activities.

Images of reality

It became a tool which uncovered and laid bare the white bones of apartheid. Lasting images of the period are of pallbearers pressing on through clouds of teargas, PW Botha[30] taking the salute at military parades, police attacking demonstrators with *sjamboks*[31], burning barricades, violent scenes of mourners clashing with police and youths fleeing for safety, a mother holding up a bloodstained shirt and police taking a smoke break while a dead body lies next to them. We live with these memories.

1994 saw the beginning of a new era, both within the country, with its first democratically elected government, and within photography, since the war waged through the image had been won. During the 1970s and 1980s South African photography was characterized by the conscious application of social documentary photography to effect political change. This meant that more creative and aesthetic applications were relegated to the sidelines. Ironically, the demise of apartheid left South African photographers each with his or her own creative crisis. Freed from their collective political purpose, photographers were forced to redefine their individual photographic identities and aims.

The internationally-imposed cultural boycott of the 1980s had isolated writers and photographers from international discourse about art-related issues and events. This affected not only the artists but also the institutions that promoted art within the country. Consequently, even as late as the mid-1980s, photography was still not generally recognized as an art form. However, institutions like the South African National Gallery, which hosted and sent on tour major photographic exhibitions, and tertiary institutions, which taught photography as Fine Art, were instrumental in establishing photography as a serious art form. By the early 1980s most tertiary institutions had established photographic courses which were taught on an equal footing alongside the disciplines of painting and sculpture.

As South Africa rejoined international cultural debates and exchanges, photographers schooled in a fine art tradition injected new spirit and energy into the medium. The number of overtly political images dwindled and photographers became concerned with exploring the potential of the medium as a vehicle for self-expression. Contemporary works reveal artists' autobiographical concerns with the self and the politics of body, gender and identity. The constraints of the conventional photographic image are explored by the use of surface manipulation, the multiple series, photomontage, photoconstruction and the diverse employment of hand-mixed photo emulsion. Aesthetic considerations now underpin the documentary image with a heightened awareness of the edges of the frame and the potential of colour.

The influence of the mega-exhibition is evident in the increased use of installation. Conventional photographic studios now enliven their images by the use of the traditional technique of hand-colouring, fashionable in the 1930s and 1940s. Vibrant work by street photographers, who number in the region of 40 000, do a brisk trade in montaged portraits rich in symbolism, cross-cultural referencing, iconography and language.

Through its accessibility and with its roots firmly embedded in the everyday experience of global culture, photography has taken its place as being the chosen medium of our time.

Kathleen Grundlingh
Curator
South African National Gallery
Cape Town, South Africa

Photograph DRUM ©
Drum Magazine.
Death in the dark City.
Alexandra, April 1956.

18. During 1960 in Sharpeville, a township of greater Johannesburg, a protest was held against the « pass laws » that enforced the carrying of identity documents. It ended in tragedy, with the police opening fire and killing 69 peaceful protesters and injuring hundreds more.

19. Eli Weinberg, *Portrait of a People* (International Defence and Aid Fund for Southern Africa, 1981).

20. Ernest Cole (1940 - 1990) left school at the age of 16 in protest against the Bantu Education system (the discriminatory education system for blacks). He was employed at *Drum* in 1958 as a darkroom assistant. In order to ensure the publication of his book, *House of Bondage*, he went into exile in 1966.

21. Ernest Cole. 1967. *House of Bondage.* Random House.

22. Leon Levson (1883 - 1968), an immigrant from Lithuania, started his career as an apprentice photographer at 13 years of age. He travelled widely and is known to have met Alfred Steiglitz. His proficiency as a painter greatly influenced his photographic work.

23. Ranjith Kally was born in Isipingo, KwaZulu-Natal, in 1925. After working in a shoe factory he joined *Drum* in 1956. He has been an Associate of the Royal Photographic Society since 1967.

24. Afrapix, a photographers' collective, was established in 1982 and served as a resource centre for community, student and labour organizations. It disbanded in the early 1990s.

25. Omar Badsha (b. 1945). A self-taught photographer active in the trade union movement, and a founding member of Afrapix.

26. David Golblatt (b. 1930). A freelance photographer whose works have been exhibited extensively both locally and internationally. A retrospective of his work was held at the South African National Gallery in 1984.

27. These photographers all belonged to Afrapix at some stage and their work was used by numerous community organizations and the alternative press.

28. *South Africa: The Cordoned Heart.* 1986. prepared for the Second Carnegie Inquiry into Poverty and Development in Southern Africa. The Gallery Press.

∧
Photographer PETER MAGUBANE / DRUM ©
The lost children of the golden city.
Drum Magazine. Johannesburg, ca. 1957.

29. *Beyond the Barricades: Popular*
Resistance in South Africa. 1989.
An Aperture Book in Association with
the Centre for Documentary Studies,
Duke University.

30. PW Botha: Prime Minister of
South Africa (1978 - 1989).

31. Sjambok: leather whip used by
the South African Police.

Bibliography :

Conrad Lighton, Arthur Elliott. 1956.
10.000 Pictures Tell a story.
AA Balkema.

Dr AD Bensusan. 1966.
Silver Images, History of Photography
in Africa. Howard Timmins.

Eli Weinberg,
Portrait of a People. 1981.
International Defence and Aid Fund
for Southern Africa.

Jurgen Schadeberg. 1996.
Images from the Black 50's.
Jurgen Schadeberg.

Peter Magubane, *Magubane's South Africa*
(Alfred A. Knopf, 78).

South Africa, The Cordoned Heart. 1986.
Prepared for the Second Carnegie
Inquiry into Poverty and Development
in Southern Africa. The Gallery Press.

Beyond the Barricades : Popular Resistance in
South Africa 1989
An Aperture Book in Association with the Centre
for Documentary Studies, Duke University,.

Comrades and cameras

Pierre-Laurent Sanner

Photographers have taken part in all the struggles and political battles which have taken place in South Africa. Trade unionists, members of the Communist Party or simply activists, they have put their cameras at the service of what they saw as a just cause, sometimes risking their lives. Their pictures have travelled the world and awoken sleeping consciences, revealing to them the worst excesses of a regime which lasted until the beginning of the Nineties. Photographs of comrades who contributed to the fall of apartheid are still alive in everyone's memory.

PETER MAGUBANE

South Africa
b. Vrededorp, Johannesburg, 1932
– lives in Johannesburg

Peter Magubane, who grew up in Sophiatown, embarked upon his photographic career in 1954 when he joined Drum magazine and later the Rand Daily Mail. He was a committed opponent of the injustices and atrocities of the apartheid regime. He was detained in 1969 and spent 586 days in solitary confinement. In the 80's and 90's he worked in New York for Time magazine. He is currently working at the magazine's Johannesburg office. In 1997 Peter Magubane received the Lifetime Achievement Award from the prestigious Mother Jones Foundation. An internationally acclaimed photographer, he has published a dozen books on the people and events of South Africa.

Photographer
PETER MAGUBANE / DRUM ©
Cops (Big Brother is watching you).
Drum Magazine.
Sophiatown, February - March 1955.

« The day that apartheid was abandoned as the official policy of the South African government, photographers - and many others as well - suddenly lost one of their main orientations. Before that moment, there was no doubt as to the nature and identity of the enemy. The lines had been clearly drawn, with good on one side and evil on the other. After, these certainties no longer existed. » David Goldblatt's words, spoken in August 1993 at the official opening of the exhibition *Through a Lens Darkly* at the South African National Gallery (SANG) in Cape Town, announced the end of an era of militant photography engaged in a struggle against apartheid. Eleven years earlier, in 1982, a small group of photographers had created Afrapix, whose objectives were to expose the atrocities of a regime that had been in power since 1948 and, just as importantly, to foster and train a new generation of black photographers. At that time, South Africa was experiencing the worst years of its turbulent racial history. As particularly intimate witnesses of the events of the period, photographers felt the imperative necessity of testifying to their involvement through images: « Photographing the struggle in South Africa is also to participate in that struggle. No longer simple observers, photographers are active forces of change. »[1]

An examination of the work produced during Afrapix's brief existence (the agency closed in 1990), reveals examples of militant and engaged South African documentary photography, characterized by archetypal images of social struggle. Beneath these images can be discerned the enthusiasm, doubts, regrets and victories of Afrapix's « comrade photographers ».

Pierre-Laurent Sanner is a graduate of the National Political Sciences Institute. A photographer, he published, with Maria Malagardis, *Rwanda Le Jour d'Après* (1996). He received a Lavoisier research grant from the Ministry of Foreign Affairs to study politically committed photography in South Africa at the University of the Western Cape's Mayibuye Centre.

1. CASA (Culture in Another South Africa) Conference and Festival. 1989. « In Our Own Image » (afterword) in *The Hidden Camera, South African Photography Escaped from Censorship*. Amsterdam: Uitgeverij Bert Bakker and Stichting CASA.

The raised hands are clenched, the gazes determined; the images of heroes and martyrs are silkscreened onto a multitude of T-shirts, banners and posters; familiar songs and slogans ring out from a multitude of voices: the scene could be any one of a hundred South African union rallies, peace demonstrations or women's union meetings of the 1980s. For the photographers of the period, such as Gideon Mendel, these events were of prime interest.

Mendel began his career within the UDF.[2] One of his first works, a portrait of Moses Mayekiso, was used to illustrate tracts demanding the liberation of the imprisoned union leader. Images such as these had few aesthetic pretensions, for they were intended to touch the political consciousness of the viewer, to « communicate a political message and contribute to the ongoing struggle »[3]. As Peter McKenzie put it, « with all respect due to technical competence, militant photography should be free from all aesthetic bonds and concern itself only with the force of its social impact ».[4]

According to Chris Ledochowski, « Entire days were spent attending the meetings of one union or another; we were highly committed and wanted to change the course of history with our cameras. » Among the cultural events that accompanied the second annual congress of Cosatu (umbrella body for South Africa's principal trade unions, instituted in 1985) was a series of photographs illustrating the history of the union movement in the country. This type of documentary photography was inspired by Eli Weinberg's pioneering work some 40 years earlier. In the preface to *Portrait of a People*[5], Weinberg wrote of his hope that « these

images will serve to show that the movement of resistance to apartheid in South Africa has always existed and will continue to exist ». Weinberg's commitment to the movement was that of both an engaged photographer and a militant activist. A member of the South African Communist Party in 1936 and a union organizer, he participated in strikes, documented the forced relocation of populations, demonstrated against the infamous « pass » for township blacks and photographed many of the legendary militants of the period, including Albert Luthuli, Walter Sisulu, Ruth First and Yusuf Dadoo.

As a pioneering photographer, Weinberg worked alone. By the 1980s, South African photographers had established a number of agencies, such as Dynamic Images, The Brotherhood, Vakalisa, The Black Society of Photographers, and the aforementioned Afrapix. All shared a common objective of revealing the hidden face of the country and its struggles for social justice and equality. In the words of the Afrapix founders, « In recent years, South African photographers have given expression to 'another' South Africa. Afrapix was created out of their desire to co-ordinate documentary photography and use it as an effective tool for social change ».[6]

The first assembly of anti-apartheid South Africans working in the arts field took place at Gaborone in June 1982.[7] The event was of crucial importance, for beyond the exhibition of the works of different generations of photographers, there emerged a collective awareness of a common identity and a common commitment to the same causes.

2. Mendel, Gideon. Lecture at the Michaelis School of Fine Art. 26 May 1997, Cape Town. The UDF or United Democratic Front was a non-racial popular movement set up in August 1983 as an umbrella body for more than 600 organizations fighting against apartheid.

3. Interview with Omar Badsha. September 1997. Cape Town.

4. *Staffrider*, Vol. 5 , No. 2. 1989. Johannesburg.

5. Weinberg, Eli. 1981. *Portrait of a People, A Personal Photographic Record of the South African Liberation Struggle*. London: IDAF (International Defence and Aid Fund for Southern Africa).

6. CASA. 1987. *Apartheid - A Vigilant Witness. A Reflection on Photography*. London: Zed Books.

7. Culture and Resistance Festival. June 1982. Gaborone, Botswana.

Photographer Λ
PETER MAGUBANE / DRUM ©
*Demonstration. Drum Magazine.
Sophiatown, February - March 1955.*

Photographer ALFRED KUMALO © >
*Black Jack (municipal cop) with dog.
Drum Magazine.
Benoni, November 1956.*

Images of reality

The work of David Goldblatt, one of the fathers of South African documentary photography, hung next to those of his successors: Weinberg and Badsha, Lesley Lawson, Judas Ngwenya, Wendy Schwegman, Mxolisi Moyo, Peter McKenzie and Jimi Matthews. For Paul Weinberg, « Gaborone taught photographers a new language and consolidated their commitment to the struggle ».

The experience also resulted in the creation of the Afrapix agency or, as it was known at the time, the Afrapix Collective. Meetings were held in the offices of the Council of South African Churches in Johannesburg, during which photographers defined their professional identity and objectives. There was a common desire to testify to the injustice and atrocities of the government, distribute images of resistance, and contribute to the development of politically engaged documentary photography. The alternative press which had appeared following the student revolt of June 1976 and the ensuing cultural renaissance, joined in the movement. Periodicals such as *Grassroots*, *New Era*, *Spark*, *Sound Stone* and above all, *Staffrider*, illustrated their pages with the works of enthusiastic and militant photographers. From 1982 to 1987, Omar Badsha and Paul Weinberg, in collaboration with *Staffrider*, organized a series of photography exhibitions which served as forums for an exchange of similar and conflicting points of view and contributed to the emergence of new talent.

Conscious of the fact that in South Africa, photography was traditionally an activity accessible only to middle-class whites[8], the Afrapix photographers organized and ran workshops for the black population throughout the country. The government's segregationist policies, which touched every level of the private and public lives of the country's black population, had ordained that they should receive a second-class education. Since it was impossible for a black person to receive university-level training in photography in the schools reserved for them, Afrapix decided to address the problem directly. The slogan of its grassroots programme was « Each One Teach One », meaning that each of its staff photographers had undertaken a commitment to share his or her knowledge of photography with someone else who needed the skills.

Cedric Nunn, Santu Mofokeng, Pax Magwaza, Judas Ngwenya and Rashid Lombard were among the young self-taught black photographers who took up the challenge. For Nunn, the project also signified a fight against what he termed « visual illiteracy » by developing a trained eye and critical vision capable both of analysing the images put out by apartheid and creating counter-images to attack it.

The apartheid regime was particularly sensitive to the power of images, and feared any which conveyed the slightest hint of rebellion. The first South African television station, which was created only in 1976, was of course heavily censored[9]. In reaction to the saturation of the country's media by the government's self-serving propaganda, politically committed photographers reacted with what they termed « morally honest propaganda »: images showing what the government wanted to hide. It was nevertheless not until 1987 that they were able to organize the exhibition called *The Hidden Camera: South African Photographers Escaped from Censorship* and, two years later in 1989, the publication in England of the book *Beyond the Barricades*. With these two events, the work of an entire generation of photographers whose images had been censored throughout the 1980s was finally revealed. *Beyond the Barricades*, like *Portrait of a People*, contained dramatic images of blood and tears, showing the determination of activist leaders and the arbitrary abuse of power of the South African government.

In the crisis years of the early 1980s, the South African government began reinforcing its arsenal of legislation restricting civil rights and freedom of expression. A national state of emergency was decreed in 1985, 1986 and 1988. After their long period of mobilization in the cause of the abolition of apartheid, the country's photographers began filming scenes of civil unrest and addressing their images to the international community. The photographs of this period are often dramatic and occasionally shocking images of violence captured in the very instant of its explosion.

Fire engulfs a vehicle overturned by an angry mob. Faces are bathed in tears and blood. A woman picks up a rock and takes aim at a nearby policeman, who cocks his rifle. A face distorted by teargas. A group of men carry the coffin of an assassinated student on their shoulders. Images of a township funeral which has been transformed into a battlefield. Images which repeat themselves over and over again, from the frontline of a nameless, bitter war in which photographers are daily risking - and sometimes losing - their lives. The access to the townships is now difficult, when not totally forbidden to members of the press. Censorship, however, is everywhere, ordained by a complex tangle of legislation and decrees. The National Key Points Act, a masterpiece of arbitrary legislation, forbids the photographing of « sensitive or strategic sites » without defining what or where they are. Anyone can be arrested for filming anything. Rare images from this period occasionally appear in the international press, but almost never in South Africa. For the government, images of the struggle and resistance of the people shouldn't exist, and it does everything in its power to assure that they don't.

DAVID GOLDBLATT

South Africa
b. Randfontein, South Africa 1930
– lives in Johannesburg.

David Goldblatt was born in South Africa in 1930 of Lithuanian parents who fled the late 19th century persecutions of Jews in the Baltic States. In 1963 David Goldblatt closed the family business in Randfontein to set himself up as a freelance photographer in Johannesburg. He later became joint editor of *Leadership SA*, then artistic director of the magazine *Millenium*. In 1989 he founded the Market Photo Workshop in Johannesburg, which became a vibrant focus for photographic creativity. He is one of the fathers of documentary photography in South Africa and the author of numerous publications.

8. Interview with Paul Weinberg. May 1997. Cape Town.

9. Harber, Anton. 1994. *Censorship* in Harker, Joseph, ed., *The Legacy of Apartheid*. The Guardian: London.

10. Magubane, Peter. 1996. Enwezor, Okwui, ed., In/Sight: *African Photographers from 1940 to the Present*. Guggenheim Foundation: New York.

11. Liebenberg, John. June 1990. *The Rainy Season* in *Full Frame, South African Documentary Photography*, Vol. 1, No.1. Johannesburg.

12. See footnote 3.

13. See footnote 6.

14. Sontag, Susan. 1983. *Sur la Photographie*. Editions Seuil: Paris.

15. Tillim, Guy. December 1990. *War in Natal* in *Full Frame, South African Documentary Photography*, Vol. 1, No. 2. Johannesburg.

16. Weinberg, Paul. Lecture at the Michaelis School of Fine Art. 12 May 1997.

17. Badsha, Omar, ed. 1986. *The Cordoned Heart: Twenty South African Photographers*. (Prepared for the Second Carnegie Inquiry into Poverty and development in Southern Africa.) Gallery Press: Cape Town.

∧ Photographer DAVID GOLDBLATT ©ca. 1955/60
Family at Lunch, Wheatlands Plots, Randfontein.
Courtesy of the South African National Gallery.

Photographers are the daily targets of army and police brutality: Peter Magubane is arrested and sentenced to 586 days in prison. When he is finally released, the government forbids him the use of a camera for five years. In 1976, he is one of the few photographers to cover the high-school student uprising of Soweto. His film is confiscated by the police and he is sentenced to 123 more days in prison.[10] For more than ten years, John Liebenberg photographed another hidden war in Namibia, where South African government soldiers engaged in merciless combat with the independent troops of Swapo (South West African People's Organization). His scenes of the conflict earned him death-threats and at least one assassination attempt by two gunmen who, after missing him, escaped in their car.[11]

Some of the assignments were difficult to stomach, and often dangerous to photograph: the mutilated corpse of a tortured child; the riot police, clubs and teargas at the ready; the angry mobs and burning, overturned cars. Many of these photographers were so close to the action that one expected them to appear in the foreground of their own pictures. The motto of those times was « Get as close as you can to your subject »[12] while the slogan, « If you're not close enough, you're not good enough » became standard operating procedure.[13] Photographers began placing their lives on the line: « Danger and voyeurism: war photographers cannot avoid being intimately involved in the murderous activity that they capture in images ».[14] In 1990, nearly ten years after this observation by Susan Sontag, Guy Tillim, a young Afrapix photographer, wrote that « ... One of the things I understood when I was photographing the fighting in Natal was that cameras are perceived as threats. A threat for the people you photograph, and sometimes for yourself ».[15] Like many of his colleagues, Paul Weinberg admits that he was never particularly excited about dodging police bullets and clouds of teargas: « I don't like violence and I've never felt like a dyed-in-the-wool news photographer. We found ourselves in a combat situation and we just did our jobs ».[16]

Very few politically committed South African photographers escaped a phase of militancy. But in addition to denouncing the injustices of the government, they also channelled their energy and talent into producing first-class documentary photographs. In terms of style, many of these photographers had been strongly influenced by American documentary photography of the 1930s, and particularly the photographers who had been commissioned by the Farm Recovery Act. After receiving a grant from the Carnegie Foundation in 1983, more than 20 South African photographers began systematically documenting the effects of poverty on the country's population. Their photographs were published in *The Cordoned Heart*[17] edited by Omar Badsha, and many were selected to appear in an exhibition of over 400 images which accompanied the Second Conference on Poverty and Development in South Africa, organized by the Carnegie Foundation in 1986.

<

>

Photographer
DAVID GOLDBLATT © ca. 1955/60
Wedding on a Farm near Barkly East.
New Year's Day Picnic,
Hartebeespoort.
Courtesy of the
South African National Gallery.

The commitment of photographers to the disenfranchised classes remained unwavering, as with their images they « ... revealed the deplorable realities that must be confronted and rectified ».[18]

If the sense of dramatic urgency conveyed by these photographs was less immediate than in the past, this was perhaps because the photographers' approach had also changed. In documenting their subjects, photographers began addressing larger questions of origins, motivations and history. In the end, as Paul Weinberg discovered, « photography often leaves you with more questions than answers ». The imagery was social and humanistic: by patiently immersing themselves within a particular context, photographers recorded the existence of their subjects within their own universe.

A procession of uprooted families: men, women and children, each with their pitiful bundle of possessions, and in the background, the smoking ruins of their homes. The hopeless atmosphere of the overcrowded urban hostels, filled with men separated from their villages and families. The run-down, poorly-equipped schools of the townships and the dead-end lives of their students, destined for unemployment or menial jobs. In a study commissioned by the Carnegie Foundation, David Goldblatt investigated the conditions governing the lives of the workers living in the homelands, the rural tribal settlements created by the government. His book, *The Transported, a South African*

Odyssey,[19] reveals that many of the township residents were obliged to spend six and even eight hours a day travelling from their homes to their jobs in Johannesburg or Pretoria. The book was illustrated by Goldblatt's photographs, which contributed a supplementary dimension of objective reality to the information supplied by the people he interviewed.

The photographer Paul Weinberg began exploring the theme of people's attachment to the land, a subject which for Weinberg « also offered the possibility of developing a series of metaphors illustrating the degree to which the struggle for land was rooted in the history of South Africa »[20]. The results of his ten years of patient exploration formed the nucleus of the exhibition *Through a lens darkly*, organized by the National Gallery of Cape Town in 1993. Weinberg's book, *Back to the Land*, published in 1996, deals with the same theme.[21]

By the end of the 1980s, documentary photography had become one of the favourite means of expression of South African photographers. At the same time, photographers like Lesley Lawson, at one time herself a member of Afrapix, began to question the orientations of photography. For Lawson, the time had come to enlarge its range and scope, for « ... like poetry or music, photography is a form of communication. No-one expects a poet to continually write the same words, or a musician to endlessly repeat the same measure, and if this were the case, people would simply stop paying attention ».[22]

18. See footnote 14.

19. Goldblatt, David. 1989. *The Transported, A South African Odyssey.* Aperture: New York.

20. See footnote 16.

21. Spark, No. 2. Documentary Photography.

22. Weinberg, Paul. 1996. *Back to the Land.* The Porcupine Press. Johannesburg.

Images of reality
OMAR BADSHA

South Africa
b. Durban, South Africa 1945 – lives in Pretoria

Omar Badsha was raised in an Indian Muslim family. Self-taught, he inherited his father's talent as a painter and, later, his uncle's taste for photography. He was 31 years of age when he first started taking photographs. In December 1975 he bought his first camera, a simple Pentax, and began photographing his immediate environment: the Grey Street neighbourhood, the true heart of the Indian community in Durban, as well as the trade-union meetings he attended as an activist and leader. He did not immediately think of becoming a photographer, thinking instead of his camera as a tool at the service of the struggle against apartheid: « We all started out as professional revolutionaries determined to overthrow the State … » At the beginning of the Eighties, he founded, with Paul Weinberg, the Afrapix collective, which brought together the major politically committed South African photographers of the time. Together they organized photographic training workshops and numerous exhibitions, supplied photographs to the alternative Press, collaborated with the literary protest magazine *Staffrider* and published the book *Beyond the Barricades*. Since the ending of apartheid Omar Badsha has, like many others, abandoned trade-union meetings for more personal research. Thanks to a stay in India, he has started a documentary project on the Indian communities in South Africa and the links with their country of origin.

∧
Photographer OMAR BADSHA ©
Durban, South Africa, ca. 1960.

During the same period, photographers increasingly sought to reconnect with their roots and origins. Santu Mofokeng and Paul Weinberg decided to return home to Pietermaritzburg and Soweto, their respective birthplaces. Describing the experience in *Going Home*,[23] Weinberg wrote that « Documentary photography is conditioned by an a priori choice of a subject, such as poverty or war ... I've never been as close to the people I've photographed as here; at the same time, its a way of rediscovering myself ». For Santu Mofokeng, returning to Soweto enabled him to show « the human aspects, the dehumanizing forces, the suffering, the courage, the resistance and the beauty which people manage to maintain against great odds ».[24] His objective was to capture a vision of perfectly normal people living in a totally abnormal context, and to render them in their dignity and pride. He also placed a high value on professional excellence: « it is only when I am good at what I do that I can be of use to society ... By participating in the organized struggle for social justice I am also involved in the struggle for self-realization. »

Paul Weinberg and Santu Mofokeng first met in 1985 in the context of the *Staffrider* exhibitions and the activities of Afrapix. Both individuals embody the triumph of documentary photography as well as its limits. As Weinberg recalls,

« Most of us had few aesthetic imperatives. Photographers from outside of South Africa were practically absent: the government refused to let them into the country. We were the only ones around, and we knew that our work would be published, so we weren't too concerned about its quality ».[25] Afrapix ceased its activities in 1990. Its photographers have taken widely different directions, some opening their own agencies and others pursuing their ideal of communicating their skills and knowledge to others. Today, as South Africa heals its old wounds, photographers are channelling their energy into the exploration of other realms of experience and returning to personal projects begun 15 years earlier. As a pastime, photography has become widespread and accessible to more of the population. Street photographers have made their appearance in many of South Africa's cities, and photography in general has been accepted as an art. As a new South African society emerges, there are constantly new subjects to document. Jurgen Schadeberg, a former editor of *Drum* magazine, adopts a philosophical tone when describing the situation: « Where are the new images of the cities, towns, vacation spots, religious celebrations and social life? South Africa is going through a period of deep change and our photographers should be documenting them. »

Pierre-Laurent Sanner

23. Weinberg, Paul, and Mofokeng, Santu. March 1990. *Going Home* in *Leadership SA*, Vol. 9.

24. Mofokeng, Santu. June 1990. *Going Home* in *Full Frame* Vol.1, No. 1. June 1990.

25. See footnote 8.

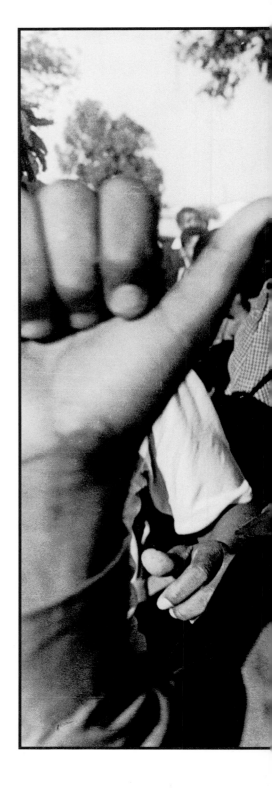

GUY TILLIM

South Africa
b. Johannesburg, South Africa 1962 – lives in Cape Town

Guy Tillim began taking photographs in 1986 and then joined Afrapix, a collective of South African photographers. From 1986 to 1987 he worked as a news photographer for Reuter and Agence France Press. He has been working on a number of projects including reports in Rwanda, Afghanistan, Korea, Guyana and recently in Namibia

Photographer GUY TILLIM © 1988
Courtesy of the South African National Galery.

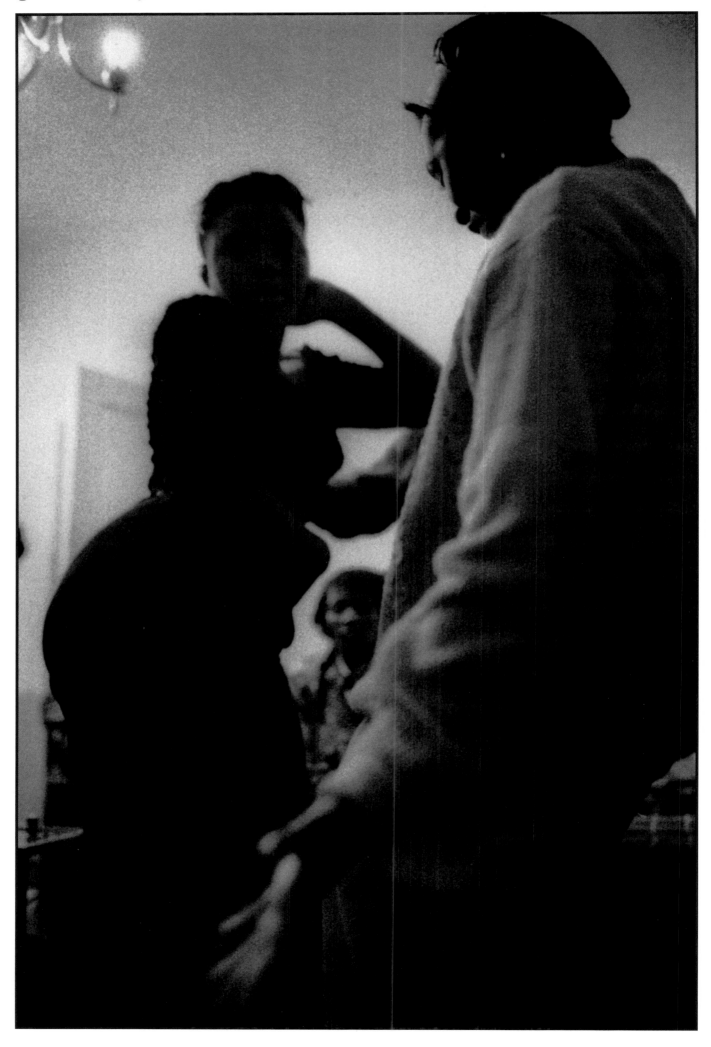

Trajectory of a street-photographer

Santu Mofokeng

To be a photographer in the 1980s in South Africa when one was Black was no easy task. Santu Mofokeng had to draw on all him will-power and strength which his vocation afforded him to stay the course. What interests him is the life of township folk. It is his desire to understand them and to penetrate into their daily universe which drives him to exhume old photographs from the turn of the century, suddenly revealing to him a piece of his own history.

« Capturing and recounting the world of omens, premonitions, cures and superstitions that is authentically ours, ... looking at reality without the limitations that rationalists ... through the ages have tried to impose on it to make it easier for them to understand ... Disproportion is part of our reality too. Our reality is in itself out of all proportion. »

GG Marquez interview
The Fragrance of the Guava,
London : Verso, 1983.

As far as I can recall there are no photographs of me as a baby. My first encounter with the camera was in the early 1960s when I was seven or eight years old. The person behind the camera was an itinerant journeyman photographer who plied his trade on a Lambretta motor-scooter. He came to our house at the behest of my mother, to photograph me and my younger brother one cold morning. She wanted to memorialize the jackets she had sewn for us with bits of leftover material from the garment factory where she worked. She was proud of her handiwork. We were happy for the warmth we got from these coats of many colours, although we regretted that our jackets did not carry any store labels.

Let me confess that envy is one of the motivations that steered me into the photography business. A few friends and peers at primary school had cameras. I noticed that they were very popular and had no problems approaching girls and chatting them up. They always had loose change jangling in their pockets.

Santu Mofokeng was born in 1956 in Johannesburg.Disturbed by the gap which existed between his photographs and the people featured in them, he decided to change direction and make a compilation of old family photographs from the townships of Johannesburg. In a South Africa prone to deep political upheavals and in search of a new identity, and with the discovery of these photographs from another era, witnesses to a story never written, Santu Mofokeng seems to be exploring his own history and giving new direction to his photographic work.

< Photographer SANTU MOFOKENG ©
Joubert Park, Johannesburg.
South Africa, 1993.

Images of reality

The first camera I ever owned had probably « fallen off the back of a truck ». I was 17 years old and in high school. It was in a dismal state of disrepair, so I couldn't do anything to it to make it worse. I paid for it to be repaired with my own money, which I had earned from the commission for the sale of a complete set of Collins encyclopaedias during the school holidays in 1973. I had this camera for only two years before my neighbour came to borrow it (in my absence) from my sister. I never saw the damn camera again.

In those two years, however, I cherished that camera. It helped me overcome my awkwardness around strangers. I got invited to parties and social gatherings. My social status was enhanced. Everywhere I went strangers would approach me to have their photograph taken or simply to talk, all because I was lugging a camera around. Conversations revolved around the features of the camera. They would appraise the value of the camera according to weight or the width and length of the eye (lens). They would ask me whether I could shoot colour or black-and-white or both, and whether the lens could see in the dark. I was often asked if I could shoot photographs inside a house, or when it was cloudy or windy or raining. Cameras had an aura of mystical fascination for a lot of people. People would stop me just to gape at the apparatus or to look through the viewfinder. It was as though the act of looking through the camera transformed and enchanted the landscape or person through the viewfinder. To be photographed was a privilege they paid for - except friends, acquaintances and relatives.

Cameras in whatever condition were difficult to come by because they were said to be too expensive. They were considered rather complicated. When you did chance upon one it carried with it a kind of an invisible DO NOT TOUCH sign, like the legend of the skull and crossbones with the words DANGER/INGOZI emblazoned beneath them, or the « zigzag » sign one might find on a power station. Our ignorance about how cameras operated gave them an irresistible allure. Cameras were the preserve of specialists; the press, men on «government business», a few rich families and educated people. This probably explains my artificial social elevation. Looking back, I am still amazed that a schlemiel like myself made a career of photography.

I have always been nervous around machines, including cars (I do not drive), computers, answering machines, microwave ovens and any new technology. Part of my paralysis around things mechanical reflects the experience of an impoverished upbringing: « Leave other people's things be, I cannot pay for the damned thing to be fixed ». And later: « You think this lens was made in Soweto? »

I began to learn the photography trade as a street photographer. As a roving portrait or street photographer you charged a deposit for each and every exposure you made for a client. You then hoped you had enough business to finish a roll of film or as many rolls of film as possible in a weekend so you could come back the next weekend with the finished prints in order to collect the balance. You had to sell all the exposures you made, including the « lemons » that came about through sloppy technique, glitches in the print and processing laboratory, or as a result of using outdated films. You could make enemies for life if you did not return all the exposed prints you made of the subject.

In the language of the township, photographs were not developed, they were washed. Technical mishaps such as over- or under-exposure were considered « burns ». « Why did you burn my face so much? Why am I so black? I don't like his (read the photographer's) pictures because he burns people ». Cropping was considered particularly ominous. I remember my mother-in-law's response when she saw an image I had made of my wife suckling Kano, my son. (This is an image I really like.) Her comments were very dark, they smacked of a Freudian foreboding: « Why did you chop my daughter's head off? » Let me add that my mother-in-law is a God-fearing and a deeply religious person.

Tardiness in returning photographs could cost you your reputation and business, perhaps even a beating. Most township people felt vulnerable and exposed when they gave you permission to take (or make) an image of them. Many felt that their « shade » (the new anthropology term), « seriti/isithunzi » (in the vernacular), or « soul » (the old missionary term), was implicated in the process. They feared that their essence could be stolen or their destiny altered by interfering with the resulting image or images: « Cameraman, why are you taking so many photos of me?

What are you going to do with the rest of them? » Often I found myself at pains to explain why I had to make many exposures or to do a re-shoot. I imagine that my early experience as a street photographer explains why I still use comparatively very little film on professional assignments.

If all went well, clients paid me the balance due and took their photographss. Most of these images found their way into family albums. Photograph albums in the townships are cherished repositories of memories. The images in these albums are similar to those in albums the world over: weddings, birthday parties, school trips, portraits - special occasions of one sort or another. They are treasuries of family history, visual cues for the telling of stories. The images are mostly of happy, smiling people, dressed to party and surrounded by food and drink. The more formal portraits are crafted to foreground what might be called *petit bourgeois* or suburban sensibility: everyone and everything must look its best. Sometimes the moment memorialized is the presence of the camera! Going through township photograph albums can sometimes be a tortuous journey for a photographer. Some people consider it impolite if you decline to participate in the ritual of looking through the albums when you visit, a kind of induction into the family's history.

In spite of the popularity I gained by having a camera, I still did not consider photography as a career. The reasons were many, the main one being I was not making a lot of money. « Hey, Santu! On the weekend of ... (Friday, Saturday or Sunday) I/ we are celebrating our wedding anniversary/21st birthday/ unveiling of a tombstone etc., etc ... I/We would like to invite you to be there. Be sure to bring your camera and don't worry about film. I/We will provide the films and I/We am/are going to pay for processing and printing myself/ourselves! Or, I know someone/brother/cousin/girlfriend who works at the processing and printing laboratory. You don't have to worry. Come and enjoy yourself, you can bring your girlfriend and some of your friends along...! » The real meaning of the invitation was that I was not going to be paid. Pressing the shutter was not considered work! As soon as I finished matric I went to work as quality control tester in a pharmaceutical laboratory. It took me four years before I decided to forego a career in pharmacy because of boredom.

SANTU MOFOKENG

South Africa
b. Johannesburg 1956
– lives in Johannesburg

Santu Mofokeng began his photographic career in Adcock Ingram's laboratories. From 1985 onwards, he was a freelance photographer and a member of Afripix. He received the prestigious Mother Jones Award for Africa. He joined the Department of African Studies at the University of the Witwatersrand (Johannesburg) in 1988 and began doing historical research. *Black Photo Album, Look at me, 1890-1950* is the first phase of this « archaeological » study. Santu Mofokeng continues exploring and chasing shadows, trying to create metaphors for his biography. Referring to his work « Chasing Shadows », Santu Mofokeng has written: « I was searching for something which refused to be photographed. Perhaps I was chasing shadows. »

< Photographer SANTU MOFOKENG ©
White City Jabavu, 1986.
Dukathole, Germiston, 1988.

Images of reality

I took a job as an assistant in a newspaper darkroom. This career move cost me a 50 per cent cut in wages. I began as a « donkerkamer assistent », no promotion and no future, just a dead-end position. Only white people could be apprenticed as photographers. I would be asked to show the new white employees their way around the darkroom and the next thing I knew, I was taking orders from them!

In South Africa at the time, « technician » was a status reserved for whites or « coloureds ». Occasionally a black person could be employed as a technician in the more progressive foreign companies. But, as an « assistent » in a pro-government newspaper, I was a dogsbody to every photographer, freelance journalist or anyone else who was chummy with the department's secretary. In that newspaper there were no black photographers, only coloured reporters who also made pictures in order to illustrate their stories. Government policy on the « colour bar » was followed to the letter.

In the first few months as darkroom assistant I learnt more about life in my country than in my 12 years of schooling. For instance, that «black skin and blood make beautiful contrast». This from a conversation overheard in the photography department office: « Come check this, china! Isn't this beautiful? » says one very famous South African photojournalist to an Indian accounts clerk. He is referring to a colour transparency. The tranny depicts a corpse, an ANC cadre bleeding in death, lying on asphalt near a curb. A casualty in what is now known as the Silverton Siege (Pretoria). « I don't get it, » responds the clerk. « I see nothing beautiful in this. This is ghoulish, man! » « You know fuck-all, china! This is a masterpiece. There is nothing as beautiful as black skin and blood! It makes a beautiful contrast. There's nothing like it, china! »

For four years I wormed my way around as a darkroom man, at various newspapers in and around Johannesburg. I also began to do free-lance work as a photographer, mainly covering sport and social events. I took the abuse and insults that came with the job. I was once told by the managing editor of the mining house newspaper that « Black is not beautiful, only hard work is !» I did not mind hard work, but I refused to « Clean up! » after the white paste-up artists (who sat gossiping and knitting) at the machines they had been using. I was promptly fired! I then accepted a job at a right-wing English language newspaper. For a long time I could not bring myself to write the name of this newspaper in my CV. All this time I was reading whatever books were available to me, in order to learn photographic theory and technique. When I felt confident enough as a photographer and darkroom technician I left newspaper work in order to apprentice as a photographer's assistant in an advertising outfit.

Gradually, I gained confidence that I had the technical wherewithal to brave the free-lance market. Unfortunately, not everyone agreed. When I asked my bosses at a Christmas luncheon what future I had as a photographer, one replied that I could at least join the throng of black photographers at soccer matches! Even the company I worked for could not conceive of giving me a commission to do a shoot, in spite of my proven abilities in the studio when the resident senior photographer was not available.

Ironically, in the light of my professed Black Consciousness politics, the person who nurtured me as a freelance photographer was a white man, David Goldblatt.

At the time I was still not sure what kind of photography I wanted to do but, for reasons I could not explain, I enjoyed his documentary work above anything anyone else was doing at the time. This education was valuable, though it came to an abrupt end when I lost all my camera equipment in a mugging incident. While I missed the camera and equipment, I considered myself lucky to escape with my life - together with the model, a friend I was photographing to make a pin-up for a society magazine. I escaped by rolling down a mine slime-dump on to a motorway.

I went back to work as «donkerkamer-assistent» in the newspaper where I had begun my career. Within a few months I was fired because I was carrying too many books into the workplace! While the security officer was going over the books, he discovered a photograph of a very young Dr Beyers Naude and Revd Makhalemele, which I had brought to work in order to make copies for a friend. Once the leader of the Dutch Reformed Church, Beyers Naude had broken away from his Afrikaner upbringing by taking a stand against apartheid. He was banned for his insolence, and was ostracized from the Afrikaner community. The security chief of the company took an uncommon interest in the image and confiscated it. When I asked to have it back, he told me he had given it to the Security Police so they could investigate the legality of my position, considering that I was in the possession of a picture of a banned person, and that during a national state of emergency.

I joined the Afrapix Collective in 1985. I had no work, no equipment and no resources. Afrapix gave me a home. It provided me with money to buy a camera and film in order to document Soweto and the rising discontent in the townships. Their confidence in me was in some ways misplaced, seeing that I was less interested in the «unrest» than in the ordinary life in the townships. Nevertheless, I became an Afrapix member and contributed to the education programme the group was preparing for unionized workers. A short time later I joined *New Nation*, an alternative newspaper, as photographer. A photojournalistic career in those days was not without hazards, not all of which came from police bullets and batons. I was once nearly «necklaced» by comrades at a night vigil in Emndeni (Soweto) after being branded an informer simply by asking permission to take pictures of the proceedings. At another time, while documenting the 1987 mine strike, I fell into the hands of scab workers. An angry mineworker confronted me: « Do you know what is happening out there? People are being killed for not joining in the strike! From whom did you get permission to take our pictures? »

I protested my innocence: « I am only a messenger, » said I! In a chilling tone he says, «You are coming with us. We are going to deal with you in the hostel! You are not getting out!» My tongue became very dry. I was trapped inside the bus with a menacing group of scab labourers baying for my blood! And I had managed to shoot only one exposure! Security guards at the mine offered little solace. One of the white security guards callously suggested that they should let the scabs deal with me, whichever way they saw fit! But for the insistence of one Paul Weinberg, a photographer who refused to leave the mine without me, I would be dead.

A few months after this incident I left photojournalism to concentrate on documentary work. When I resigned from *New Nation*, I was leaving the universe in which my pictures had to function as « weapons of struggle ».

Photographer SANTU MOFOKENG ©
Preparing sheep-heads, Dukathole, 1989.

I was unhappy with the propaganda images which reduced life in the townships into one of perpetual struggle, because I felt this representation to be incomplete. I came to work at the African Studies Institute (now called IASR), in the Oral History Project at the University of the Witwatersrand.

This move was frowned upon by a few friends, who considered it a sign of lack of commitment. My work at the institute involved documenting worlds that did not usually feature in the «struggle» images of South Africa so beloved of American and European audiences: rural communities, marginal coloured communities threatened with resettlement, etc. In addition to this work I continued with my documentation of township life - a long-term project which I had begun as a «metaphorical biography» in 1982, which is divided into small manageable chapters or definable photographic essays, e.g. « Train Church », « Soweto: Going Home », « Chasing Shadows », etc. This work was vindicated in the early 1990s when the overseas market, weary of « struggle images » of sjambok-wielding « Boer » policemen ,

began to ask for ordinary pictures of everyday life in townships. Suddenly my pictures of quotidian African life - of shebeens, street-soccer and home life, which had been considered unpublishable in the 1980s - now found commercial favour. My credentials as a « struggle » photographer were restored.

It was not until I had my first solo exhibition that I really began to ponder my role as photographer. *Like Shifting Sand*, the exhibition, explored not only the townships, where the focus of the struggles for liberation were well documented, but rural landscapes as well. I had some reservations about the way the show was received by the majority of people in the black communities. I soon realized that a lot of people in the townships could not relate to the realities that were inherent in my photographs. One comment from a visitor who signed his name as Vusi haunts me: « Making money with blacks ».

That simple comment forced me like nothing else ever had, to question the value of my work. I began to understand that the messages I was trying to send, however singular and different

from others that came before, would always be overshadowed by the perceptions and assumptions about South Africa that viewers bring with them. The other thing that became clear to me as a result of Vusi's comment was that in my pursuit of the art I was not paying enough attention to the narratives and aspirations of the people I was photographing. I had either forgotten, neglected or disregarded my early beginnings. I had simply graduated into being a professional photographer without first pondering the meaning of this switch. I had not thought about my own responsibility in the continuing, contentious struggle over the representation of my country's history.

This inspired me to change my methods. Where assumptions and projections were once an implicit part in my professional work, I now began to enlist the participation of the communities where I worked. Soon after, in the show *Distorting Mirror/Townships Imagined*, I juxtaposed images « of » the township (public/political) with images « in » the township (private/personal).

I was looking at images of the township which I had been making for the public media and contrasting them with those I had been making as a street photographer, that is, images people chose to value, to treasure, to conserve: ultimately to show or display and pass on to their children. This is how I began to explore the politics of representation. And it was not until I was doing research for that project that I became aware of the urban family portraits that were made at the beginning of this century. These images were slowly disintegrating in plastic bags, tin boxes, under beds and on top of cupboards and kists in the townships. And because they lay outside the consciousness of the education system, including the museums, galleries and libraries in this country, I found them enigmatic. These solemn images of middle- and working-class black families, crafted according to the styles (in gesture, props and clothing) of Georgian and Victorian portrait painting, portray a class of black people which, according to my education, did not exist at the time they were made! My quest for an explanation for this omission in my history education made me appreciate the magnitude of the crime of apartheid: « For the struggle for power is the struggle of memory against forgetting » (Kundera). And as I examine old family albums, I feel I have come full circle.

Santu Mofokeng

Photographer SANTU MOFOKENG ©
Motouleng Caves / Surrender Hill,
Clarens, Easter Weekend, 1996.

Photographer ANDREW TSHABANGU ©
< Twilight on Klip Town.
Cooked food sellers, Joubert Park, 1995.
Cooked food sellers, Joubert Park, 1994.
∧ Children in twilight city.

ANDREW TSHABANGU

South Africa
b. Soweto, South Africa 1966 – lives in Johannesburg

Andrew Tshabangu is one of the new generation of South African photographers who are experiencing all the difficulties involved in moving into a post-apartheid era in a violent world, where equal opportunities in life and social justice do not yet exist. His work takes the form of social reportage which displays great sensitivity to the distress of others.

AKINBODE AKINBIYI

Nigeria
b. Oxford,UK 1946 – lives in Berlin

Akinbode Akinbiyi studied at Ibadan University (Nigeria), Lancaster (England) and Heidelberg (Germany). He taught himself photography in 1972 and has been working free-lance since 1977. Akinbiyi is fasci-nated by Africa and travels there at least once a year. He is an avid wal-ker who records the elements of daily life with his eagle eye, capturing the black-and-white verticality of South Africa or the brutality of the streets of Lagos without judgement. He depicts reality, gently and calmly.

ALIOUNE BÂ

Mali
b. Bamako, Mali 1959
– lives in Bamako

Alioune Bâ has been the photographer for the Mali National Museum since 1983 and has to his credit several major projects aimed at highlighting the Malian cultural heritage. His photographs show daily attitudes and gestures, everyday objects, light on mosque walls: every detail is important in his extremely poetic work.

< Photographer ALIOUNE BÂ © 1996
Nangoyo Mosque, Mali.

PHOTOGRAPHER ALIOUNE BÂ © 1996 >
The bowl of milk.

Photographer ALIOUNE BÂ © 1996 V
The Great Djenné Mosque, Mali.

HOUSSEIN ASSAMO

Djibouti
b. Djibouti 1963 – lives in Djibouti

Houssein Assamo Abdillahi Rayalé is a lover of silence and wide open spaces. He is currently preparing several photo-stories on young people and khat, odd jobs, and traditional means of transport.

< Photographer
HOUSSEIN ASSAMO © 1996
The Assal lake.

Photographer >
HOUSSEIN ASSAMO © 1996
Djibouti-city.

Photographer ∨
HOUSSEIN ASSAMO © 1996
Djibouti, the port.

ABDOURAHMAN ISSA

Djibouti
b. Djibouti ca 1960
– lives in the USA

Abdourahman Issa has done numerous photo-stories about Djibouti and official and society events in the capital. He moved to the United States in 1996.

Photographer
ABDOURAHMAN ISSA © 1996
Djibouti.

AMIN MAHAMOUD AHMED

Djibouti
b. Djibouti 1968 – lives in Djibouti

Amin Mahamoud Ahmed was taught photography by Abdallah Kayari. He has been working for the newspaper *La Nation* since 1992. The paper regularly publishes unusual photos taken by him under the heading « Amin's flashes ». He is preparing photo-reports on the Djibouti-Ethiopian train and on Somalian refugees in Djibouti.

∧ Photographer
AMIN MAHAMOUD AHMED © 1996
The Djibouti-city market.

∨ Photographer
AMIN MAHAMOUD AHMED © 1996
Djibouti-city.

RAMADAN ALI AHMED

Djibouti
b. Djibouti 1970 – lives in Djibouti

Ramadan Ali Ahmed is a technician in a photo studio in Djibouti-city. He is interested in the various printing processes, macrophotography and « experimental photography ».

Λ Photographer
RAMADAN ALI AHMED © 1996
Tadjoura.

V Photographer
RAMADAN ALI AHMED © 1996
Khat hawkers in Djibouti-city.

DORRIS HARON KASCO

Ivory Coast
b. Daloa, Ivory Coast 1966
– lives in Abidjan, Ivory Coast

« The madmen of Abidjan », the fruit of three years work, are ruthless evidence of a denial of reality, or worse still, of a collective blindness that rejects these nightly figures onto the city streets. Since then, Dorris Haron Kasco has spent time with the destitute children on the streets and has just taken part in a collective work to portray them.

Photographer
DORRIS HARON KASCO © 1993
The madmen of Abidjan.

In search of an aesthetic

Recherche d'une esthétique

Photographer
ROTIMI FANI-KAYODE © 1989
Every minute counts.
(Ecstatic Antibodies series.)

Apart from South Africa, which has economic wealth, numerous photographers and laboratories, and is more oriented towards contemporary American and European culture than towards its own continent, most African countries do not have any photographers whose quest is primarily aesthetic. Such examples are few and far between and are often the result of the diaspora and its contact with the major international aesthetic trends. The most typical example is Rotimi Fany-Kayodé, the Nigerian photographer who lived in New York and London. His work, situated within current world trends, is often linked to a search for identity that sometimes even caricatures his own culture of origin: as though the quest for identity only applies to those who are culturally, intellectually and geographically distanced from their roots. On the other hand, his work also wholly integrates the individual, if not individualistic, vision of the photographer turned artist, in specific western terms. That said, the output of a few specific photographers and the example of South Africa prove that, when given the information and the material means, there is no shortage of African talent in the aesthetic field. Which proves that there is more to African photography than portrait photography.

PMSL & JLP

ROTIMI FANI-KAYODE

Nigeria – UK
b. Ifé, Nigeria 1955 – d. London 1989

Born into a family with considerable political and religious influence, Rotimi Fani-Kayode left Nigeria for England after the military coup in 1966. He went on to study art at the University of Georgetown in Washington DC and then at the Pratt Institute in New York, and was deeply marked by this period of contact with the African-American community. In 1982 he returned to England, where he shared the greater part of his life and work with Alex Hirst.

A founder-member of Autograph, the black photographers' association, he was also active in the Black Audio Film Collective and the campaign against HIV/AIDS. In his life, as in his work, his distinctive identity was something he made no effort to conceal; and while his stated aim was to create pictures that would shake the established order, he threw eloquent light on the affinities between cultures and people, with the Africa and Nigeria that had never left him looming ever larger in his work - that same Africa to which he was intending to return when death stepped in on 21 December 1989, after Fani-Kayode had had only only seven years of creative activity.

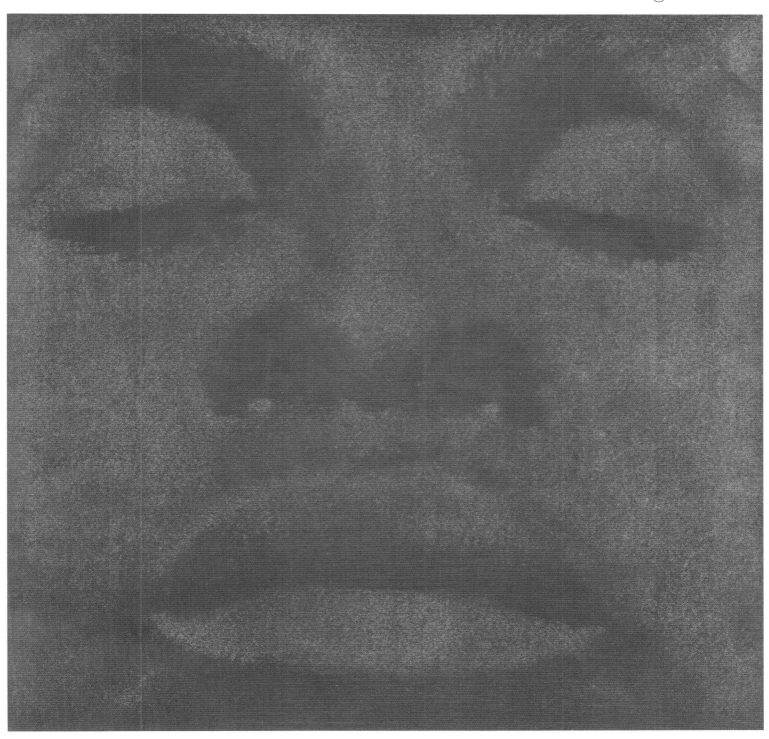

Photographer
ROTIMI FANI-KAYODE ©
Mother's milk, 1983.
Bronze head, 1987.
Lorne, gum bichromate, 1989.

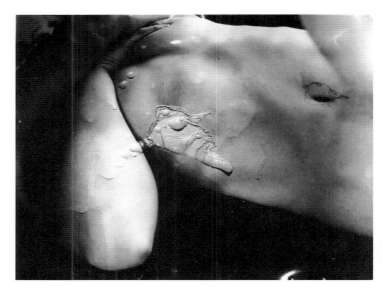

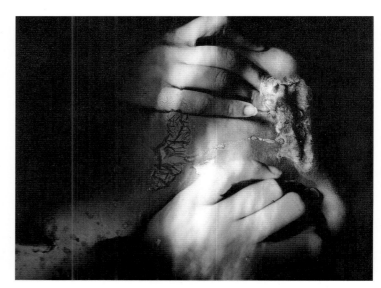

JULIA TIFFIN

South Africa
b. Cape Town, South Africa 1975 – lives in Cape Town

Julia Tiffin completed her Fine Arts degree in 1997. Of the photographs shown here she writes: « I wanted to photograph the body. I began with hands, for I find that hands are an integral part of the beauty of the human body. But photographically the results were disappointing. They weren't exact. I had to stress the silvery aspect of beauty. I had to scrape, burn, work right inside my pictures. But in spite of everything, beauty still did not come out real. It did not match my experience of life. So I burnt the skin, poured acid on the surface of the body, soaked the prints in stagnant water. They decomposed, went mouldy, stank.

It was finally beginning to become real. Via this process I rediscovered authentic sensations, sensations I recognised. I wanted to go further and look at this decomposition, this ugliness as a version of beauty. Out there beyond the process of putrefaction. So I rephotographed these shreds of decomposing paper. Painful burns to the skin, the flesh, the body and the heart emerged transfigured amid the sombre tones of the silver salts. I live in a country of violence: violence of the heart and the flesh, of the places that bear the marks of our lives. »

Photographer JULIA TIFFIN © 1996
Beauty & Decay I-IV.

In search of an aesthetic

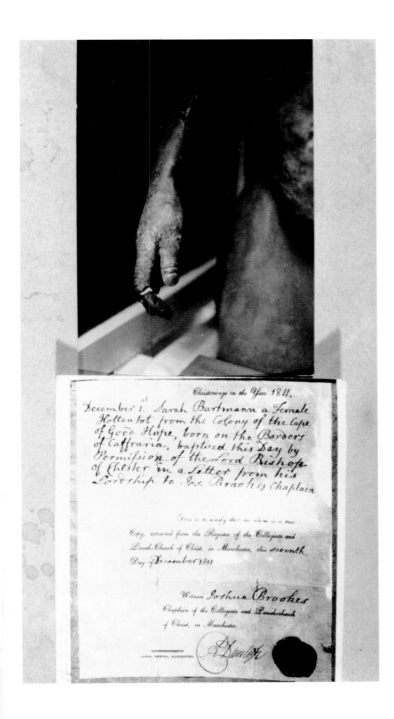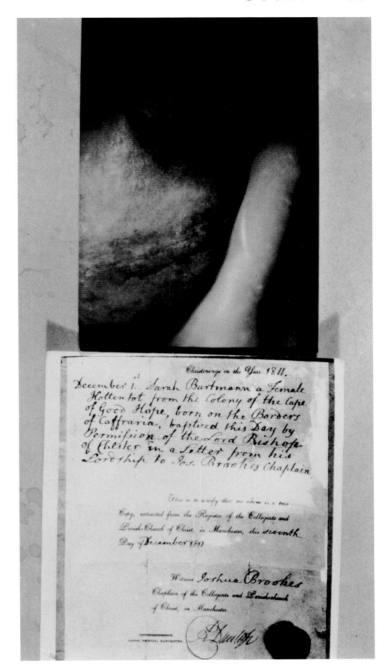

PENNY SIOPIS

South Africa
b. Vryburg, South Africa 1953 – lives in Johannesburg

Born in 1953 in Vryburg, in South Africa's Northwest Province, Penny Siopis now teaches at the University of the Witwatersrand in Johannesburg. Here she presents a dramatically intense account of a moulding of the body of Saartjie Bartmann, a Catholic Khoi woman from the Cape, on display in its wooden cage in the Paris Natural History Museum. « This woman had been brought to Paris to be 'shown'. Then she had been 'forgotten' and died wretchedly in France in January 1916. Nobody ever claimed the body or called for its return .»

Photographer PENNY SIOPIS © 1997
Eye.

CATHY PINNOCK

South Africa
b. Johannesburg, 1967 – lives in Westdene, South Africa

A graduate of Johannesburg's National School of the Arts and of Rhodes University in Grahamstown, Cathy Pinnock looks here at the landscapes of the Cape and, more especially, their strange varieties of succulents: she first photographs them in black-and-white, then handpaints the negative, and finally prints in colour - a process that captures perfectly the harsh beauty of this rugged terrain. Cathy Pinnock works as a photographer for the *Saturday Star* and is also a member of the Yip Photography agency.

Photographer CATHY PINNOCK © 1991
Eastern Cape.

Photographer OBIE OBERHOLZER ©
< Hotazel, drankwinkel.
  Nothern transvaal farmer, Rian du Toit.
> Sugarcane worker, Nkulu.

OBIE OBERHOLZER

South Africa
b. Pretoria, South Africa 1947 – lives in Pretoria

After a course in graphic design at the University of Stellenbosch, Obie Oberholzer studied photography at the Bavarian State Institute of Photography in Germany. In its use of contrast, colour, landscapes and people, his South African « notebook » reveals a committed, highly personal aesthetic that embraces both the violent and the quirkily humorous. He has done much to document disappearing traditional ways of life in the Cape, and some of his work has been published in popular book form.

Nelson Mandela delivers his first public speech, on the eve of his release. Grand Parade, Cape Town 11·02·1990

Photographer CHRIS LEDOCHOWSKI ©
< *Madiba delivers his first public speech in 27 years, on the day of his release. Grand Parade, Cape Town, 11 February 1990. Hand-coloured photo with ceramic frame by Chris Ledochowski made in collaboration with Joe Faragher.*

< *KTC Squatter camp, Guguletu, Cape Town, 1984. Hand-coloured photo with ceramic frame by Chris Ledochowski made in collaboration with Joe Faragher.*

∧ *Purple rain Day, Burg Street, Cape Town 1991. Photocolor dyes, watercolor with ceramic frame by Chris Ledochowski made in collaboration with Joe Faragher.*

< *Religious office, Manenberg, Cape Town, 1992. Colour solution, watercolour and ceramic frame, created in collaboration with Joe Faragher.*

CHRIS LEDOCHOWSKI

South Africa
b. Pretoria, South Africa 1956 – lives in Cape Town

Born into a Polish immigrant family, Chris Ledochowski studied in Swaziland before taking a degree at the Michaelis School of Fine Art at the University of Cape Town. As director and cameraman for the independent audiovisual agency Afroscope, he recorded the high points of the struggle of South Africa's trade unions and working classes during the 1980s. He was also a member of the Afrapix Collective, but without ever abandoning his independence of thought and vision. He has spent almost 20 years photographing the daily life of the townships of the Cape and celebrating the humanity and dignity of their inhabitants. In 1980, at the request of his subjects, he began to add watercolour and oil paint to his photos - a return to the tinted portrait traditionally favoured in the Cape's townships. During the same period he has been meticulously recording the ornamental and mural paintings of the townships.

In search of an aesthetic

ZWELETHU MTHETHWA

South Africa
b. Durban, South Africa 1960
– lives in Cape Town

Zwelethu Mthethwa grew up in Durban before moving to Cape Town. He completed a Fine Arts degree at the Michaelis School of Fine Art and a Masters in the Art of the Image at the Rochester Institute of Technology in the USA. He photographs people living in the townships.
« Most photographers use black-and-white for pictures of informal housing, so as to get a dark, gloomy atmosphere. I chose colour because it provides a greater emotional range. My aim is to show the pride of the people I photograph. I love the richness of the jumble of styles and the cheap materials used to decorate the houses. »

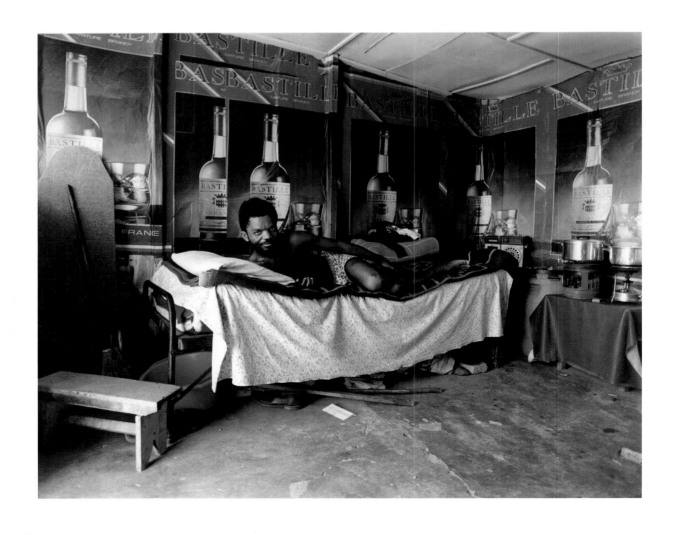

Photographer ZWELETHU MTHETHWA © 1995-96

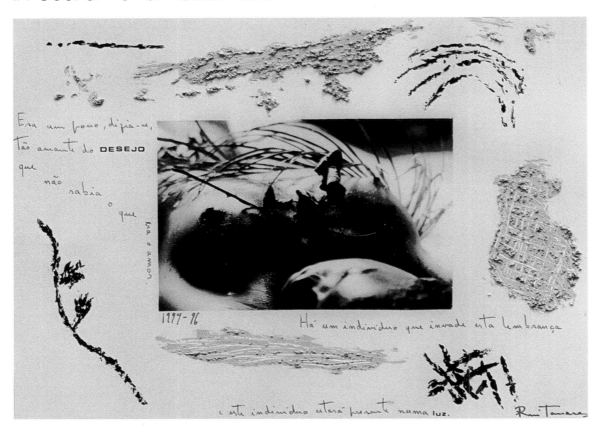

Photographer RUI TAVARES ©
From the series The Time of Flowers : Guilt
The enchanted garden.
The serpent's egg.

RUI TAVARES

Angola
b. Germany 1971 – lives in Lisbon, Portugal

Rui Tavares always adds paint, floating sentences or superimposed images to his black-and-white negatives or prints. «My work is experimental; the result is often a surprise and there is a high factor of chance. Witchdoctor? Magician? Alchemist? I don't know ...». He is also preparing his final thesis in architecture.

Joe's Yard

There are some people who seem to be made of cardboard, hobo philosophers who shamble between inspired speeches and mechanistic mental constructs, expounding on mankind's woundedness. Seeking followers, they preach freedom, seeking to be teachers, they forbid all teaching. They are ill at ease with themselves, but even more so with those others who are deaf to their prophecies - people who exist only in reacting to a context or a situation deliberately created for this purpose. They live out the anger of the world, which becomes for them something sublime.

If Joe's Yard had not existed, Joe Ramangelissa Samb, alias Issa Samb, alias Joe Ouakam, might have been one such. Years and years of an endlessly discoursing yard overflowing with contradictory shapes were captured for this single instant in their totality: a single image in which eyes for seeing and feet for walking find nothing left to comprehend. A ruin-yard, ruin of a work constantly in danger from itself, yet safe within the enclosure of a patch of land he called untouchable - magic. At last Joe could stop talking, at last he could let his world talk, a world made up of his own pictures and those of others who had accepted not the talk but the yard and its volley of words. There the crazy man, the student and the friend made objects that could aggregate around a rite expiating all the images and signs in the world. Who? Which? What? All were becoming a reality. And finally the work and its signature melted away into doubt, the accumulation of doubts. Their destinies were putrescence or a simple burying whose shroud would give shape to the object to come.

« Joe's corpse » - a hanged dummy wrapped in the national flag - was the yard's abstract guardian. Now it lies in a pizza parlour with a menu of ironclad ideas.

Wali Wala

BOUNA MEDOUNE SEYE

Sénégal
b. Dakar, Senegal 1956 – lives in Dakar

Bouna Medoune Seye studied in Marseille, France, then returned to live in Dakar. Fighting to gain artistic recognition for African photography, he has a sometimes disconcerting approach to the aesthetics of framing and composition that points to the strength and originality of his personality. As co-curator with Bertrand Hosti of the Dakar Month of Photography in 1992, he brought Mama Casset, the ageing portrait photographer of the Dakar Medina, to the attention of the public. Working in a range of creative fields - painting, photography, cinema - he attempts to pin down a kind of uncertainty running through the world in which he lives. His first short film, *Bandit-Cinema*, was made in 1994 and was followed by *Sai Sai By* in 1995.

Photographer
BOUNA MEDOUNE SEYE © 1995
Joe's Yard.
Joe's Yard in Dakar - captured here on film by Seye - was a gathering place for artists, writers and intellectuals, presided over by the fevered imagination of Joe. Today it is a « pizzeria ».

ANTÓNIO OLE

Angola
b. Luanda, Angola 1951
– lives in Luanda

António Ole shifts between several forms of expression: painting, sculpture, video and photography. Deeply marked by his country's eventful past, he is inspired by Angolan historical recollections and reality: colonization, the civil war, malnutrition, the demographic explosion in the capital and social rifts. Graduate of the American Film Institute in the USA, António Ole directed several documentaries on Angola from 1978 onwards and has naturally turned to photography. Softly-lit images capture the mysterious atmosphere of ruined palaces, portraits of rural people with unsettling gazes, traces of water and salt on the sun-cracked earth. He also creates elegant photomontages with saturated colours which he calls « accidents along the way ».

Photographer ANTÓNIO OLE ©

SERGIO AFONSO

Angola
b. Luanda, Angola 1976 – lives in Lisbon, Portugal

Sergio Afonso belongs to the second generation of an Angolan family of photographers. The brothers José Antonio, Rui and Joaquim Pinto Alfonso have been taking pictures since the 1950s and are owners of Foto Ngufo, Luanda's most fashionable photographic studio. Sergio Alfonso divides his time between Luanda and Lisbon, where he is completing his university studies.

Photographer SERGIO AFONSO ©

Indian Ocean

Océan Indien

En route to India

Tristan Bréville

In its early days photography in Mauritius obeyed the same rules as elsewhere, with Europeans producing portraits, landscapes and other pictures we would now describe as strictly for tourists. The most striking historical development was surely the systematic photographing of all new immigrants at the Coolie Ghat, the point of arrival; dating from the beginning of the century, this practice marks the official adoption of photography as a means of checking and controlling the island's population groups.

In January 1840, Ferdinand Worhnitz, a civil servant returning from a voyage to Europe, arrived in Port Louis with a wooden crate weighing over 18 kg. Inside it was one of the first photographic cameras, along with all the materials necessary for the preparation and development of photosensitive plates. The camera, itself made of wood, consisted of two units. The first and smallest, equipped with a lens manufactured by Charles Chevalier, was designed to slide into the second and larger unit. By adjusting its length, it was possible to obtain a focused image. The word « photograph » had not yet been coined: the images were known as daguerreotypes, a word derived from the name of the inventor of the process, the Frenchman, Louis Daguerre. Owning one of these cameras was one thing; using it was another. In the days that followed his arrival, and with infinite patience, Worhnitz began attempting to produce images with his new camera, as his bemused family and friends looked on. The rumour that it was possible to capture reality in images spread through the town like wildfire, and the story soon appeared in the local press:

The enthusiasm and perseverance of one of our compatriots, Mr Worhnitz, has permitted us to appreciate the prodigious discovery of Mr Daguerre. Among the excellent images that were produced before our eyes, one of the most interesting was a view of the town's theatre and Catholic church.

Le Cernéen, February 27, 1840.

According to this information, it would appear that the first series of photographs of Mauritius was taken on 25 or 26 February 1840. On 15 January of the same year, *Le Mauricien*, a local daily newspaper, reprinted an article that had previously appeared in *La Gazette des Tribunaux,* relating a « public demonstration of the daguerreotype process ».

His awareness of the importance of photography in the Mauritian heritage led the photographer Tristan Bréville to establish the Museum of Photography and the island's first photographic agency.

< UNKNOWN photographer ©
Curepipe, Mauritius.
Courtesy of Marie-Noelle &
Tristan Bréville.
Port-Louis Museum
of Photography.

On 16 June another article discussed one of the first applications of the new invention at length:

We are pleased to announce that in the skilled hands of our young engraver J Dureau, the wonderful invention of Mr Daguerre is destined to become more than a simple luxury or an amusement for the idle rich. Mr Dureau has informed us of his intention of employing the daguerreotype in a work of the highest interest, aided by several amateur artists who have joined their talents to his. Our readers will be pleased to learn that Mr Dureau has the intention of publishing a complete collection of views of the principal monuments and landscapes of the Island, in the form of lithographic engravings of daguerreotypes. It is well known that this process affords the highest degree of veracity and precision. The first series of images, which should be appearing soon, will include views of the Catholic church and Protestant temple of Port Louis, the church at Pamplemousses and that of Mon Plaisir. We are certain that Mr Dureau's new publication will be enthusiastically received by the public.

On 1 May 1841, less than a year after the article's appearance, Dureau's work was published. Soon after, the first photographic studios opened in Port Louis:

Daguerreotype portraits. Perfect likenesses produced in one minute. Enquiries at Erny and Tardieu's, Rue Touraine at the Corner of Bourbon Street from 10 o'clock to noon.

It was thus that in 1843 the first photographic studio in Mauritius announced its opening. The price of a daguerreotype portrait was ten piastres. Studio portraits required the subjects to remain completely still for minutes on end. This immobility was assured by a system of neck and head clamps, and specially-designed chairs. As a selling point, the two first photographers to open studios in Port Louis (they were also the first in the entire Indian Ocean region), emphasized the speed with which their process was completed.

One of them, the photographer Evariste Letourneur, boasted « without charlatanism » that he could produce a portrait « 15 seconds faster than any other photographer in the colony, and at cheaper prices ». In effect, Letourneur charged six piastres for a portrait.

The advertisement marked the beginning of stiff competition among photographers which was reflected in constantly-diminishing prices: at Mr Lemaire's studio, a portrait cost 350 francs; Mr Soleil demanded 250 francs, while Baron Séguier offered smaller-format likenesses for even less, as did Mr Giroux.

During the same period, two English photographers, the Trood Brothers, established a studio at 46 Rue Saint Georges in Port Louis. On 14 August 1844, they placed the following advertisement in a local paper:

For those in town for the races, daguerreotype portraits are available at C & J Trood's of London between the hours of 7 and 4 o'clock. The Trood Brothers would like to remind you that the most considerate of gifts is a portrait of your loved ones. Prospective clients may examine examples of their work at Mr Forer's shop in Chaussé or at the Trood studio at 46 Rue Saint-Georges.

The brothers, who were ambitious and enterprising, organised a public demonstration of the latest photographic techniques on 11 November 1844. At the time, a painted portrait executed by one of the artists on Cathedral Square or Rue de la Comédie cost a minimum of 20 *piastres*, and only the wealthy could afford them. The Trood Brothers understood that photography was destined for the common people. Their studio, located on Rue Saint-Georges, a well-frequented street between the racetrack at the Champ de Mars and the more formal Rue du Government, was chosen to attract a modest clientele, many of whom used it as their preferred route to the hippodrome. Out of purely historical interest, they also photographed the poverty and miserable living conditions of the thousands of newly-freed slaves who had gathered in the capital. Without knowing it, the Trood Brothers had invented documentary photography; others would soon follow in their footsteps.

On 4 January 1845, an elegantly-dressed man left India on board the schooner *Juliana*. Soon after his arrival in Port Louis, the following advertisement appeared in *The Mauricien* on 19 February 1845:

Hand-coloured daguerreotype portraits at 3, 4, and 5 piastres each. Reproduction of paintings, artists' portraits, sculptures and medallions. Views, landscapes, etc. Funerary portraits: Enquirers should address Mr Léger at the Duviviers' Residence, Rue Desforges.

Like many of his colleagues, Jules Léger, the photographer in question, often travelled to other localities on the island in the exercise of his profession. As a period news article related:

It is 5 o'clock in the morning and Port Louis is awakening. At the Duviviers', where he lodges, the photographer Léger is preparing his baggage by lantern-light. The sight of his daguerreotype camera causes his fertile imagination to picture all that lies ahead of him far from the capital. Today, his destination is the south of the island, and in particular, Grand-Port.

Bibliography:

Tristan Bréville, Edouard Maunick, Yvan Martial. 1993. *Le Temps d'une île*. Éditions du Pacifique.

Yvan Martial, André de Kervern et le Musée de la Photographie. 1991. *Les Cartes Postales de Maurice*. Éditions du Pacifique et Édition Didier Millet.

Siegfried Sammer. 1962. *Romantic Mauritius*.MTTB.

Allistair Mac Millan. 1914. *Mauritius Illustrated*. Édition W.H.L. Collinridge Londres.

Gabriel Gentil. 1914. *Maurice Pittoresque*. The Standard Printing Establishment.

Florence Nairac. *Trou d'Eau Douce*.

Claude Pavard. 1994.*Mémoires de couleurs*.

UNKNOWN photographer ©
Portrait of a young Indian,
(Mauritius immigration records).
Courtesy of Marie-Noëlle
& Tristan Bréville.
Port-Louis Museum of Photography

Léger's professional voyages were carefully prepared; advance notice of each leg of his journey always appeared in the local press:

Mr Léger has the honour of informing the inhabitants of Grand-Port that he will be in Mahébourg on 8 June next, and that his celebrated hand-coloured portraits will be available at the price of 6 to 8 piastres each.

From town to town, Léger photographed the entire island and produced literally albums-full of images. Far-ranging and exceptionally mobile, he often extended his activities beyond the confines of Mauritius: in August 1845 he made a brief voyage to Réunion, where he was the first photographer on the island, and on 15 September of the same year, he left for the Seychelles on the schooner *Joséphine Loizeau*. Léger was also the first photographer to work in the region of Cape Town, South Africa.

Léger's exceptional wanderlust finally resulted in his finding himself on the quay at Port Louis one Sunday morning in February 1853. A huge crowd of family and friends had come to bid farewell to some 200 voyagers leaving for Australia in search of gold. Among those leaving was Léger himself, ever in quest of new horizons to photograph.

Mauritius, situated on the maritime trade routes to India, was a decisive factor in the dissemination of photography throughout the Indian Ocean. By 1859 ten studios, modelled after those of Paris and London, were serving the island's 320 000 inhabitants. Devaux, the owner of one of the capital's most modern lithography presses, opened a daguerreotype studio on the first floor of his Rue Royale offices. The quality of his work was exceptional: the images were treated with gold chloride, a unique process which preserved them from fading with the passage of time. As photographic techniques evolved, daguerreotype images were supplanted by emulsion-based paper negatives.

The negatives, which could be used to produce positive images, opened the way for mechanically-produced photographic illustrations, a technique that was mastered early on by the printer, Maisonneuve. The island's specialist for portraits in visiting-card format (a fashion launched in Europe by Disdéri) was Chambray. After opening a daguerreotype studio in 1854, he adopted the new technique of negative-based images and caused a sensation by discovering a method of transferring colour to the positive paper print of his images. His work was so successful that after a brief partnership with Lecorgne from 1861 to 1863, he left Mauritius for Paris, where he opened two studios, the first of which was located at 25 Avenue Montaigne and the second on the premises of the Grand Hotel, 12 Boulevard des Capucines. Acly and Lecorgne, two partners, were the first photographers to work for the government of Mauritius, from which they obtained a contract to produce identity photographs of the Indian, African and Chinese immigrants disembarking where the government immigration office at Coolie Ghat. This was one of the world's first examples of a government using photography for administrative ends: the thousands of portraits taken over the ensuing years are today conserved in the archives of the Gandhi Institute.

From 1860 to 1870, more than a dozen new photographers established themselves in the capital. Among these were J Newman (Rue de l'Hôpital); Acly and Squire (on the corner of Rue de la Reine and Rue Bourbon); F Lacombe; W Tunks; J Galland (19 Rue de la Chaussée); MA Thomas (66 Rue Bourbon); Rondeau and Lagunière; M Richard (Rue des Casernes); Saunier and Britter (who acquired the Chambray studio after the latter left the island); M Moco (Rue du Rempart); E Raoul (also on the Rue du Rempart); JP Joseph (installed in the Baissac Pharmacy in Mahébourg); G Pierre and S Paul, who had been trained by Lecorgne (26 route des Pamplemousses) and M Florian (45 Rue Moka). The latter photographer, equipped with a camera capable of taking twelve photographs at a time, offered visiting-card format portraits at four *piastres* the dozen.

< UNKNOWN photographer © 1862
Indian immigrants in the village of Antoinette, Mauritius.
Courtesy of Marie-Noëlle & Tristan Bréville
Port-Louis Museum of Photography.

∧ UNKNOWN photographer © 1864
Slaves from Mozambique living in Mauritius
Courtesy Marie-Noëlle & Tristan Bréville
Port-Louis Museum of Photography

∨ Photographer TRISTAN BRÉVILLE ©
Lives in Rose Hill, Mauritius.

The list of other photographers and their sometimes novel techniques that succeeded over the following years can only be partial: ML Berenger and his method for reproducing images on enamel; S Dupuy, who introduced the gelatine-silver bromide process to Mauritius in March 1881; the painter Gustave Corret who, along with his assistant Charles Drenning (1857-1920), acquired Chambray's former studio, renamed *La Photographie Mauricienne*, and who photographed the aftermath of the catastrophic hurricane of 1912; Alexandre Rambert, who opened La Photographie Parisienne studio in Port Louis in 1884; Joseph Gabriel Gentil (1872-1956), who opened the Fine Arts Studio near Victoria Station in 1901 and who, like M Réhaut at the Rose-Hill Photographic Studio and the publishers Vidal, Audusson and Appavoo, created numerous photographic postcards; Edley Lemême, a skilled colourist; and the Halbwachs family, a veritable dynasty of photographers since the turn of the century: Rodger Halbwachs (1893-1970), an expert in stereoscopic views who photographed the yacht races in Mahébourg Bay in 1915 and was the author of *Les Monuments de l'Ile Maurice*, published in 1930; his nephew, Philippe Halbwachs (1922-1981), the representative for Hasselblad cameras in Mauritius and who, like his uncle Rodger, photographed the entire island; and today, Yves Halbwachs, born in 1949, a pioneer of marine photography.

Tristan Bréville

Photographer YVES PITCHEN © 1990 ∧
*Young woman of Indian origin,
Mauritius*

Photographer YVES PITCHEN © 1990 >
Afternoon, Mauritius.

YVES PITCHEN

Mauritius
b. Lubumbashi, Democratic Republic of Congo 1949
– lives in Rose Hill, Mauritius

Born and raised in Zaïre of a Belgian mother and a Mauritian father, Yves Pitchen went on to study photography at the National School of Architecture and the Visual Arts in Brussels. Since 1979 he has lived and worked in Mauritius, building up a personal file of over 500 6 x 9 photos of island life and the varying facets and customs of a population comprising Indians, Chinese, African Creoles and a handful of Europeans.

31. Année.
15.5 ep. 192 h.

Razolonjatovo

The Great Island

Frédéric Izydorczyk

Lying midway along the route to the Indies, sole pathway for trade with Asia, the island of Madagascar discovered photography at the same time as Europe: before the turn of the century studios catering to a wealthy local clientele were proliferating. At the same time that the studios were specializing in family portraits, the French presence and the setting up in 1896 of the National Geographical and Hydrographical Institute led to the growth of photography of a technical and military nature. Today's younger generation of photographers seeks to portray their homeland with a new sensibility, one with roots in both social concern and reportage.

Madagascar's first professional photographer was named Razaka. Born in February 1871 in Antananarivo, he opened a studio located in his home in the city of Ambatonakanga on 1 January 1889. After Razaka's death in 1939, his son Jean Jafetra continued in his father's footsteps and opened a studio in Besarety. From portraits to marriages, Razaka photographed the entire local aristocracy.

Gradually, photographing individuals and important events became fashionable. In response to the increasing demand, a number of other young photographers (among them, Rajaofera, Ramilijoana, Ramarcel, Razafitrimo, Rakotoarivony and Maurille Andrianarivelo) opened their own studios. By 1894, portrait photography had spread across the entire island. Even today, many of the great families of Madagascar still possess portrait albums dating from this period.

Slavery in Madagascar was abolished in 1896, when the island became a French colony. The new law had an enormous impact upon the aristocratic slave-owning families, who generally considered manual labour to be an unacceptable activity. Some of them, such as the Ratompoarivelo family, nevertheless broke with the ancestral tradition and began farming their own land - previously cultivated by slave labour.

Frédéric Izydorczyk lived in Madagascar for several years, working with the island's artists and photographers.

In December 1996, three photographers - Ramily, Pierrot Men and Dany Be - carried out research into the history of photography in Madagascar. Appeals in newspapers and over the air, research into family albums and visits to existing studios yielded, after some months, a collection opened to the public at CITE, in the centre of Antananarivo.

< Photographer
RASOLONJATOVO © 1924
Young man of 31 from the Ramaroson family, photographed 15 September 1924.
Rasolonjatovo died leaving no descendants.

∧
Photographer RAZAKA © 1920
The Malagasy photography pioneers in 1920 in Razaka's studio in Antananarivo. In the first row, the third from the left, Razaka senior. Standing, the first from the left side, Jean Razafitrimo. Photography collected by Ramily in February 1997.

∧
Photographer RAZAKA © 1892
In 1892, in Antananarivo, Razaka photographed this musician in his studio, a zejy voatavo player, traditional instrument from the Betsileo. One of the oldest photographs collected by Ramily.

∧
Photographer RAZAKA © 1889
IIn his studio in Ambatonakanga, in 1889, Razaka senior (left) and his brother Jafetra are photographed by Razaka's son.

Photographer RAZAKA © 1919 >
Razaka's son is riding down the Galliéni staircase in Antananarivo on his bike, photographed by his father in 1919.

As a consequence, they were excluded from the closed circle of the local aristocracy - despite their financial success. A number of period photographs of this new class of moneyed, working aristocrats, testify to their newfound wealth.

Following the arrival of the French, the private photographic studios were complemented by the activities of various government agencies. Despite their primary mission of documenting Madagascar's rich and varied physical aspects, their activity contributed to the development of photography in the country. In 1896 the French colonial government created the Institut Géographique et Hydrographique National (IGN). Prior to the creation of an infrastructure of roads and bridges, French army topographers and engineers systematically photographed and mapped the island. By the 1950s, the colonial government was concentrating on social and economic progress, and the island's road system was notably improved. After Madagascar's independence, the IGN became the present-day FTM.

Many of these images were taken by photographers attached to the colonial administration between 1896 and 1905. Although with a few exceptions the photographers were French, their names remain unknown. Other photographs are from the ANTA archives.

The ANTA (formerly the Service Général de l'Information) was created in 1946 at Ambohidahy, near Lake Anosy, by the colonial governor, De Coppet. Among its other activities, the Service archived a wide variety of photographs of Madagascar, ranging from political subjects to cultural and anthropological themes. Today, ANTA's photographic archives cover the period from 1905 to 1990.

RAZAKA

Madagascar
b. Antananarivo, Madagascar 1871 – d. Antananarivo 1939

Razaka was one of the first photographers in Madagascar. The existence of a substantial, wealthy aristocracy helped the spread of photography and on 1 January 1889 he opened his Razaka Studio in his house at Ambatonakanga, in Antananarivo. On his death the studio was taken over by his son.
The presence of ten or so big studios made photography a major business in Madagascar: it is known that the silver bromide process that was to oust the difficult wet plate technique was in use there before it reached Cape Town.

ANTA's archives also contain photos which appeared in many of the country's illustrated periodicals, such as the *Madagascar Review*, the 1931-1941 issues of *L'Ile Rouge* (renamed *Croix de Lorraine* during World War II), the postwar *Rouge et Or*, the postcolonial *Bleu et Or* and *Vaoyao*. The photo-safaris organized by the Association of French Journalists in 1927 and 1937 are also part of the ANTA archives.

In 1992, the ANTA was denationalized; at present, it is a private company. Along with the ANTA, the London Missionary Society (LMS) is another rich source of photographic documents concerning Madagascar: the illustrations which appeared in *Voyages Autour du Monde* (1860-1914) are from the LMS archives.

The years from 1957 to 1960 were marked by the creation of a national film agency which sporadically attempted to document the emergence of the new republic. The agency was directed by Robert Lisan, and the cameramen were for the most part French nationals.

In the 1950s, a new generation of photographers and studios made their appearance on the island, among them Studio Fily, Photo Stavy, Photo Kall, Photo Monde and Photorex. During this period Madagascar was still governed by the French, who had imposed a system of photographic censorship: among all the existing studios, only Express Photo was authorized to photograph street scenes.

Although the reasons for this strict limitation of photographic activity were never clearly explained, it would appear that France was desirous of avoiding images capable of « compromising » its colonial policies in the eyes of the international community. In addition, Madagascar was - and still is - an extremely rich and strategically located island. The tragic events of 1947, marked by violence, social unrest and military repression, are among the unfortunate expressions of this reality.

In the 1970s, photographers such as Pierrot Men, Dany-Be and Ramily, left the confines of their studios and began taking news photos. Today, they continue their struggle to publish images of the realities of life in Madagascar throughout the world.

Frédéric Izydorczyk

Photographer G RAZAFITRIMO Jr © 1918 >
28 January 1918.
From the Ramaroson family album.

V Photographer G RAZAFITRIMO Jr © 1916
Birthday photo: b. Friday 15 September 1893, photographed 15 September 1916.
From the Ramaroson family album.

G. Razafitrima fils
RUE CARAYON, TANANARIVE

28 Janvier 1918

∧ Photographe J RANDRIA ©

J. Randria, a Merina living among the Bara people, worked with the products of Louis Lumière. With Ramilijaona he was one of Antananarivo's great portraitists, working from his Randria Studio on the Boulevard Labigorne in Antananarivo.

∧ Photographe J RANDRIA ©

Four friends from Madagascar. The first is Madagascan, the second Indian, the third African, the fourth Chinese (representative of the island's population).

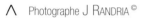

∧ Photographer J RANDRIA © 1914
Late December 1914.
From the Ramaroson family album.

Photographer J RANDRIA © 1916 ∧
20 August 1916, at 4.40 in the afternoon.
From the Ramaroson family album.

< Photographer J RANDRIA © 1932
House at Ihosy (south of Fianarantsoa) in 1932.
Georges Raveloson Collection.

Photographer J RANDRIA © 1916 >
Let us be forever united!
6 January 1916.
From the Ramaroson family album.

Soyons toujours unis!... _6/2/16._

Impanotoamaizina, Eundi 24 Août 1925

MAURILLE ANDRIANARIVELO

MADAGASCAR
b. Antananarivo, Madagascar 1871 – d. Antananarivo 1969

Andrianarivelo, a member of the Panama revolutionary group later responsible for the 1947 uprising, set up his Rill Studio in Moramanga, a district of Antananarivo. Like everybody else, he was subject to French regulations limiting outdoor photography. Forbidden to take pictures in town, he worked only in his studio.

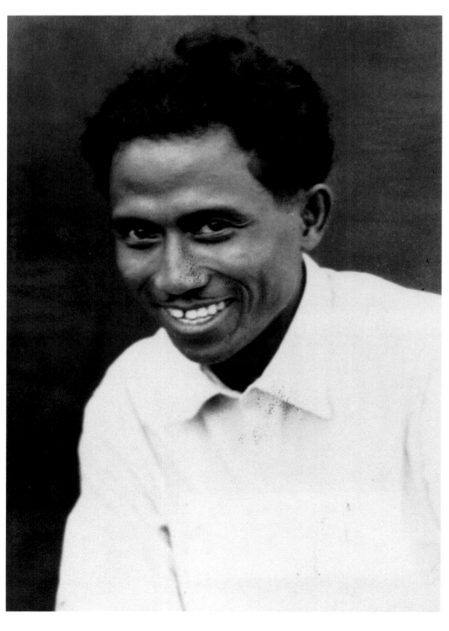

< Photographer
ANDRIANARIVELO ° 1925
A family portrait taken by Andrianarivelo in Tamatave, 24 August 1925.
This wealthy family was accompanied by their photographer on their trips to the country.

< Photographer
ANDRIANARIVELO ° 1954
Self-portrait of the photographer taken in 1954 in his workshop the Studio Rill, the first photographic laboratory to be installed in Moramanga just after the bloody repression carried out by the French military (MDRM 1947).

Photographer
ANDRIANARIVELO ° 1954 >
Maurille Andrianarivelo photographs his assistant in 1954. Leaving the Studio in his car, he often travelled across the country of Moramanga (about 120 km from Antananarivo towards the east coast, in the Toamasina) to take identity photographs.

∧ Photographer RAMILIJAONA © 1922

RAMILIJAONA

Madagascar
*b. Antananarivo, Madagascar 1887
– d. Antananarivo 1948*

Photographer, politician and writer, Ramilijaona began taking photographs in 1894. He later set up one of the island's largest studios and his pictures featured in many Madagascan family albums, characteristically showing family groups posed against imposing classical backdrops. One senses in his subjects a degree of refinement indicative of a rich and complex culture. Ramilijaona was also recognized abroad, being awarded medals in Antwerp in 1930 and Paris in 1931. He was the first photographer to establish a studio in the central part of the island, at Fianarantsoa.

< Photographer RAMILIJAONA © 1930
Vintage photograph of the Ratompaorivelo family.

∧ Photographer RAMILIJAONA © 1935
Self-portrait of the photographer.

Photographer RAMILIJAONA © 1930 >
Young lady with an umbrella.

Photographer RAMILIJAONA © >
*In the studio at Antananarivo, cousins
from the city (above) and from the
country (first now) come together in
front of Ramilijaona's lens.*

∨ Photographer RAMILIJAONA © 1930
The album of the Ratompoarivelo family.

Photographer RAMILIJAONA © 1931 ∧
In 1931, Ramilijaona was already out of his studio, photographing ceremonies and family gatherings.

< Photographer RAMILIJAONA © 1930
The Ratompoarivelo family.

DANY-BE

Madagascar
b. Antananarivo, Madagascar 1934
— lives in Antananarivo

Born in Antananarivo in 1934 into a Protestant family, Daniel Rakotoseheno, known as Dany-Be, rapidly came to be seen as a rebel. He joined the French Army in 1956 and became an assistant photographer for 18 months. Thanks to this experience, Dany-Be became a photographer for the *Courrier de Madagascar* in 1959, the country's main newspaper at the time. Too free-thinking, he had to leave the paper during the first major demonstrations in 1971. In 1974 he created his first private agency, SARY, with his friend Lucien Rajaonina. His career then followed the ups and down of the island's political life: he photographed the major political events, spent some time in prison for «causing disruption» and had all his negatives confiscated, but always picked up his camera again when he got out. Defining himself as a photo-journalist, Dany-Be sees himself as a humble witness to Madagascan society.

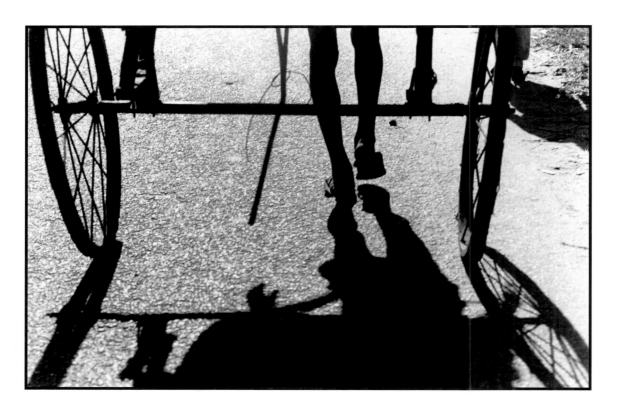

∧ Photographer DANY-BE © 1996
Madagascar's age-old means of transport: the rickshaw, Toamasina.

< Photographer DANY-BE © 1994
Tongon-tromby (ox's hoofs) at an Antarandolo butcher's.

Photographer DANY-BE © 1971 >
The revolt of the homeless children of the Zoma neighbourhood.
When it was featured on the front page of a daily paper, this photograph by Dany-Be generated real public concern over the plight of the children the authorities were seeking to evict from the Zoma neighbourhood.

RAMILY

Madagascar
b. Antananarivo, Madagascar 1939 – lives in Antananarivo

Ramily lives in Itaosi, a working-class area a few kilometres from the city centre. His studio is probably the busiest one in the capital as all the professional photographers have their prints processed there. Ramily started his career in 1957 as a laboratory worker at Photoflex and shot a few holiday landscape photographs with an old Agfa camera. Eleven years later he decided to leave his first employer and start working on commissions: he photographed weddings, christenings and all sorts of family ceremonies. He also opened a small bookshop/newsstand in town. Meanwhile he was still capturing the horizons of the Great Island on film with a newly-acquired Rolleicord 6 x 6. Despite the arrival of colour film on the Madagascan market, Ramily carried on working in black-and-white. « Black-and-white is easier, colour is technical, black-and-white is artistic. » From 1978, a year after the waves of nationalization began, Gaétan Baranger entrusted him with the Bureau for Aerial Photography orders. «Aerial shots are very expensive and it's an important test of confidence to ask me to develop and print shots like that.» Ramily waited until 1985 before exhibiting his photographss with those of his old friend, Dany-Be.

∧ Photographer RAMILY © 1973
Bessa-Lola, on the Horombe plateau, Ihosy.

< Photographer RAMILY © 1973
The Horombe plateau.

∧ Photographer DADDY © 1997
Table football player.

Photographer DADDY © 1992   >
*Zoma market attendant,
in the rain at daybreak.*

DADDY

Madagascar

b. Toamasina, Madagascar 1968 – lives in Antananarivo, Madagascar

Photographer at the daily paper *L'Express* since 1995, Daddy is also a choreographer and stage director. He discovered photography when he was nine, thanks to an average format Zeiss Ikon camera which belonged to his father. At the end of 1992, Daddy met Ramily while he was studying medicine. The latter taught him how to print black-and-white photographs in his Itoasy laboratory. From January 1993, Daddy did his own prints. He now divides his time between *L'Express*, advertising commissions and more personal work.

∧ Photographer DADDY © 1997
Old newspaper vendor in the streets of Antananarivo.

Photographer PIERROT MEN © >
Roundabout on the Fianarantsoa road.

Photographer PIERROT MEN © >
Soatanana.

Pierrot Men

Madagascar
b. Midongy, Madagascar 1954 – lives in Fianarantsoa, Madagascar

Chan Hong Men Pierrot, known as Pierrot Men, was born in South Midongy, Madagascar, in 1954, son of a Franco-Madagascan mother and a Chinese father. In Chinese, Men means « light »; a prophetic name for this lover of shadow effects. He discovered photography somewhat by chance when he bought an old Minolta for « next to nothing » while he was learning to paint with Léon Fulgence, his lifelong friend. He runs a photolaboratory in Fianarantsoa. Pierrot Men loves photography and the alchemy of the darkroom. In 1994 he won the first prize of the Mother Jones Leica competition. He recently accompanied John Liebenberg, a South African photographer, on a journey all over south-western Madagascar. Today, Pierrot Men is documenting the life of the white village of Saotanana.

∧
Photographer PIERROT MEN ©
Cold-drink vendor at a football match.

The Anthropometry of memory

Wilhiam Zitte

An overseas territory of France since 1946, Reunion has moved through the technical advances of the 19th and 20th centuries at the same rate as Europe itself. Apart from the TV images in colonial photography, local photography initially focused on such technical innovations as bridge-building and the coming of the railway. More recently, French government support for photography has led to the blossoming of an original artistic approach in a new generation of photographers trained to international standards.

The oldest photographs in my family album date from 1955. A photograph taken by my father when I was four months old shows me seated in a Gol-chair in the garden of our house in Saint-Benoit, Montée College. Another portrait of myself, this time in a chrome baby-buggy, was taken by Madame Grandmaison, a professional photographer who worked in Saint-Benoit in the 1950s. Reproductions of this photograph were sent to various members of my family.

Among other family photographs that remain in my memory, the most unforgettable were those of my grandmother Louise, and above all, an identity photograph of my great-grandmother Babadine. The haunting expression in her eyes came back to me as I discovered a series of anthropometric portraits in the archives of the Museum of Natural History in Saint-Denis in 1993. Dating from 1863, and attributed to Désiré Charnay, these remarkable photographs sparked my decision to delve deeper into the history of photography in Reunion.

The first cameras arrived on the island in the early 1860s. The economy of Reunion was at that time prosperous owing to the cultivation of sugar-cane, its principal cash crop. A prized possession in France's growing colonial empire, the island was the subject of a remarkable series of photographs taken by Rondeau and Parent in 1861, and preserved today in the Archives Départementales de La Réunion. The subjects of these photographs were the island's most spectacular sights and noteworthy monuments, as well several of its principal sugar-cane mills. The entire series of photographs, collated in an album entitled *Album des Vues de Bourbon* and dedicated to « The Sugar Manufacturers and Merchants of Reunion », was sold to wealthy colonial residents.

∧ Photographer
MME GRANDMAISON ©
Wilhiam Zitte as a young child.
William Zitte Collection.

\> UNKNOWN photographer ©
late 19th century
Babadine 'looking into space'.
William Zitte Collection.

< Photographer
J EYCKERMANS ©1870-80
Nanny and child.
Private collection.

Wilhiam Zitte was born in Saint-Benoit in 1955 and is now a painter in Saint-Leu. His graphic work often incorporates photographic elements relating to memory, history and the island's Creole character. At the request of René-Paul Savignan and working with Gilbert Albany and Bernard Leveneur, he has prepared an initial history of photography in Reunion, with special attention to the Creole question.

Indian Ocean

These photographs constitute the first precisely dated historical evidence of photographic activity in Reunion. They sparked an interest in the discipline and encouraged the use of the new technique as a means of artistic expression: in fact, several local artists turned from painting to photography. Among them was the artist François Cudenet, who temporarily abandoned his easel and opened one of the first professional photographic studios. Several examples of his work are preserved in private collections and at the Centre des Archives d'Outre Mer in Aix-en-Provence. Other pioneer photographers active in the early 1860s include the painter Louis Antoine Roussin, Eyckermans, Chambay, Eugene Bidache and Lamele.

In 1863, Reunion was the object of its first news story illustrated with photographs: Louis Simonin, a journalist for the magazine *Le Tour du Monde*, wrote a praise-filled article about the island. His text was illustrated with a series of etchings executed by Lamele after photographs taken by Bevan. Also in 1863, Désiré Charnay produced a strange and fascinating series of anthropological photographs, some of them representing individuals with serious physical disabilities. Although Reunion would often be a subject for photographers in the latter half of the 19th century, these portraits were among the first systematic photographic studies of the island's inhabitants.

Photographic activity in Reunion increased during the Second Empire (1852-1870). Whether they were French colonials or indigenous inhabitants of the island, little is known of the lives of those pioneer photographers, and only the fragile evidence of their images testifies to their existence.

As photography became more widespread, members of the upper classes had their portraits taken in visiting-card format, as was the fashion in Europe during the latter half of the 19th century. Precious copper-hinged leather or red velvet-covered family albums still contain these faces from another age, these garments in the latest styles from Paris. African or Indian servants occasionally appear in certain photographs, recalling the slavery that had existed on the island in the not-so-distant past. Anonymous dark-skinned nannies hold the hands of fair-skinned and well-born children, their gazes caught for eternity in the fleeting moment of posing for the photographer.

In the years between 1870 and 1880, an increasing number of photographic albums containing selected views of Reunion were published.

Among the most interesting were those of the prolific photographer, Charles Saunier, whose work has been preserved in the Archives Départementales de La Réunion, La Bibliothèque Nationale and the Centre des Archives d'Outre-Mer. The island's capital, Saint-Denis, as well as its principal cities of Saint-Paul and Saint-Pierre, are often represented, along with the warm water spas at Salazie and Cilaos, whose healthy climate and spring waters were reputedly effective against tropical diseases such as malaria. Charles Saunier also meticulously documented the gradual transformation of the island's transportation system, including the construction of the first railroad. Symbols of modernity and technological progress, the bridges and viaducts designed by the celebrated French engineer Eiffel, were also abundantly photographed by Adolphe Blondel, one of the team of colonial engineers responsible for the construction of the railroad line and port facilities. Many of Blondel's photographs are preserved in the Fonds de la Société de Géographie and the Cabinet des Estampes of the Bibliothèque Nationale. Blondel also produced a series of ethnological and anthropological photographs documenting the very mixed origins of the island's inhabitants. Many of his original glass-plate photographs were projected during lectures organized by the island's Geographical Society. Georges Richard, another photographer active during the same period, produced a remarkable series of images (most of which are preserved at the Centre des Archives d'Outre-Mer) of Reunion's most picturesque sites from 1887-89. His style, innovative and original, prefigures the tourist photographss so common today.

The last decade of the 19th century was especially rich in photographic activity. Among the best examples were the photographs taken from 1895-1897 by Henri Mathieu, a member of the colonial army posted in Reunion. Today kept in a private collection, many of his photographs were later published as a highly popular series of postcards. Richeville Lauratet, another exceptional photographer of the period, captured intimate scenes of a family dressed in their best clothing, gathered around their table for lunch. His original glass-plate negatives are today preserved in the Centre des Archives d'Outre-Mer. The works of other amateur photographers[1] active during the same period are also to be found in museums.

At the turn of the century, professional photographers such as Richard, André Blay and André Albany, had opened studios in which they immortalized first communions, marriages and important social events.

Photographer DÉSIRÉ CHARNAY © 1863
Madagascan and Mozambique women from Reunion.
Reunion Natural History Museum.

Photographer HENRI MATHIEU © 1895-97
Old man.
Private collection.

Photographer DÉSIRÉ CHARNAY © 1863
Mozambique men from Reunion.
Reunion Natural History Museum.

1. Among them are Octave Dumesgnil, Zampierro, Eruida, Claude Marion and several immigrant Indian photographers.

2. *Ile de la Réunion: Trura Kartié; Entre Mythologie et Pratiques,* Editions de la Martinière, 1994.

Indian Ocean

Photographer EUGÈNE BIDACHE ©ca.1860 >
Rue de l'Eglise, Saint-Denis.
Reunion Departmental Archives.

Photographer HENRI MATHIEU ©1865 >
Mr Augier de Maintenon, Navy Commissioner
Mr Payen, Colonial Pharmacist First-Class,
and servant, at home.

Photographer RICHEVILLE LAURATET FILS ©ca.1905 >
Wedding in Saint-Denis.

Photographer FRANÇOIS CUDENET ©1861 >
Straw huts at Saint-Pierre.
Overseas Archives Centre.

Photographer HENRI MATHIEU ©ca.1900 >
Church of the Port.

Photographer CHARLES SAUNIER ©1880 >
Bridge on the river Mât'
Reunion Departmental Archives

The career of André Albany was typical: born in the village of Saint-André, he learned the techniques of photography as a young man and mounted his first exhibition at the age of 20. In 1926 he was awarded a government scholarship and went to Paris, where he enrolled in a school of photography while at the same time working as a press photographer for several studios. After obtaining degrees in still and film photography, he returned to Reunion in 1939. Active until the 1970s, André Albany remains a landmark in the history of photography in Reunion.

With the transformation of Reunion into an administrative Department of France, professional photographers became more numerous. Itinerant photographers also appeared throughout the entire island. In the 1960s, photographic studios and shops could be found in practically every village, offering services ranging from portrait and special events photography to film development, cameras and related products. Among the best known were Photo Eclair in Saint-Paul, Photo Lux in Saint-Louis, Photo Cristal in Saint-Pierre, Photo Max and Photo Maurice in Saint-André. A number of other studios were owned by members of the island's Chinese community, such as Fend Hong in the port district and Chane Chi-Kune's Maximin studio in Saint-Louis. The latter, in partnership with Jean Colbe, was the first to offer colour developing services, a practice which became widespread in the 1980s with the introduction of «mini-labs». Colbe arrived in Reunion in 1949 and worked as a journalist and press photographer specializing in sport and politics. After obtaining a Kodak franchise, he began a freelance career in 1957. He published a series of scenic postcards and worked as a commercial photographer in advertising and heavy construction.

In the 1970s, a new generation of press photographers emerged - among them, Daniel Ubertini, Bruno Testa, René Laï-yu, Mamode Loussadjee and Jean-Claude Feing. Creative photography, practised by talented amateurs such as teachers and architects, also flourished and was shown in various exhibitions.

The 1980s and 1990s were marked by a veritable explosion of cultural and artistic activity. Collections were compiled by a number of institutions and agencies, such as the Fonds Régional d'Art Contemporain, the Departmental Archives, the Natural History Museum, the Stella Matutina Museum, the Historical Museum of Villèle, the Leon Dierx Museum and the departmental art collection. Local institutions and cities such as Saint-Benoit actively acquired, commissioned, archived and distributed works of art and, increasingly, the work of photographers such as Antoine du Vignaux and Thierry Fontaine.

From 1989 to 1994, Jean Bernard, Karl Kügel and Bernard Lesaing were commissioned by the Island's Urban Planning Board to photograph physical and cultural transformation in three localities: La RiviËre des Galets, Piton-Saint-Leu and Trois-Bassins. The results, archived in 32 albums and 92 compact disks, are today preserved in the Stella Matutina Museum.[2] The project also included a training programme for apprentice photographers, whose numbers included Philippe Gaubert, René Paul Savignan, Jacques Bigot, Jean-Marc Grenier, Thierry, Isriss Issop-Banian, Gilles Tricat and Nathalie Véchot - all of whom have since launched careers in photography or image-related activities.

The Professional Education Centre of Reunion offers specialized courses leading to a diploma in photography. Up to the present, attempts to organize a photographers' union have been unsuccessful. Associations such as the ASPIR have begun documenting the contents of private photographic archives. With the development of mass tourism, illustrated postcards and promotional images of the island - often the work of Nour AhKoun or Gélabert - have multiplied. At the same time, new technologies are rapidly appearing in educational contexts such as the School of Fine Arts, in much the same manner as in Europe.

Wilhiam Zitte, in collaboration with
Gilbert Albany and Bernard Leveneur

354

RENÉ-PAUL SAVIGNAN

Reunion
b. Le Port, Reunion 1970
– lives in Reunion.

« I like sharing life's little moments with people», René-Paul Savignan says tentatively. «Not as a peeping Tom out to get photos, but when there's a personal story in the making. » After spending the years 1992-94 as a trainee with the BKL (Bernard, Kugel, Lesaing) Association, responsible for training a large number of Reunion's young generation of photographers, Savignan took as one of his first subjects the growing of rice in the Ambatondrazaka region of Madagascar; he used the results of this exercise for an exhibition titled *Brisure (Broken Rice)*. He is currently working with South African photographer Andrew Tshabangu on religions in South Africa.

Photographer
RENÉ-PAUL SAVIGNAN © 1994-95
Rice fields, Ambatondrazaka,
Madagascar.

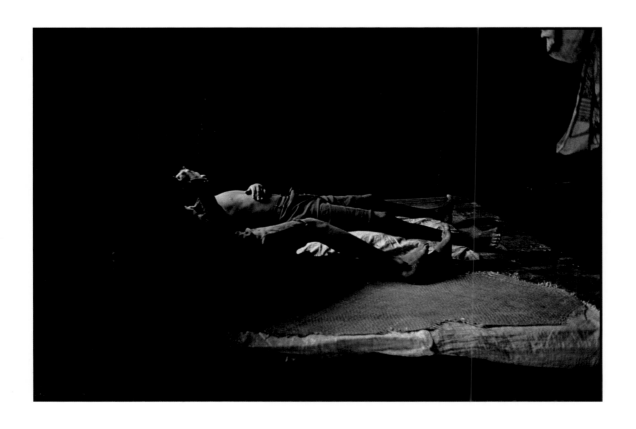

Photographer
PHILIPPE GAUBERT © 1995
Madagascar Prisons: Toamasina.

PHILIPPE GAUBERT

France – Reunion
b. Marseille, France 1967 – lives in Madagascar

Philippe Gaubert was born in Marseille in 1967 and in 1990 moved to Reunion, where he studied for three years in the BKL (Bernard, Kugel, Lesaing) Association's image workshop. He now works with various official bodies and cultural associations in Reunion, dividing his time between the island and Madagascar, where he collaborates on numerous assignments with Pierrot Men.
« I don't use an ethnological approach,» he says, « and I don't analyse. I just share life's stories via my own language: photography .»

Raymond Barthes

Reunion
b. Antananarivo, Madagascar 1957
– lives in Reunion

Born in Antananarivo, Madagascar, in 1957, Raymond Barthes now lives in Sainte-Marie de la Réunion. While studying at the Toulouse School of Art he decided to devote himself to photography. On his return to Reunion in 1980, he was appointed official photographer at the Reunion Departmental Archives. His personal work, both documentary and artistic, is marked by a somewhat naïve vision of the beauty, the shifting impressions and the mystery of the world around him. In the work presented here he uses everyday Polaroid views of Reunion to transform exoticism into fantasy.

Photographer
RAYMOND BARTHES © 1995
The yellow cruise. ∧

Diaspora

La diaspora

Shreds of identity

Simon Njami

Those who find themselves forcibly displaced and uprooted suffer traumas that are located at the very heart of their personal quest. Self-definition and memory - whether the memories are dreamed or real - become the basic components of a simultaneously inner- and outer-directed schizophrenia. At this point art - photography - becomes the terrain for an uprooted individual's questioning, the medium for self-investigation focused as much on the exploration of one's body and skin as on the development of a pictorial alphabet of memory. Afflicted with this feeling of original loss and working within an egocentric aesthetic which, whatever the subject, is basically self-referential, the photographers of the African diaspora seek with their pictures to regroup the scattered elements of their own history. A history which, for good reason, will never be the one they have lived. A virtual world that will never have a reality other than the one they make up for themselves day by day.

The moment the problem of the diaspora is looked at in terms of Africa's distant descendants (and we shall initially concern ourselves with those whose exile goes back centuries), the race question arises. And while there can be no ignoring its present complexity in racially mixed countries - unless, as in the darkest days of Europe's inhumanity, systems of genealogical definition are resorted to - we may become confused as to the very nature of our intended subject. Even if, today, skin colour plays an undeniable role in the Americas, we still have the task of establishing the conditions under which new identities and loyalties can be formulated. In all its multiplicity and complexity the diaspora maintains an ambiguous relationship with Africa. Colonial Africa followed different paths under the aegis of its various colonizers; and we find these same colonizers in the United States, the Caribbean and South America.

Photographer
PATRICE FÉLIX TCHICAYA © 1997

The difference, however, is that while Europeans in Africa have always felt themselves on foreign territory - with South Africa, a special case, as a possible exception - they immediately felt at home in the New World and demanded of the other exiled peoples, mostly black, that they justify their presence in countries where they started out on the same footing as the rest of the population. We shall examine here only the ordeal of slavery, which was to contribute psychologically to the way in which black groups would come to define themselves. As official religions, Spanish, Portuguese and French Catholicism, and Anglo-Saxon Protestantism, provide the first examples of reappropriation and personal restructuring on the part of black populations: the religious syncretism to be found among the various African exile groups in the New World - for even largely Protestant black Americans have turned their ceremonies into something far removed from Anglo-Saxon Puritanism - is certainly the most notable form of opposition to their masters.

Uprooted Africans had to come up with the same kind of syncretism, the same ability to reconcile contradictions, to get by in everyday life, to anchor themselves in an elsewhere which, over the decades and centuries, came to be truly theirs. The voyage of Christopher Columbus is now more than 500 years in the past, and the Mother Africa to which different groups could lay claim during the Congo Square revels in New Orleans or capoeira sessions in Brazil - and which helped them stand up to the implacable logic of slavery - was quickly reduced to the status of myth, when not actually rejected out of hand by successive generations whose integration became more and more a fact of life.

Whether we like it or not, what the various groups of the diaspora had in common was slavery. Dehumanized, reduced to mere beasts of burden and denied any shred of individuality, they had but this single factor on which to build their varying identities, this umbilical cord with which to reconstruct an individuality that would allow them to survive. Their relationship to Africa was both romantic and charged with conflict. Their relationship to the race question, itself linked to their continent of origin, only rounded out the overall picture. So the initial phase of reappropriation centred on a struggle for equality.

PATRICE FÉLIX TCHICAYA

Congo – France
b. Paris, France 1961
– lives in Paris

Patrice Félix Tchicaya is of mixed Corsican and Congolese birth, his father being the great writer Tchicaya U Tam'si. He works as a photographer, but also writes, directs and makes videos. Fashion photography allows him to bring an incisive eye to bear on a reality he treats as a form of scenario. After spending several years in London, he now lives in Paris.

DAVID DAMOISON

Martinique
b. Malakoff, France 1963
– lives in Valderies, France

David Damoison's mother is French, his father from Martinique. His photographic work is largely focused on black life, mainly in the Caribbean. He also works as a book and magazine illustrator.

Photographer
DAVID DAMOISON © 1992-93
Caribbean.

Diaspora

In Haiti, for example, which became a republic by defeating Napoleon's troops, and in the United States, where the Civil War was at once followed by struggles for civil rights, it seemed that the universal precondition was the restoration of the black person's original dignity. Thus the runaways to be found all along the Caribbean's coastlines - those slaves who had broken the taboos and reclaimed their stolen liberty - are now romantic figures. Yet even at the turn of the century the hypothetical return to Africa was no longer on the agenda. Apart from the excesses of Marcus Garvey and his boat for Africa at the beginning of the 20th century, the struggle of diaspora blacks had become a political one in their new countries. With slavery abolished, they saw the goal as recognition of their rights here and now - and in the countries they were living in. It was in this context that photography came to play a part.

As in Africa, the representation of blacks after Daguerre's invention came into use was designed to meet anthropological and ethnological, not to say propagandist, requirements. Europeans set out to provide images of blacks that matched those already generally accepted. Photography was thus to become the scene par excellence of a representational battle whose echoes still resound today, notably in the current heated debate in British photographic circles. Yet what reality could truly seize the identity of the diaspora, apart perhaps from a kaleidoscopic approach within which images cluster together without intermingling? Artists such as Kobena Mercer, Stuart Hall and Georges Lipzick have gone into what seems to be the fundamental problem of the African diaspora as a whole: that of trying to redefine oneself, to invent a hybrid identity which, painlessly and without conflicts other than those resulting from the pangs of creativity, combines the relationship with the present and the relationship with the past - and one's historical origins with the bodily, sensory memory that makes us all the fruit of a long and complex process.

Despite today's marked revival of interest in Africa, or at least in a powerful affirmation of black and African culture - with all the limitations this implies - Africa was no longer the original source when diaspora photography appeared on the scene. The pioneers were more concerned with capturing the everyday reality of life around them, with restoring their peoples' lost beauty and dignity. These early pictures were meant to counter the anthropological clichés: they were photos of neighbourhoods, a form of local reporting, and images of communities, bearing the implicit - and undeniably successful - message that « black is beautiful ».

RENÉ
PEÑA
GONZALES

Cuba
b. Cuba 1957 –
lives in Havana, Cuba

René Peña Gonzales, the « weirdo »
of Cuban photography, takes his
inspiration from the surrealistic reality of his native island. He has produced such series of photos as
Chronicles of the City (1991), *The
Cook, the Thief, his Wife and her
Lover* (1995), *The Blue Dakota
Rituals and Self-portrait* (1996).

Photographer
RENÉ PEÑA GONZALES © 1995
*The Cook, the Thief, his Wife
and her Lover.*

Diaspora

Then came a long period of waiting: for the process of reappropriation to take effect, for a painful psychoanalysis to bear fruit, for the emergence of another style of photography, one that was more individualistic or at least existentialist and egocentred. Fully existing means attaining a relative harmony between the different elements of our make-up. The more complex the sum of our personal components, the more obsessional our quest. The goal of this quest is to arrive at a result which, while being the slowly-matured product of a past laid bare, will not be something new. The use made of the voodoo cult by the young Chinese-Jamaican photographer Albert Chong is a good illustration of this. What each person has to do now is establish a synthesis of the place he or she lives in, their friendships and love affairs, and their attitude to a society in which circumstances have compelled their involvement. One of the miracles of displacement and inner fragmentation is that they inevitably lead to original solutions and arrangements which, in this area more than elsewhere, are vital to survival.

From this point on, belonging to and appropriating a specific space becomes the sole guarantee of our rights as citizens. For citizenship, with its concomitant notion of participation, is the only concept to which we can actively apply our free will. The trap involved in any process of social integration is the inevitable dismemberment of the ego. A feeling of having betrayed, having forgotten or - even more so - of having got lost, is what might emerge from the sum of the experiences of the new generation of the diaspora. It is interesting to note here that it is in contemporary photography - most of whose practitioners have opted for approaches related to the plastic arts or, as in the case of David Damoison, for the creation of a kind of family album that transcends borders while remaining clearly limited to the Caribbean (with a brief incursion into Africa) - that this tension is most fully expressed. For photography is image and deliberate revelation, even if the image, in terms of what it reveals, is never simply a surface reading of the elements that show up on the film.

In the UK, the photograph is endlessly revelatory. The subject matter, the focus, the degree of contrast opted for, systematically lead us back to the photographer, to that subjective vision behind the framing, the pose - to the underlying message, in other words. When Ajamu the photographer takes himself as subject, disguised as a blonde, he is transmitting a message about the representation of himself. He is illustrating the expression of the eternally unfinished quest for identity. His sexuality, his blackness and his view of British society are all ways of situating himself on the social checkerboard and sending out his message. Until quite recently photography in Africa was a way of bearing witness, of reflecting people's reality in terms of their everyday lives or their fantasies; but for the Africans of the diaspora it had very quickly become a means for exploring identity, via self-portraits or the reconstruction of a family that was at once imaginary and very close, as in the work of David Zapparoli.

AJAMU

Jamaica – UK
b. Huddersfield, UK 1963
– lives in London

Ajamu belongs to that committed 1980s generation of black English photographers whose work is founded on the search for self-redefinition. He is the creator of the character Miss Tissue, his «queer» blonde double who seems to embody the aesthetic basis of his creative work while revealing another side of himself. « Since the beginning of the 1990s I've been experimenting and taking risks so as to cross and push back all those borders built into the contemporary theoretical debate on race, sexuality and representation. »

Photographer AJAMU © 1997
Miss precious Rhourbourgeua.

These photographs are the product of a thought-process both productive and obsessional, narcissistic and socially-oriented, one that creates a kind of autobiography in pictures. The duty, or destiny, of the Africans of the diaspora is to find the connection between all those drives that make them what they are - and this via a schizophrenic search for the reconciliation of opposites, for totalling up at some single point their present consciousness and their past, history, tradition and exile. Let there be no mistake about my use of the word exile here: I am not referring to that romantic, vaguely ethnographic vision founded on nostalgically perceived sorrows and languishings. The human beings of the diaspora are always - and increasingly so for the new African generations - born on the soil on which they live. In referring to exile we appeal to notions going beyond what is immediately perceptible, beyond some truncated reality.

The bodily and gestural memory mentioned earlier is the sole legitimate driving force of this exile - this exile from oneself, so to speak, with its ceaseless call for return. The self so ardently pursued here is often no more than a jumbled collection of images, clichés, memories or historical fragments; a hallucinatory conception of the world, oneself and one's environment. The creator's strength lies in making richness out of this chaos, in bringing order to this global sensory disorder. Here we can assert, with Derrida, that in our postmodern world any true, solid work of construction necessarily requires a violent process of deconstruction, destruction and challenging accepted truths. Truth is always someone else's truth and the creative artists of the diaspora will no longer settle for this. Where age-old Africa has had the misfortune to bog down in notions of belonging and legitimacy, the diaspora - necessarily suspect, wounded in its flesh and its past while challenged in its present - had no way out beyond its capacity to say no.

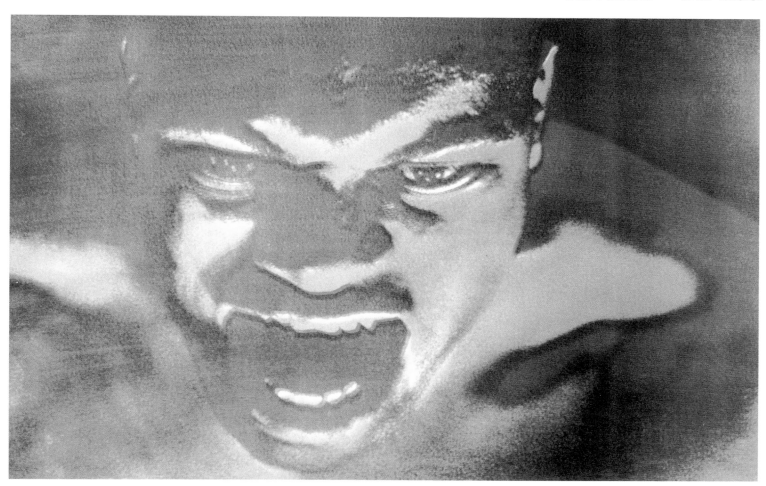

This is the capacity to which these photographers bear witness. Each in his or her own way is exploring the mysteries of identity and memory, either through scrupulous, meticulous observation of the self - a self which then becomes an outlet for other histories - or through memories of places, traditions and ancestral practices. On the one hand there is the body become object, a body denied, mocked, endlessly deformed as if better to reveal its true nature; and on the other hand, things and places that suddenly seem gifted with speech. In a word, humanized.

Simon Njami

Photographer
ROSE-ANN MARIE BAILEY ©
Accused.

ROSE-ANN MARIE BAILEY

Jamaica – Canada
b. Claredon, Jamaica 1971
– ives in Toronto, Canada

In her photographs Rose-Ann Marie Bailey sets out to provide understanding and a more profound vision of the beauty and culture of her people by exploring the sweetness, bitterness and acidity of black-berries. Her obsession with light has led her to concentrate on the texture and lustre of her subjects' skins. Rose-Ann Marie Bailey also works in video and made a short film in 1998.

373

L'endroit des Salines.
Au débarcadère du Soleil aveuglant
les esclaves des voyages précédents
toilaient la nouvelle cargaison
d'ÊTRES brûlés par le Sel
les embruns & les silences dé vent.

MANGO#1 [les bateaux de
l'horrible voyage]

Dans le liquide de son ventre
elle l'avait emmené jusqu'aux
rivages maîtres de l'Antille.

Canada : New Pathways

African-Canadian photographers have started taking risks in the technical field. They are using a broad range of supports and unusual printing methods to produce their images, thus giving expression to ideas going well beyond what is generally expected of black culture. Working on a basic image, David Zapparoli and Stella Fakiyesi try out various supports, colour pencils, additional images and found objects, then photograph the result. Rose-Ann Marie Bailey goes back to the origins of photographic printing, using the gum bichromate technique. Each stage of their work sees the original become more abstract. Thus photography, initially used to record facts, has become a tool for creating an area of consciousness, for evoking individual memories and for encouraging greater cultural understanding between communities. It is also a means for deconstructing stereotypes.

This generation of photographers has to confront both black and white viewers and their perception of negritude or the status of the black artist. Attention should be paid to their work, in the interests of creating a cultural context conducive to increasing public understanding of their approach, making their voices heard and communicating their relationship with the contemporary world. The principal challenge they face is that of exploring and mapping new pathways that lead beyond their present frontiers, so that their contribution can assume its full meaning and scope.

Orla La-Wayne Garrigues

SERGE EMMANUEL JONGUÉ

Guyana – Canada
b. Aix-en-Provence., France 1951
– lives in Montreal, Canada

Son of a Guyanese father and a Polish mother, Serge Emmanuel Jongué is a photojournalist and writer. Objets de mémoire (Memory things) is a group of ten photos of which only a part is shown here. « Thus things give us back, as a mirror image, feelings at their most intense - an animistic zone, a mental landscape in which contemporary and mythical memories intermingle .»

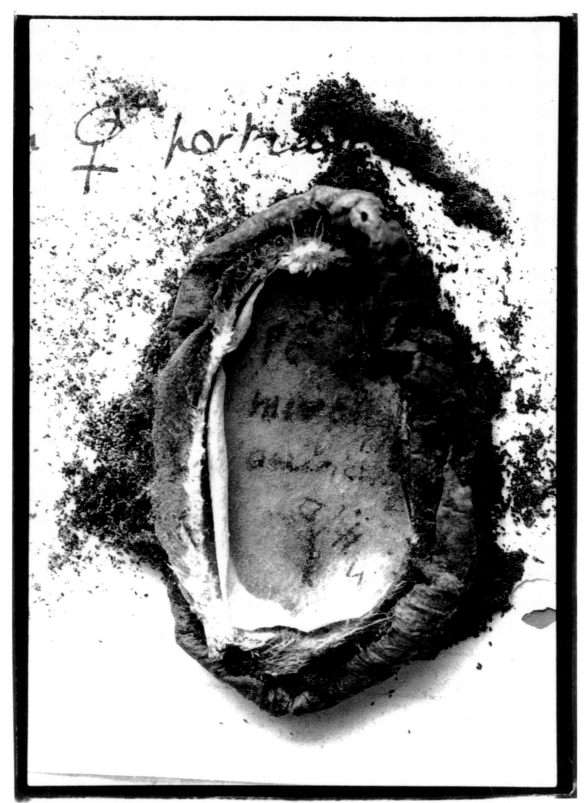

Par l'infamie d'Arkansas & de
Mississipi conjurés, elle était
devenue enfermée des horizons.
VIEILLE, La MÈRE flétrie, la
femme américaine [l'ancienne
africaine]

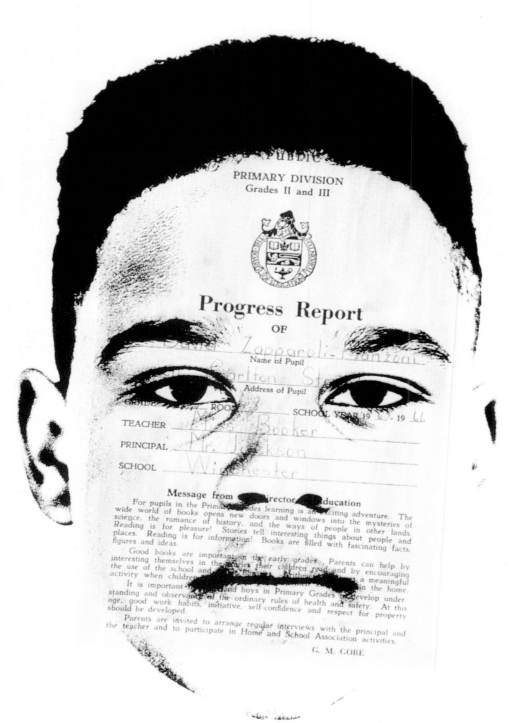

DAVID ZAPPAROLI

Canada
b. Toronto, Canada 1957
– lives in Toronto

Influenced by the documentary approach, Zapparoli's primary intention is to lay bare hitherto unexplored or inadequately treated features of society. Since 1992 he has been focusing on the effects of the environmental and ancestral elements of the self. His photographs combine portraits of his family and objects drawn from his childhood, to which he adds the faces of children with whom he can identify in terms of race or social class.

Photographer
DAVID ZAPPAROLI © 1992
Report card.

STELLA FAKIYESI

Nigeria — Canada
b. Lagos, Nigeria 1971
— lives in Toronto, Canada

Stella Fakiyesi's work sets out to dismantle the stereotypes of which she sees black women as victims. She works mostly in black-and-white, adding collage and interpolations of colour. Of herself she says, « As a young black woman artist, I see the coming millennium as a chance to redefine myself and take a fresh look at the way I am perceived by the world. »

Photographer STELLA FAKIYESI ©

Framing black photography in America

Deborah Willis

The first photograph taken by a black American dates from 1840 and marks the beginning of a long tradition whose main areas of focus have never really changed. The initial results were portraits and reportage by itinerant photographers whose aim was to provide an alternative view of a black people just released from slavery. In parallel with these «classic» pictures there grew up a militant photography that would later be associated with the civil rights movement. From 1930 onwards photojournalism was predominant, but in the 1970s the acceptance of photography into university courses gave rise to a new generation of photographers whose work combined aesthetic considerations, social and political commentary and introspection.

African Americans shaped the practice of photography from its origin in 1839, and have participated in its history as daguerreotypists, documenters, journalists, artists, studio photographers and subjects. The larger American public was fascinated with the daguerreotype as soon as Louis Jacques Mande Daguerre (1787-1851) publicized the process in France in 1839. The French inventor, Nicephore Niepce (1765-1833), had produced the earliest extant photographic image made by a camera obscura in 1827. After the death of Niepce, Daguerre successfully fixed an image and announced to the Paris press his discovery, which he named - after himself - as the daguerreotype in January of 1839.

Newspapers in the spring of 1839 published accounts of Americans experimenting with the daguerreotype process. It was on 19 August 1839 that Daguerre publicly announced the process and published a manual of instructions. By late August newspapers in Paris and London were describing Daguerre's process in detail. *The Great Western*, one of the fastest known transatlantic steamers of the period, is noted for carrying aboard the French and English newspapers with descriptions of the daguerreotype process, which arrived in New York on 10 September 1839.

Deborah Willis, a graduate of New York's Pratt Institute, is the leading authority on black American photography. Curator of photography at the Schomburg Center in New York from 1980 to 1992, she then joined the Smithsonian Institution's National African Museum Project in Washington as collections coordinator. Herself a photographer, she has directed many exhibitions, taught in various American universities and published many books, including *Lorna Simpson* (1992); *Black Photographers: 1840-1940*, Garland, 1989; *The Portraits of James VanDerZee* (1993); *Picturing Us, African American Identity*, New York Press, New York, 1994; and *The Family of Black America*, Crown Trade Paperbacks, New York, 1996. She lives and works in Washington DC.

< Photographer FOSTER STUDIO ©
Kids in Philadelphia, ca. 1900.

379

Diaspora

Six months after the public announcements of the process in Paris, Jules Lion, a free man of colour, lithographer and portrait painter, exhibited the first successful daguerreotype views in New Orleans. His exhibition - the first publicized exhibition of a work by a black photographer - was held on 15 March 1840 in the Hall of the St Charles Museum in the city of New Orleans. The exhibition was reported to have drawn a large crowd and was organized and sponsored by the artist. Even though many of those African Americans were still enslaved, there were numerous free black men and women who had established themselves as daguerreotypists, photographers, inventors, artists and artisans, and who had gained local and national recognition in their respective cities. Portraits of prominent and lesser-known African Americans were produced regularly in galleries and studios throughout the country as portraiture became more and more popular as a method of creating a likeness. Most of the photographs taken at this time were not intended for publication or public presentation, but prominent citizens and other families from all walks of life thought it important to have their likenesses preserved for posterity.

During most of photography's early history, images produced by African American photographers were idealized glimpses of family members in romanticized or dramatic settings. Many African American photographers sought to integrate elements of romanticism and classicism, as the painters of previous centuries had done. Most photographs taken in the early years were made to commemorate a special occasion in the sitter's life, such as courtship, marriage, birth, death, graduation, confirmation, military service, anniversaries, or achieving some social or political success.

A number of these early photographers recorded celebratory as well as dispiriting moments within their communities. Many owned and operated studios in small towns and major cities, while others worked as itinerants. They photographed the prosperous, the labourers, and the poor, and they documented the activities of l9th-century abolitionists and 20th-century civil rights activists.

Stereotypical photography was prevalent during this period. To reinforce stereotypical notions about African Americans a large number of studios owned by white proprietors created staged photographs in which black children were presented as lazy; these images often also placed children in scenes with alligators. Images of men and women of African descent were sold to perpetuate myths.

In photography's first decade, the 1840s, James Presley Ball (1825-1905) and Augustus Washington (1820-?), operated successful galleries in Cincinnati, Ohio and Hartford, Connecticut. Ball and Washington were active abolitionists who often used their photographic skills to expose the inhumane institution of slavery and promote the activities of the abolitionist movement. Between 1869 and 1899, numerous photographers and itinerants flourished in the North. Studios opened for business which produced paper prints as well as tintypes, these being the newer and faster processes of the period.

At the turn of the century photography expanded in a variety of ways. Newspapers, journals and books published photographic images. Courses in photography were offered in schools and colleges, and correspondence courses were available. A noted educator in photography was CM Battey (1873-1927), an accomplished portraitist and fine art photographer. Battey founded the Photography Division at Tuskegee Institute, Alabama, in 1916.

In 1917, Crisis magazine highlighted Battey in the Men of the Month column as one of the few coloured photographers who had gained real artistic success. The most extensive series of portraits of African American leaders from the l9th and early part of the 20th century was produced by CN Battey. His photographic portraits of John Mercer Langston, Frederick Douglas, WEB DuBois, Booker T Washington and Paul Laurence Dunbar were sold nationally and produced in two formats: postcard and poster.

Between l900 and 1919, African American photographers flourished in the larger cities. They produced photographs of rural and urban experiences, as well as images of architecture and leisure.

Addison Scurlock (1883-1964) of Washington, DC, Howard University's official photographer, opened his studio in l911, which he operated with his wife and sons until 1964. His sons, Robert and George, also worked in the studio. In New York City, James Van Der Zee (1886-1983), undoubtedly the best known of black studio photographers, captured the spirit and life of New York's Harlem for over 50 years.

During the period of the Harlem Renaissance, through the Great Depression and Franklin D Roosevelt's WPA (Works Progress Administration) years, photographers began to exhibit their work widely in their respective communities. In the 1920s, young black photographers who viewed themselves as artists, moved to the larger cities seeking education, patronage and support for their art. Harlem was a cultural mecca for many of these photographers.

James Latimer Allen (1907-1977) produced genre portraits of African American men, women and children. He published and exhibited his works in art journals and galleries. He also photographed such writers of the period such as Alain Locke, Langston Hughes, Countee Cullen and Claude McKay. Photographers active between 1920 and 1940 included students of CM Battey such as PH Polk (1898-1985) of Tuskegee, Alabama. PH Polk opened his first studio at Tuskegee in 1927. The following year he was appointed to the faculty of Tuskegee Institute's Photography Department, photographed prominent visitors such as educator, Mary McLeod Bethune, and activist-artist, Paul Robeson, and made extensive portraits of scientist-inventor George Washington Carver.

Richard S Roberts (1881-1936) of Columbia, South Carolina, opened his studio in the early 1920s. He had began by studying photography through correspondence courses and specialized journals. When he opened his studio he advertised that his studio took superior photographs by day or night. Twin brothers Morgan (1910-1993) and Marvin Smith (1910) were prolific photographers in Harlem in the 1930s and early 1940s. They photographed members of the community, its famous and infamous, and their cameras also captured political rallies, breadlines during the Depression, families and Lindy Hoppers in the *Savoy Ballroom*. Robert H. McNeill (b. 1917) created a comprehensive documentary record of African American life in Washington during the 1930s and 1040s. Frequently working with the black press such as the *Pittsburgh Courier*, *Washington Afro-American*, and *Chicago Defender*, McNeill's photographs documented that African Americans living in a segregated city survived - even thrived - by creating their own social and community organizations.

The Farm Security Administration (FSA) began in 1935 as the Resettlement Administration, an independent coordinating agency that inherited rural relief activities and land-use administration from the Department of the Interior, the Federal Emergency Relief Administration and the Agricultural Adjustment Administration. The FSA photography project generated 270 000 images of rural, urban and industrial America between 1935 and 1943. Many of the heavily documented activities of the FSA were of black migrant workers in the South. In 1937 Gordon Parks (b. 1912) decided that he wanted to be a photographer after viewing the work of the Farm Security Administration photographers. He was hired by the FSA in 1941 and during World War II worked as an Office of War Information correspondent. After the war, he was a photographer for Standard Oil Company. In 1949 he became the first African American photographer to work on the staff of Life magazine.

Roy DeCarava (1919) is the link to contemporary street photography. He studied art at Cooper Union in New York City, the WPA Harlem Art Centre, and the George Washington Carver Art School. In 1955, DeCarava collaborated with Langston Hughes in producing a book entitled *The Sweet Flypaper of Life*, which depicted the life of a black family in Harlem. In 1954 he founded a gallery which became one of the first in the United States devoted to the exhibition and sale of photography as fine art. Also noted for his jazz photography, DeCarava in 1963 founded the Kamoinge Workshop, a group of concerned black photographers. Members included Shawn Walker, Lou Draper, Anthony Barboza and Ming Smith.

From the 1930s to the 1960s, photographers began working as photojournalists for local newspapers and national magazines marketed for African American audiences such as *Our World*, *Ebony*, *Jet*, *Sepia* and *Flash*. Only a few African American photojournalists, notably Gordon Parks and Roy DeCarava, were employed for the larger picture magazines such as *Life* and *Sports Illustrated*. Most of them learned photography while in the military and studied photography in schools of journalism.

This period also encompassed the beginning of reportage and the documentation of public and political events. In the 1930s smaller handheld cameras and faster films aided photographers in expressing their frustration and discontent with social and political conditions within their communities.

The civil rights movement's activities were well documented by photographers such as Moneta Sleet Jr (New York/Chicago) and Jack T Franklin (Philadelphia). During the the early 1960s to the 1970s, the active years of the civil rights and black power movements, a significant number of socially committed men and women became photographers. They set a different standard in documenting the struggles, achievements and tragedies of the freedom movement. SNCC (Student Non-Violent Coordinating Committee) photographers Doug Harris, Elaine Tomlin and Bob Fletcher were in the forefront of documenting the voter registration drives in the South; Robert Sengetacke, Howard Bingham, Jeffrey Scales and Brent Jones photographed, in the North and on the West Coast, the activities of the Black Panther Party and desegregation rallies. Between 1969 and 1986, six African American photographers received the coveted Pulitzer Prize for photography. The first to win the award was Moneta Sleet Jr (1969) for photographs of Mrs Coretta Scott King and her daughter, and of the funeral of Dr Martin Luther King Jr.

In the 1970s universities and art colleges began to offer undergraduate and graduate degrees in photography. African American photographers began studying photography and creating works for exhibition purposes. Outside the academy, others studied in community centres and workshops. These photographers began to explore and redefine the photographic image. They respected the photograph as a document, while simultaneously looking at it as a metaphor. The symbolic and expressive imagery of the works produced in the 1980s and 1990s is concerned with offering sociological and psychological insights into the past. Many of the themes explored by these photographers focused on their own families and communities and were informed by personal experience. They created symbolic works that were referential to social issues such as racism, unemployment, child and sexual abuse, death and dying. The viewer becomes a participant by being asked to contexualize his or her own experiences with the visual references offered by the photographer and in so doing creates his or her own historical perspective, interpretation, or meaning.

Photographer ∧
GORDON PARKS © ca. 1942
Mrs Ella Watson, judge, with her three children and her adoptive sister. Washington DC.

Photographer >
ROBERT MC NEILL © ca. 1942
Washington DC.

Clarissa Sligh, Lorna Simpson, Jeffrey Scales, Coreen Simpson, Albert Chong, Fern Logan, Carrie Mae Weems, Pat Ward Williams, Willie Middlebrook, Roland Charles, Chester Higgins, Stephen Marc, Carla Williams, Christian Walker and Lynn Marshall-Linnemeier are just a small number of the photographers who began creating works in this genre in the 1980s.

All are engaging storytellers who have discovered the intersection of the private and public in art. A number of contemporary photographers challenge contemporary art practices and as photographer-writer Rick Bolton states, these photographers have created « a new social basis for ar »[1]. They are photobiographers who use appropriation, multiple printing, fabric, straight images, and manipulated photographs to make compelling visual statements about modern-day culture, as well as create narratives about the collective history in multi-ethnic America. The contemporary photobiographers employ themes relating to identity, spirituality, gender, family, race difference and stereotyping. Some of the artists are concerned with the implications of historical and contemporary references to women and have offered new strategies in incorporating their personal perspectives in the construction of their work. Many of the photographers mentioned in this essay create provocative and sensitive visual references to their African American cultural experience. Some use text to create tension and set up a paradigm relating to the transformative nature of the medium.

Albert Chong uses family photographs, religious icons and animal remains to explore ritual as it is translated into art. He likens the task to that of archeologists in unearthing the past to explore family history. Chong is strongly conscious of composition and form. The exact placement of cultural objects has a significance which reveals his roots: born in Jamaica of African and Chinese ancestry, Chong imbues his works with references to all three cultures. The photographs of Albert Chong are highly individualized, spiritually oriented images. Coreen Simpson makes portraits that speak to us about the experience of young black men and women living in New York City. Many are oversized images that are highly stylized as the photographer and her subject create a visually expressive dialogue. Jeffrey Scales records commonplace scenes and occurrences within his community of Harlem, while simultaneously speaking out about cultural and social problems. His portraits of young and older men seek to explore the relationships that exist between men. He is concerned about the stereotyping of black men and how they are perceived in the culture by their peers and others.

Photographer GORDON PARKS © ∧
Saturday afternoon, 7th Street and Florida Ave. Washington DC, 1942.

Photographer ROBERT MC NEILL © >
The Savoy Ballroom, NYC.

1. Bolton, Richard, ed. 1990. *The Contest of Meaning: Critical Histories of Photography*, p. xii. Cambridge, Massachusetts: The MIT Press.

Diaspora

Fern Logan re-examines her family relationships in her art. Using the cyanotype, also known as the blueprint process (a printing process based on the light-sensitivity of iron salts), Logan investigates memories from her past, speaking with a warm voice and using old letters and imagined responses. Looking back at old photographs of her son, she raises provocative issues about his and her American childhoods and the irony of their fate. Her insight is written on the print as the photograph is submerged. The issues raised are difficult and are presented in order to evoke a 20th-century consciousness of miscegenation. Coming to consciousness in the context of the issues presented within her own family, Logan stimulates an open discussion about race, racism, denial and domination.

Lorna Simpson focuses on the construction of meaning and values by juxtaposing text and image. Her style creates a format for her critical examination of race and gender. She focuses specifically on the notion of invisibility, representing black women as survivors, protagonists and victims. Simpson's work is rooted in the tradition of African American storytelling and her work incorporates visual narratives that border on biography. Coiffure, 1991, is a self-conscious piece. It consists of three black-and-white large-scale photographs hung as a triptych. The images include the back of a woman's closely-cropped hair, a segment of a long braid wrapped in a spiral and the back of an African mask. They are combined with ten engraved plaques which bear short phrases referring to hair. Using black hair, Simpson explores the evocative potential representations of black people by placing the images and text in a manner that invites them to refer to each other.

Family experiences form the core of inspiration for Clarissa Sligh's work. Her work is layered with political, familial and racially charged messages. Using family photographs and archival references, she directs her audience's gaze towards sociological relationships centred on experiences in African American communities in the l9th and 20th centuries. Sligh is the keeper of her family album of photographs and other memorabilia. She places her family history within the larger context of American history. In shifting attention away from her personal experiences, she is able to analyse other shared experiences of black children across the generations. She is cognizant of the role she plays in preserving her family history. Sligh's work is important not only because she addresses the realities of racism and sexism in a direct, yet not confrontational, style, but she is also an accomplished storyteller. The search for representation continues throughout Sligh's work in pieces such as Reading Dick and Jane with Me. « My work is a journey toward self-change which itself is self-healing. »

The act of creating my visual statements requires that I work from a place I push against. I begin by trying to be clear with myself. I struggle to develop a correct relationship to myself, a continuous cycle requiring passage through darkness my 'shadow areas', as well as through light. » Sligh looks carefully at her own relationships with her family as she re-examines the lives of men, women and children in general. Historical and social perspectives are closely related to the images of photo-artist Clarissa Sligh. Her work is provocative and historically introspective.

In What's Happening With Momma Sligh creates an artist's book with her photographic diaries by restating personal childhood and adult experiences. In this book, she tells a story as she sits on the steps with her older brother. The story becomes a mystery story that unfolds while their mother is in labour. Laura Marks observes that « Sligh's working process is more like therapy than like the process of creating an artefact. Sligh uses photography as a means of self-examination and self-healing. But her art does more than that: it also examines and heals the cultural body ».[2]

Christian Walker incorporates family snapshots within his own contemporary images. He reprints them with superimposed images of reproductions of Madonna and Child and paints over the surface with raw pigments. « In his series, Bargaining with the Dead, Christian Walker uses the format of the family photograph album to « document » a history of the extended or archetypal African American family. He amplifies this format with paint and pigment as well as vintage rephotographed images: his manipulations emphasize the artistic rather than the technical aspects of the medium. At the centre of Walker's fictive dramas are his own kin, whose lives also fit the paradigm of fortitude in the face of physical change, and embody the fragile nature of life. » Through his compositions and formal manipulations, Walker examines social structures in the family. Walker, citing Bargaining With the Dead, writes: « It concerns the charged emotions surrounding the deaths of my parents in 1985. It is a photograph album of sorts, of the extended black family ... The central images follow my mother from age 19 to 55, yet they are larger, in the sense that they comment on the journey of a black woman through life. Each photograph of her not only shows her physical changes and the depth of her struggle, these images also reveal her strength and fortitude. »

This is a series of biographical family photos, inspired by grief at the death of both of his parents.

Photographer GORDON PARKS © >

2. Marks, Laura U. 1991. Healing the Cultural Body in Photography Center Quarterly No. 50.

Diaspora

Walker's family portraits and art historical images (Gothic Madonnas, etc.) evoke the artist's own family ties and comment on the exclusion of African-American and African imagery - and therefore « culture » - from history. They also expose the overlay of social meanings on a personal and emotional history. This links Walker's meditations on race and society to his own biographical experience.

Carla Williams' photographs captivate as they explore the photographer's imagination and her fascination with the human body. Williams' subject is her own body, which she has documented continuously for over ten years. Her self-portraits are conscious references to the photographic tableaux of the 19th century. She allows the viewer to explore the notion of being an object of desire by photographing her body at difference stages in her life. She projects the fragmented and whole body and this representation can be viewed as linking her past and her future. Her body is linked to her culture and she is interested in the experience of the female body as both subject and object of desire.

Carrie Mae Weems' current work, in which she creates sequential photographs and insightful text that examines the experiences of women in general and black women specifically, bring to life the overlapping of fantasy and lived experiences. In her work, all gesture is metaphor.

The black American photographers of the 19th and 20th centuries respond to their own lives and their communities in ways that have much in common. Some of them communicate an emotional message that goes beyond the self-representation to investigate the African American experience in photography in a new way. Many of the photographers working today respond to social issues beyond the sometimes insular photographic community. They comment on politics, culture, family and history from internal and external points of view. The fact that many of these photographers have probably witnessed social injustice has not clouded their vision. In interpreting these works, the viewer is open to multiple readings, including satire, humour, parody and testimony. The issues addressed in contemporary photography and the interpretations which flow from it blend to create exhilarating visionary biography of African American life.

Deborah Willis
Curator of Exhibitions
Center for African American History
and Culture
Smithsonian Institution
Washington, DC

Photographer CARLA WILLIAMS © 1998

The image and religious syncretism

Maria Lucia Montes

In painting and subsequently in photography, the representation of black people has always fallen victim to an ideology of otherness. Exoticism, ethnology and anthropology have all helped establish a stereotype corresponding - at best - to that of the « noble savage ». In Brazil it has taken a long time for the descendants of the slaves to create, via photography, images of - and for - themselves: images that are still deeply marked by the country's distinctive religious syncretism.

Down the centuries the representation of black people has been a vehicle for different points of view. From Greek art down to 19th-century Japanese screens, the image of black people has been the logical outcome of a vision that may see them as idol or fetish - but never as mirror image.

The « exotic » approach, with its capacity to incorporate the fascination and horror generated by such otherness, is the first step towards conferring the status of fetish: the other is dehumanized visually, transformed into an object identifiable by fixed characteristics but lacking the qualities that make each of us a unique being within the immense chorus of humanity's differences.

In the 19th century a new invention impinged on this system of representation: photography bolstered exotic imaginings with the illusion of realism that was then permeating the emerging scientific mentality. There was even a choice between the German tendency - romantic inspiration based on the pre-eminence of culture - and the Anglo-Saxon and French tradition of emphasizing the advance of civilization. The infant discipline of anthropology made ample use of this new art of the image, using photographic evidence as proof of truths then regarded as scientifically irrefutable.

Maria Lucia Montes teaches at the University of São Paulo and is an associate of Emanoel Araújo, director of the Pinocateca do Estado in São Paulo.

< UNKNOWN photographer © ca. 1870
Benjamin de Oliveira,
on the day of his marriage to Victoria.
Courtesy of Emanoel Araújo

Diaspora

It goes without saying that despite their scientific pretensions, these initial photographs of black people gave rise to thoroughly tendentious readings ultimately rooted in the 18th-century curio collection mentality. They were primarily designed for what we might call the vast Museum of Natural History of Humanity, whether the image in question was that of a slave in Brazil or of ethnic groups recently brought into the European colonial orbit on the African continent.

This serves to illustrate the extent to which, throughout history, the representation of black people has been an arbitrary process founded on the assigning of a single role: that of an object viewed so as to deprive it of its essential humanity.

It is vital that we distance ourselves from the Eurocentric way of seeing that has always marked this approach. The man who has perhaps made the greatest contribution to renewal here is the French ethnological photographer, Pierre Verger. His pictures from the United States, Brazil, Africa and Asia reveal an entire planet in which black people, no longer a mere figment of the European imagination, acquire the full force of their hitherto disregarded humanity. This way of seeing does not postulate an archetypal «black man»; it offers us, instead, flesh-and-blood black men and women, varying in their characteristics and forms of ethnic expression, as well as in the scars left by forced incorporation into a civilization incapable of perceiving them other than as primitives or slave-objects.

His photos also reveal something African cultures have managed to preserve or reinvent in the new world: a certain capacity to express freedom. Their gods and rites, their dances and finery lay bare a body language revelatory of a world view that colonialism and slavery have not succeeded in destroying. Through these pictures the African diaspora is seeking to recreate its own history.

However, the real revolution was to take place when blacks themselves got behind the lens, free for the first time to create the image they wanted and - as they can rightly proclaim to the whole world - to give of themselves and for themselves. To look at themselves!

Sometimes, as in the pictures of Januário Garcia, the black individual is a kind of punctuation mark amid all the colours of Rio de Janeiro, an icon of the ongoing cultural and ethnic mix that is the heritage of all Brazilians. Garcia's lens captures the precise moment of ecstatic, explosive joy in the midst of a Carnival parade. These pictures connect with the tradition of a Brazilian photojournalism in which black people have been ever-present - even if their presence has been mostly ignored.

Closer examination leads us back from Januário Garcia to an earlier group of photographers of African origin who started out in the black militant press in the early 1930s: here we can rediscover, for example, the work of Anísio C de Carvalho, in Bahia.

This movement also included Vantoen Pereira Júnior, Carla Osório and Roberto Esteves. Their pictures bear the mark of a past continuing on into the present, against a backdrop of favelas and shanties as crammed with black people as the outbuildings of the great houses during the slave era; against a backdrop of canefields where the work makes one wonder if slavery really has been abolished in Brazil. And there are, too, the photos of street children, which make it clear that abandonment and fear have a colour in Brazil: the black colour of the victims of a perverse discrimination that does not speak its name, concealed beneath the proverbial warmth of the Brazilian people. Yet even here - with these shocking truths looking us in the face - the frank gaze, the pride and dignity barely salvaged, the broad smile of a child given back the right to dream, reveal a confidence and understanding telling us that, between blacks, these black images can be created.

Other images in a different style convey another form of beauty, with no loss of this potent underlying preoccupation to affirm an identity one is proud of. Bauer Sá's delicate, strangely powerful portraits echo the anxious, mythic quest embarked on by Rotimi Fani-Kayodé on the other side of the Atlantic; and there is no coincidence here, for both are equally rooted in the urge to safeguard an identity.

Other photographers take yet another road in their search for a cultural heritage that obstinately refuses to die: the heritage that breaks through on the fringes of the samba carioca dance - those luminous moments captured by Walter Firmo, that indefatigable chronicler of Rio de Janeiro life - in the relaxed disorder of the hillside favelas and in the suburban houses where the heroes of popular Brazilian music live. Heroes called Pixinguinha, Cartola, Clementina de Jesus. Simple people like all Firmo's neighbours, with Firmo capturing them on the spot in all the ordinariness of the everyday or in their moments of elation: at a wedding or just there on their doorstep, when they're taking a break or preparing a saint's day candomblé.

We find these roots again in the feast-day celebrations photographed by Eustáquio Neves among the Arturos, an authentic contemporary community of runaway slaves in Minas Gerais State. There the cult of the ancestors blends into devout veneration of Catholic saints.

UNKNOWN photographer © ca. 1870 ∧
A group of old African porters in Bahia, Brazil.
Courtesy of Emanoel Araújo.

UNKNOWN photographer © 1932 >
The battalion sets off, 9 July 1932.
Courtesy of Emanoel Araújo.

Um grupo de Velhos carregadores africanos, Bahía (Brazil)

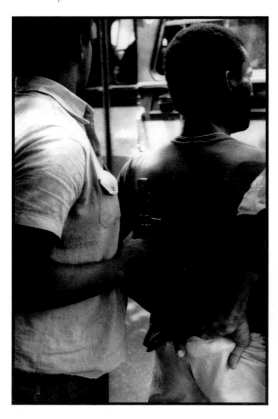

Photographer ∧
ANÍSIO C. DE CARVALHO © 1979
Arrest in Salvador.

∧ Photographer
ANÍSIO C. DE CARVALHO © 1965
Bobby Kennedy visiting Alagados Uruguay in Salvador: a favela built on a rubbish dump in the bay of Bahia.

Images of accumulated memory, of time's successive strata, these snapshots bring precision and poetry to their capturing of history's slow interminglings, superimposing images of a still-living African heritage and the traditional worship of another God that people have learnt to love. Through this work of recording memory the photographer himself gradually rediscovers his origins - just like the Arturo children whose likeness he captures and who, at the feet of the elders, learn to decode the language of the ancestral drums and the deepest meaning of the feast-days whose celebration they in turn will perpetuate.

These very same traditions, of which black people are the conscious inheritors, emerge with great sharpness from the extraordinary ceremonies of the Brotherhood of Nossa Senhora da Boa Morte (Our Lady of a Happy Death) at Cachoeira, in Bahia State. In recent years Adenor Gondim has devoted a substantial part of his photographic work to the Brotherhood. As with the Arturos, the Catholic faith is the filter through which these black elders learnt to revere their voodoo goddess, Orixá - and so long ago that they can no longer distinguish between the Virgin Mary, the white Iáiá and the black Naná, Iemanjá and Oxum, mothers of all of us and sources of forgiveness. Then, just as on the pre-abolition plantations, come the sound of the drum, and the dance, as stirring today as they were then. All this is stamped on Adenor Gondim's powerful images: images that immortalize the wisdom of these gazes that have already transcended death itself, immortalize the rich attire, the profusion of gold bracelets and necklaces worn by these black women we cannot help but identify with the ancestral power of Orixá or the white Virgin.

And then there are the photos of Luis Paulo Lima, taken during a candomblé ceremony in São Paulo: again the same gods - or rather their successors - are there in person, exploding into the image in that suspended moment of giddying possession, as all-powerful Orixá bestrides her disciple, passing on to him those cosmic forces to which, as the ancestral traditions teach, he has always belonged. Streaks of light shaping the contours of a dream, these pictures are a powerful means of penetrating to the deep, intimate significance of the religious experience as enacted in the Afro-Brazilian tradition.

All different approaches, then; but approaches whose very diversity gives us access to the true, contradictory features of an authentic, flesh-and-blood black person; one with a body and soul, one finally delivered from the imaginings of that other who, like some perverse demon, was driven to assert his identity by transforming black people into phantasmagorical beings, by stealing the substance of their souls and refusing them the right to be the subject of their own gaze. Now a black way of seeing constructs these black images, a way of seeing inevitably marked by a spark of indignation or, sometimes, of respectful surprise; yet a way of seeing that remains shot through with compassion and warmth. This is the friendly, affectionate scrutiny of someone photographing their own people - working within the family so to speak - and reaching out in a gesture of solidarity and tenderness. Images of simple people, common folk, blacks caught in moments overflowing with humanity. Images as simple as truth, as simple as the ebb and flow of life. Utter clarity, black on white in a flash of eternity, black images shot through with a thousand colours of hope.

Maria Lucia Montes

ANÍSIO C DE CARVALHO

Brazil
b. Bahia, Brazil 1930 – lives in Salvador, Brazil

Grandson of a Portuguese landowner and an African slave, Anísio C de Carvalho was born in 1930 in Conceição da Feira, Bahia, and can be considered one of Brazil's first photographers of African descent. His photographic training began at age twelve with Léon Rozenberg, in Salvador. In 1968, he was hired by the new daily *Jornal da Bahia*. Some of his photographs were censored during the dictatorship years of 1960-1980.

∧ Photographer ANÍSIO C DE CARVALHO ©
Alagados Uruguay in Salvador, a favela built on a rubbish dump in the bay of Bahia, 1963.

Photographer ANÍSIO C DE CARVALHO © >
Cosme de Faria, defender of the poor in Salvador, 1970.

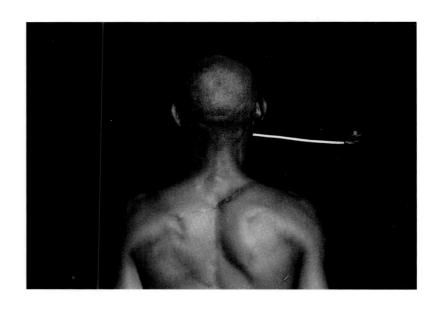

BAUER SÁ

Brazil
b. Salvador, Brazil 1950
– lives in Salvador

Bauer Sá lives in the city of
Salvador, where he was born in
1950. His photographic explora-
tions take a poetic approach to
the question of black people and
the African divinities they venerate.

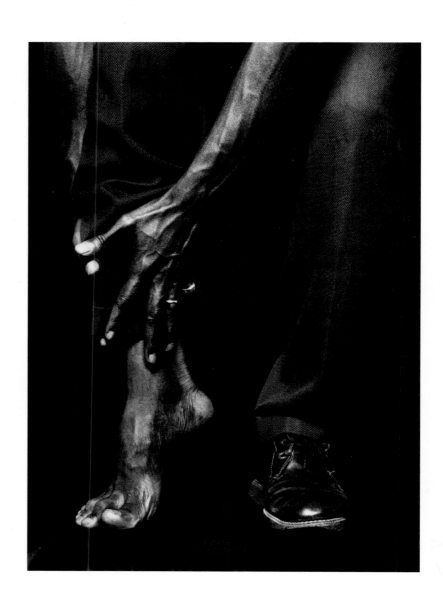

FIGHTING COCK

Photographer BAUER SÁ © ca. 1995
< *Cachimbo I (Pipe I).*
Feet.
∧ *Fighting Cock.*

EUSTÁQUIO NEVES

Brazil
b. Juatuba, Brazil 1955
– lives in Belo Horizonte, Brazil

Born in 1955 in Juatuba, in the state of Minas Gerais, Eustáquio Neves currently lives in Belo Horizonte. After finishing his studies in chemistry, he took up photography in 1979. Social issues are at the heart of his work: the Arturos community, urban chaos, urban runaway slave communities. He manipulates his finished prints, subjecting them to chemical processes and manual interventions.

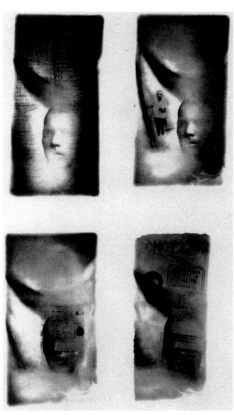

Photographer EUSTÁQUIO NEVES © 1996

Urban chaos.
Self-portrait.

∧ Photographer EUSTÁQUIO NEVES ©
Black Maria 1998.
Series, after carnaval 1997.
> *Arturos community 1996.*

∧ Photographer VANTOEN PEREIRA JR. ©
Siesta.
Woman in the afternoon.
Old man.
> *The Lapa neighbourhood at night, Rio 1996.*

VANTOEN PEREIRA JR

Brazil
b. Rio de Janeiro, Brazil 1960
– lives in Rio

Vantoen Pereira Jr was born in Rio de Janeiro in 1960. He has been a photographic reporter and film technician since 1980 and is a founding member of the ZNZ photographic agency. This work in the genre of photoreportage is published in the main Brazilian papers and magazines.

WALTER FIRMO

Brazil
b. Rio de Janeiro, Brazil 1937 – lives in Rio

Walter Firmo, born in the suburbs of Rio with a carioca in his soul, is described in the following terms by Lena Frias: « A wily, smooth-talking Mulatto. If you didn't know better you'd take him for one of those black guys who are perfect for livening up the conversation over a cold beer at the local café. Then suddenly you realize you're in the presence of an artist who interprets and re-reads the malicious twists and turns of Brazilian difference ».

<< Photographer WALTER FIRMO ©
My mother on the edge of Amazonia, ca. 1950.
∧ *Pixinguinha the musician 1964.*

Diaspora

Photographer WALTER FIRMO ©
The artist Arthur Bispo do Rosário.

CARLA OSÓRIO

Brazil
b. Bahia, Brazil 1972 – lives in Vitória, Brazil

Carla Osório was born in 1972 in Salvador de Bahia. After studying journalism and public relations at the Federal University in Espirito Santo State,
she worked as a press reporter and photographer in Vitória, the state capital. Her exhibition *Black People in Espirito Santo* drew considerable attention during the first Festival of Black Art in Belo Horizonte in 1995.

Photographer CARLA OSÓRIO © 1995-96 ∧
Black people in the state of Espirito Santo. >

JANUÁRIO GARCIA

Brazil
b. Montes Claros, Brazil
– lives in Rio

Januário Garcia was born in Montes Claros, Minas Gerais. He lives and works in Rio de Janeiro. « Music, fiesta and shouting are part of our Afro-Brazilian culture. Every expression represents thousands of people who dance and sing the same song to the same rhythm at exactly the same time during the Carnival. »

 Photographer JANUÁRIO GARCIA ©
Cries and trances at the Carnaval.

CHARLES SILVA DUARTE

Brazil
b. Contagem, Brazil 1965 – lives in Brazil

Charles Silva Duarte was born in Contagem, Minas Gerais State, in 1965. Completely self-taught, he has been working as a press photographer since 1986. His personal work focuses on such social issues as street children and African echoes in Minas Gerais popular festivals.

FICHA
DE SINUCA
150:00

∧ Photographer CHARLES SILVA DUARTE ©
Festival.
< *Bar in Contagem.*

LITA CERQUEIRA

Brazil
b. Bahia, Brazil – lives in Brazil

Born in Bahia State, photographer Lita Cerqueira is known for her work with several Brazilian film-makers, and for her Postcard series, begun in 1993.

Photographer LITA CERQUEIRA © ∧
Street painter in Salvador de Bahia.

ADENOR GONDIM
Brazil
b. Rui Barbosa, Bahia, Brazil 1950 – lives in Salvador, Brazil

Adenor Gondim was born in Rui Barbosa, Bahia State, in 1950. He now lives in Salvador, working as a freelance photographer-reporter. The religious themes explored in his work include the *Brotherhood of Our Lady of a Happy Death in Cachoiera*, and *Holy Week in Bom Jesus da Lapa*.

∧ Photographer ADENOR GONDIM ©
Holy Week in Bom Jesus da Lapa

Photographer ADENOR GONDIM ©
Holy Week in Bom Jesus da Lapa.
The Brotherhood of Our Lady
of a Happy Death in Cachoiera

∧
>
>

DENISE CAMARGO

Brazil
b. São Paulo, Brazil 1964
– lives in São Paulo

Denise Camargo was born in
São Paulo in 1964. After obtaining a master's degree at the
University of São Paulo (USP),
she worked as a photographer-
reporter for several national dailies based in that city. She is
currently editor-in-chief of the
picture magazine, *Iris*.

Photographer DENISE CAMARGO ©
Asylum in São Paulo.

LUIZ PAULO LIMA

Brazil
b. Porto Alegre, Brazil 1955 – lives in São Paulo, Brazil

Born in 1955, Luis Paulo Lima is a native of Porto Alegre, in the State of Rio Grande do Sul. He lives in São Paulo. After studying history at the Catholic University of São Paulo (PUC), he is now a press photographer and film-maker. He also works on personal projects, notably the photographic representation of movement in the dances of the candomblé, a ceremony of African origin.

Photographer LUIS PAULO LIMA ©
Candomblé in São Paulo.

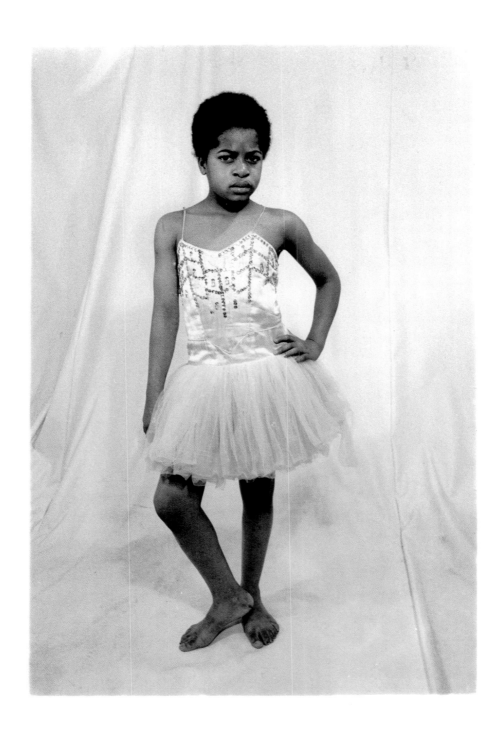

ROBERTO ESTEVES

Brazil
b. São Paulo, Brazil 1958 – lives in São Paulo

Born in the State capital, Roberto Esteves began working as a photographer in 1977. In 1997, during a course in basic photography for teenagers at the Sesc Pompéia, he suggested to his street children pupils that he should photograph them in poses they had chosen for themselves: he also listened to what they had to say about their lives.

Photographer
ROBERTO ESTEVES © 1997
Portraits of street children, São Paulo.
Child of 10 dressed as a ballerina.
Cristian, a mentally ill 17-year-old,
dressed as an executive.

∧
>

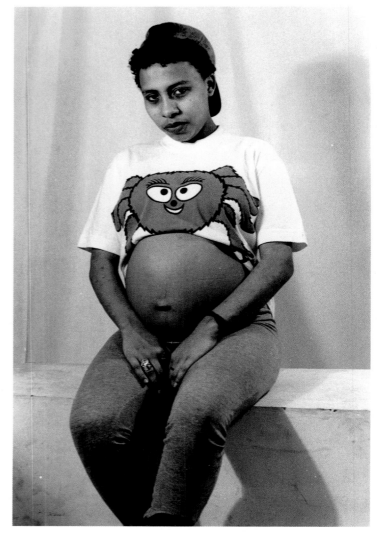

Photographer ROBERTO ESTEVES © 1997
Portraits of street children, São Paulo.
Josénildo, aged 13.
Mariza, aged 16, pregnant.
Thiago and his friend , aged 17 and 16, dressed as girls. ∧
>

biographies

Steven Abiodu Thomas
PORTRAIT PHOTOGRAPHERS - *b. Accra, Ghana*
Famous for his painted screens of the 1940s.
Pages. 108-115 (in the text)

Alex Agbaglo Acolatse - BEGINNINGS
b. Kedzi, Togo 1880 - d. Lomé, Togo 1975
In 1914 he opened his studio in Lomé. One of the earliest African photographers, he began by taking outdoor photographs of groups of people, the city's monuments, and important political events between 1920 and 1940. He stopped taking photographs in 1953.
Pages. 43-44-106 (in the text)
Pages. 42-45-46-47 (photographs)

Sergio Afonso - IN SEARCH OF AN AESTHETIC
b. Luanda, Angola 1975 – lives in Lisbon, Portugal
As a young man in his early twenties, he represents the second generation of an Angolan family of photographers who own the Foto Ngufo studio, the most fashionable in Luanda.
Page. 314 (in the text)
Pages. 314-315 (photographs)

A Foto - THE OFFICIAL PRESS AGENCIES
Luanda, Angola 1949- still active
The official photographic and audio-Visual agency which was privatised in 1991.
Pages. 197-212 - Pages. 212 to 215

Afrapix - AGENCY - *South Africa 1982 – 1992*
Afrapix was an independent agency of politically committed photographers which closed down when apartheid ended.
Pages. 248-253-256-257-261-267

Drum magazine - IMAGES OF REALITY
South Africa, 1950 – 1985
This South African magazine, established in the 1950s, became an exciting meeting-place for the best writers and photographers of the time. A magazine published under the same name today bears no resemblance to the original.
Page. 19-244-246-248-261
Page. 242 to 273

The Aguiar Brothers - BEGINNINGS - *Togo*
Page. 44

Nelson Ankruma Events
PORTRAIT PHOTOGRAPHERS - *b. Ghana, 1954*
A studio specializing in painted screens.
Page. 116

Rui Assubuji - IMAGES OF REALITY
b. Cabo Delgado, Mozambique 1964 – lives in Maputo
Worked in television as a cameraman, later receiving training at the Centro de Formação Fotográfica in 1968.
Page. 240
Pages. 238-240-241

Autograph - AGENCY - *UK, London 1987*
Association of black British photographers founded in about 1987 by Rotimi Fani-Kayodé, David A Bailey and Minika Baker. The association today is run by Mark Sealy and protects the rights of black photographers.
Page. 292

Joseph Moïse Agbojelou
PORTRAIT PHOTOGRAPHERS
b. Védo, Benin 1912 – lives in Porto-Novo, Benin
An itinerant outdoors photographer who later worked in a studio, he has portrayed Benin from the Thirties up to the present day, covering weddings, funerals, political ceremonies, trivial events and portraits.
Page. 84
Pages. 84 to 87

Amin Mahamoud Ahmed - IMAGES OF REALITY
b. Djibouti 1968 – lives Djibouti
Page. 284

Ramadan Ali Ahmed - IMAGES OF REALITY
b. Djibouti 1970 – lives Djibouti
Page. 285

Ajamu - DIASPORA
b. Huddersfield, UK 1963 - lives in London, originally from the Caribbean
He belongs to the 1980s generation of black English photographers. He created the character Miss Tissue, who was his double, thereby placing himself at the centre of the contemporary debate on race, gender and identity.
Page. 370
Pages. 370-371

Akinbode Akinbiyi - IMAGES OF REALITY
b. Oxford, UK 1946 – lives in Berlin, background Nigerian
Since 1977, he has been working as a freelance photographer in Europe and in Africa, where he regularly returns to work.
Page. 274
Pages. 274 to 277

Daniel Attoumo Amichia
PORTRAIT PHOTOGRAPHERS
b. Behine, Ghana about 1908 – d. Grand-Bassam , Ivory Coast 1994
Practised as an itinerant photographer and, using natural light, specialized in family portraits or photographing members of the professions in Grand-Bassam society. He opened a studio after the Second World War.
Page. 88
Pages. 88 to 91

Mohamed Amin - IMAGES OF REALITY
b. Tanzania 1943 – d. Comoros islands 1996
Pages. 232-234-235

Maurille Andrianarivelo - Indian OCEAN
b. Antananarivo, Madagascar 1871– d. Antananarivo 1969
Opened Studio Rill in 1947, one of the first photographic workshops on the island.
Pages. 327-334
Pages. 334-335

AMAP/ANIM - THE OFFICIAL PRESS AGENCIES
Bamako, Mali 1960 - diminished output since 1991
AMAP (Malian Press and Advertising Agency) was set up at independence, operating on the base provided by the former colonial ANIM (Malian National Information Agency). Under Modibo Keita and Moussa Traoré, it developed into the official government agency, with 15 photographers spread across every region of Mali.
Pages. 19-197-198
Pages. 196 to 201

ANTA - THE OFFICIAL PRESS AGENCIES
Antananarivo, Madagascar 1928 - less active since 1974
This Press agency has a unique photographic collection. Unfortunately it has seen minimal activity since 1974.
Pages. 197-219-327-328-330
Page. 219

Houssein Assamo - IMAGES OF REALITY
b. Djibouti 1963 – lives in Djibouti
Pages. 280-281

FAK Awortwi - PORTRAIT PHOTOGRAPHERS
Ghana
Page. 107

Cornelius Yao Augustt Azaglo
PORTRAIT PHOTOGRAPHERS
b. Palimé, Togo 1924 - lives in Korhogo, Ivory Coast
He regularly cycles off with his box camera to take pictures of peasants in the village squares. He also photographs them in his Studio du Nord in Korhogo, which he opened in 1955.
Pages. 19-93-100-175
Pages. 100 to 103

Alioune Bâ - IMAGES OF REALITY
b. Bamako, Mali 1959 - lives in Bamako
His highly personal work is imbued with great poetry. He captures everyday gestures, objects, light, contours on a dried earth wall. He has been a photographer with the National Museum of Mali since 1983.
Page. 278 - Pages. 278-279

Omar Badsha - IMAGES OF REALITY
b. Durban, South Africa 1945 - lives in Pretoria
In the early 1980s, with Paul Weinberg, he founded the Afrapix collective, which brought together the most prominent politically committed photographers in South Africa. Of Indian origin, he has been working amongst the Indian communities of South Africa for many years.
Pages. 248-254-256-257-260
Pages. 260-261

Rose-Ann Marie Bailey - DIASPORA
b. Jamaica 1971 - lives in Toronto, Canada
Her obsession with light has led her to concentrate on the texture and lustre of her subjects' skins. She is also a film-maker.
Pages. 373-374
Pages. 372-373

Oladélé Ajiboyé Bamgboyé
b. Nigeria, 1963 - lives in London
He studied chemistry at Strathclyde University in Glasgow as well as information science at Glasgow's Slade College of Fine Art, before continuing with cinematographic and video studies at the London Institute.

Mamadou Barry
b. Kan Kan, Guinée, around 1930 - lives in Kan Kan

Raymond Barthes - Indian OCEAN
b. Madagascar 1957 – lives in Ste Marie, Reunion
Appointed photographer of the Departmental Archives of Reunion. Since 1980 he has been involved in documentary work.
Page. 360 - Pages. 360-361

Tchekoro Bezissi
b. Kano, Nigeria around 1897
At the age of 15 he started working as a general assistant in the studio of Wilson Stafford who, captivated by his artistic feeling, initiated Bezissi into laboratory techniques. Around 1916 he enrolled in the British Army, in whose service he died at the age of 28. The few pictures which he took are to be found in Nigerian homes. His famous « courbes » photographs remain etched in memory.

Franck Bitemo - PORTRAIT PHOTOGRAPHERS
b. Brazzaville, Congo 1971 - lives in Brazzaville
Works in a personal and amusing style portraying the youth of Brazzaville.
Page. 163
Page. 162

Bobby Bobson
b. Durban, South Africa 1928 - lives in Durban
Bobby Bobson opened his studio in the 1950s. The series of potraits taken in the 1970s mainly represent Zulu people. His son, Vicky is now running the studio.

Bedros Boyadjian - PORTRAIT PHOTOGRAPHERS
b. , Armenia, 1868 – d. Addis Ababa, Ethiopia 1928
Photographer of the emperor Menelik.
Pages. 133 to 146 - Pages. 136 to 148

Haigaz Boyadjian - PORTRAIT PHOTOGRAPHERS
b. Alexandria, Egypt 1901 - d. Addis Ababa, Ethiopia 1941
Photographer of the empress Zawditu.
Pages. 133 to 146 - Pages. 133 to 148

Torkom Boyadjian - PORTRAIT PHOTOGRAPHERS
b. Addis Ababa, Ethiopia 1920 - d. Addis Ababa, 1987
Photographer of the emperor Haile Selassie.
Pages. 133 to 146
Pages. 136 to 148

Tristan Bréville - INDIAN OCEAN
As a photographer, he became aware of the importance of photography as an element of the cultural heritage of Mauritius and established the Museum of Photography in Mauritius as well as the first photographic agency.
Page. 319 - Page. 323

James K Bruce-Vanderpuye
PORTRAIT PHOTOGRAPHERS
b. Accra, Ghana 1901 - d. Accra 1989
Opened the Deo Gratias Studio in 1922. He recorded the 1948 riots in Accra.
Pages. 109-110
Page. 107

José Cabral
b. Mozambique - lives in Maputo, Mozambique
Has worked as a photographer for the INC Cinematographic Institute and the newspapers *Noticías* and *Domingo*. In 1986 he taught photography at the Centro de Formação Fotográfica.
Page. 240

Denise Camargo - DIASPORA
b. São Paulo, Brazil 1964 - lives in Riode Janeiro, Brazil
She is currently editor-in-cheif of the magazine *Iris* in Brazil.
Page. 418

Anísio C de Carvalho - Diaspora
b. Bahia, Brazil 1930 - lives in Salvador, Brazil
Considered to be one of the top Brazilian photographers of African origin.
Pages. 392 to 395
Pages. 394-395

Mama Casset - Portrait photographers
b. St Louis, Senegal 1908 - d. Dakar, Senegal 1992
All the Dakar bourgeoisie passed through the well-known African Photo Studio, situated in the medina of Dakar, between 1946 and 1980.
Pages. 19-52-58-60-80-93-175
Pages. 78 to 83

Salla Casset
b. St Louis, Senegal 1910 - lives in Dakar, Senegal
Mama Casset's brother set up his studio, Senegal Photo, in the medina of Dakar in the 1960s.

Lita Cerqueira - Diaspora
b. Salvador, Brazil – lives in Brazil
Lita Cerqueira is known for her work with several Brazilian film-makers.
Page. 414
Page. 414

Joel Alirio Chiziane
b. Mozambique 1964 - lives in Maputo, Mozambique
Reporter with the Mozambican Information Agencies (AIM).

Albert Chong - Diaspora
Carribean American photographer from the West Coast, originally from Jamaica (Chinese).
Page. 370

Ernest Cole
b. South Africa 1940 - d. USA 1990
Joined *Drum* magazine in 1958.
Page. 246

Congopresse - The official press agencies
Kinshasa, Democratic Republic of Congo 1950 - less active since 1970
Congopresse was the official image-producing agency of the Belgian Congo.
Pages. 19-197-209
Pages. 208 to 211

Daddy - Indian Ocean
b. Toamasina, Madagascar 1968 - lives in Antananarivo
As photographer with the daily *L'Express* since 1995, he also works in various other artistic fields such as theatre, dance and fashion.
Page. 345
Pages. 344-345

David Damoison - Diaspora
b. Malakoff, France 1963 - lives in France, originally from Martinique
Most of his work revolves around the black world, mainly the Caribbean.
Pages. 367-370
Page. 367

Dany-Be - Indian Ocean
b. Antananarivo, Madagascar 1934 - lives in Antananarivo
A photo-journalist since 1959, he says that he wishes to be a modest witness of Madagascan society.
Pages. 330-340
Pages. 340-341

JP Decker - Beginnings
Sierra Leone
Photographed the British headquarters in Sierra Leone, Gambia, Ghana and Nigeria for the Colonial Office in London.
Page. 37

Mountaga Dembélé - Portrait photographers
b. Bamako, Mali 1919 - lives in Bamako
He is a schoolteacher who, in the course of his various appointments, took photographs in his spare time in many regions of Mali
Pages. 119 to 122
Pages. 118-121

Depara - The awakening of a vision
b. Kbokiolo, Angola 1928 - d. Kinshasa, Democratic Republic of Congo 1997
Having photographed the night-clubs and bars of Kinshasa in the 1950s, he became the official photographer of Franco, the famous Zairean singer, from 1954 onwards. He retired in 1989.
Page. 179
Pages. 178 to 181

Alpha Bacar Diallo
Kouroussa, Guinea
Itinerant photographer.

Félix Diallo - Portrait photographers
b. Kita, Mali 1931 - d. Kita 1997
He learned about photography in Bamako in 1951 but returned to Kita to open the first studio there in 1955.
Pages. 120-123
Pages. 122-123

Mody Sory Diallo
b. Conakry, Guinea - lives in Conakry
Photographed Camp Boiro (the dictator's military torture camp) in 1984 after Sékou Touré's demise.

Serge Dibert-Bekoy
b. Central African Republic 1966 - lives in Bangui, Central African Republic
Introduced to photography at school at the age of eleven, he completed training courses in medical photography in France. Back in Bangui, with very basic equipment for colour development, he began work on his photographic project, which was to depict his country as it is today, going beyond the bounds of taboo.

Doudou Diop - Beginnings
b. St Louis, Senegal 1920 - lives in St Louis
After an apprenticeship in the army in 1954, he opened the Studio Diop in St Louis. The studio is no longer operational.
Page. 58

Alioune Diouf - Beginnings
St Louis, Senegal 1910 - lives in St Louis
Formerly Clerk of the Court, he photographed the neighbourhood of Sor in St Louis.
Page. 58

Roberto Esteves - Diaspora
b. São Paulo, Brazil 1958 - lives in São Paulo
He trained and photographed street children.
Pages. 392-422
Pages. 422 to 425

Stella Fakiyesi - Diaspora
b. Lagos, Nigeria 1971 - lives in Toronto, Canada
As a woman involved in the affairs of the black Canadian community, her work (in black-and-white) attempts to break down the stereotypes which, in her opinion, render Black women victims.
Page. 374-377
Page. 377

Rotimi Fani-Kayodé - In search of an aesthetic
b. Ifé, Nigeria 1955 - d. London, 1989
He was amongst the founders of Autograph (Association of black English photographers) in London. The body, both physical and spiritual, Western and African, is central to his questionings.
Pages. 291-292-392
Pages. 290 to 293

Patrice Félix Tchicaya - Diaspora
b. Paris 1960 - lives in Paris, originates from Congo Brazzaville.
In his fashion photography, he takes an incisive look at reality.
Page. 366
Pages. 364 to 366

Walter Firmo - Diaspora
b. Rio do Janeiro, Brazil 1937 - lives in Rio de Janeiro
Walter Firmo interprets and re-reads the malicious twits and turns of Brazilian difference.
Pages.392-404
Pages. 404 to 407

Samuel Fosso - Portrait photographers
b. Cameroon 1962 - lives in Bangui, Central African Republic
Since 1975, in addition to his studio work, he has been producing an original series of self-portraits.
Page. 19-164
Page. 164-165

Antoine Freitas - Approaches
b. Angola, 1919 - d. Kinshasa, Democratic Republic of Congo 1990
Antoine Freitas settled in Kinshasa in 1932. He was an itinerant photographer from 1935 onwards, criss-crossing the whole Congo region with his box camera, taking portraits of villagers in the most remote provinces.
Page. 18

Georges Manteya Freitas
b. Kinshasa, Democratic Republic of Congo - lives in Kinshasa
Eldest son of Antoine Freitas, he took of photography in the 1970s.

Oscar Mbemba Freitas
b. Kinshasa, Democratic Republic of Congo - lives in Kinshasa
Youngest son of Antoine Freitas, he is known for his sport photographs. He has been a senior reporter with a weekly news magazine until the 1970s. Today he photographs society subjects.

FTM - The official press agencies
Antananarivo, Madagascar 1896 - active
Set up in 1896 in Antananarivo, the National Geographic and Hydrographic Institute (IGN) is still busy producing photographs for maps.
Pages. 216-327-328-330
Pages. 216-217

Januário Garcia - Diaspora
b. Brazil - lives in Rio de Janeiro, Brazil
Januário Garcia is known for his photographs of the Carnival.
Pages. 392-411 - Pages. 410-411

Philippe Gaubert - Indian Ocean
b. Marseille, France 1967 - lives in Madagascar.
A photo-reporter, first in Reunion and now in Madagascar.
Pages. 354-359
Pages. 358-359

Meïssa Gaye - Beginnings
b. Coyah, Guinea 1892 - d. St Louis, Senegal 1982
A photographic genius who was the most celebrated photographer in St Louis in the 1940s.
Pages. 49-51-52-54-56-60-66-67
Pages. 50-51-64 to 67

David Goldblatt - Images of reality
b. Randfontein, South Africa 1930 - lives in Johannesburg
From 1963 onwards he became a full-time freelance photographer, producing what is probably a unique photographic documentary of South African society.
Pages. 248-253-254-256-258-268
Pages. 257 to 259

Adenor Gondim - Diaspora
b. Bahia, Brazil 1950 - lives in Salvador, Brazil
A free-lance photographer known for the religious themes of his photographies.
Pages. 394-415
Pages. 415 to 417

Bob Gosani - Images of reality
b. Johannesburg, South Africa 1934 - d. 1972
Began his career as a photojournalist in 1952 with *Drum* magazine.
Pages. 242-246
Pages. 242 to 247

Jean-Marc Grenier - Indian Ocean
b. Reunion – lives in St Denis, Reunion
A reporter and photographer, he has been working with the Reunion press since 1983.
Page. 354

Mix Gueye - Beginnings
b. St Louis, Senegal 1906 - d. Dakar, Senegal 1994
Initiated into photography in the late 1920s, he opened his studio in Dakar in 1959, while at the same time taking official photographs for the Senegalese Ministry of Information and News.
Page. 54

Dorris Haron Kasco - Images of reality
b. Daloa, Ivory Coast 1966 - lives in Abidjan, Ivory Coast
He completed a long photographic essay on the mentally ill in several towns and cities of the Ivory Coast, as well as making a study over several years of abandoned and rejected children.
Page. 287 - Page. 286-287

Thierry Hoauro - Indian Ocean
Page. 354

Holm - Portrait photographers
Ghana, Accra
Opened a studio in Accra in 1883. In 1897 he became the first African photographer to be a member of the British Royal Photographic Society.
Page. 106

biographies

Francis K Honny - Portrait photographers
Ghana, Accra
Page. 110

Abdourahman Issa - Images of reality
b. Djibouti, 1960 - lives in the USA
Pages. 282-283

Alexander Joe - Images of reality
b. Harare, Zimbabwe 1951 - lives in Nairobi, Kenya
Began photography in 1975 for the *Rhodesian Herald*, covering the war of independence in Zimbabwe and later the war and famine in Mozambique. He joined AFP in 1985 as their permanent correspondent in East Africa.
Page. 230 - Pages. 230-231

Serge-Emmanuel Jongué - Diaspora
France, Aix en Provence, 1951 - lives in Montreal, Canada
In his work he creates a kind of mental landscape, combining both contemporary and mythical memories.
Pages. 374 -375

Zacharia Kaba - Approaches
b. Kan Kan, Guinea ca. 1910 - lives in Kan Kan
He is the oldest living portraitist in his country, living in the North of Guinea.
Page. 16

Ranjith Kally
b. Natal, South Africa 1925
Joined the *Drum* magazine in 1956.

Moctar Kane
b. Marseille, France 1966 - lives in Marseille
From Mauritania, this young photographer tries to photograph his ancestors, the black people of Mauritania, when he is not busy with Press reporting.

Mohamed Abdallah Kayari
The awakening of a vision
b. Djibouti 1929 - lives in Djibouti
For almost half a century, Abdallah Kayari has been photographing the city, its inhabitants and the Afar area.
Page. 192 - Pages. 192-193

Seydou Keita - Portrait photographers
b. Bamako, Mali 1923 - lives in Bamako
He made portraits of Bamako society between 1949 and 1963, displaying an unsurpassed wealth of detail.
Pages. 19-93-120-124-175
Pages. 124 to 127

Siama Kibamgu
b. Democratic Republic of Congo 1963 - lives in Kinshasa
He uses techniques such as drawing and collage to embellish the photographs brought to him by his clients, thereby producing contemporary icons.

John Kiyaya - Portrait photographers
b. Kassanga, Tanzania 1970 - lives in Tanzania
A portraitist, he mainly photographs the inhabitants of his village and the areas surrounding Lake Tanganyika.
Page. 166 - Pages. 166-167

Philippe Koudjina - The awakening of a vision
b. Togo ca. 1940 - lives in Niamey, Niger
The extraordinary chronicler of the crazy Niamey night life of the 1970s, he is today an independent, itinerant photographer who takes pictures in bars and night clubs.
Page. 175 - Pages. 172 to 177

Alf Kumalo - Images of reality
b. South Africa, 1930 – Lives in South Africa
Began his career as a photo-reporter in 1950. Formerly a photographer with *Drum* magazine, today takes press photographs.
Page. 246 - Page. 255

Philip Kwame Apagya
Portrait photographers
b. Sekondi, Ghana 1958 – lives in Ghana
Well-known for his coloured, painted backdrops. He created room dividers, seating his subject before an interior décor scene in which he or she was surrounded by a wealth of dreamed-of consumer articles.
Pages. 108-110-112-114-117
Pages. 109-111-113-114-117

Chris Ledochowski - In search of an aesthetic
b. Pretoria, South Africa 1956 - lives in Cape Town
A member of the former Afrapix group, he photographs the daily life of the inhabitants of Cape Town's townships, working colour into his pictures of current events in South Africa.
Pages. 248-254-303
Pages. 302-303

Dionysius Leomy - Beginnings
Sierra Leone, 19th Century
A black American exiled in England to escape from slavery, he left for Sierra Leone with many others. Worked in Freetown between 1880 and 1990.
Page. 36

Luis Paulo Lima - Diaspora
b. Brazil 1955 - lives in São Paulo, Brazil
Luis Paulo Lima is a press photographer ans a film-maker. He is known for his photographs of the Candomblé, a ceremony of African origins.
Pages. 394-421 - Pages. 420-421

John Liebenberg - Images of reality
b. Johannesburg, South Africa 1958 - lives in Johannesburg
Has been working freelance as a photographer-reporter since 1963. His photographs, published in various newspapers, have been used the world over.
Pages. 236-257
Pages. 236-237

Alphonso Lisk-Carew - Beginnings
b. Freetown, Sierra Leone 1887 - d. 1969
A Creole, he opened his studio at the age of 18 and became one of the most prosperous photographers in his country, doing portraits, panoramic shots of the countryside and animated views of the city.
Page. 38
Page. 41

Raschid Lombard - *South Africa*
Pages. 248-256

Gerhardt L Lutterodt - Beginnings
Freddy RC Lutterodt - *Accra, Ghana*
Started in 1870 as a photographer migrating between Freetown and Douala. Initiated his nephew Freddy RC Lutterodt (1871-1937) to photography; the latter opened the Duala Studio in Accra in 1889. His own son, Erick P Lutterodt (1884-1959), in turn opened the Accra Studio in 1904. Several photographers were trained in these studios, including Alex A Acolatse.
Pages. 43-106
Pages. 104

Peter Magubane - Images of reality
b. Johannesburg, South Africa 1932 - lives in Johannesburg
A politically committed photographer who began his career in photography with *Drum* magazine in 1955.
Pages. 19-246-248-253-256
Pages. 251-252-254

John Mauluka - Images of reality - *Zimbabwe*
Page. 223

Pierrot Men - Indian Ocean
b. Midongy, Madagascar 1954 - lives in Fianarantsoa, Madagascar
Runs three photographic laboratories in Fianarantsoa. His photographs shed remarkable light on the island of Madagascar, both traditional and contemporary.
Pages. 19-330-347-359
Pages. 346 to 349

Gideon Mendel
Pages. 248-254

Santu Mofokeng - Images of reality
b. Johannesburg, South Africa 1956 - lives in Johannesburg
A freelance photographer since 1985 and former member of Afrapix. He is presently undertaking an historical research project. *Black Photo Album, Look at me, 1890 - 1950* is the first phase of this archaeological study.
Pages. 19-265-267-269-270
Pages. 248-256-258-261-265 to 270

Billy Monk - The awakening of a vision
b. Cape Town, South Africa 1937 -
d. Johannesburg, South Africa 1982
Formal photographic training played no part in Monk's turbulent life yet he captured, with a tragic sensitivity but without self-indulgence, the nightlife of Cape Town in the years 1960 to 1970.
Pages. 19-188
Pages. 188 to 191

Zwelethu Mthethwa - In search of an aesthetic
b. Durban, South Africa, 1960 -
lives in Cape Town, South Africa
He has produced an extraordinary series of colour portraits of township inhabitants. He teaches photography at the University of Cape Town.
Page. 304
Pages. 304 to 307

Kok Nam - Images of reality
b. Maputo, Mozambique 1939 - lives in Maputo
After working in a commercial laboratory from 1957, he became a reporter from 1966 onwards for the *Diário de Moçambique* and the *Semanário Voz Africana*, participating in setting up the newspaper *Tempo* in 1970.
Pages. 239-240

Agence Nataal - Agency
Senegal, 1993 - 1996
A young agency of Senegalese photographers bringing together, among others, Mamadou Touré Mandémory, Touré Béhan and Djibril Sy. Being associated with the daily *Dakar-Soir*, they contributed to the prominent position of photography in Senegal.

Eustáquio Neves - Diaspora
b. Juatuba, Brazil 1955 - lives in Belo Horizonte, Brazil
In 1986, he began work on a series of very personal portraits in black-and-white whose subjects were drawn from the community of slave descendants, the Arturos. He is now working on collages and photomontages centred on the theme of the city.
Pages. 394-398 - Pages. 398 to 401

Ambroise Ngaimoko - Studio 3Z
Portrait photographers
b. Angola 1949 - lives in the Democratic Republic of Congo
He set up his 3Z studio in Kitambo in 1971, where he still works today.
Pages. 102-103

Obie Oberholzer - In search of an aesthetic
b. Pretoria, South Africa 1947 - lives in Pretoria
His South African « notebook » is characterized by a uniquely personal aesthetic.
Page. 301 - Pages. 300-301

António Ole - In search of an aesthetic
b. Luanda, Angola 1951 - lives in Luanda
Works in several media, including painting, sculpture, video and photography, which tends towards documentary photography.
Page. 312 - Pages. 312-313

FF Olympio - Beginnings
Page. 44

José Ondoa - Approaches
b. Yaoundé, Cameroon 1938 - lives in Yaoundé
An independent reporter, he opened his photographic studio in 1984, shutting it down in 1989.
Page. 22

Onicep - Agency
Niamey, Niger 1960 - reducedl output since 1980
The National Publishing and Press Office was at its zenith at independence. Many photographers travelled the length and breadth of Niger covering the political and cultural events of the country.
Page. 197

Alex Osei - Portrait photographers
b. Accra, Ghana 1905 - d. Accra 1985
Page. 108

Carla Osório - Diaspora
b. Bahia, Brazil 1972 - lives in Vitória, Brazil
She works as a press reporter and photographer.
Pages. 392-408 - Pages. 408-409

Alfredo Paco
b. Maputo, Mozambique 1962 - lives in Maputo
Young photo-reporter.

Papillon
b. Haïti ca. 1920 - lives in Miami, USA
His photomontages link the personality of the subject with objects which may be emblematic of them, in a naïve vision which lifts daily occurrences into a different dimension.

Narandar Parekh - Portrait photographers
Page. 158

Gordon Parks - Diaspora
Pages. 381-383-387

René Peña Gonzales - Diaspora
Page. 369 - Page. 369

Vantoen Pereira Jr - DIASPORA
b. Rio de Janeiro, Brazil 1960 - lives in Rio de Janeiro
A reporter-photographer, he is a founder member of the ZNZ photographic agency.
Pages. 392-402
Pages. 402-403

Cathy Pinnock - IN SEARCH OF AN AESTHETIC
b. Johannesburg, South Africa 1967 -
lives in Westdene, South Africa
Cathy Pinnock brings together photography and painting, most notably in a series on the vegetation of the Cape. At present she works as a photographer at the *Sunday Star*, a local newspaper.
Pages. 19-298
Pages. 298-299

Yves Pitchen - INDIAN OCEAN
b. Lubumbashi, Democratic Republic of Congo 1949
- lives in Mauritius
Since 1979, he has produced personal work on Mauritian life and its various communities (Indian, Chinese, European, African, Indonesian and mixed-race).
Page. 325
Pages. 324-325

Khamis Ramadhan - IMAGES OF REALITY
b. Nairobi, Kenya 1965 - lives in Nairobi
Since 1992 he has been working as a freelance reporter-photographer. His photographs are used in African newspapers in Europe and East Africa.
Page. 229
Pages. 225-227-229

Ramily - INDIAN OCEAN
b. Antananarivo, Madagascar 1939 - lives in Antananarivo
A studio photographer since the 1960s, working in the popular neighbourhood of Itaosy, some kilometres from the centre of Antananarivo, he has also produced striking landscape work.
Pages. 330-342
Pages. 342-343

Ramilijoana - INDIAN OCEAN
b. Madagascar, 1887 - d. Madagascar 1948
He began photography in 1894 and set up one of the most important studios on the island. He worked in his studio and outdoors, photographing all the Malagasy aristocracy.
Pages. 327-336
Pages. 336 to 339

Ricardo Rangel - THE AWAKENING OF A VISION
b. Maputo, Mozambique 1924 - lives in Maputo
From 1952 to 1984, he worked for several Press organizations. He founded the Centro de Formação Fotográfica (CFF) in 1983, where almost all Mozambican photographers were trained. During the 1960s, he executed a remarkable series of photographs of night in Maputo.
Pages. 186-239-240
Pages. 186-187

Razaka - INDIAN OCEAN
b. Antananarivo, Madagascar 1871 - d. Antananarivo 1939
On 1 January 1889, he opened his studio in his home in Antananarivo. His son took over on his death.
Pages. 327-328

Bauer Sá - DIASPORA
b. Salvador, Brazil 1950 - lives in Salvador
He is involved in aesthetic research based on a poetic approach to the question of the black people and their African divinities.
Pages. 392-396 - Pages. 396-397

Abderramane Sakaly - PORTRAIT PHOTOGRAPHERS
b. St Louis, Senegal 1926 - d. Bamako, Mali 1988
Born in St Louis in Senegal, he moved to Bamako in 1956, starting up a studio which was very fashionable in the 1960s and 1970s.
Pages. 120-129 - Pages. 128 to 131

Sergio Santimano - IMAGES OF REALITY
b. Maputo, Mozambique 1960 - lives in Maputo
Worked as a photo-reporter on the weekly *Domingo* and later at the Mozambican Information Agency, AIM.
Page. 240

René-Paul Savignan - INDIAN OCEAN
b. Le Port, Reunion 1970 - lives in Reunion
Runs a photographic laboratory at Le Port where, since 1992, he has produced a great deal of work on Reunion.
Pages. 354-356 - Pages. 356-357

Jurgen Schadeberg - IMAGES OF REALITY
b. South Africa 1931 - lives in South Afrca
Worked for *Drum* magazine from 1950 to 1959.
Page. 244-261 - Page. 247

Bouna Medoune Seye - IN SEARCH OF AN AESTHETIC
b. Dakar, Senegal 1956 - lives in Dakar
A photographer, film director and painter, he has established himself in the capital, Dakar, as an original personality, creating a unique world through his art.
Page. 311 - Pages. 310-311

Malick Sidibé - THE AWAKENING OF A VISION
b. Soloba, Mali 1936 - lives in Bamako
Opened his studio in Bamako in 1956, while at the same time producing astonishing reportage photographs about the youth of Bamako in the Sixties and Seventies.
Pages. 19-120-122-182
Pages. 182 to 185-294-295

Charles Silva Duarte - DIASPORA
b. Contagem, Brazil 1965 – lives in Brazil
His personal work focuses on such social issues as street children and African echoes in Minas Gerais popular festivals.
Page. 412
Pages. 412-413

Penny Siopis - IN SEARCH OF AN AESTHETIC
b. Vryburg, South Africa 1953 - lives in Johannesburg
Known for her achievements in the plastic arts, she has increasingly introduced photography into her works.
Pages. 296-297
Page. 297

Studio Jiro - PORTRAIT PHOTOGRAPHERS
Addis Ababa, Ethiopia 1945 – active
Studio Jiro was the studio frequented by the middle classes of Addis Ababa. Georges ran it until 1955 when he handed over to the Armenian Jirary K Makjan, known as Jiro, who ran it until 1974.
Pages. 145-146-152
Pages. 152-153

Studio Shamir - PORTRAIT PHOTOGRAPHERS
Addis Ababa, Ethiopia around 1945 - active
Made its reputation through portraits with touching up and the application of water colours.

Doro Sy - PORTRAIT PHOTOGRAPHERS
b. St Louis, Senegal 1930 - lives in St Louis
Having been initiated into photography in 1950 while on a course in Paris, he opened Doro Sor Photo in St Louis in 1954.
Page. 58

Syli-Photo - Onacig - THE OFFICIAL PRESS AGENCIES
Conakry, Guinea 1961 - has slowed down its activities since 1986
At independence in 1958, the colonial photographic collection was attached to the Ministry of Information and Ideology. In 1961 the agency Syli-Photo was set up, working for the State before being incorporated into ONACIG (National Board of Guinea Cinema) in 1986. Moustapha Wally was the director in charge of Sily-Photo from 1961 to 1966. The most active reporters of the agency were Amadou Bah, Élisa Camara, Samoura and Wouly Barry.
Pages. 197-203
Pages. 202

Adama Sylla - BEGINNNINGS
b. St Louis, Senagal 1934 - lives in St Louis
A researcher at the St Louis Museum who opened his studio in the Guet N'Dar fishing quarter of St Louis in 1963.
Page. 60

André Nonga Tassembedo
b. Burkina Faso 1952 - lives in Bobo-Dioulaso, Burkina Faso
Initially a reporter, he subsequently opened his studio in 1977 in Bobo-Dioulaso.

Rui Tavares - IN SEARCH OF AN AESTHETIC
b. Hamburg, Germany 1971 - lives in Lisbon, Portugal
He always works on his negatives or black-and-white prints with paint, and superimposes images and texts.
Page. 309
Pages. 308-309

Julia Tiffin - IN SEARCH OF AN AESTHETIC
b. Cape Town, South Africa 1975 - lives in Cape Town
A Fine Arts graduate, she does very personal work, exploring the concept of metamorphosis and using her own body as the subject.
Page. 294

Guy Tillim - IMAGES OF REALITY
b. Johannesburg, South Africa 1962 - lives in Cape Town
An independent photo-journalist and former member of the Afrapix group, he was a correspondent for AFP and Reuters between 1986 and 1987.
Pages. 248-257-263
Pages. 262-263

Mamadou Touré Béhan
b. Dakar, Sengal 1961 - lives in Dakar
A founding member of the Agence Nataal, he has depicted Senegalese society's daily life since 1989.

Boubacar Touré Mandémory
b. Dakar, Senegal 1956 - lives in Dakar
This self-taught photographer creates a very contemporary vision of the African city by playing with perspective, depth of field and colour.

Andrew Tshabangu - IMAGES OF REALITY
b. Soweto, South Africa 1966 - lives in Johannesburg
This young South African photographer was noticed by Santu Mofokeng at the University of the Witwatersrand. He is one of the post-apartheid generation of politically committed photographers.
Pages. 19-273
Pages. 272-273

Naita Ussene
b. Mozambique 1959 - lives in Maputo, Mozambique
Has been working as a photo-reporter for the magazine *Tempo* since 1975.
Page. 240

António Valente
b. Mozambique 1955 - lives in Maputo, Mozambique
Freelance reporter.

James Van Der Zee - DIASPORA
Page. 113

Paul Weinberg - IMAGES OF REALITY
South Africa
Page. 254-256-257-258-261-269

Eli Weinberg
b. Latvia 1908 - d. Dar-es-Salaam, Tanzania 1981
A militant and independent photographer, he produced portraits of the leaders of the South African struggle and covered all the demonstrations in the early apartheid period.
Pages. 246-254

Negash Wolde Amanuel
PORTRAIT PHOTOGRAPHERS
b. Ethiopia 1931 - d. Addis Ababa, Ethiopia 1988
Page. 150
Page. 151

David Zapparoli - DIASPORA
b. Toronto, Canada 1957 - lives in Toronto, originatlly from the Caribbean
A documentary photographer, he works on image associations.
Pages. 372-374-376
Page. 376

Studio Addis Zemen - PORTRAIT PHOTOGRAPHERS
Pages. 154-155

bibliography

Ajamu. 1994 .*Black Bodyscapes*. Birmingham: David A Bailey.

Rui Assubuji. 1991. *Pa Ublie; Diario di Campo*. Italy: INCA/CGIL.

Olivier Aubert, Text by Patrick Pichot. 1995. *De L'exil au refuge*. Paris: Cimade.

Alioune Bâ, Antonin Potoski. 1997. *Photographies: 1986-1997*. Bamako: Centre Culturel Français de Bamako.

Omar Badsha, text by Heather Hughes. 1985. *Imijondolo — A photographic Essay on Forced Removals in South Africa*. Johannesburg: Afrapix.

Roger Ballen. 1994. *Platteland — Images from Rural South Africa*. Rivonia: William Waterman Publications.

Anthony Barboza. 1980. *Black Borders*. New York: Anthony Barboza.

Anthony Barboza. 1983. *Introspect: The Photography of Anthony Barboza*. New York: The Studio Museum in Harlem.

Dr A D Bensusan. 1966. *Silver Images — History of Photography in Africa*. Cape Town: Howard Timmins.

Bruce Bernard. 1994. *De l'humain et de l'inhumain — Le voyage photographique de George Rodger*. London: Phaidon Press Limited.

Skip Berry, Nathan Irvin Huggins, Gordon Parks. 1991. *Photographer*. New York: Chelsea House Publishers.

Bill Akwa Bétote. 1996. *Corps instrumental*. Paris: Espace Art Reflex.

Zarina Bhimji. 1992. *I will Always be Here*. Birmingham: Ikon Gallery.

Pascal Blanchard, Stéphane Blanchoin, Nicolas Bancel, Gilles Boëtsch and Hubert Gerbeau. 1995. *L'Autre et Nous — Scènes et Type*. Paris: Syros et Achac.

Jacques Borgé and Nicolas Viasnoff. 1995. *Archives de l'Afrique Noire*. Éditions Michèle Trinckvel, Archives de la France Collection.

Marjorie Bull and Joseph Denfield. 1970. *Secure the Shadow — The Story of Cape Photography from its beginnings to the end of 1870*. Cape Town: Terence McNally.

A Waberi. 1996. *Regards croisés* (John Liebenberg, Pierrot Men, Yves Pitchen, Ricardo Rangel). Djibouti: Centre Culturel Français Arthur Rimbaud.

Brahim Chanchabi. 1995. *Cités & diversités: L'Immigration en Europe*. Paris: AIDDA-Diffusion Syros.

Roland Charles and Toyomi Igus. 1992. *Life in a Day of Black Los Angeles — The way we see it — L.A.'s Black Photographers Present a New Perspective on Their City*. California: UCLA Center for Afro-American Studies.

Clement Cooper. 1988. *Presence*. Manchester: Cornerhouse Publication and Clement Cooper.

Clement Cooper. 1996. Deep — *People of Mixed-Race*. Cardiff: Autograph/Fotogallery/Viewpoint.

Robert Cornevin. 1972. *Les mémoires de l'Afrique — Des origines à nos jours*, Paris: Robert Laffont.

Michael H Cottman, Photo Editor Deborah Willis, Research by Linda Tarrant-Reid. 1996. *The Family of Black America*. New York: Crown Trade Paperbacks.

Pete Daniel and Anne Wilkes Tucker. 1990. *Carry Me Home - Louisiana Sugar Country*. Photographs by Debbie Fleming Caffery. Washington: Smithsonian Institution Press.

Philippe David. 1993. *Alex A. Acolatse (1880-1975) – Hommage à l'un des premiers photographes togolais*. Lomé: Edition Halo, Goethe Institut.

Dorris Haron Kasco. 1994. *Les fous d'Abidjan*. Paris: Revue Noire, Collection Soleil.

Jean-Christophe Deberre, Dorris Haron Kasco and Nathalie Rosticher. 1996. *Cornélius Yao Augustt Azaglo, photographies — Côte d'Ivoire 1950-1975*. Paris: Revue Noire, Collection Soleil.

Bernard Descamps, text by Serge Bahuchet. 1997. *Pygmées — L'esprit de la forêt*. Paris: Marval.

Juan Manuel Diaz Burgos, Mario Diaz Leyva and Paco Salinas. 1998. *Cuba: 100 anos de fotografia, anthologia de la fotografia cubana (1898—1998)*. Mestizo A.C./Fototeca de Cuba.

Thomas Dorn. 1996. *Houn-Noukoun — Tambours et Visages*. Paris: Éditions Florent-Massot.

Roger Dorsinville and Jean-Jacques Mandel. 1991. *L'Homme derrière l'arbre: Un Haïtien au Libéria*. Paris: L'Harmatan.

Eric Easter, D. Michael Cheers, Dudley M. Brooks. 1992. *Songs of my People — African Americans: a Self-Portrait*. Boston/Toronto/London: Little Brown and Company.

Elizabeth Edwards. 1992. *Anthropology & Photography: 1860 — 1920*. New Haven: Yale University Press.

Angèle Etoundi Essamba. 1989. *Passion*. Amsterdam: Uitgeverij An Dekker.

Angèle Etoundi Essamba. 1996. *Contrasts*. AGFA.

Directed by Trevor Esward. 1987. *The Arrivants — A Pictorial Essay on Blacks in Britain*. The Race Today Collective, London: Race Today Publication.

Charles-Henri Favrod. 1989. *Étranges Étrangers: Photographie et Exotisme, 1850/1910*. Paris: Centre National de la Photographie.

Moira Forjaz, text by Amélia Muge. 1983. *Muipiti — Ilha de Moçambique*. Mozambique: Imprensa Nacional, Casa da Moeda.

Ben Forkner. 1991. *Cajun — Fonville*. Paris: Marval.

Armet Francis.1985. *The Black Triangle: The People of African Diaspora*. London: Seed.

Armet Francis. 1988. *Children of the Black Triangle: The People of African Diaspora*. London: Seed.

Roland I Freeman. 1981. *Southern Roads/City Pavements: Photographs of Black Americans*. International Center of Photography.

Roland I Freeman. 1981. *Something to Keep you Warm: The Roland Freeman Collection of Black American Quilts from the Mississippi Heartland*. Mississippi Departement of Archives.

Roland I Freeman. 1989. *The Arabbers of Baltimore*. Maryland: Tidewater publishers.

Peter Galassi, Roy DeCarava. 1996. *A Retrospective*. New York: The Museum of Modern Art.

Bernard Gardi, Pierre Maas and Geert Mommersteeg. 1995. *Djenné, il y a cent ans*. Paris: Karthala.

Remy Gastambide. 1996. *Monograph*. London: Autograph.

Amadou Gaye, texts by Eric Favereau and Leïla Sebbar. 1988. *Génération Métisse*. Paris: Syros/Alternatives.

David Goldblatt and Nadine Gordimer. 1986. *Lifetimes under Apartheid*. New York: Alfred A. Knopf Publisher.

David Goldblatt, text by Brenda Goldblatt and Phillip Van Niekerk. 1989. *A South African Odyssey: The Transported of Kwandebele*. Aperture Fondation.

Alan Govenar. 1996. *Portraits of Community: African American Photography in Texas*. Austin: Texas State Historical Association.

Alan Govenar. 1996. *Photography by Benny Joseph. The Early Years of Rhythm & Blues; Focus on Houston*, Houston: Rice University Press.

Joy Gregory. 1995. *Monograph*. London: Autograph.

Directed by Sunil Gupta. 1990. *An Economy of Signs — Contemporary Indian Photographs*. London: Rivers Oram Press.

Sunil Gupta. 1997. *Monograph*. London: Autograph.

Guy Hersant, texts by Christian Jacob. 1995. *L'Africain*. France: Filigranes Éditions.

Gudrun Honke. 1990. *Au plus profond de l'Afrique — Le Rwanda et la colonisation allemande 1885-1919*. Wuppertal: Peter Hammer Verlag.

Françoise Huguier, Text by Michel Cressole. 1990. *Sur les traces de l'Afrique fantôme*. Paris: Maeght Éditeur.

Birney Imes. 1994. *Partial to Home*. Washington: Smithsonian Institution Press.

Thomas L Johnson and Phillip C Dunn. 1986. *A True Likeness — The Black South of Richard Samuel Roberts 1920-1936*. USA: Bruccoli Clark, Algonquin Books of Chapel Hill.

Frances B. Johnston. 1966. *The Hampton Album*. New York: The Museum of Modern Art.

Directed by André-Jean Jolly, *Namibia/photographies* with John Liebenberg, Maria Gerthrud Namundjebo, Gerson Nghituwamata, Howard Buis, Djunior Svane, Pedro Vorster, Namtenya Akukothela, Tony Figueira. 1994. Paris: Revue Noire, Collection Soleil.

Musée Albert Kahn. 1995. *Albert Kahn 1860.1940 — réalités d'une utopie*. Boulogne: Département des Hauts-de-Seine.

Musée Albert Kahn. 1996. *Pour une reconnaissance Africaine, Dahomey 1930*. Boulogne: Département des Hauts-de-Seine.

Youssouf Tata Cissé. 1995. *Seydou Keita*. Paris: Centre National de la Photographie, Collection Photo Poche.

André de Kervern and Yvan Martial. 1991. *Cartes Postales du Passé — L'île Maurice*. Mauritius: Les éditions du Pacifique.

Rui Knopfli. 1989. *A Ilha de Próspero — Roteiro poético da ilha de Moçambique*. Lisboa: Edições.

Jean Lacouture, William Manchester and Fred Ritchin. 1995. *Magnum: 50 ans de photographies*. Paris: Edition de La Martinière.

Brian Lanker. 1989. *I dream a World — Portraits of Black Women Who Changed America*. New York: Stewart, Tabori & Chang.

Eric Lesdema. 1994. *Monograph*. London: Autograph.

Dave Lewis. 1997. *Monograph*. London: Autograph.

André Magnin. 1997. *Seydou Keita, monographie*. Zurich: Scalo.

André Magnin. 1998. *Malick Sidibé, monographie*. Zurich: Scalo.

Peter Magubane. 1981. *Levande Död — Sydafrika*. Stockholm: Kulturhuset.

Peter Magubane, text by David Bristow and Stan Motjuwadi. 1990. *Soweto, Portrait of a City*. Cape Town: Struik Publishers.

— Text by Carol Lazar. 1993. *Women of South Africa — Their Fight for Freedom*. Canada: Bulfinch Press.

Edouard J Maunick, Tristan Bréville, Yvan Martial. 1993. *Maurice — Le temps d'une île*. Mauritius: Les éditions du Pacifique.

Christian Maurel. 1980. *L'Exotisme colonial*. Paris: Robert Laffont.

Guy C McElroy-Richard J Powell-Sharon Patton. 1989. *African-American artists — 1880-198: Selections from the Evans-Tibbs Collection*. Seattle/London: University of Washington press.

Kobena Mercer, Derek Bishton, Jean-Loup Pivin and Simon Njami. 1996. *Rotimi Fani-Kayodé & Alex Hirst*. Paris/London: Revue Noire & Autograph.

Bouna Medoune Seye, Gilles Eric Foadey and Jean-Loup Pivin. 1994. *Mama Casset et les précurseurs de la photographie au Sénégal*. Paris: Revue Noire, Collection Soleil.

Pierrot Men and Philippe Gaubert. 1996. *À l'intérieur d'à côté*. St Denis: Artothèque.

Pierrot Men, Bernard Descamps, Text by Elie Rajaonarison. 1994. *Gens de Tana*. Antananarivo: Centre Culturel Albert Camus.

Patrick de Mervelec, Texts by Mazisi Kunene. 1996. *Regards sur l'Afrique du Sud*. Paris: Nouveau Monde Éditeur, Paris.

Charles Moore, Text by Michael S Durham. 1991. *Powerful Days –– The Civil Rights Photography of Charles Moore*. New York: Stewart, Tabori & Chang.

Jeanne Moutoussamy-Ashe. 1996. *iew-finders — Black Women Photographers*. London: Writers & Readers Publishing, Inc.

Carole Naggar. 1984. *George Rodger en Afrique*. Paris: Editions Herscher.

Eustáquio Neves. 1995. *Monograph*. London: Autograph.

Erika Nimis. 1998. *Photographes de Bamako de 1935 à nos jours*: **Mountaga Dembélé, Seydou Keita, Félix Diallo, Malick Sidibé, Sakaly, AMAP, Alioune Bâ, Emmanuel Daou**. Paris: Revue Noire, Collection Soleil.

Obie Oberholzer. 1989. *Southern Circle: Another Pictorial Journey by Obie Oberholzer*. Parklands: Jonathan Ball Publishers.

Obie Oberholzer. 1991. *To Hell'n Gone*. Cape Town: Struik Publishers.

1994. *Ile de la Réunion : Trwa Kartié — Entre mythologie et pratiques* (collectif). Editions de la Martinière.

Richard Pankhurst & Denis Gérard. 1996. *Ethiopia Photographed — Historic Photographs of the Country and its People Taken Between 1867 and 1935*. London: Kegan Paul international.

Molefe Pheto and George Hallett. 1993. *Rastafarians in South Africa, Jagtar Semplay*. London: Autograph.

Photographs by Twenty South African Photographers. 1989. *Beyond the Barricades — Popular Resistance in South Africa in the 1980's*. London: Kliptown Books.

Ingrid Pollard. *Monograph*. London: Autograph.

Ricardo Rangel. 1994. *Photographe du Mozambique*. Centre Culturel Franco-Mozambicain, Éditions Findakly.

Shanta Rao, Alemshaye. 1995. *et autres histoires de femmes*. Paris: Marval.

Jean-Jacques Renaud. 1993. *Les chasses coloniales par les cartes postales*. Paris: Éditions Le Faubourg.

Naomi Rosenblum. 1992. *Une Histoire Mondiale de la Photographie*. Paris: Editions Abbeville.

Jackie Ryckebusch. 1994. *La Réunion (1900) en cartes postales*. St André: Ocean Éditions.

Compiled and edited by **Jurgen Schadeberg**. *The Finest Photos from the Old DRUM*. Lanseria: Bailey's African Photo Archives Production.
1987. *The Fifties People of South Africa — Black life: Politics/Jazz/Sport*. Lanseria: Bailey's African Photo Archives Production .
1994. *Voices from Robben Island*. Randburg: Ravan Press-Nedbank.

Chris Schoeman. 1994. *District six: The Spirit of Kanala*. Cape Town: Human & Rousseau.

Directed by **Mark Sealy**. 1993. *Vanley Burke — A Retrospective*, London: Lawrence & Wishart.

Bouna Medoune Seye, text by **Jean-Loup Pivin**. 1994. *Les trottoirs de Dakar*. Paris: Revue Noire, Collection Soleil.

Fazal Sheikh. 1996. *A sense of Common Ground*. Zurich: Scalo.

Aaron Siskind. 1991. *Harlem — Photographs 1932-1940*.

Sunmi Smart-Cole. 1991. *The Photography of Sunmi Smart-Cole*. Nigeria: Daily Times Nigeria Ltd-Bookcraft.

Karl Steinorth. 1996. *Lewis Hine — Passionate Journey*. Zurich: Edition Stemmle.

Paul Strand, commentary by **Basil Davidson**. 1976. *Ghana: An African Portrait*. New York: Aperture Book.

Jacques Trampont. 1990. *Djibouti hier — de 1887 à 1939*. Paris: Hatier.

Wifred Thesiger. 1987. *Visions d'un nomade*. Paris: Plon.

Victor Vázquez. 1988. *Fotografías Recientes/Recent Photographs*. San Juan: Galería Latino Americana.

Text by **Abdourahman Ali Waberi**. 1997. *L'oeil nomade : Voyage à travers le pays* (**John Liebenberg, Pierrot Men, Yves Pitchen, Ricardo Rangel, Abdourahman Issa, Amin Mahamoud, Houssein Assamo, Ramadan Ali**). Djibouti: Centre Culturel Français Arthur Rimbaud.

Eli Weinberg. 1981. *Portrait of People — A personal Photographic Record of the South African Liberation Struggle*. London: International Defence and Aid Fund for Southern Africa.

Deborah Willis-Thomas. 1985. *Black Photo-graphers, 1840-1940: An Illustrated Bio-Bibliography*. New-York/London: Garland.
1989. *An Illustrated Bio-Bibliography of Black-Photographers: 1940-1988*. New-York/London: Garland.
1992. *23 postcards — Early black Photographers 1840-1940*. New York: New Press, with the Schomburg Center for Research in Black Culture.
1994. *Picturing Us — African American Identity in Photography*. New York: The New Press.

Deborah Willis-Braithwaite, Rodger C Birt. 1993. *Van DerZee — Photographer 1886-1993*. Washington: Smithsonian Institution.

Francis Wilson. 1986. *South Africa: The Cordoned Heart — Essays by Twenty South African Photographers*. Cape Town: The Gallery Press.

Tobias Wendl, Heike Behrend. 1998. *Snap Me One ! — Studio Photographers in Africa*. Munich: Prestel Verlag.

exhibitions selection

1986: *On Freedom: The Art of Photojournalism*. The Studio Museum in Harlem, New York.

1989: *Images of Silence - Photography from Latin America and the Caribbean in the 1980s*. Museum of Modern Art of Latin America, Organization of American States, Washington.

1992: *Revue Noire et la photographie africaine*. Centre Wallonie Bruxelles, (Rotimi Fani-Kayodé, Bouna Medoune Seye, Djibril Sy, Mama Casset, John Kiyaya, Django Cissé).

1993: *Ile Maurice - Singulier Pluriel*. Centre Wallonie-Bruxelles, Paris.

— *Through a Lens Darkly: Six Portofolios by South African Photographers*. South African National Gallery.

1994: *Seydou Keita*. Fondation Cartier, Paris.

— *1ères Rencontres de la photographie Africaine*. Bamako, Mali.

1995: *Malick Sidibé*. Fondation Cartier, Paris.

— *Semblantes Negros, Mitos Blancos; Black Looks, White Myths*. Johannesburg, South Africa.

— *Africa 95*, London-Birmingham-York-Cardiff.

1996 : *In/sight : African Photographers, 1940 to the Present*. Guggenheim Museum, New York.

— *Africaines — un portrait photographique*. Chapelle de l'Oratoire, Festival des trois Continents, Nantes.

— *2èmes Rencontres de la photographie Africaine*. Bamako, Mali.

1997: *PhotoSynthesis: Contemporary South African Photography*. South African National Gallery.

— *Das Gesicht Afrikas*. Gruner & Jahr Pressehaus, Hamburg.

— *Traces of Identity* (Black Canadian photographers). Toronto, Gallery 44.

1998: *L'Afrique par elle-même*. Maison Européenne de la Photographie, Paris.
— Pinacoteca de São Paulo, Brazil.
— South African National Gallery.

— *Snap Me One! Studio Photographers in Africa*. Munich.

— *3èmes Rencontres de la photographie Africaine*. Bamako, Mali.

1999: *Africa by Africa*. Barbican Center, London.
— JF Kennedy Center for the Parforming Arts, Washington DC.
— Smithonian Institute, Museum for African Art, Washington DC.

magazines

Afrapix, Quaterly, vol.1, n°2, December 1990. *Full Frame: South Africa Documentary Photography* (Jenny Gordon, David Goldblatt, Guy Tillim, George Hallett), Johannesburg.

Artrage, N°22/23, 1988; *Photo Feature: Autograph, Photographers' Association*.
Artrage, n° 25. Summer 1989.

Autograph. London, 1991/1994.

Balafon, N°131, december 96 -January 97. Franck Verdier, *Objectif Bamako*, France.
Frank Verdier. *Profession: Photographe de quartier*.

Black Renaissance/Renaissance Noire. Indiana University Press, Volume I, N°1, Fall 1996.

Camera Austria International, Austria, n°56, 1996. Sabine Vogel. *Santu Mofokeng*.

Cimaise, n°197. Alain Dister. *Black Photography in America*.

Clichés, n°61, december 1989. Alain D'Hooghe. *Elizabeth Sunday: Reflets de l'essence africaine*.

Creative Camera, n°316, June-July 1992. David A. Bailey and Stuart Hall. *Critical Decade : An Introduction*.

Drum Magazine. Since 1950. Johannesburg, South Africa.

Full Frame; *South Africa Documentary Photography*. Paul Weinberg, Roger Meintjes, John Liebenberg, Santu Mofokeng. Johannesburg.

Le Photographe, n°1520, december 94-january 95. Guy Hersant. *Trente six ans de photographie en Guinée*.
Hervé Le Goff. *L'Afrique fait son image*.

Mayibuye History & Literature Series, n°48, 1994. *A Pictorial History of the African National Congress*. Mayibuye Centre (photographs), African National Congress (text), Mzabalazo. Cape Town: The Rustica Press.

Photographie Magazine, n°78, July-August 1996. Martine Ravache. *Un photographe et son appareil: Seydou Keita*.

Photokid, Bimensuel n°3, Fall 1986. Bertrand Hosti. *Enfants du Ghana*.

Revue Noire, Paris, n°1 to 29, 1991-1998 Portfolios.
Special issues on photography:
n°3 december 1991.
n°15 december 1995.
n° 28 March 1998.

SF Camerawork, Quarterly, vol. 17, N°3, Fall 1990. *Disputed identities: US/UK*.

Ten. 8, Birmingham, Vol. II, n° 1, Spring 1991, Bodies of Excess.
Vol. II, No. 2, Autumn 1991. *Digital Dialogues; Photography in the Age of Cyberspace*.
Vol. II, n° 3, Spring 1992. Critical Decade: *Black British Photography in the 80's*.

Vrye Weekblad. Johannesburg, n°156, December 1991/January 1992.

20:20: The National Magazine for Photography and Media Education, Brighton, issue 2. Summer 1995. Portofolio, *African Identities*.
Jim Hornsby, interview with Mark Sealy, *African geezers with cameras*.

Anthology
Revue Noire

of African and of Indian Ocean

Photography

500 photographies

directed by Pascal Martin Saint Léon & N'Goné Fall
with
Frédérique Chapuis, Simon Njami, Jean-Loup Pivin, Gwénaële Guigon
and
Brazil: Emanoel Araújo, André Jolly
South Africa: Kathleen Grundlingh, Pierre-Laurent Sanner, Santu Mofokeng
Ethiopia: Denis Gérard, Richard Pankhurst, Guy Hersant
United States of America: Deborah Willis
Sierra Leone: Vera Viditz-Ward
Ghana: Tobias Wendl
Kenya: Heike Behrend
Mauritius: Tristan Bréville
Reunion: René-Paul Savignan, William Zitte

Artistic Directors: Pascal Martin Saint Léon & N'Goné Fall
Layout: Olivier Moisan
Translations: Bas Angelis, Shan Benson, Gail de Courcy-Ireland, Jonathan Kundra, Helen Laurenson,
Anne Lemieux, Sandrine Marquis, Barbara Peiker, John Tittensor.

Covers: photographies by Antoine Freitas & Zwelethu Mthethwa

© Editions Revue Noire
8 rue Cels, F - 75014 Paris
Phone: 33-01 43 20 92 00
Fax: 33-01 43 22 92 60
e-mail: renoir@club-internet.fr
http://www.rio.net/revue noire

First French edition published in by Revue Noire in 1998. ISBN: 2-909571-30-0
First Portuguese edition published in by Revue Noire in 1998. ISBN: 2-909571-43-2
Second French edition by Revue Noire, Paris, March 1999, ISBN : 2-909571-30-0
First English edition published by Revue Noire in 1999. ISBN: 2-909571-49-1

Hardcover. 432 pages
Paper: 150 gsm matt art paper
Technical Survey: Angelo Mussio
Process engraving (duotone & color 200): Seleoffset, Torino, Paris, New York
Printed in EU by Computer to Plate
by Eurografica, Vicenza, Italia